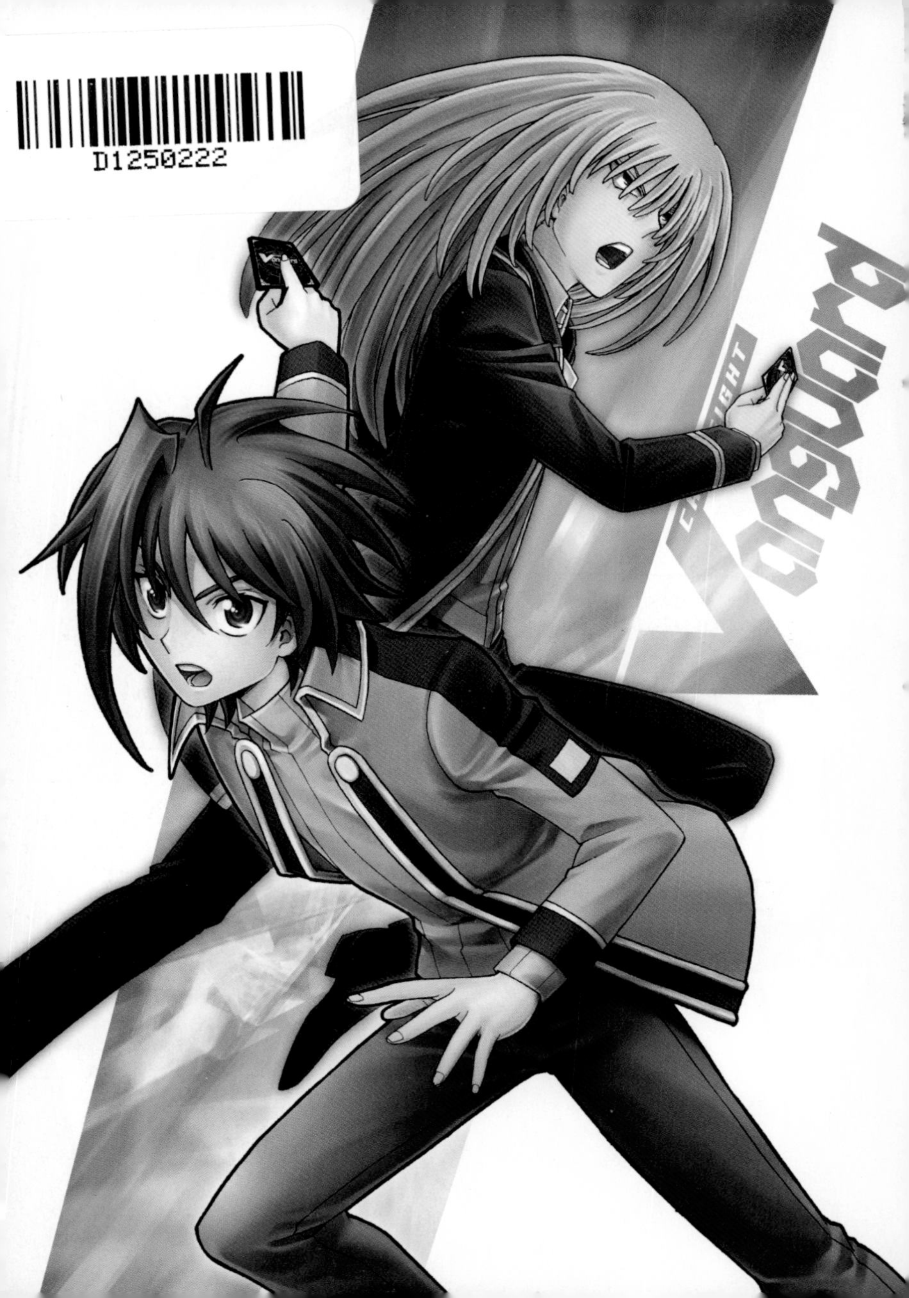
Vanguard

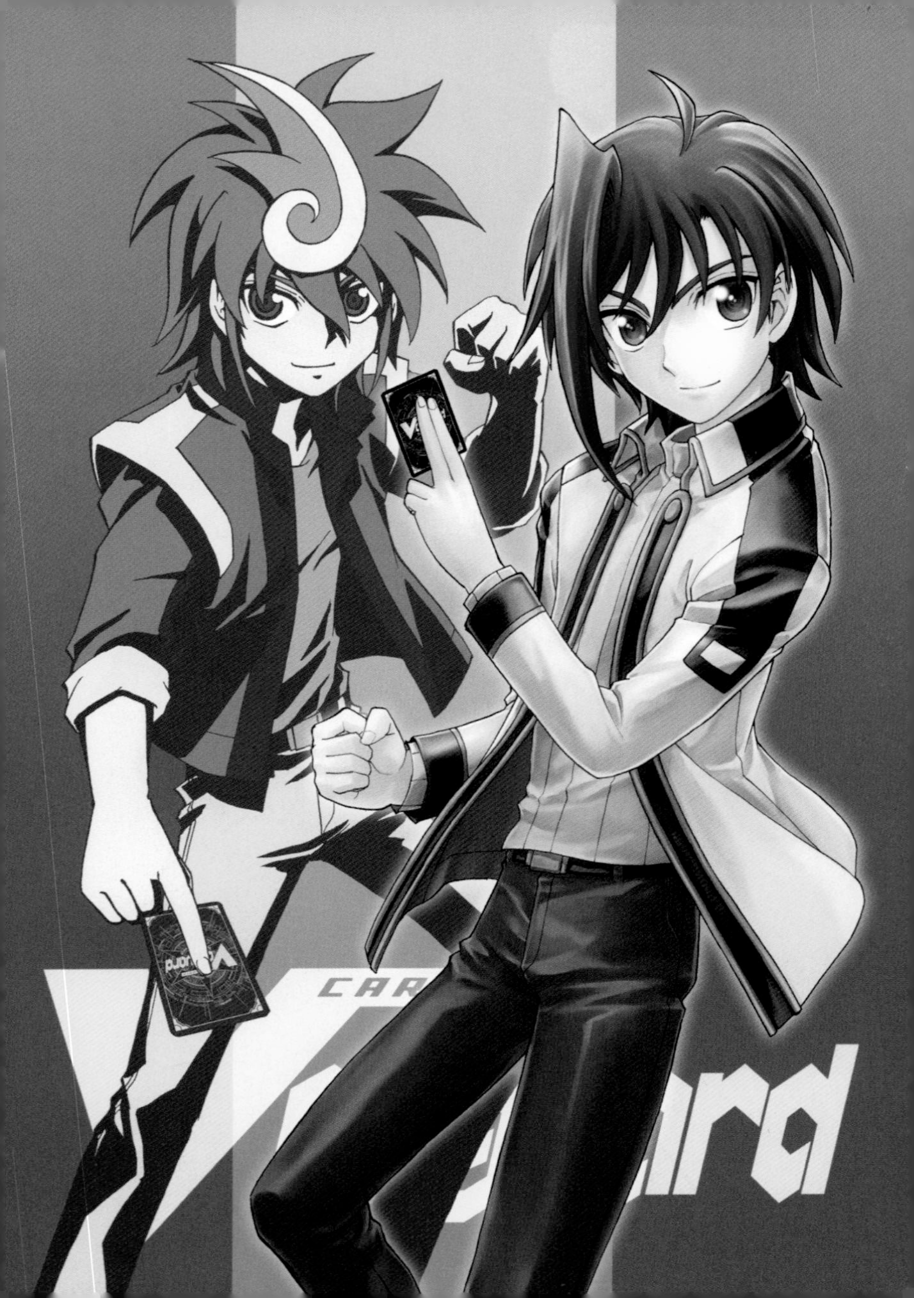

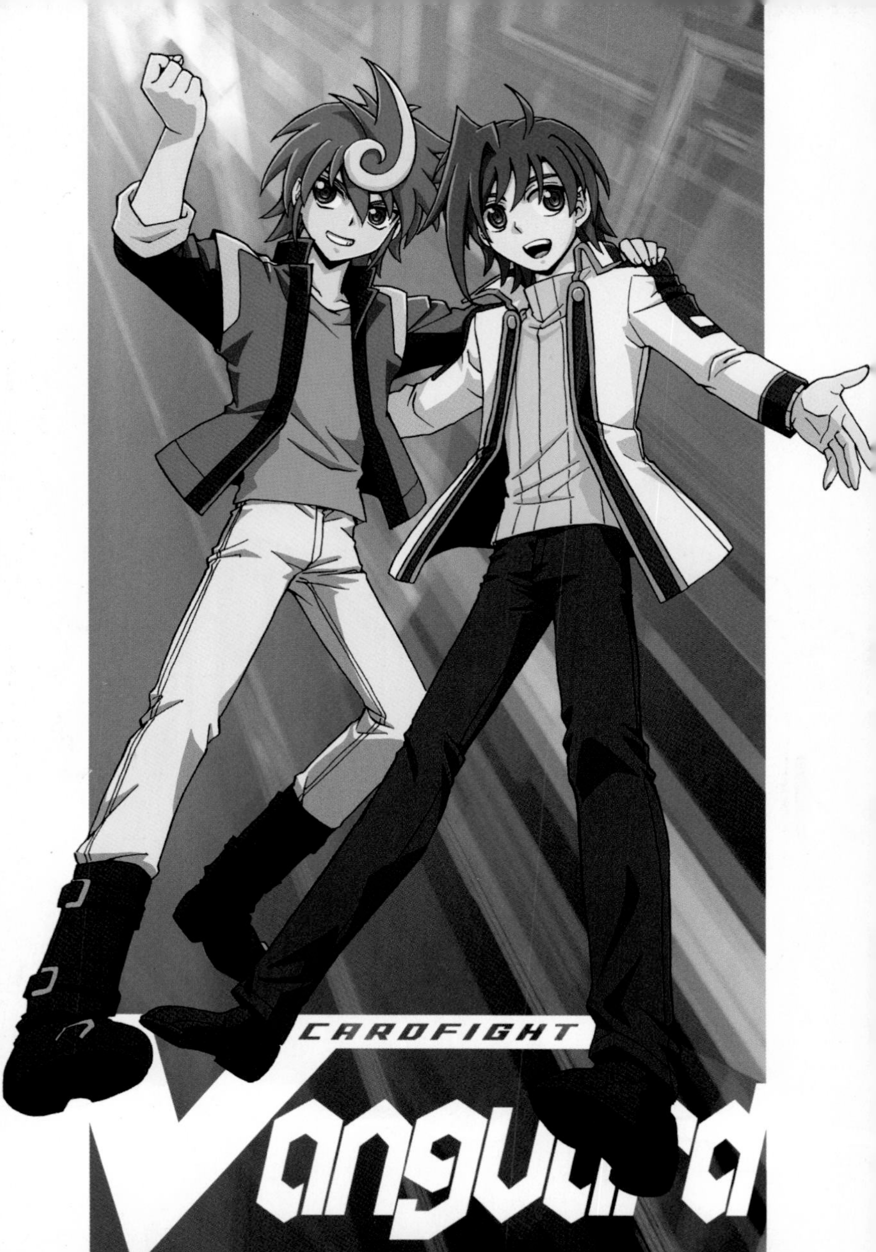
CARDFIGHT
Vanguard

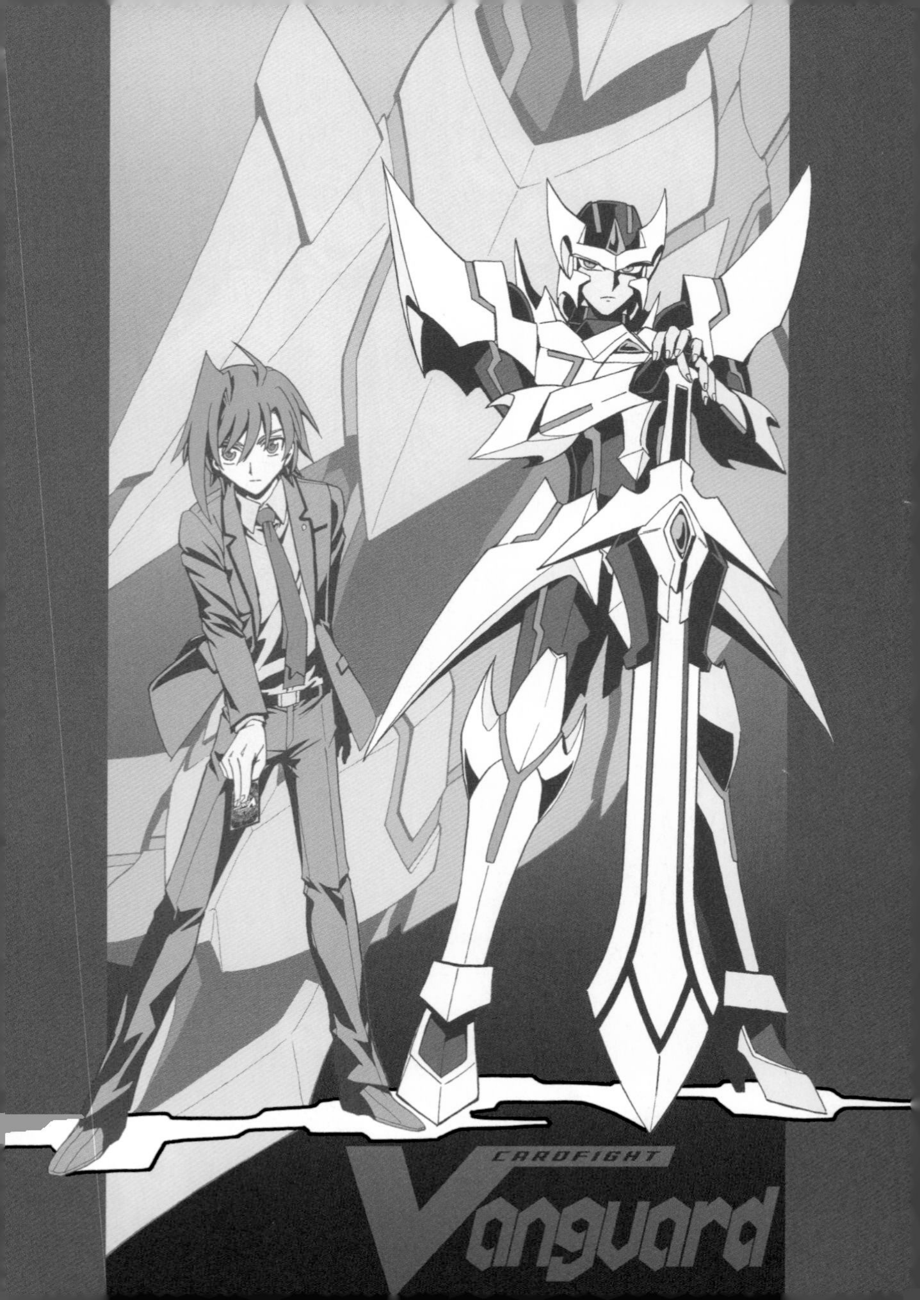
CARDFIGHT
Vanguard

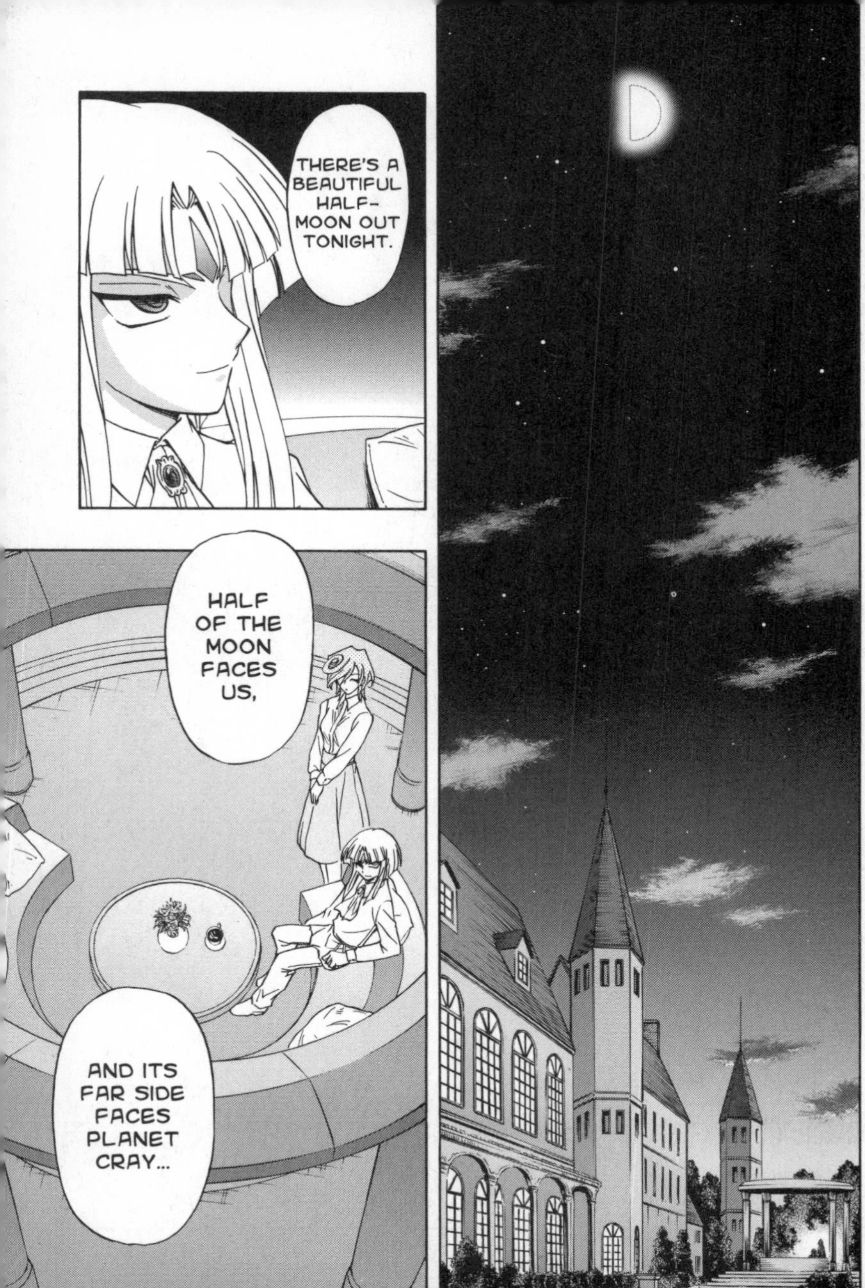
THERE'S A BEAUTIFUL HALF-MOON OUT TONIGHT.
HALF OF THE MOON FACES US,
AND ITS FAR SIDE FACES PLANET CRAY...

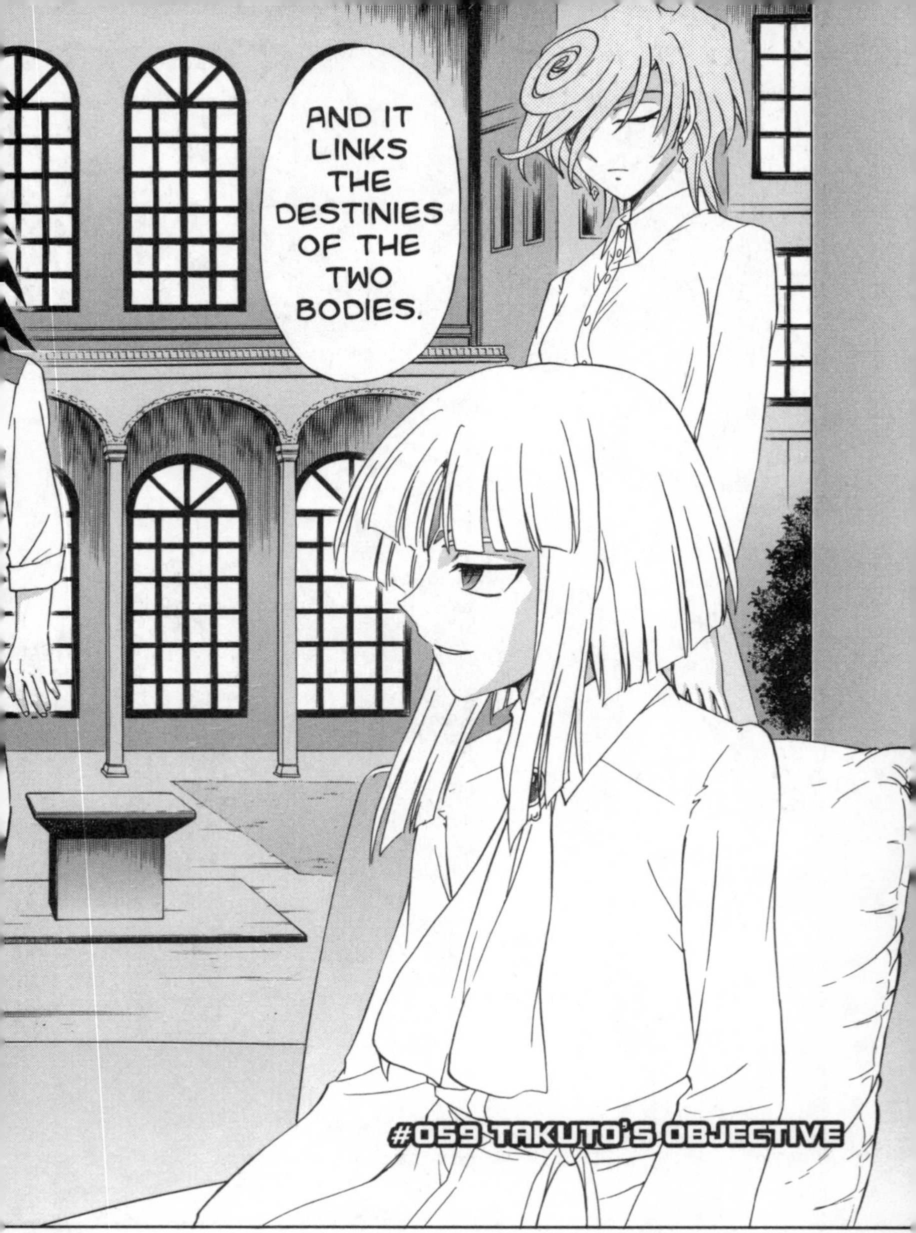
AND IT LINKS THE DESTINIES OF THE TWO BODIES.
#059 TAKUTO'S OBJECTIVE

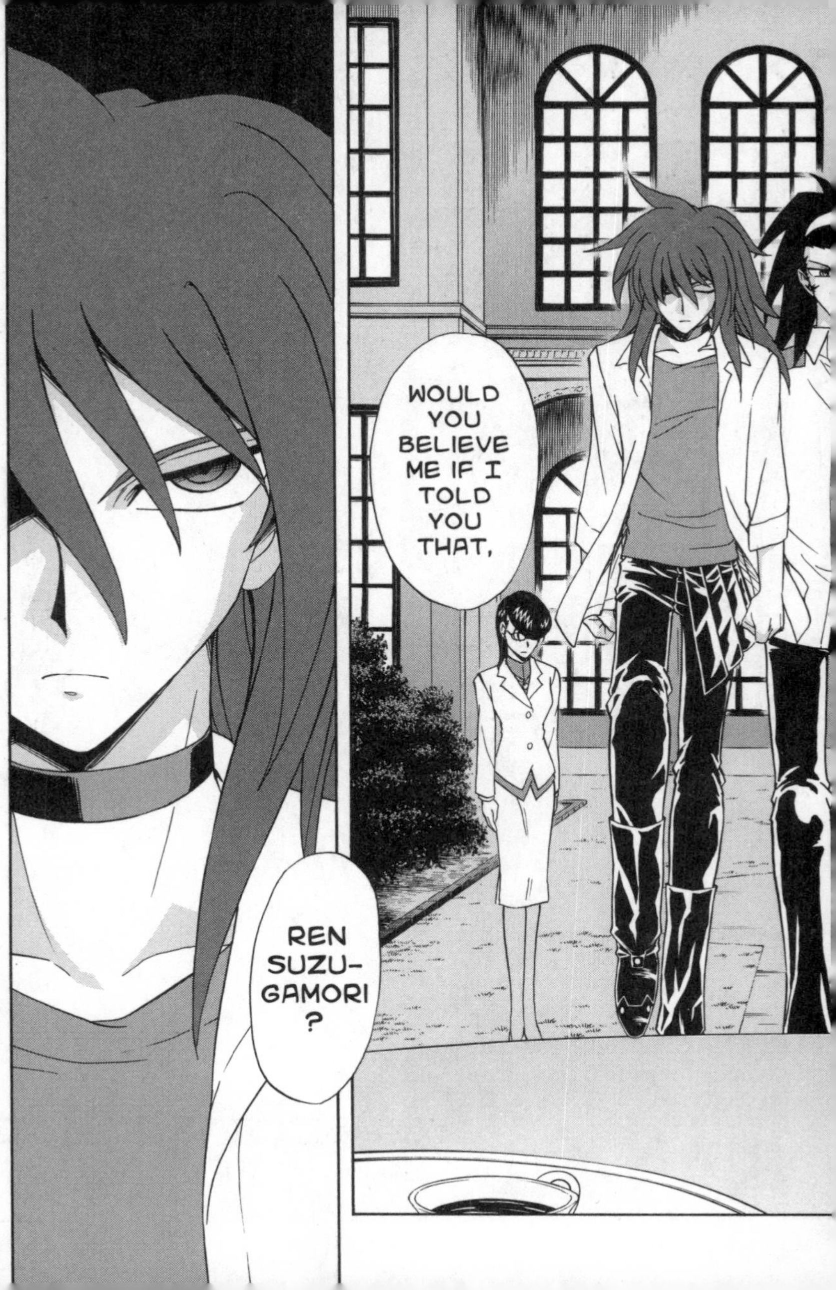
WOULD YOU BELIEVE ME IF I TOLD YOU THAT,
REN SUZU-GAMORI ?

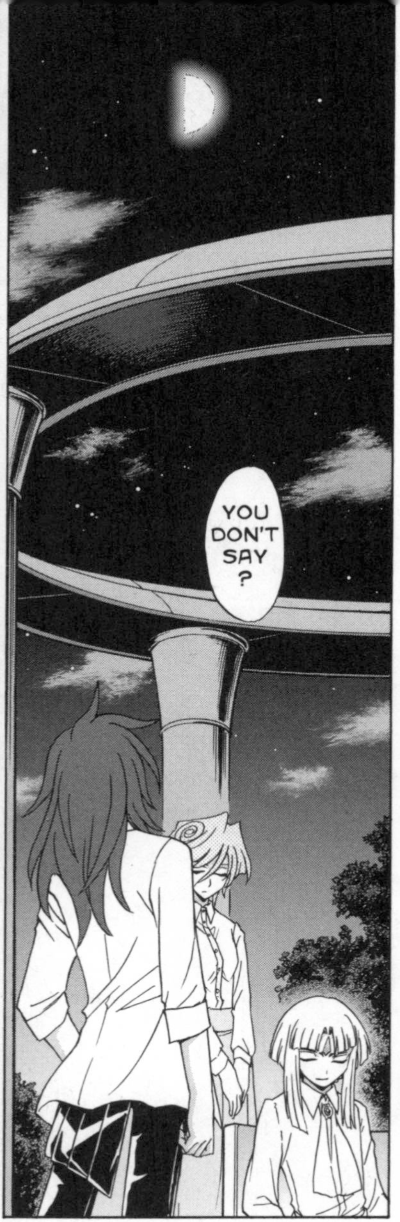
YOU DON'T SAY?
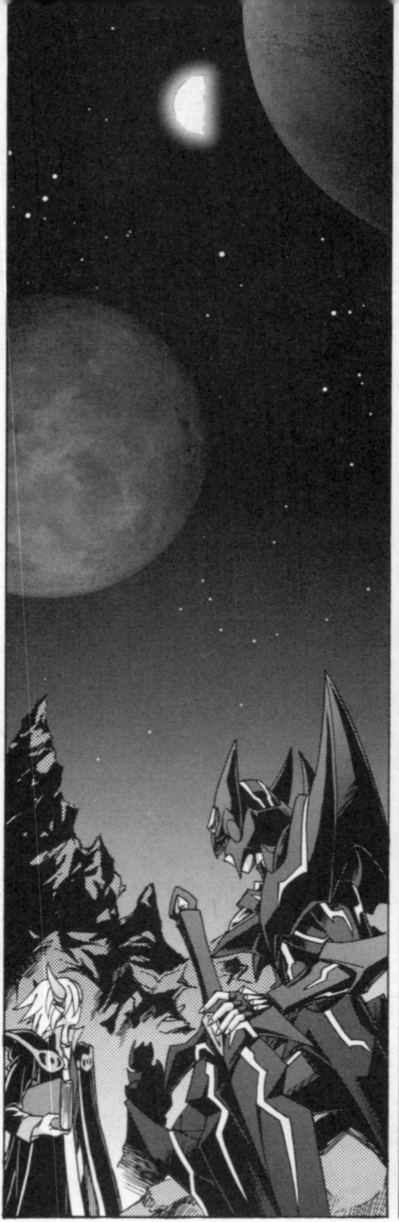

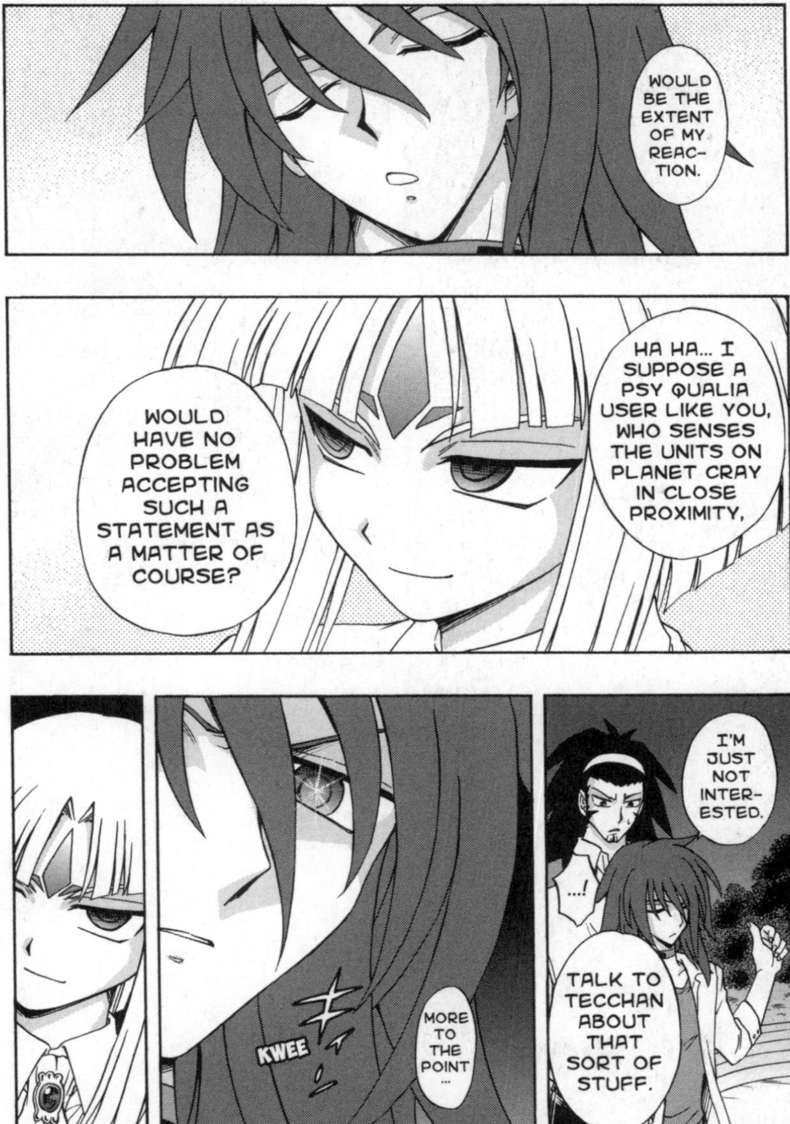
WOULD BE THE EXTENT OF MY REAC-TION.
HA HA... I SUPPOSE A PSY QUALIA USER LIKE YOU, WHO SENSES THE UNITS ON PLANET CRAY IN CLOSE PROXIMITY,
WOULD HAVE NO PROBLEM ACCEPTING SUCH A STATEMENT AS A MATTER OF COURSE?
I'M JUST NOT INTER-ESTED.
...!
TALK TO TECCHAN ABOUT THAT SORT OF STUFF.
MORE TO THE POINT ...
KWEE

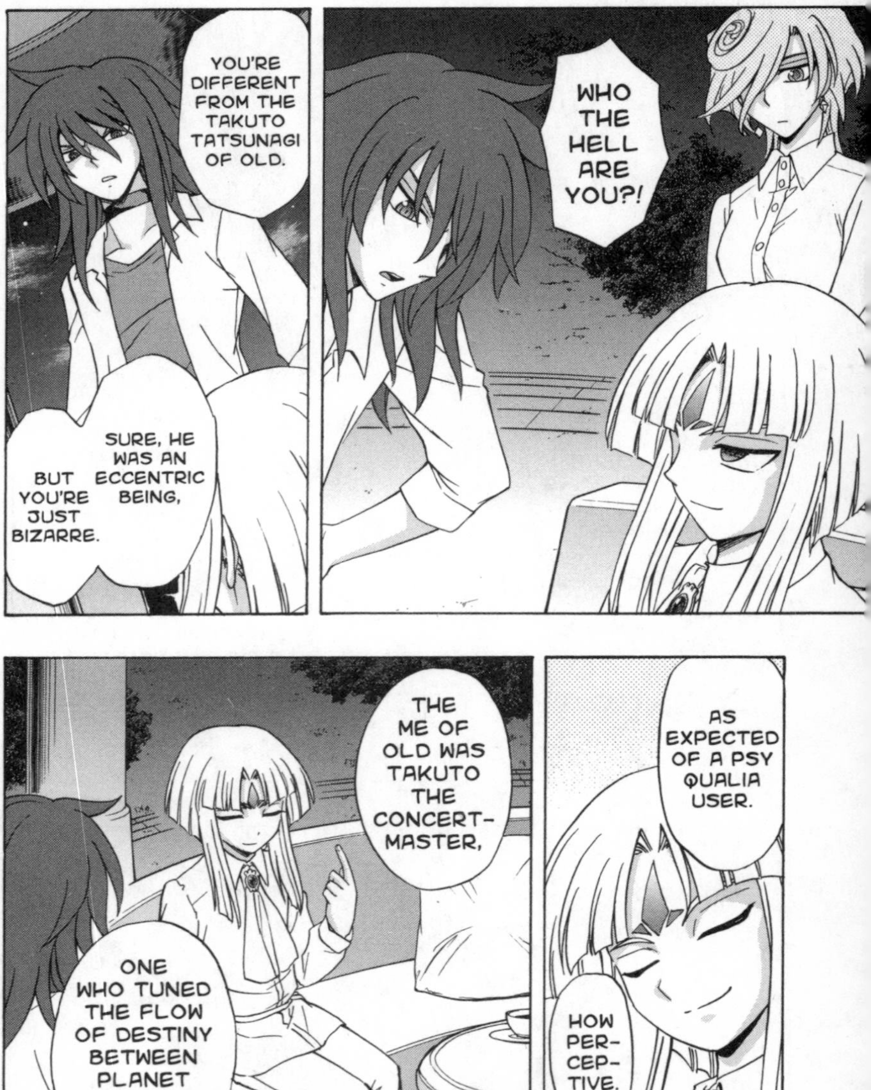
WHO THE HELL ARE YOU?!
YOU'RE DIFFERENT FROM THE TAKUTO TATSUNAGI OF OLD.
SURE, HE WAS AN ECCENTRIC BEING,
BUT YOU'RE JUST BIZARRE.
AS EXPECTED OF A PSY QUALIA USER.
HOW PER-CEP-TIVE.
THE ME OF OLD WAS TAKUTO THE CONCERT-MASTER,
ONE WHO TUNED THE FLOW OF DESTINY BETWEEN PLANET CRAY AND EARTH.

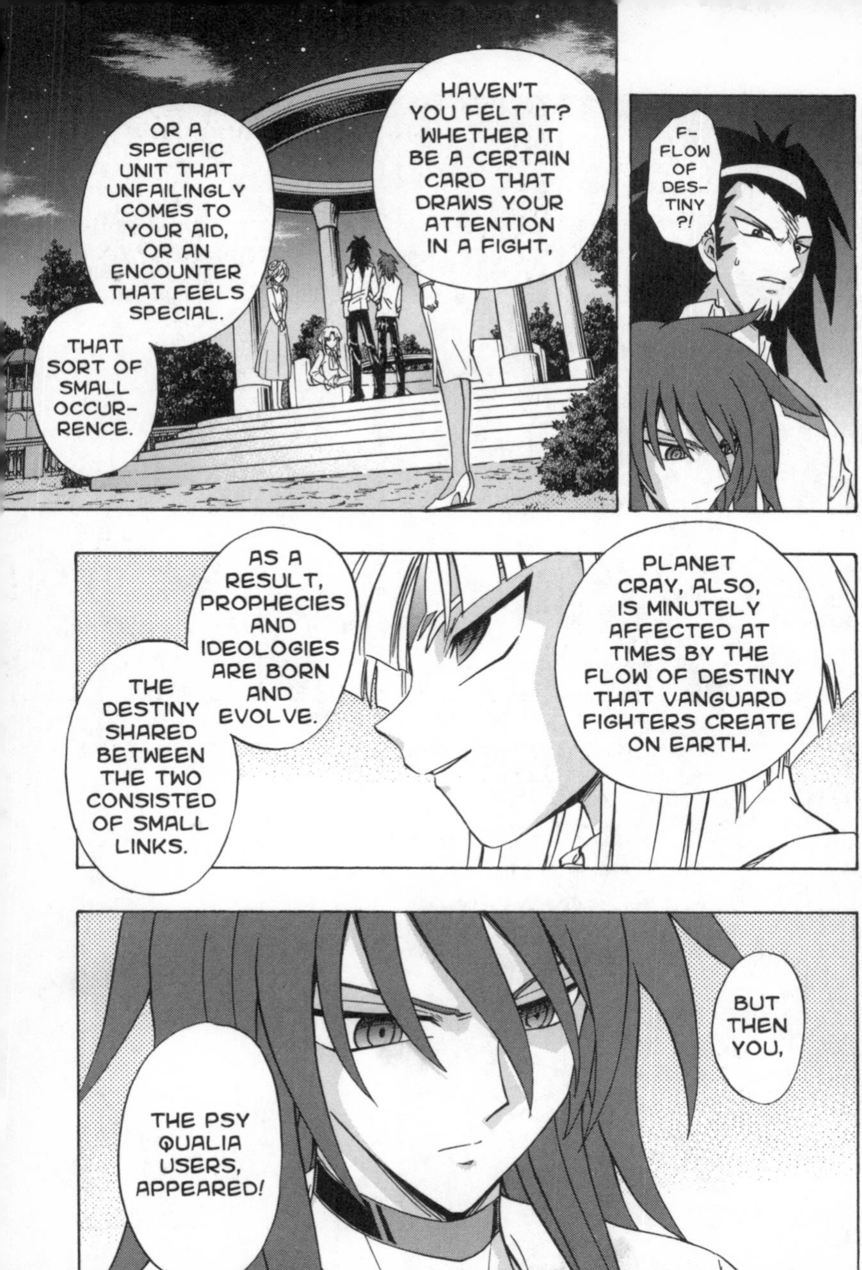
F- FLOW OF DESTINY?!
HAVEN'T YOU FELT IT? WHETHER IT BE A CERTAIN CARD THAT DRAWS YOUR ATTENTION IN A FIGHT,
OR A SPECIFIC UNIT THAT UNFAILINGLY COMES TO YOUR AID, OR AN ENCOUNTER THAT FEELS SPECIAL.
THAT SORT OF SMALL OCCURRENCE.
PLANET CRAY, ALSO, IS MINUTELY AFFECTED AT TIMES BY THE FLOW OF DESTINY THAT VANGUARD FIGHTERS CREATE ON EARTH.
AS A RESULT, PROPHECIES AND IDEOLOGIES ARE BORN AND EVOLVE.
THE DESTINY SHARED BETWEEN THE TWO CONSISTED OF SMALL LINKS.
BUT THEN YOU,
THE PSY QUALIA USERS, APPEARED!

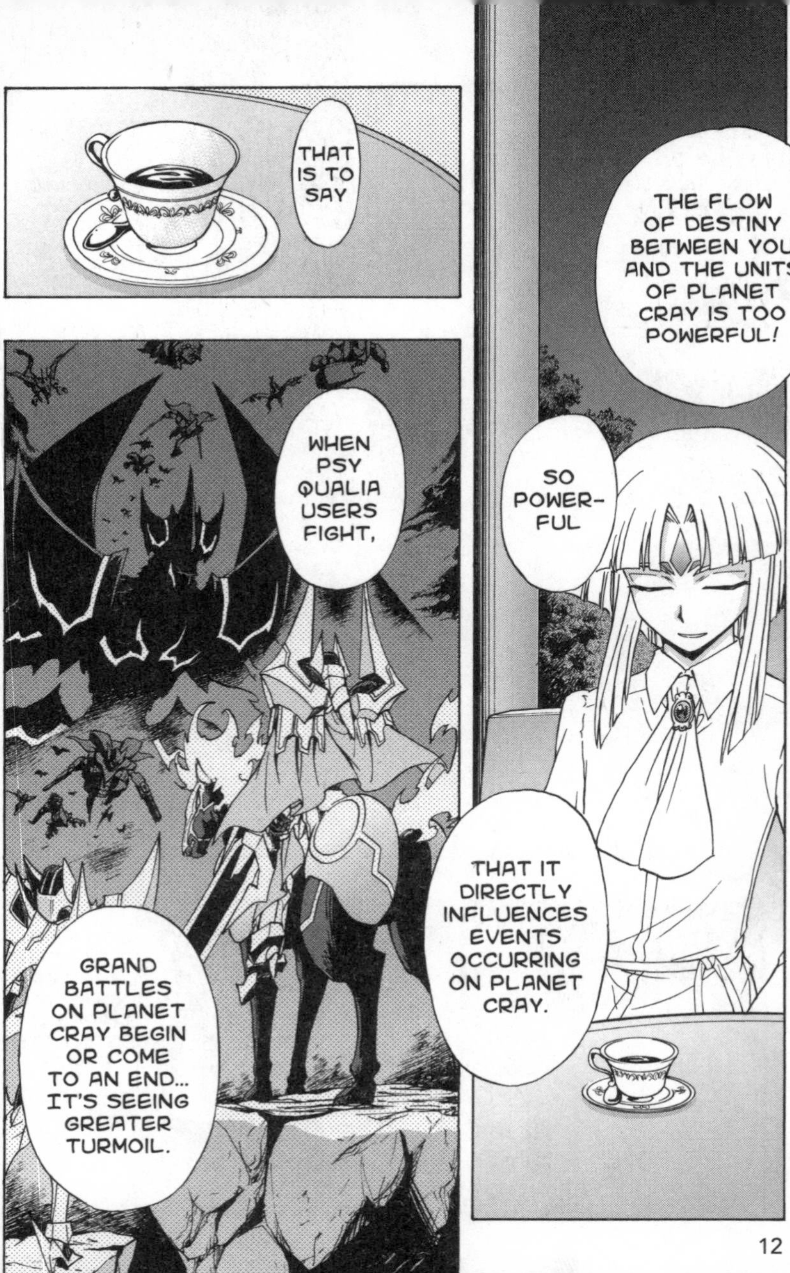
THE FLOW OF DESTINY BETWEEN YOU AND THE UNITS OF PLANET CRAY IS TOO POWERFUL!
SO POWER-FUL
THAT IT DIRECTLY INFLUENCES EVENTS OCCURRING ON PLANET CRAY.
THAT IS TO SAY
WHEN PSY QUALIA USERS FIGHT,
GRAND BATTLES ON PLANET CRAY BEGIN OR COME TO AN END... IT'S SEEING GREATER TURMOIL.

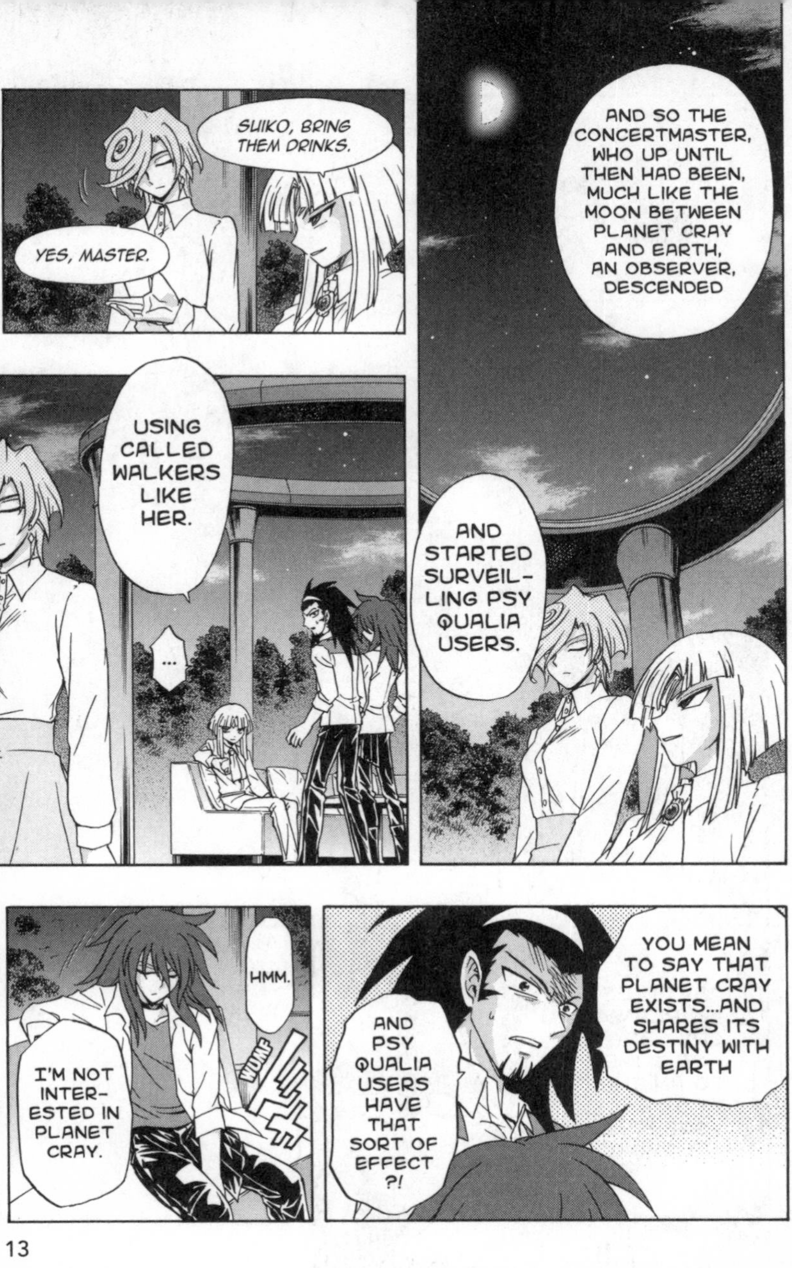
AND SO THE CONCERTMASTER, WHO UP UNTIL THEN HAD BEEN, MUCH LIKE THE MOON BETWEEN PLANET CRAY AND EARTH, AN OBSERVER, DESCENDED
AND STARTED SURVEIL-LING PSY QUALIA USERS.
SUIKO, BRING THEM DRINKS.
YES, MASTER.
USING CALLED WALKERS LIKE HER.
...
YOU MEAN TO SAY THAT PLANET CRAY EXISTS...AND SHARES ITS DESTINY WITH EARTH
AND PSY QUALIA USERS HAVE THAT SORT OF EFFECT ?!
HMM.
WUMF
I'M NOT INTER-ESTED IN PLANET CRAY.

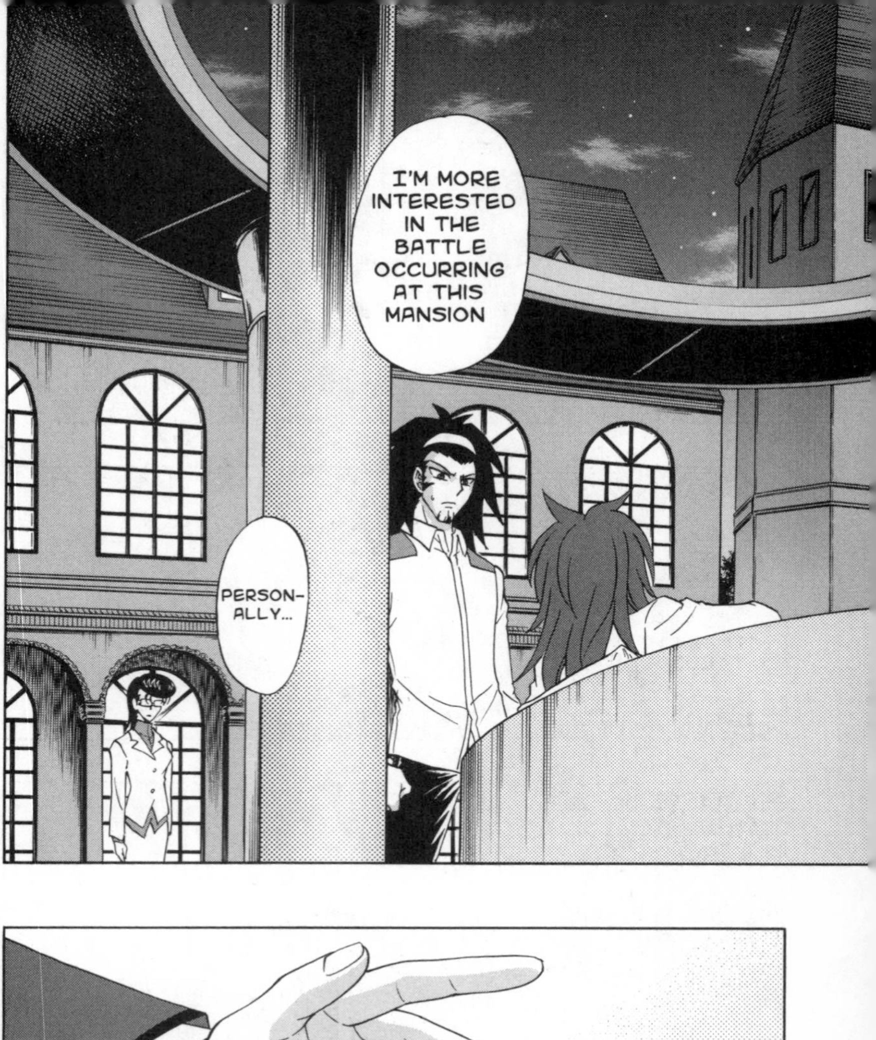
PERSON-ALLY...
I'M MORE INTERESTED IN THE BATTLE OCCURRING AT THIS MANSION

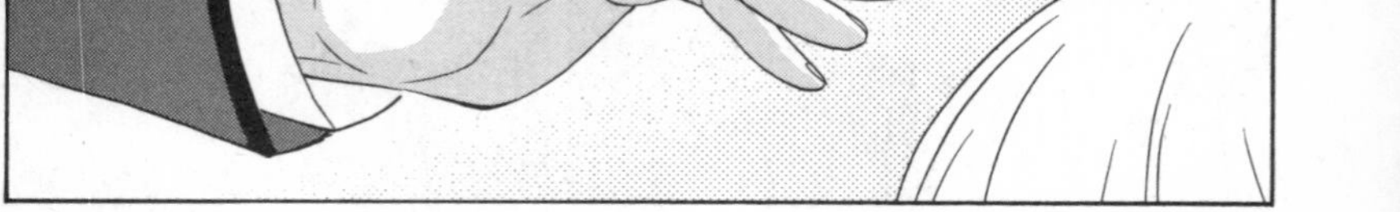

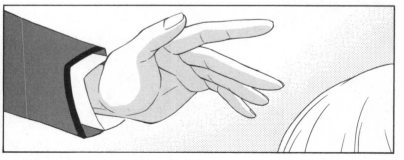

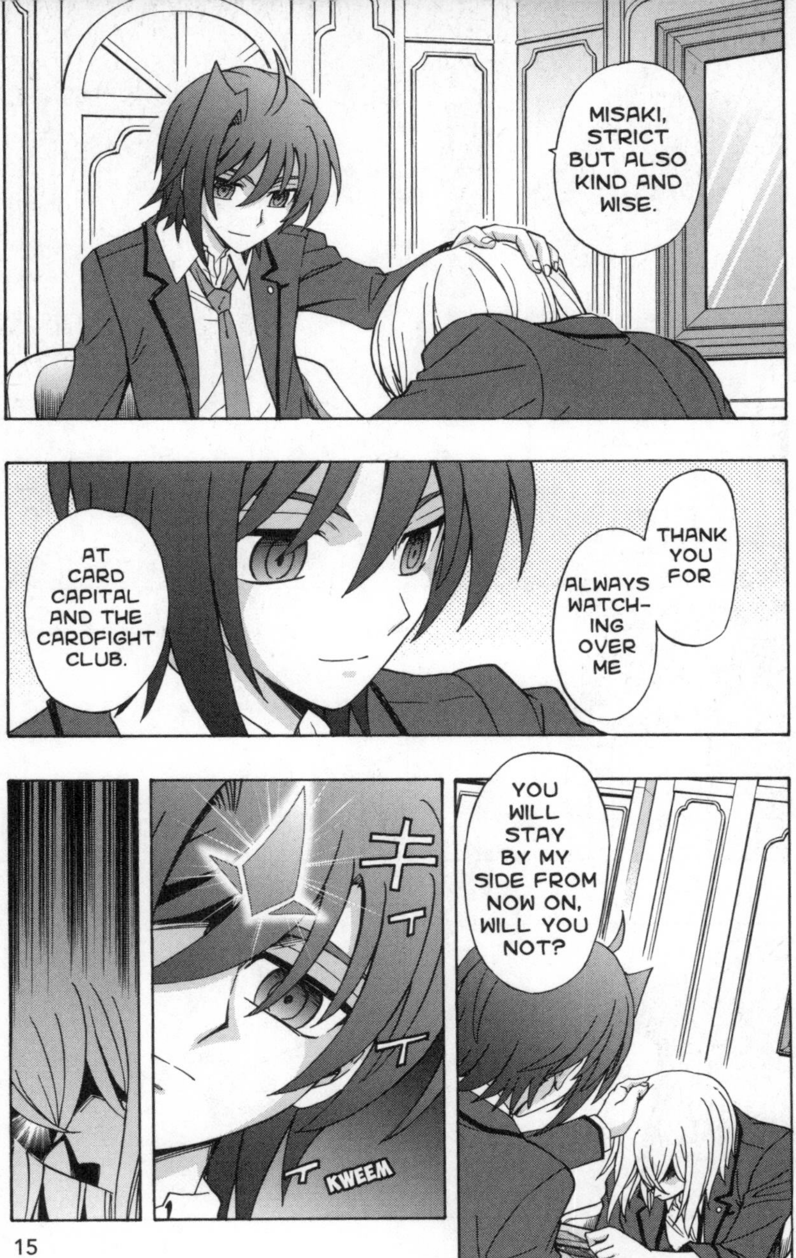
MISAKI, STRICT BUT ALSO KIND AND WISE.
THANK YOU FOR ALWAYS WATCHING OVER ME
AT CARD CAPITAL AND THE CARDFIGHT CLUB.
YOU WILL STAY BY MY SIDE FROM NOW ON, WILL YOU NOT?
KWEEM

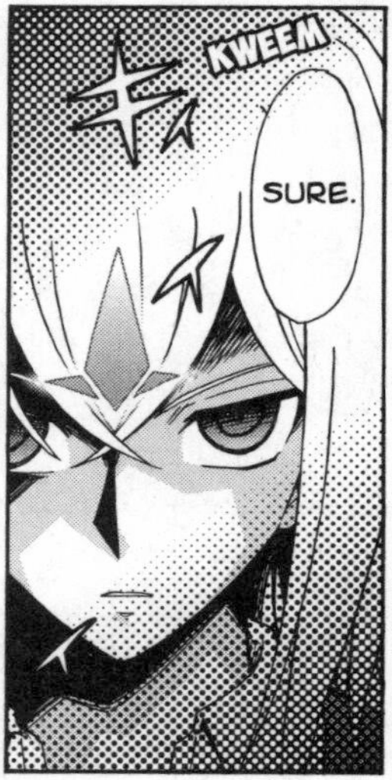
KWEEM
SURE.
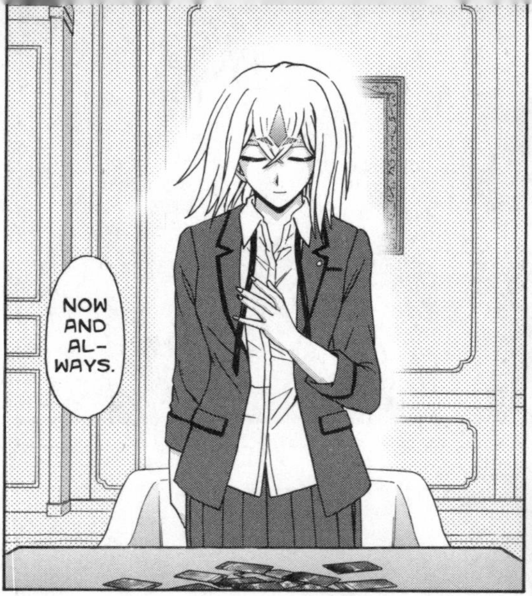
NOW AND AL-WAYS.
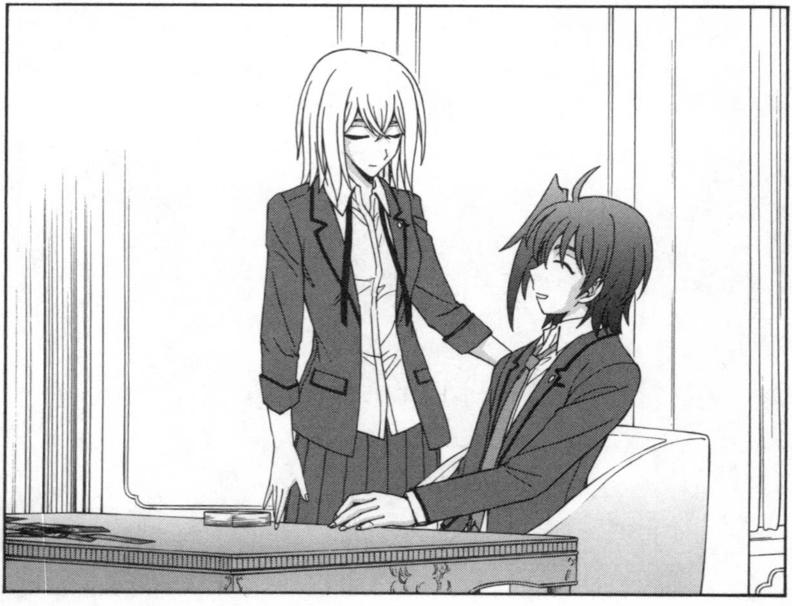

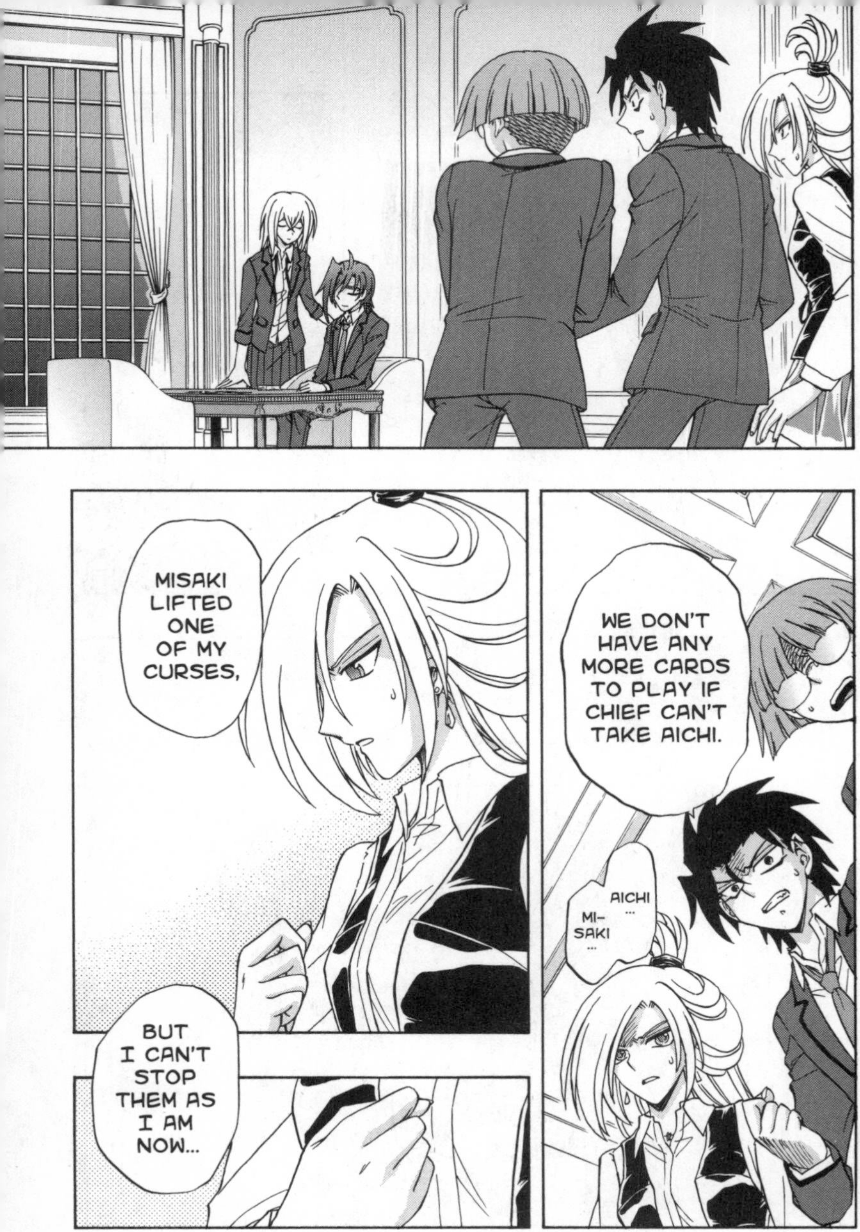
WE DON'T HAVE ANY MORE CARDS TO PLAY IF CHIEF CAN'T TAKE AICHI.
AICHI ...
MI-SAKI ...
MISAKI LIFTED ONE OF MY CURSES,
BUT I CAN'T STOP THEM AS I AM NOW...

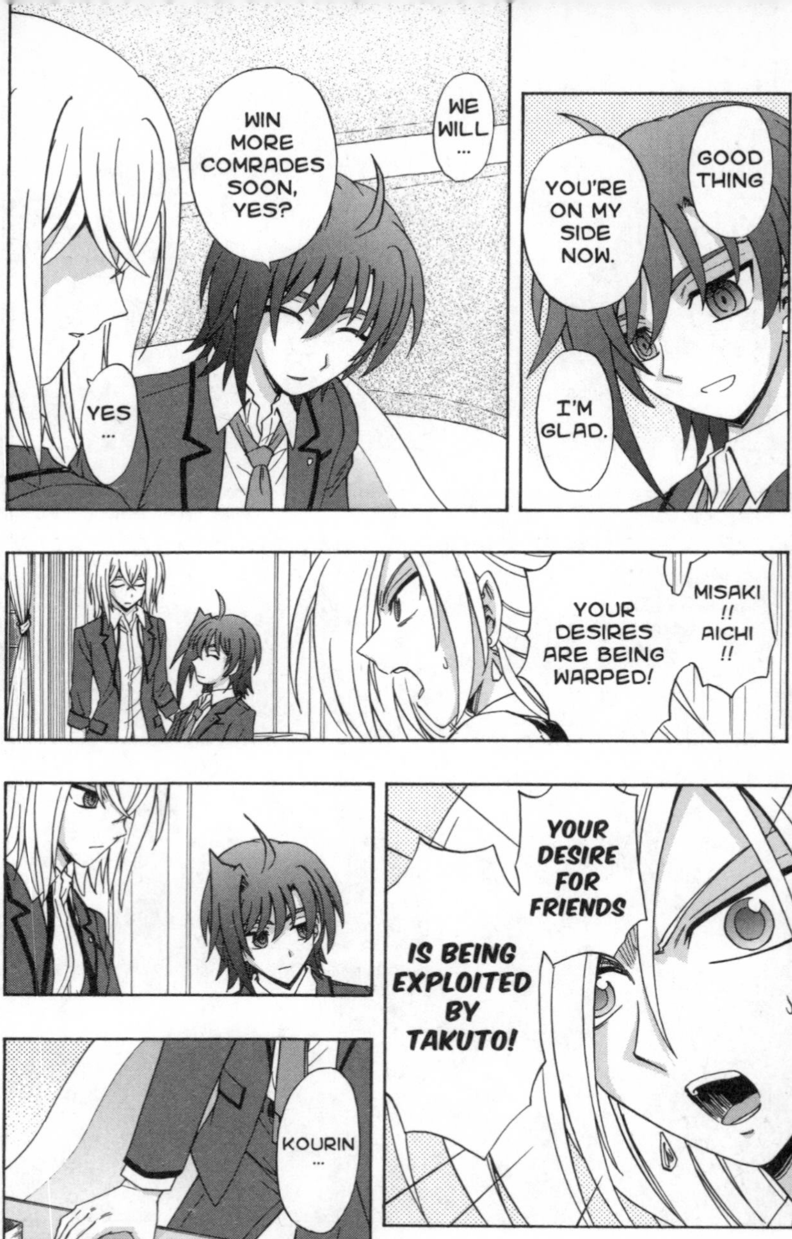
GOOD THING
YOU'RE ON MY SIDE NOW.
I'M GLAD.
WE WILL ...
WIN MORE COMRADES SOON, YES?
YES ...
MISAKI !! AICHI !!
YOUR DESIRES ARE BEING WARPED!
YOUR DESIRE FOR FRIENDS
IS BEING EXPLOITED BY TAKUTO!
KOURIN ...

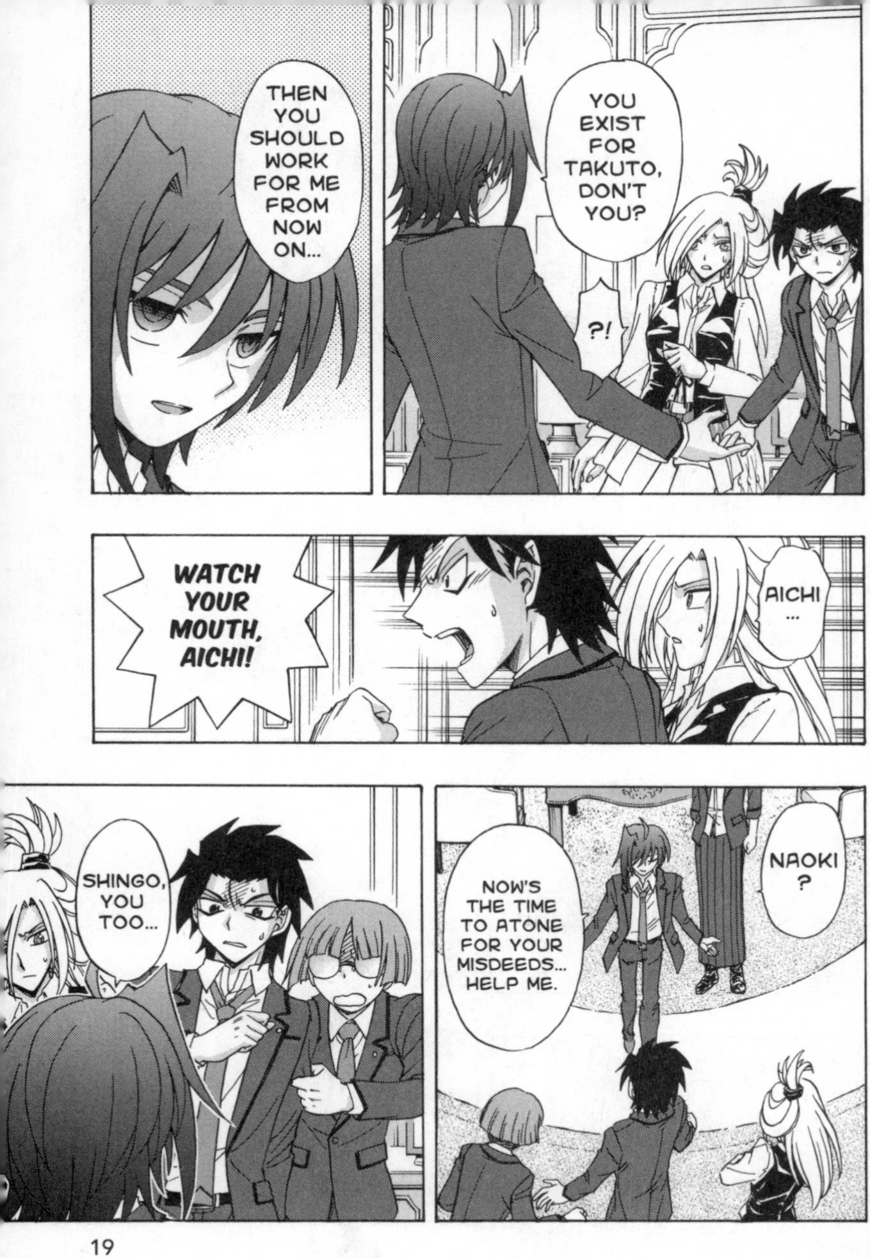
YOU EXIST FOR TAKUTO, DON'T YOU?
?!
THEN YOU SHOULD WORK FOR ME FROM NOW ON...
AICHI ...
WATCH YOUR MOUTH, AICHI!
NAOKI ?
NOW'S THE TIME TO ATONE FOR YOUR MISDEEDS... HELP ME.
SHINGO, YOU TOO...

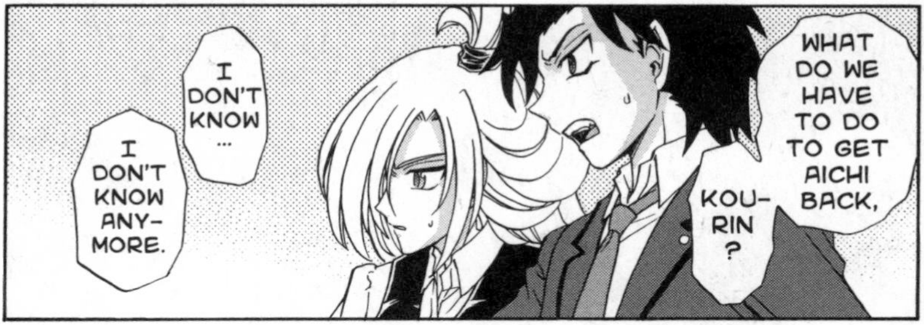
WHAT DO WE HAVE TO DO TO GET AICHI BACK,
KOU-RIN?
I DON'T KNOW...
I DON'T KNOW ANY-MORE.

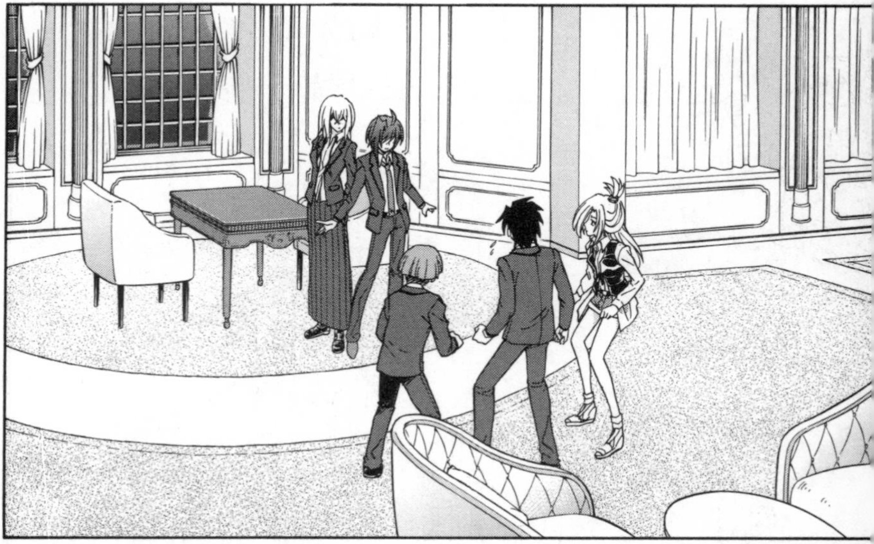

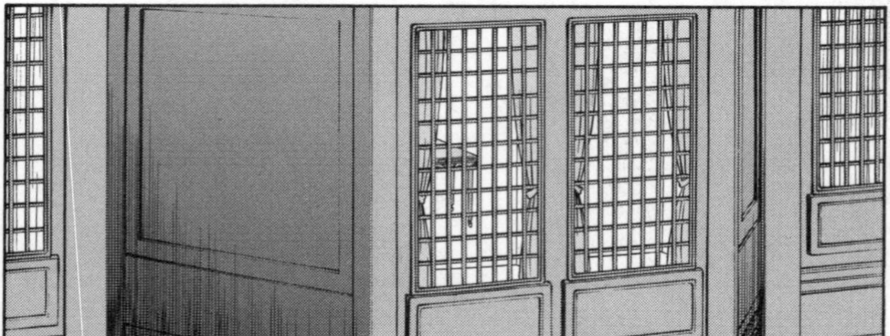

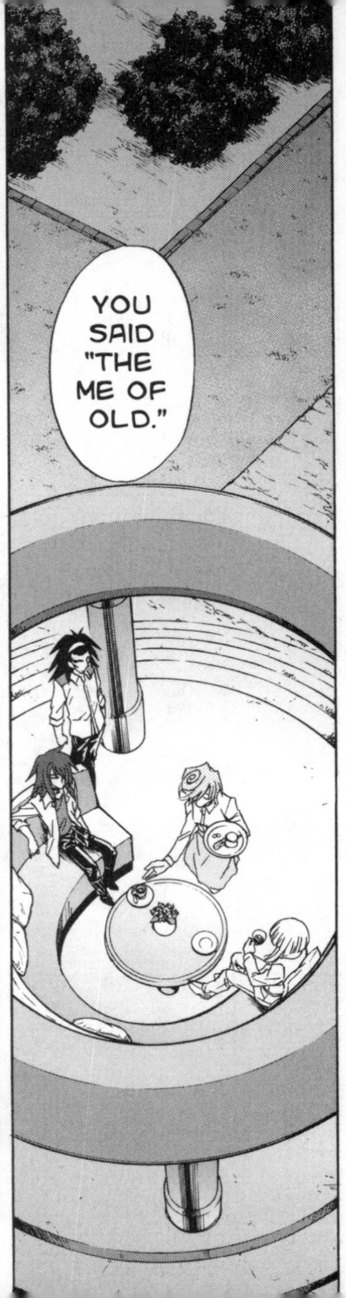
YOU SAID "THE ME OF OLD."
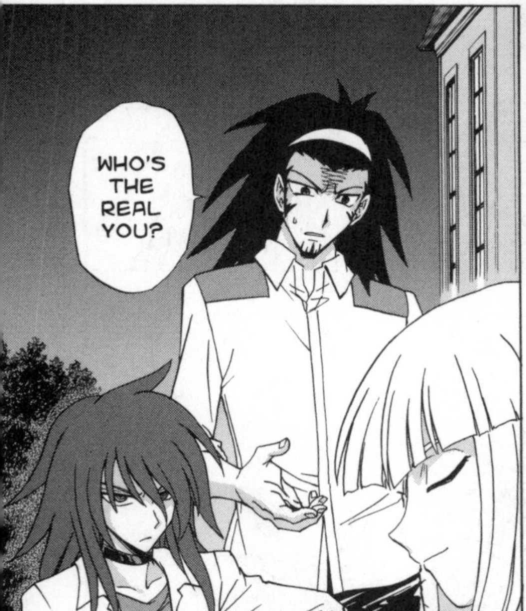
WHO'S THE REAL YOU?
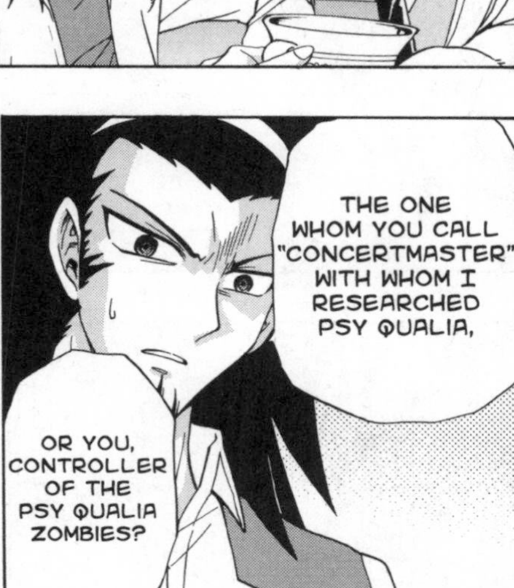
THE ONE WHOM YOU CALL "CONCERTMASTER" WITH WHOM I RESEARCHED PSY QUALIA,
OR YOU, CONTROLLER OF THE PSY QUALIA ZOMBIES?

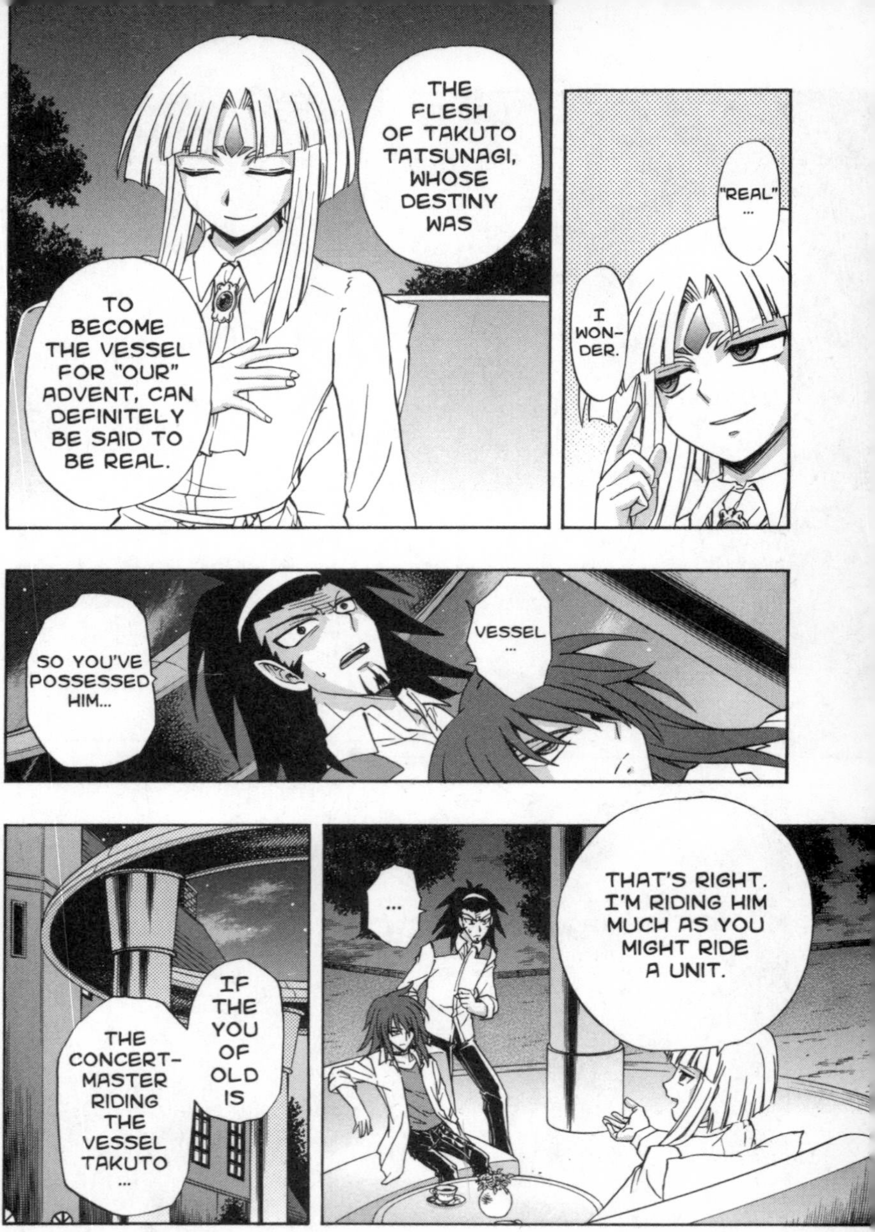
THE FLESH OF TAKUTO TATSUNAGI, WHOSE DESTINY WAS
TO BECOME THE VESSEL FOR "OUR" ADVENT, CAN DEFINITELY BE SAID TO BE REAL.
"REAL"...
I WONDER.
SO YOU'VE POSSESSED HIM...
VESSEL...
IF THE YOU OF OLD IS
THE CONCERT-MASTER RIDING THE VESSEL TAKUTO...
...
THAT'S RIGHT. I'M RIDING HIM MUCH AS YOU MIGHT RIDE A UNIT.

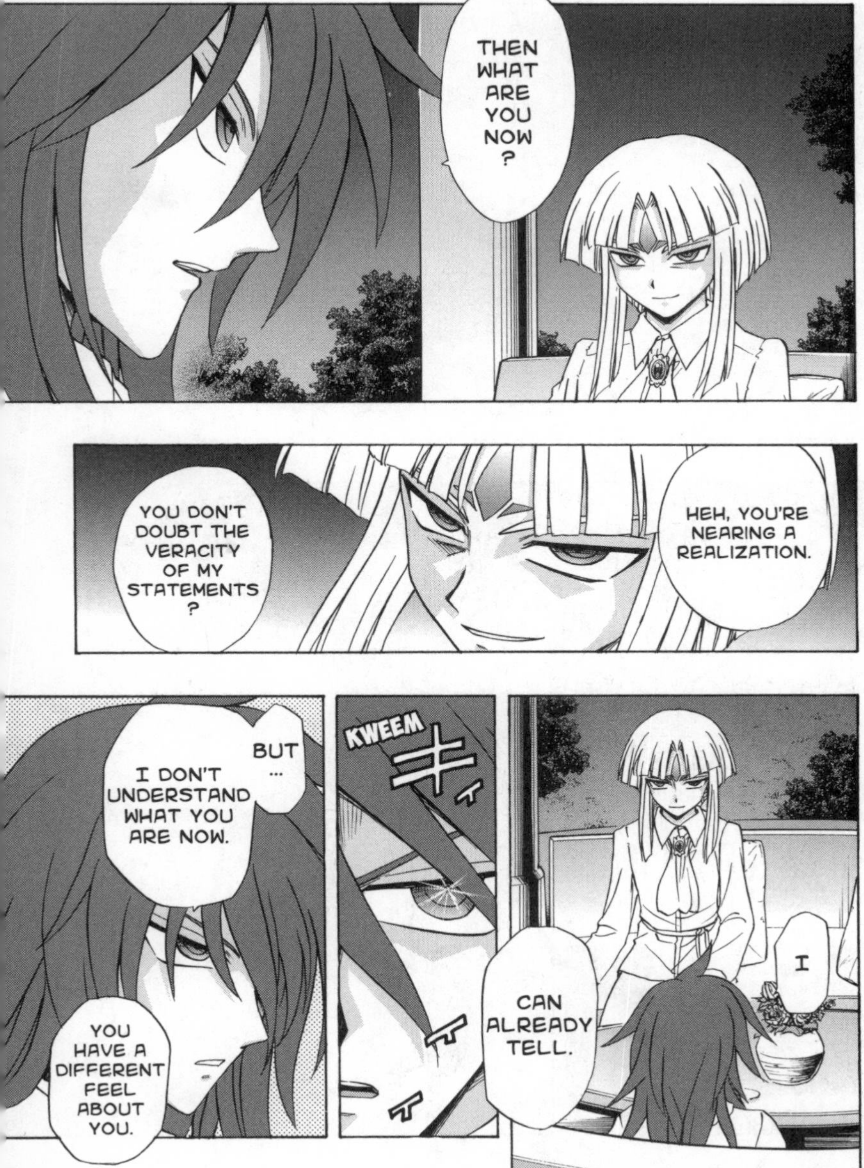
THEN WHAT ARE YOU NOW?
HEH, YOU'RE NEARING A REALIZATION.
YOU DON'T DOUBT THE VERACITY OF MY STATEMENTS?
I
CAN ALREADY TELL.
KWEEM
BUT...
I DON'T UNDERSTAND WHAT YOU ARE NOW.
YOU HAVE A DIFFERENT FEEL ABOUT YOU.

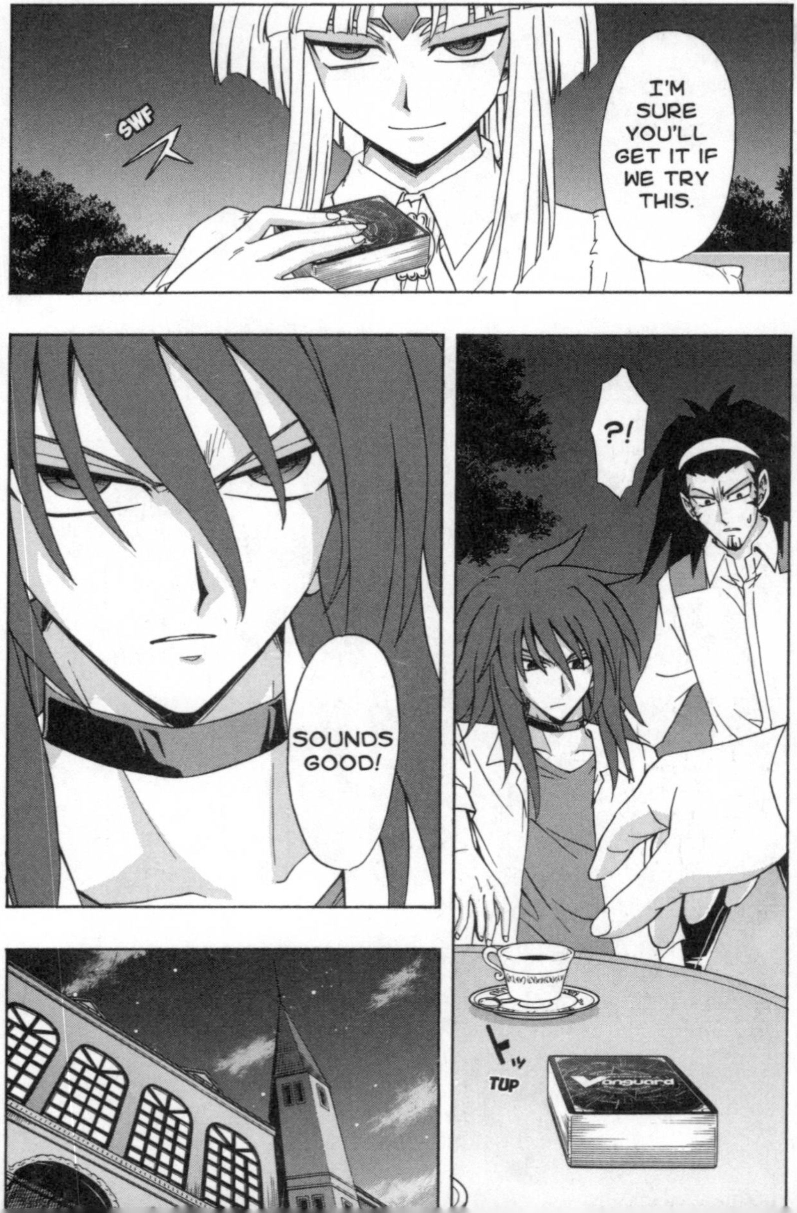
SWF
I'M SURE YOU'LL GET IT IF WE TRY THIS.
?!
SOUNDS GOOD!
TUP
Vanguard

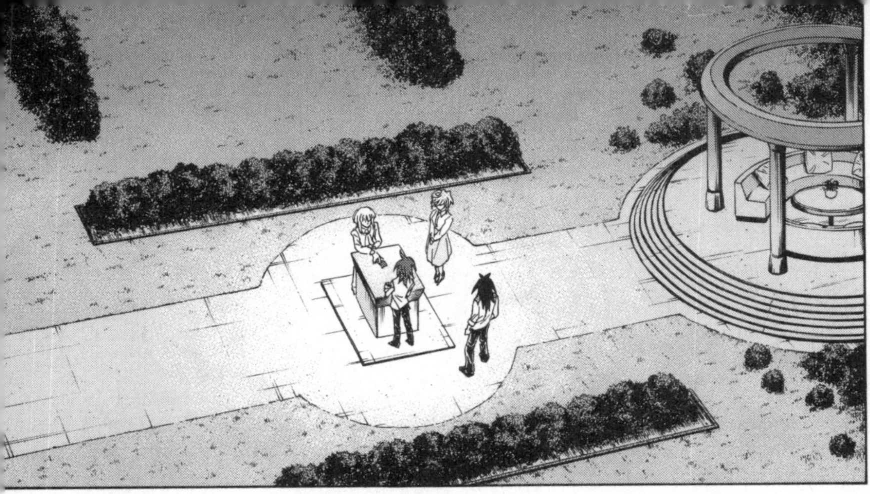

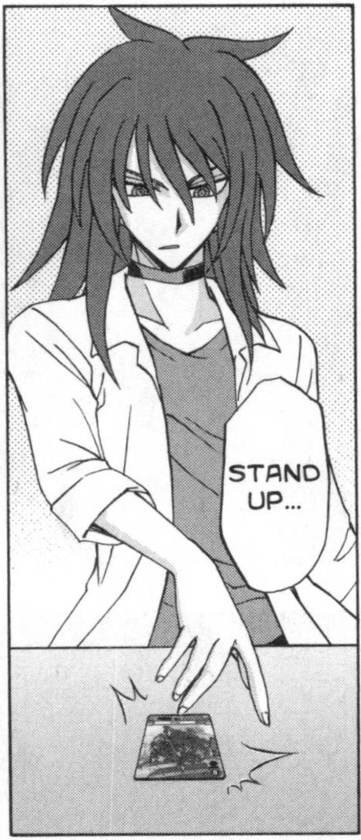
STAND UP...

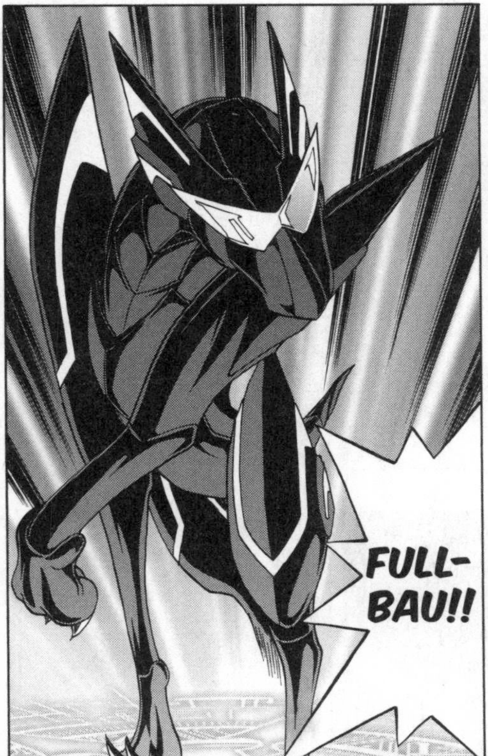
FULL-BAU!!

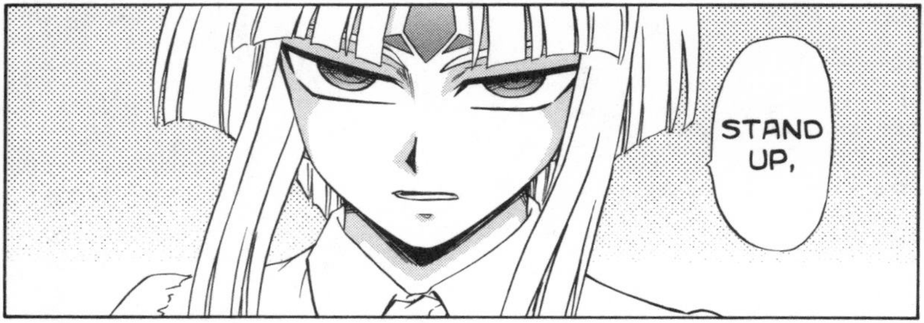
STAND UP,

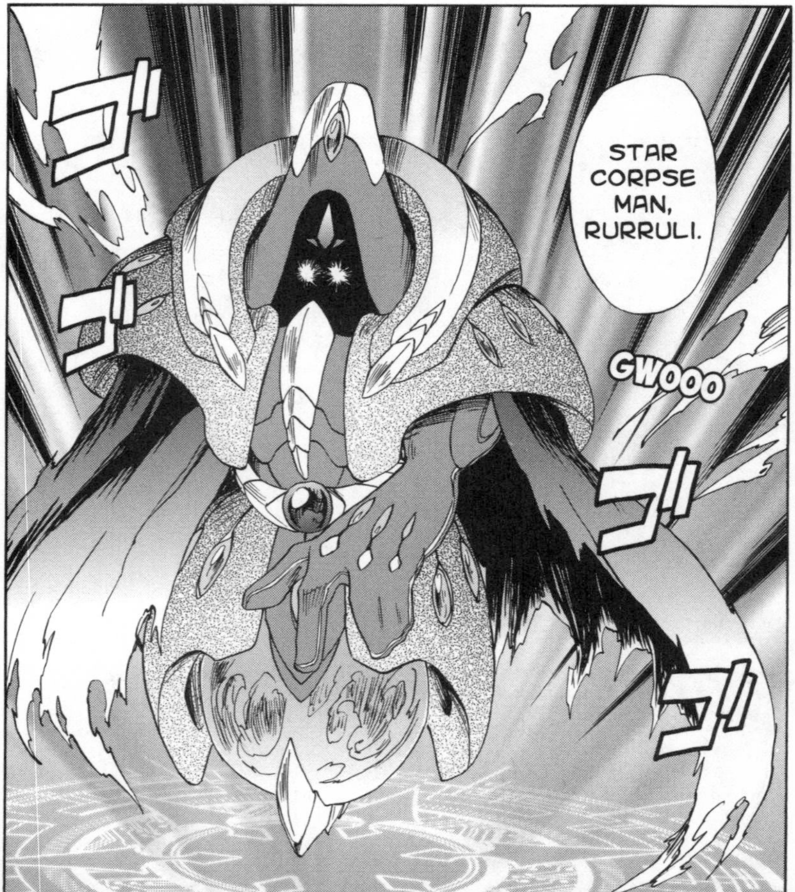
STAR CORPSE MAN, RURRULI.
GWOOO

CARDFIGHT!! Vanguard

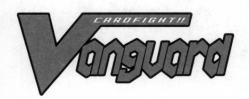

BONUS! CARDFIGHT!! Vanguard NEVER-BEFORE-SEEN IMAGE BOARDS

Releasing Mr. Akira Itou's Rough Sketches!

Borrrr-ring...
...

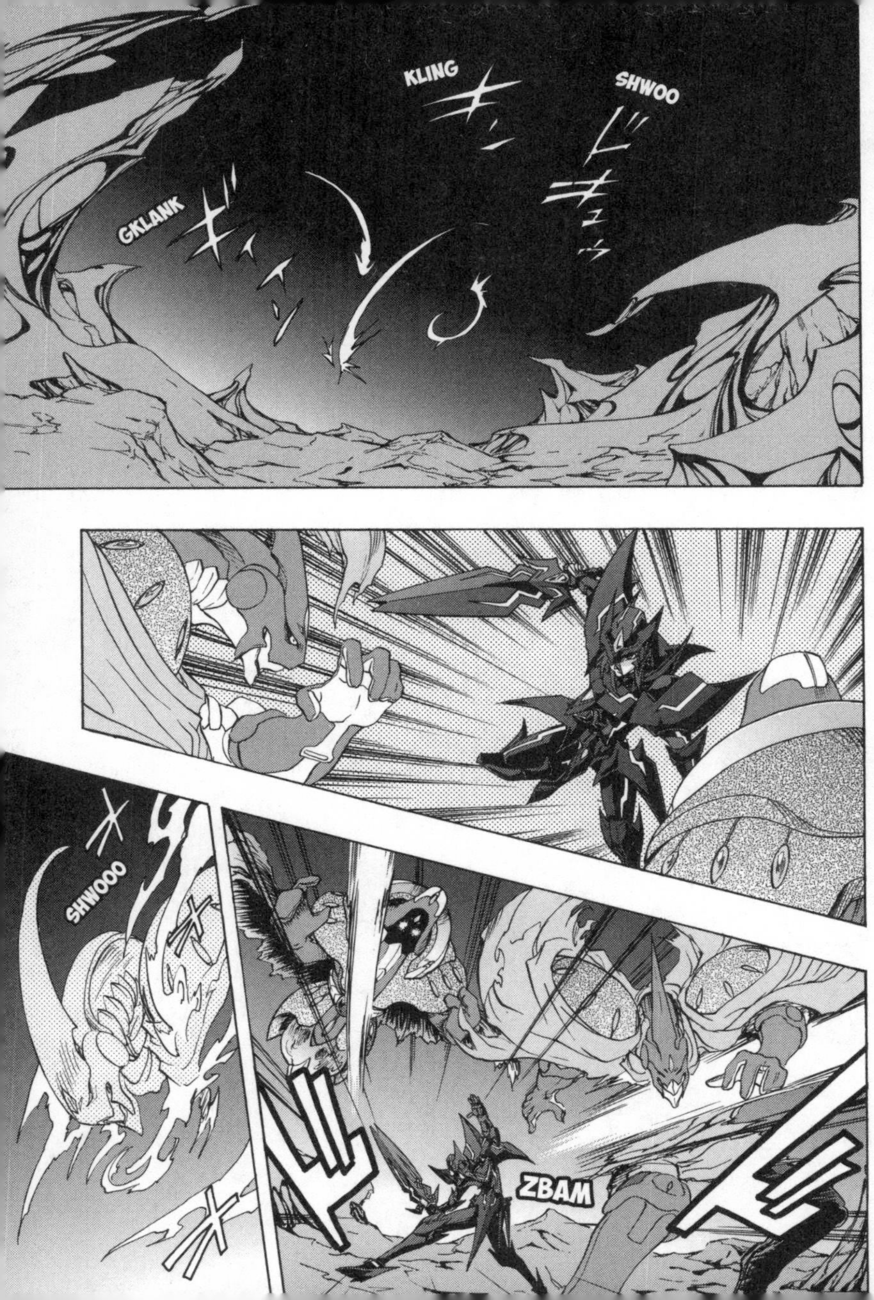
SHWOO
KLING
GKLANK
ZBAM
SHWOOO

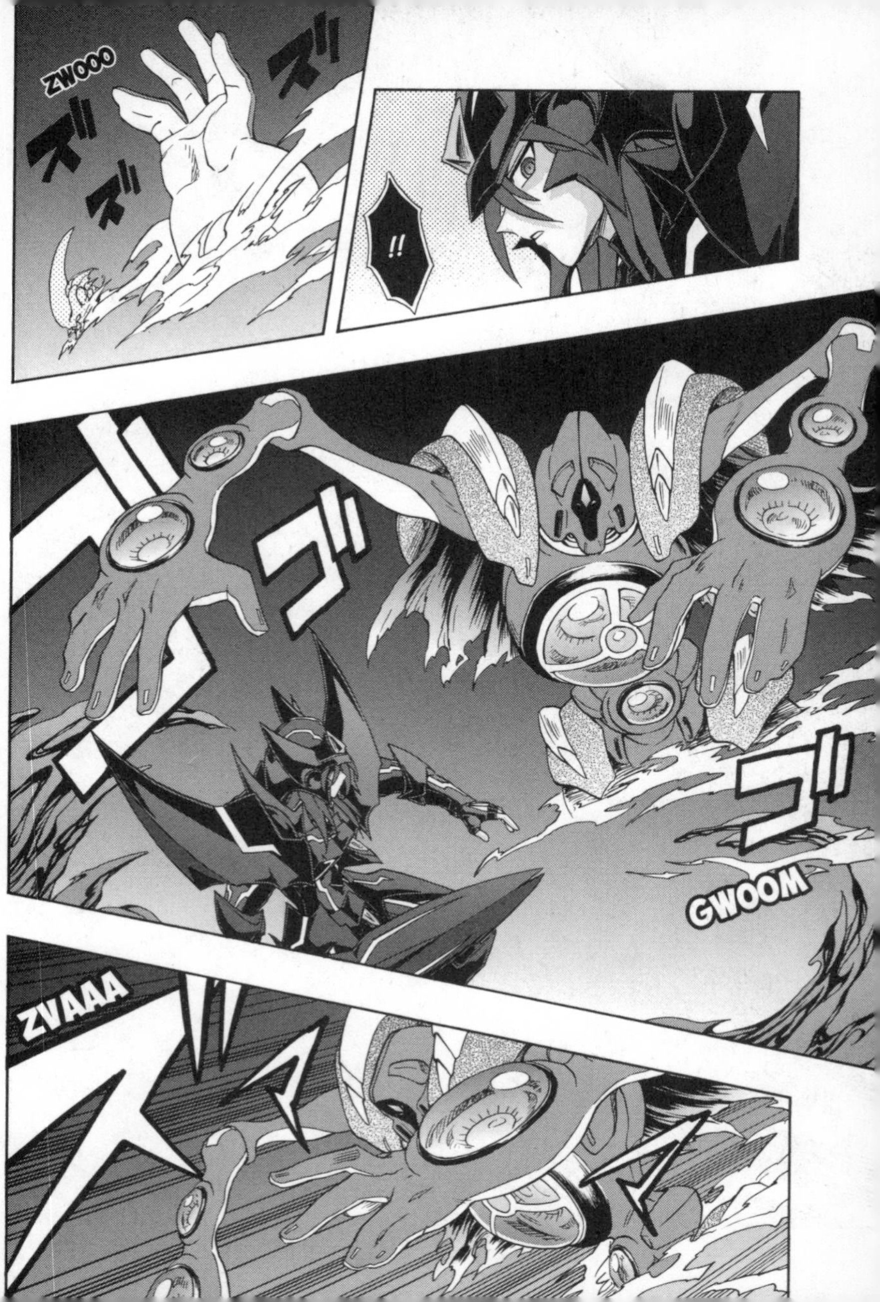
!!
ZWOOO
GWOOM
ZVAAA

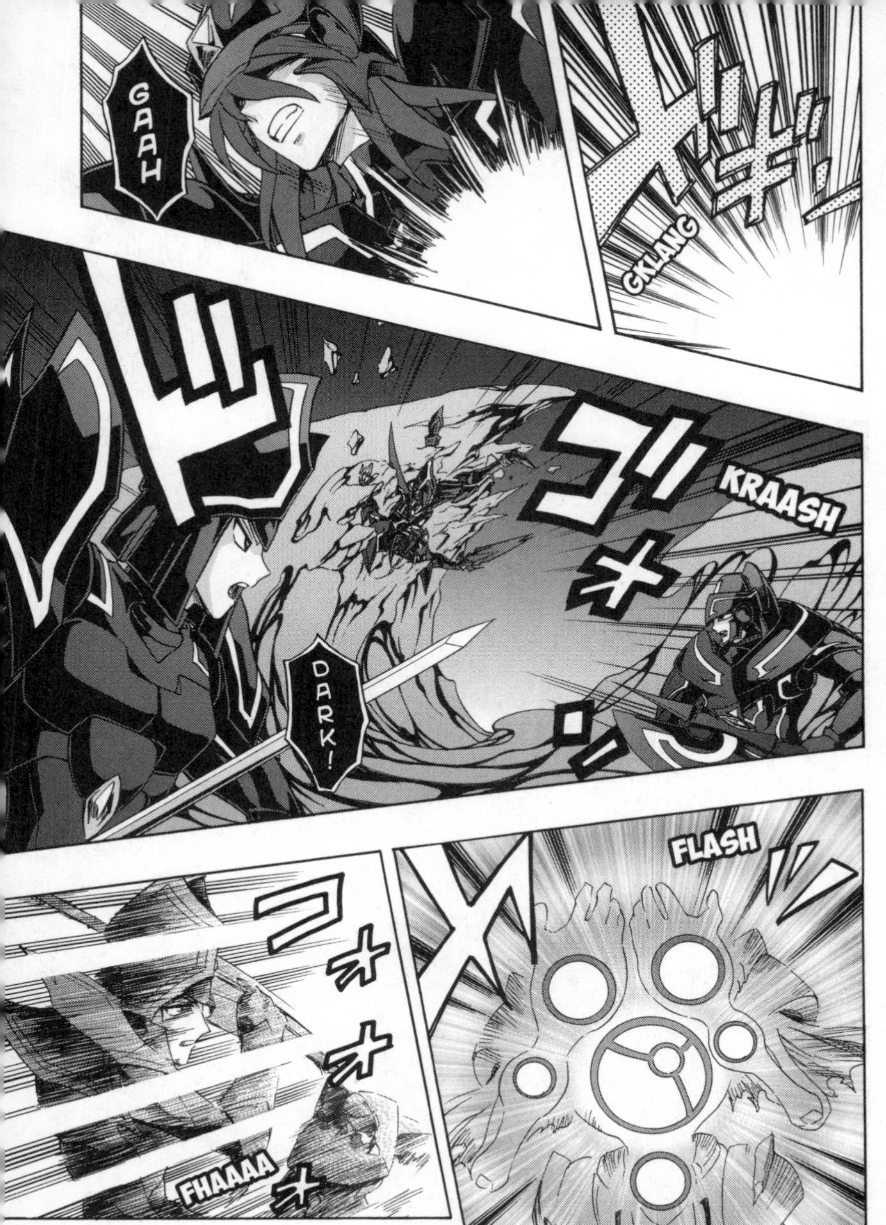
GKLANG
GAAH
KRAASH
DARK!
FLASH
FHAAAA

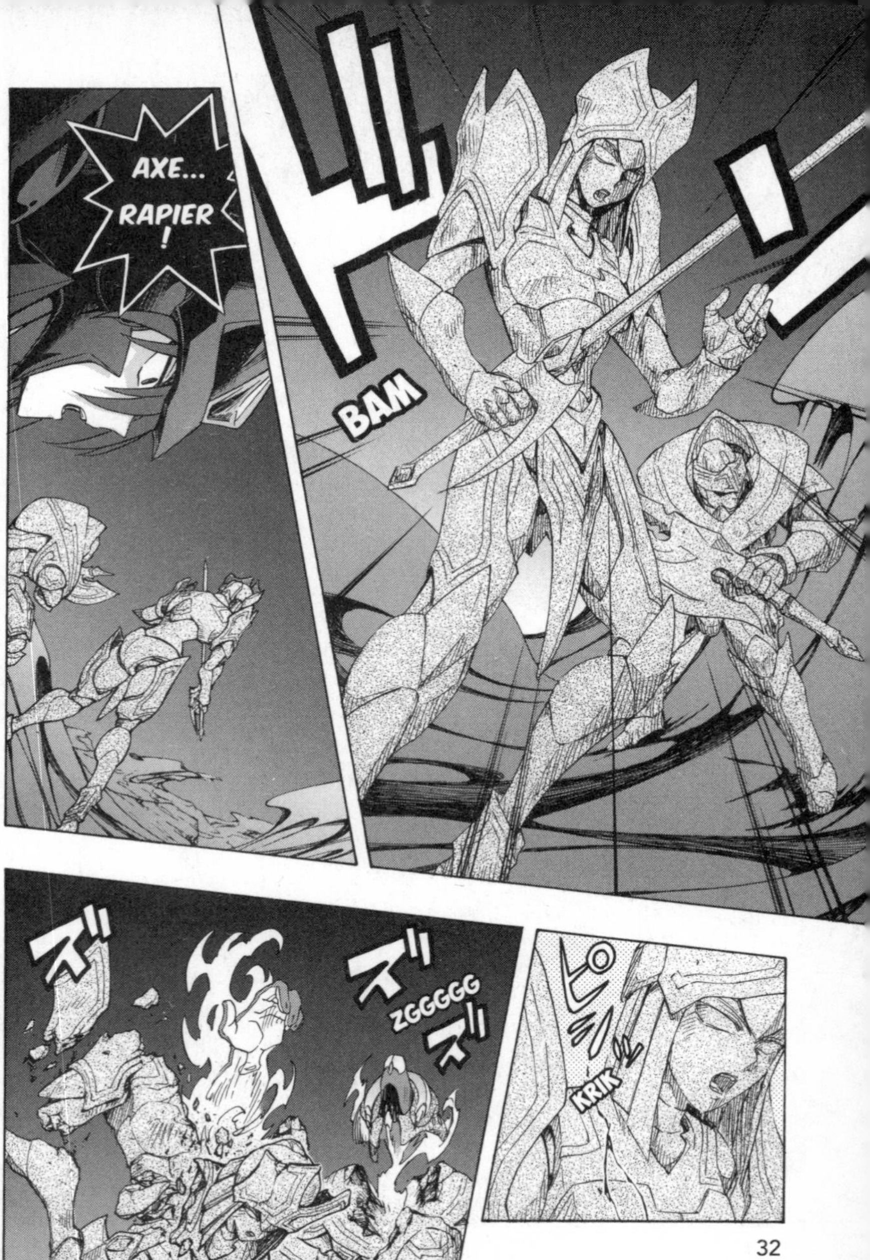
BAM
AXE...
RAPIER
!
KRIK
ZGGGGG

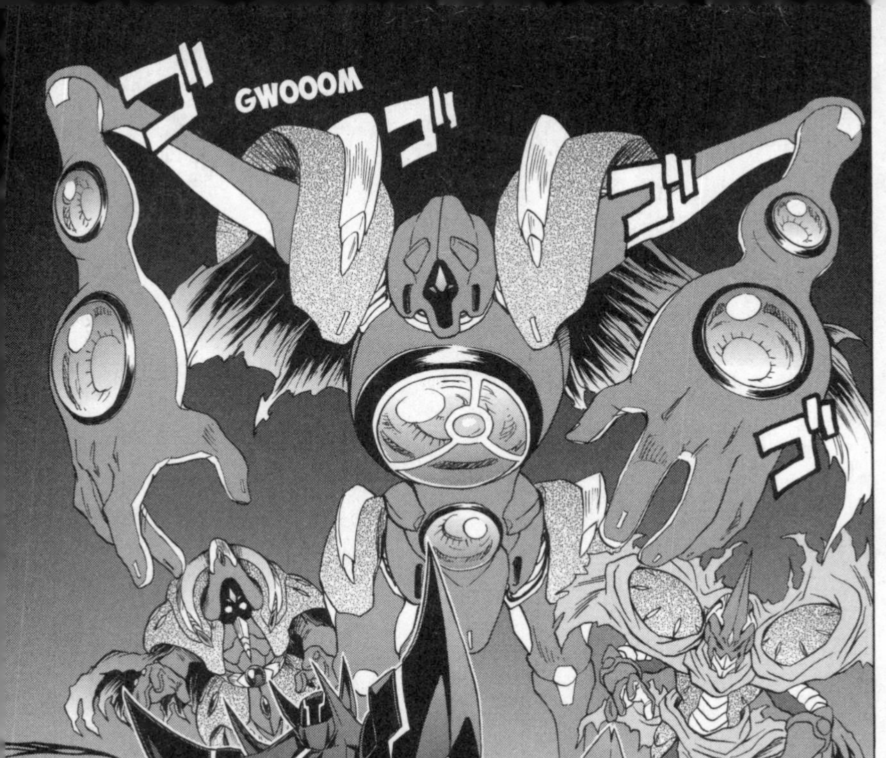
GWOOOM

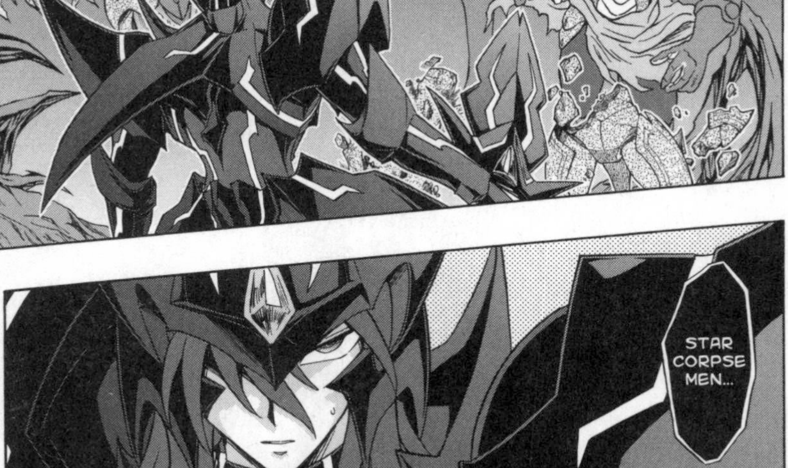
STAR CORPSE MEN...

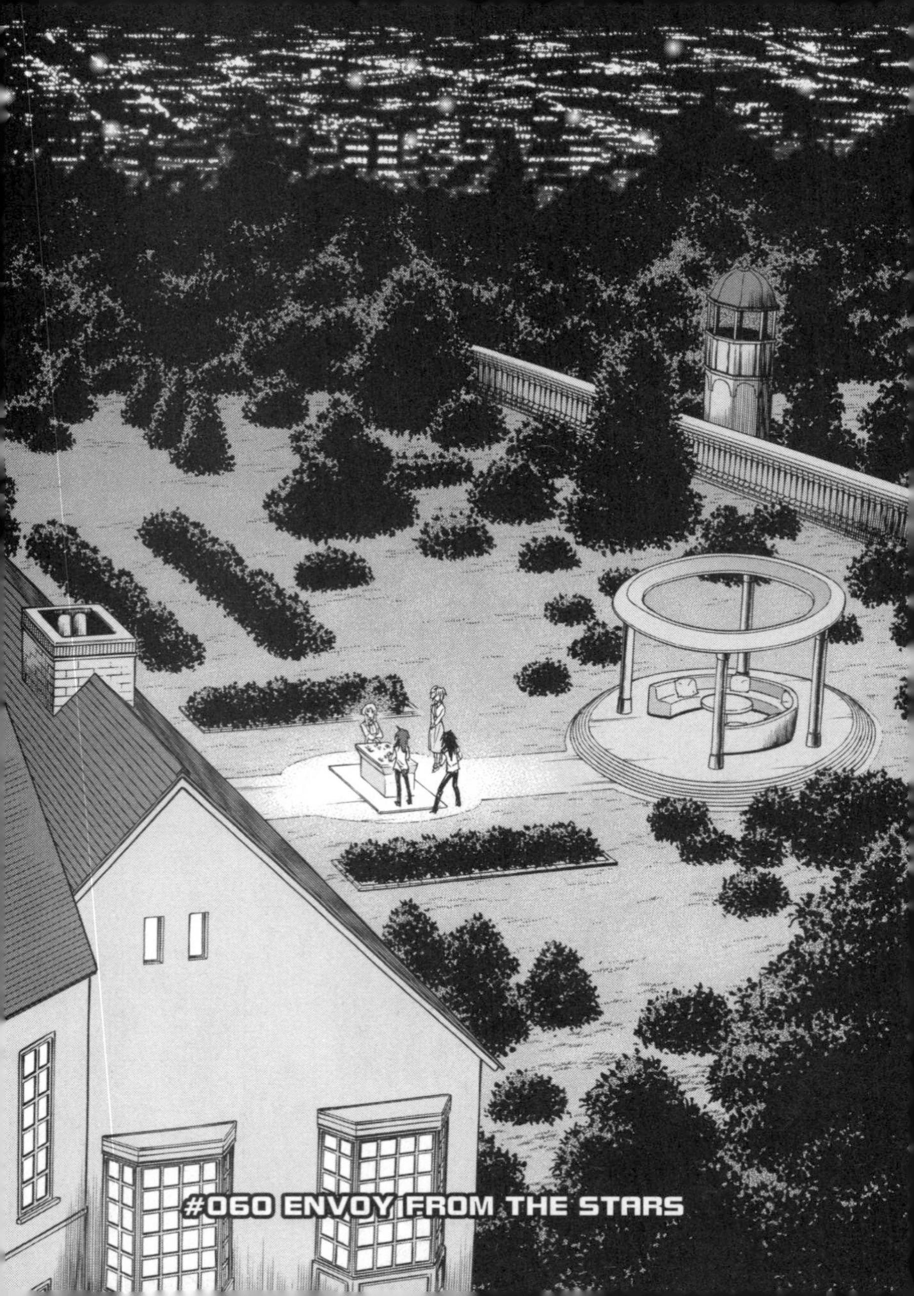
#060 ENVOY FROM THE STARS

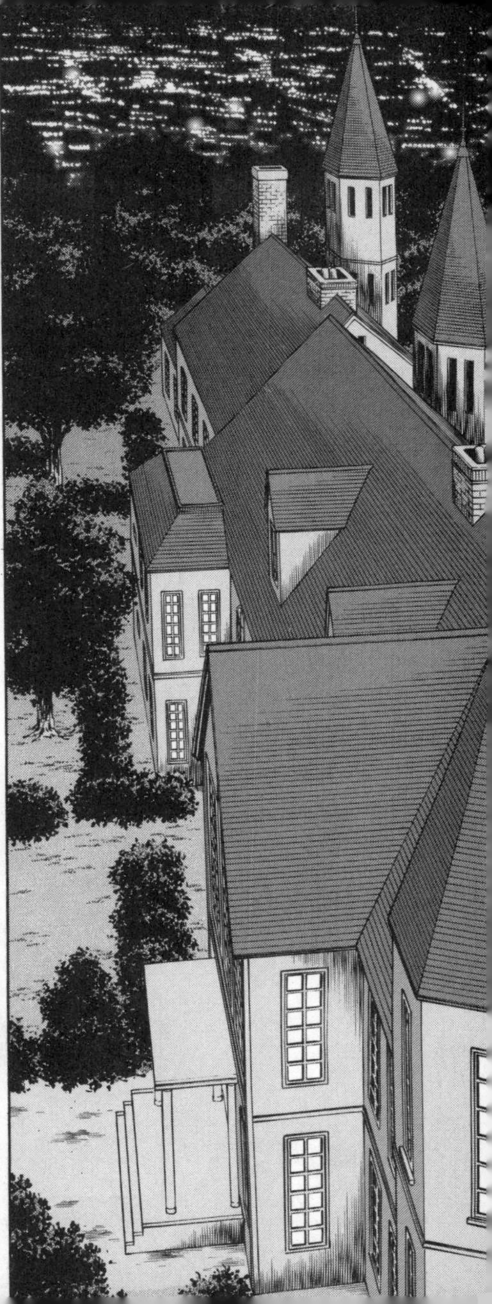
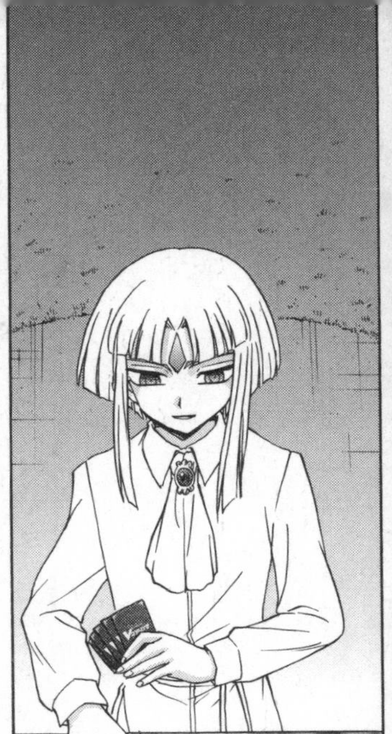
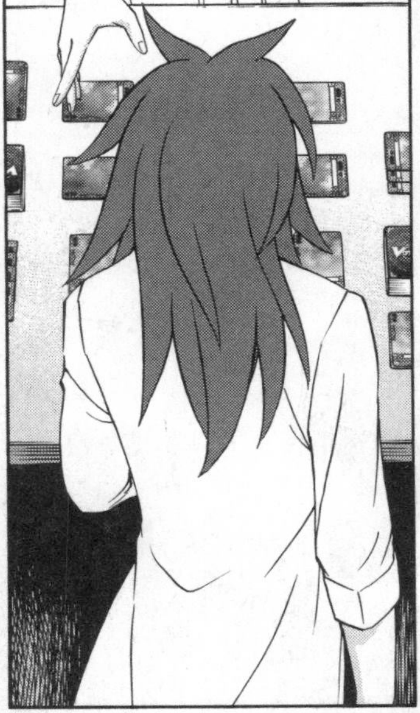

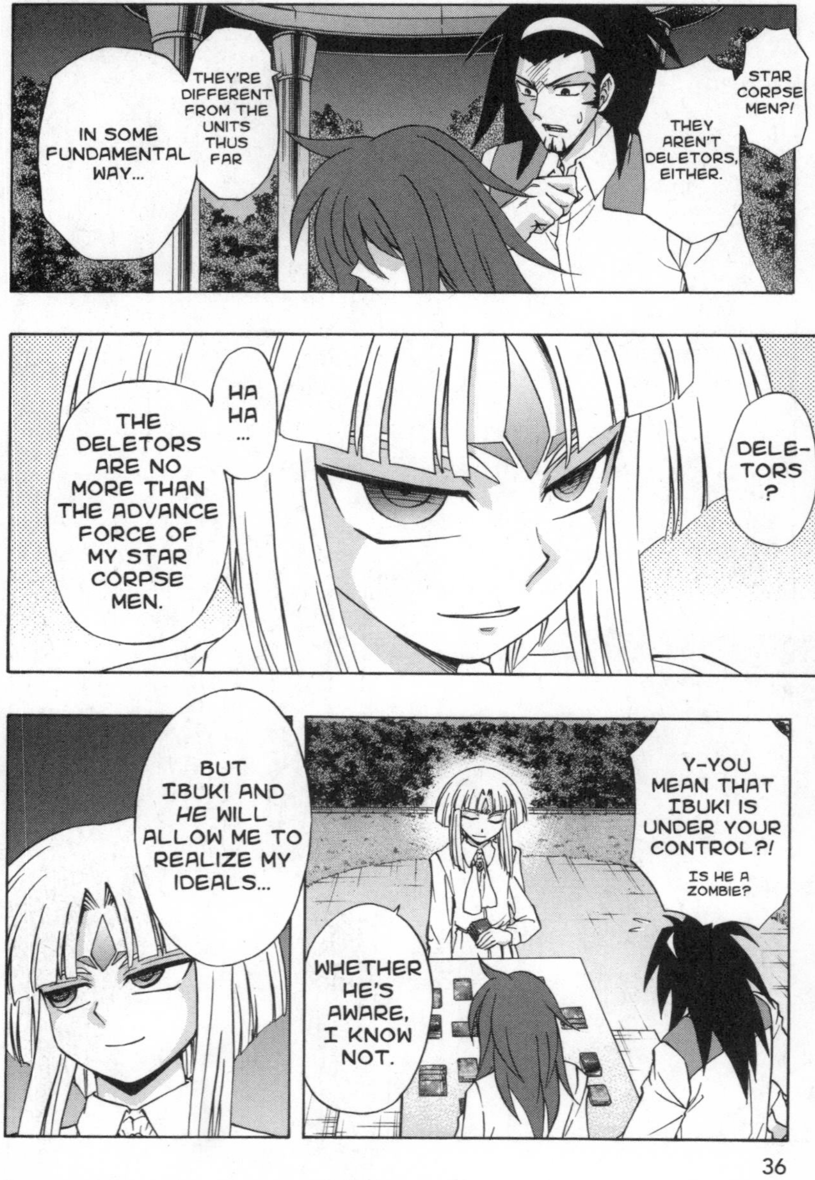
STAR CORPSE MEN?!
THEY AREN'T DELETORS, EITHER.
THEY'RE DIFFERENT FROM THE UNITS THUS FAR
IN SOME FUNDAMENTAL WAY...
DELE-TORS?
HA HA ...
THE DELETORS ARE NO MORE THAN THE ADVANCE FORCE OF MY STAR CORPSE MEN.
Y-YOU MEAN THAT IBUKI IS UNDER YOUR CONTROL?!
IS HE A ZOMBIE?
WHETHER HE'S AWARE, I KNOW NOT.
BUT IBUKI AND HE WILL ALLOW ME TO REALIZE MY IDEALS...

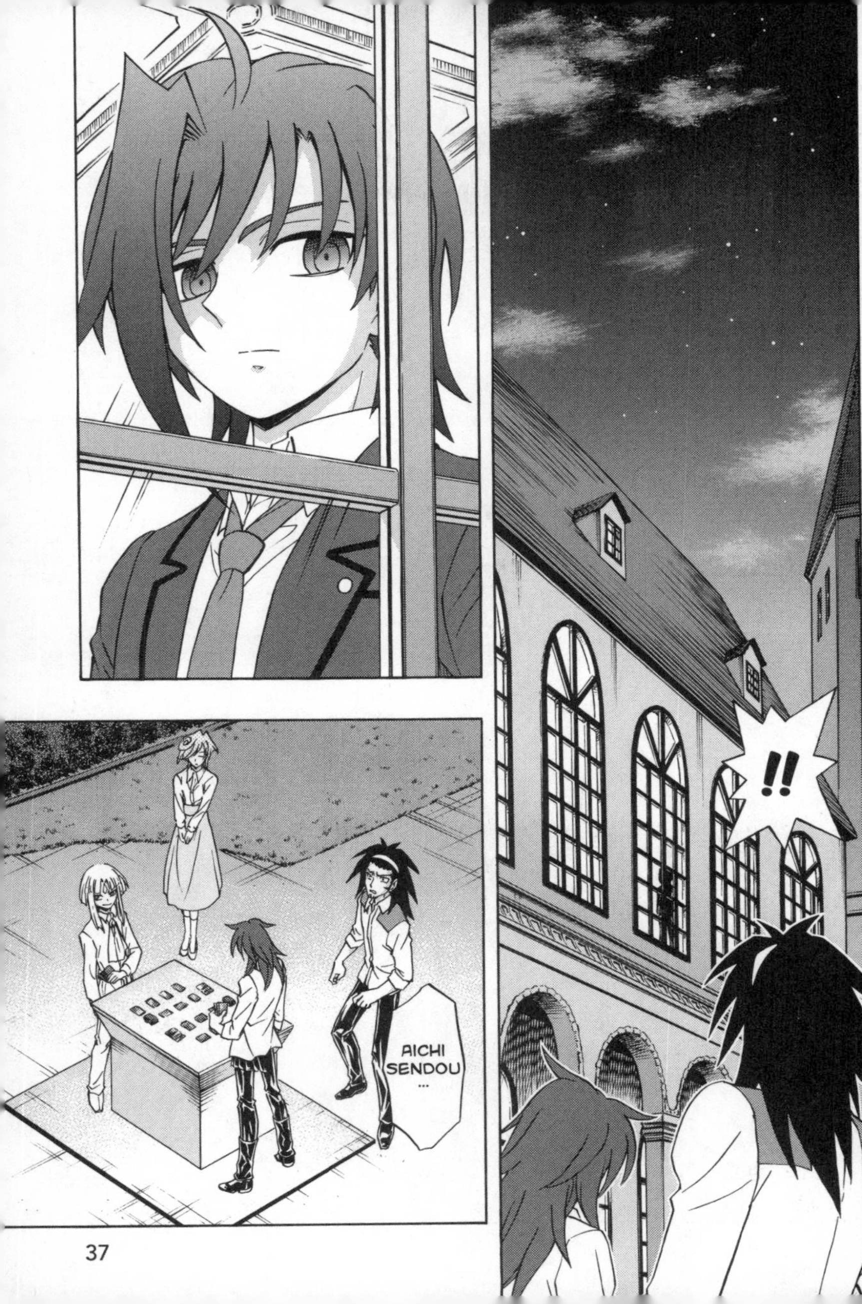
!!
AICHI SENDOU ...

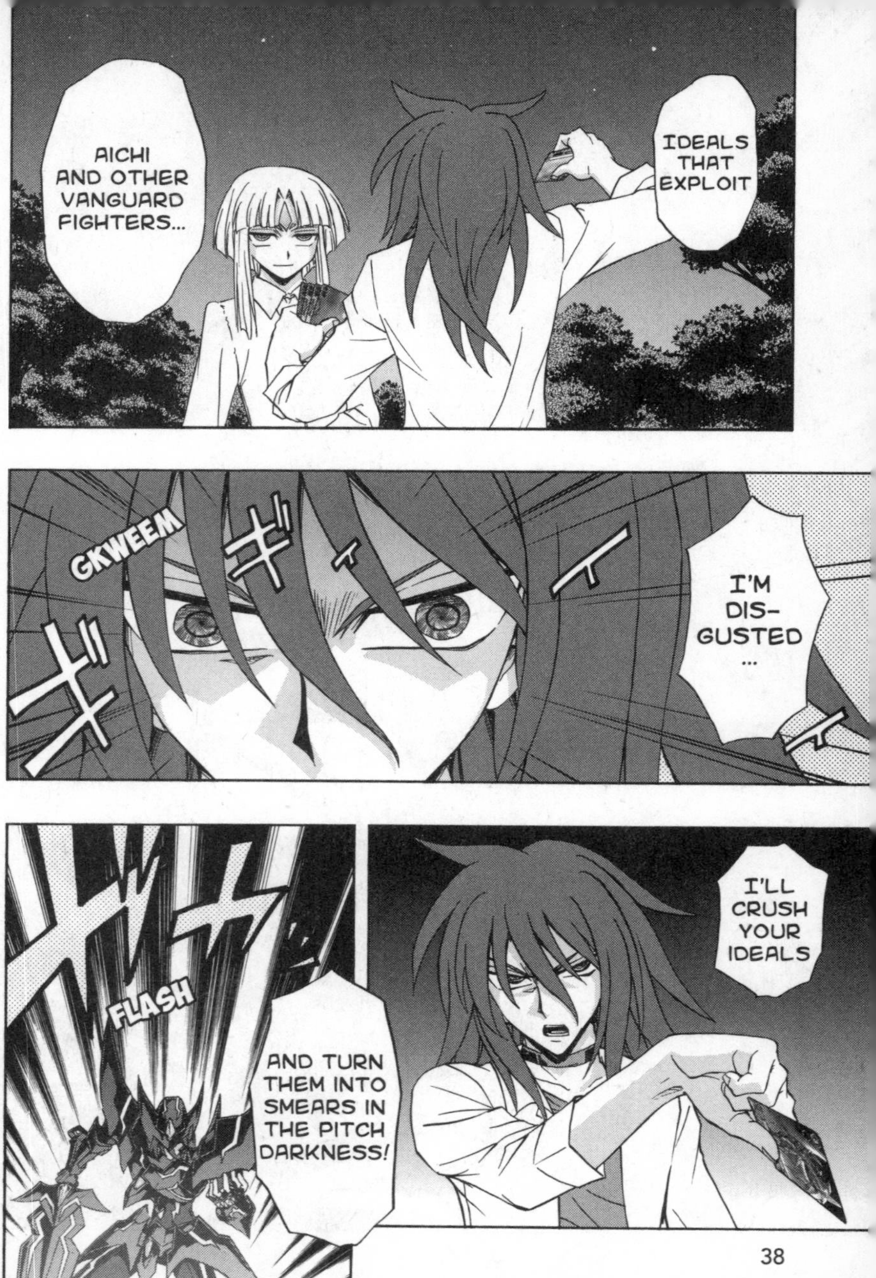
IDEALS THAT EXPLOIT
AICHI AND OTHER VANGUARD FIGHTERS...
GKWEEM
I'M DIS-GUSTED ...
I'LL CRUSH YOUR IDEALS
AND TURN THEM INTO SMEARS IN THE PITCH DARKNESS!
FLASH

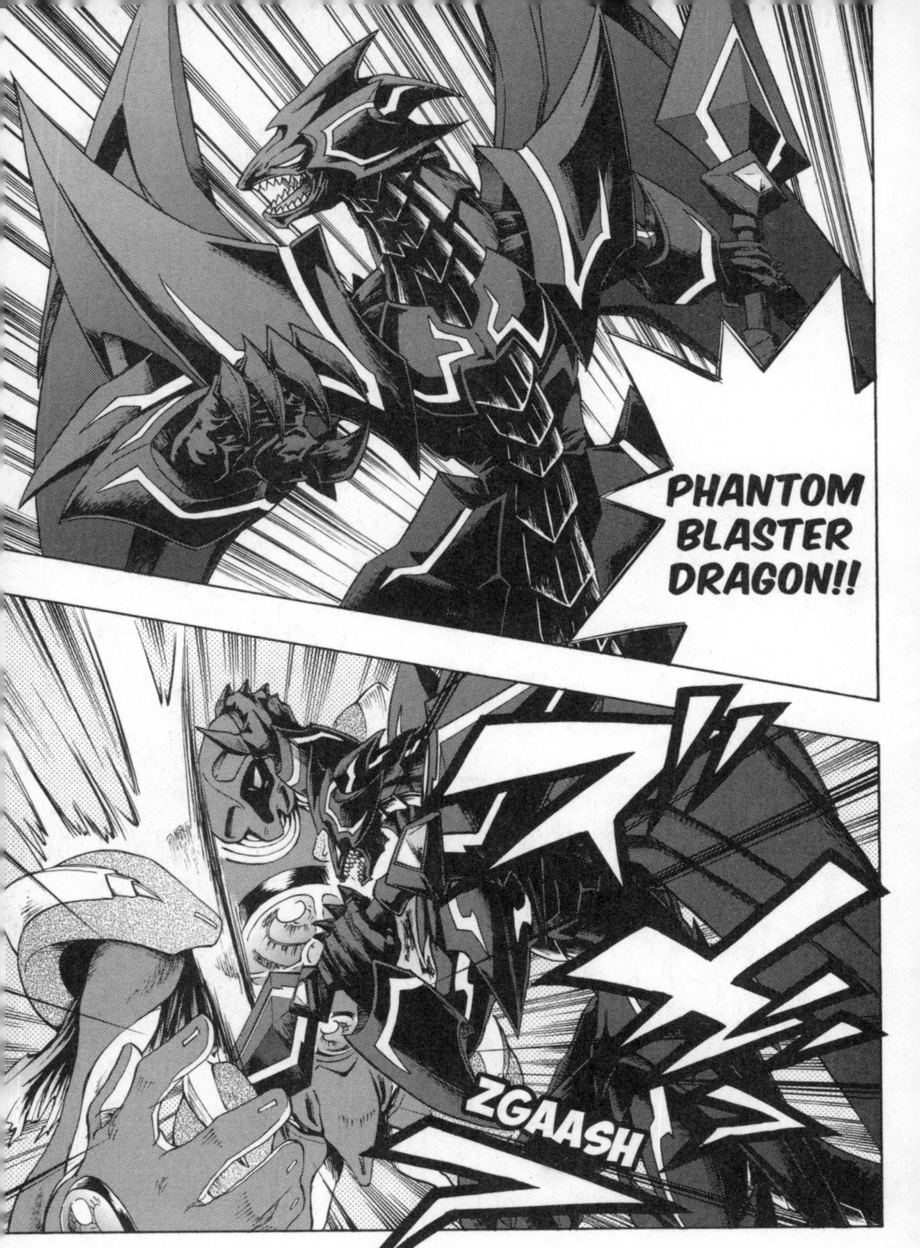
PHANTOM
BLASTER
DRAGON!!
ZGAASH

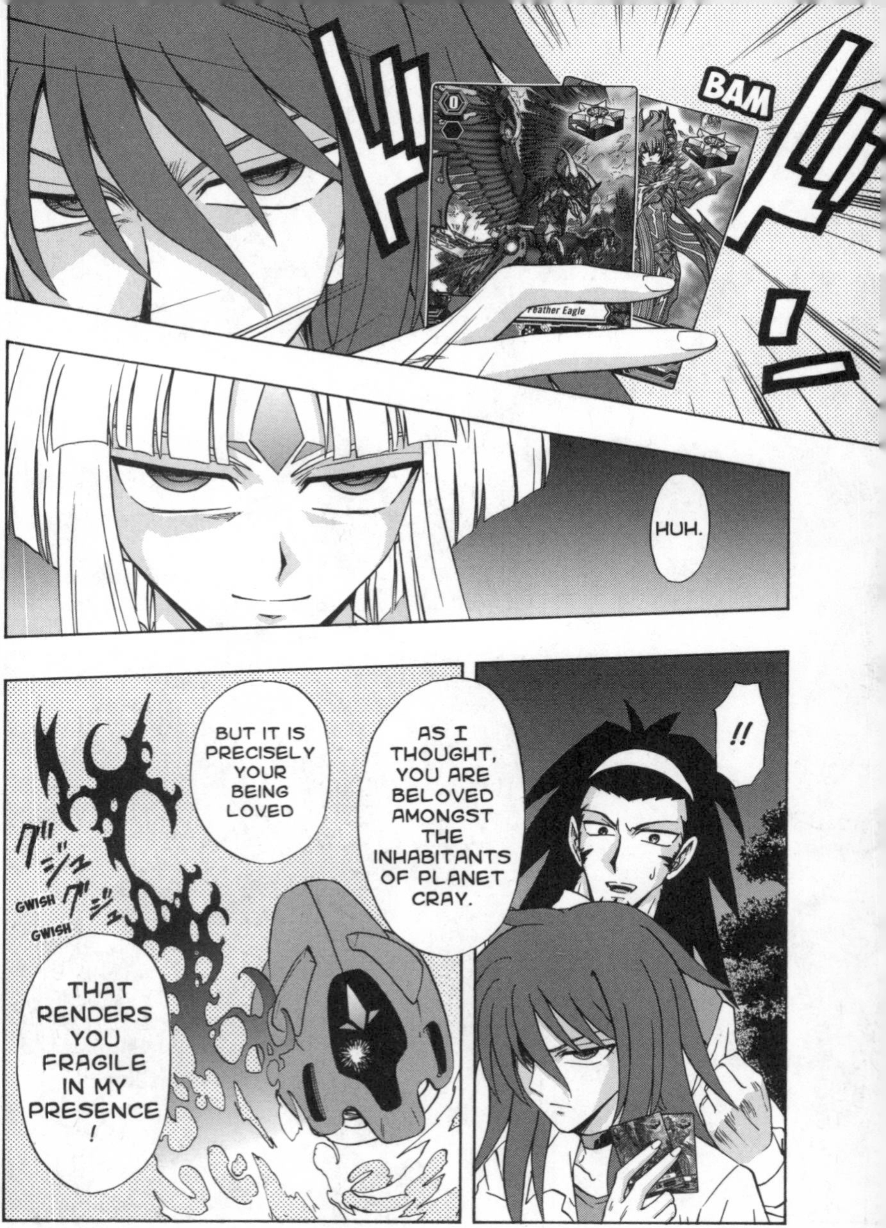
BAM
HUH.
!!
AS I THOUGHT, YOU ARE BELOVED AMONGST THE INHABITANTS OF PLANET CRAY.
BUT IT IS PRECISELY YOUR BEING LOVED
GWISH
GWISH
THAT RENDERS YOU FRAGILE IN MY PRESENCE!

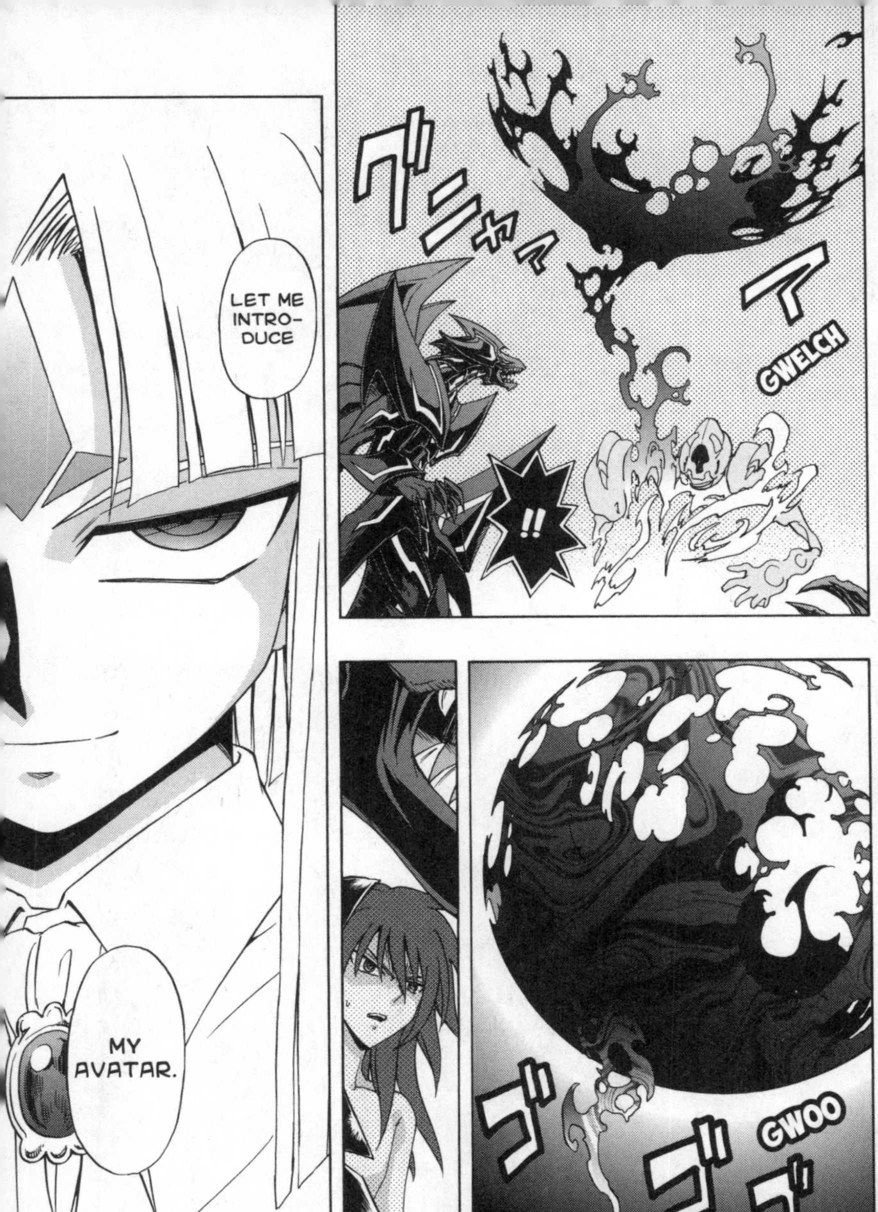
GWELCH
!!
GWOO
LET ME INTRO-DUCE
MY AVATAR.

PLAN-ETARY CORPSE KING,

DUN

DUN

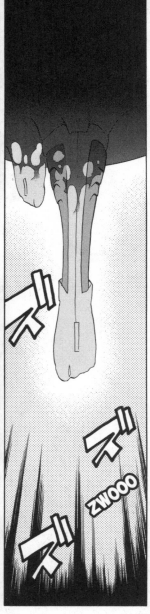

ZWOOO

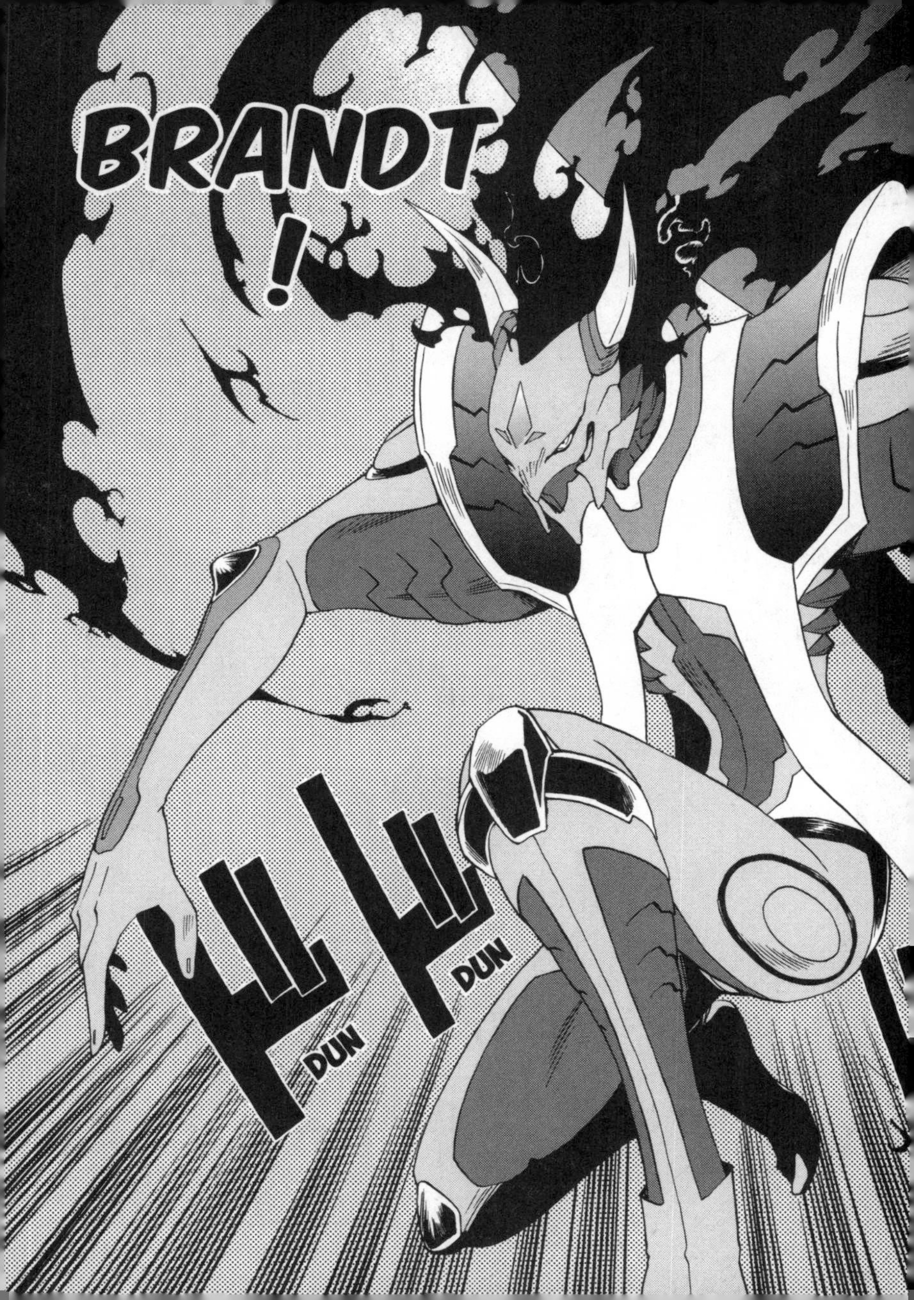
BRANDT!
DUN
DUN

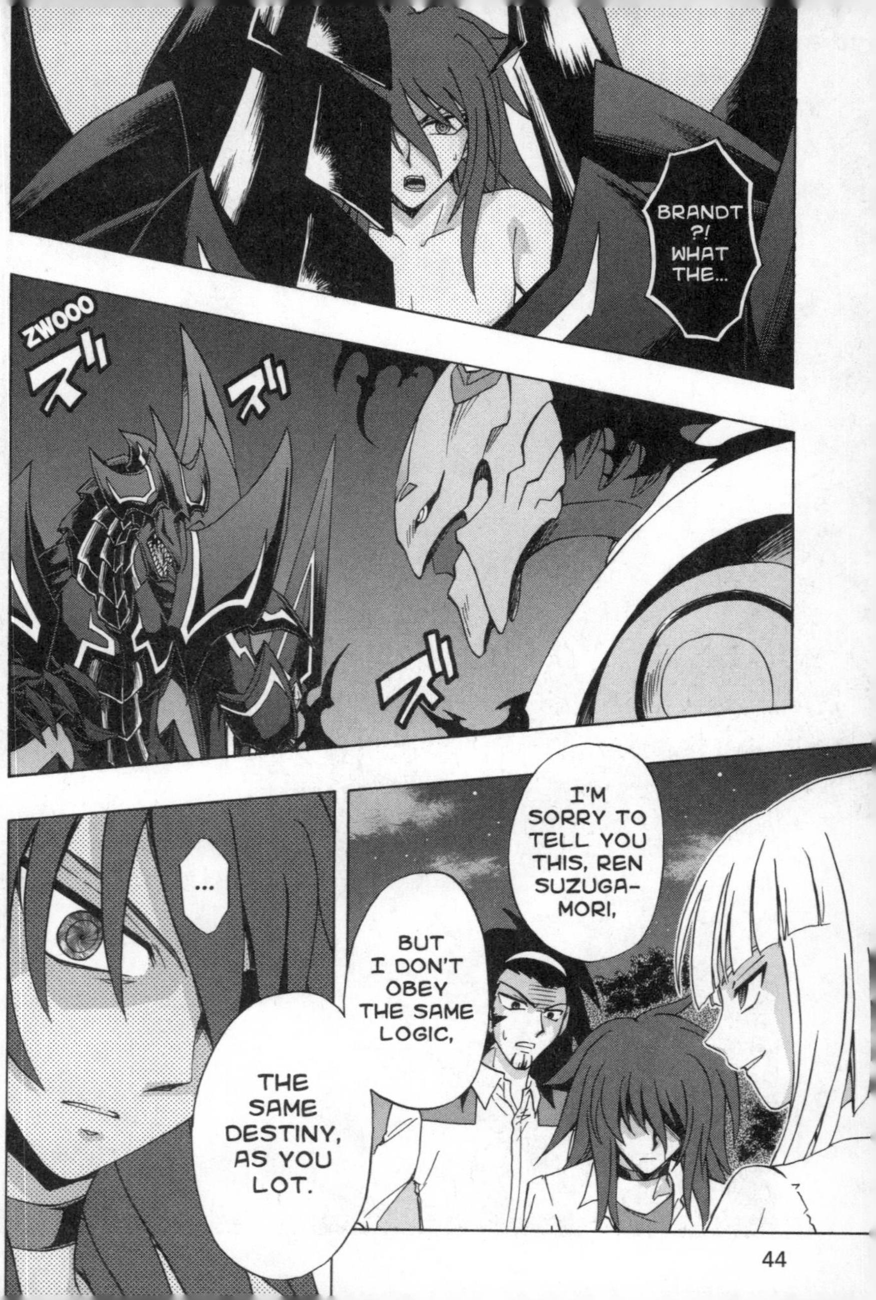
BRANDT?! WHAT THE...
ZWOOO
I'M SORRY TO TELL YOU THIS, REN SUZUGA-MORI,
BUT I DON'T OBEY THE SAME LOGIC,
THE SAME DESTINY, AS YOU LOT.
...

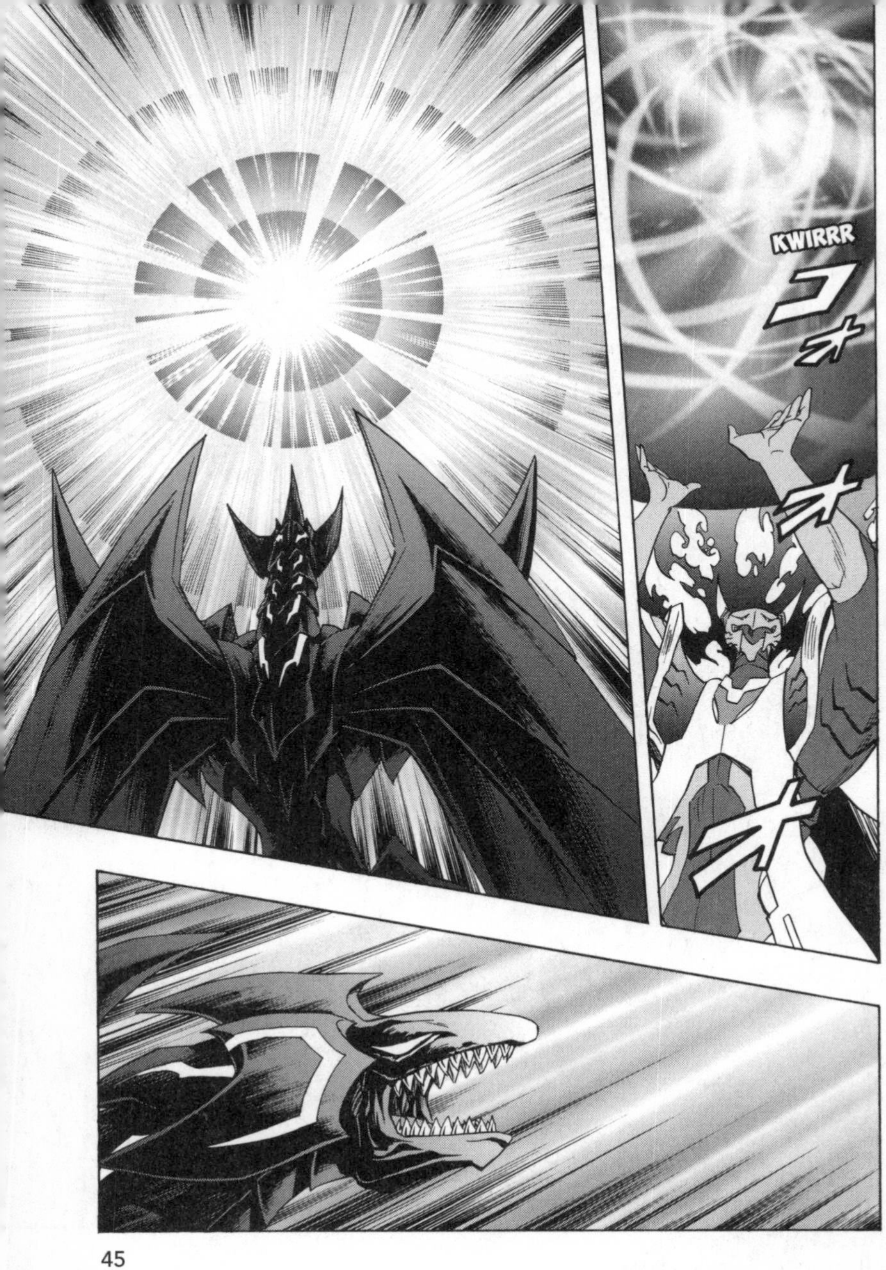
KWIRRR
コォオオ

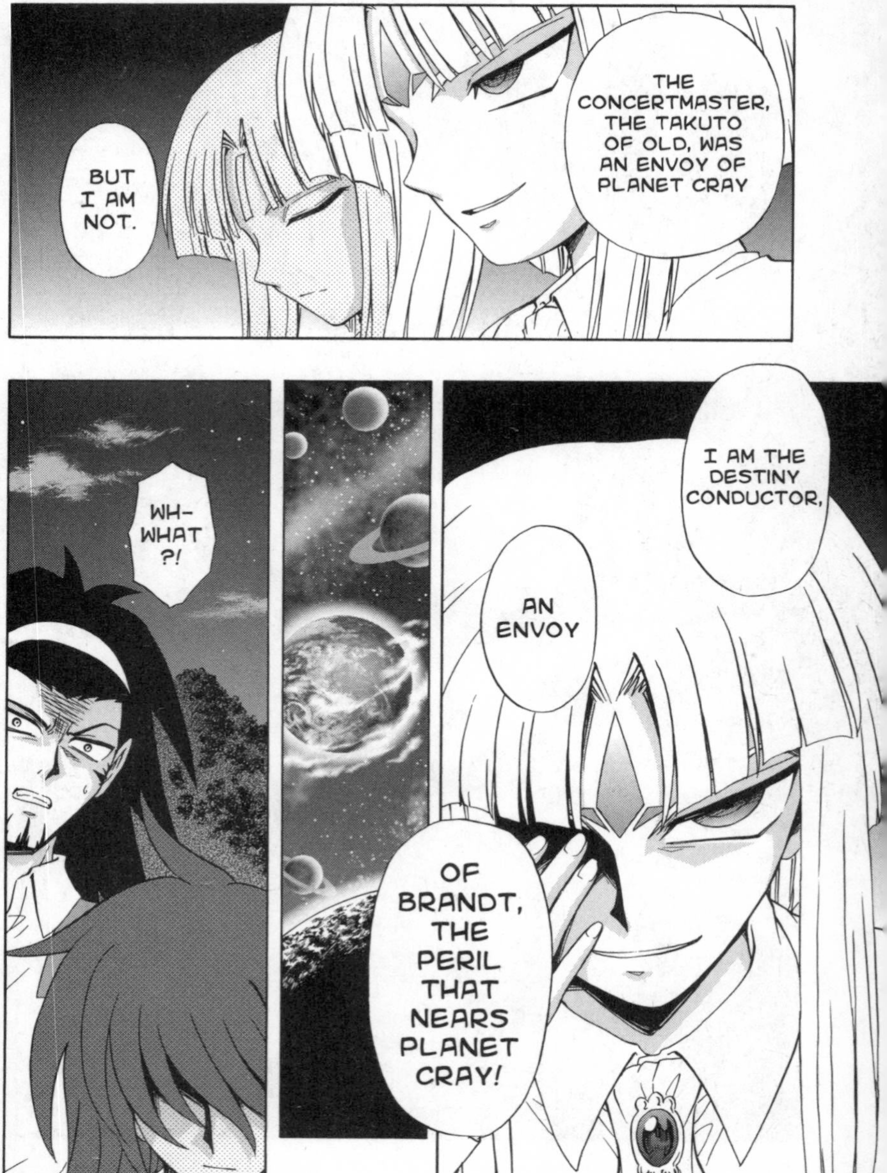
THE CONCERTMASTER, THE TAKUTO OF OLD, WAS AN ENVOY OF PLANET CRAY
BUT I AM NOT.
I AM THE DESTINY CONDUCTOR,
AN ENVOY
OF BRANDT, THE PERIL THAT NEARS PLANET CRAY!
WH-WHAT?!

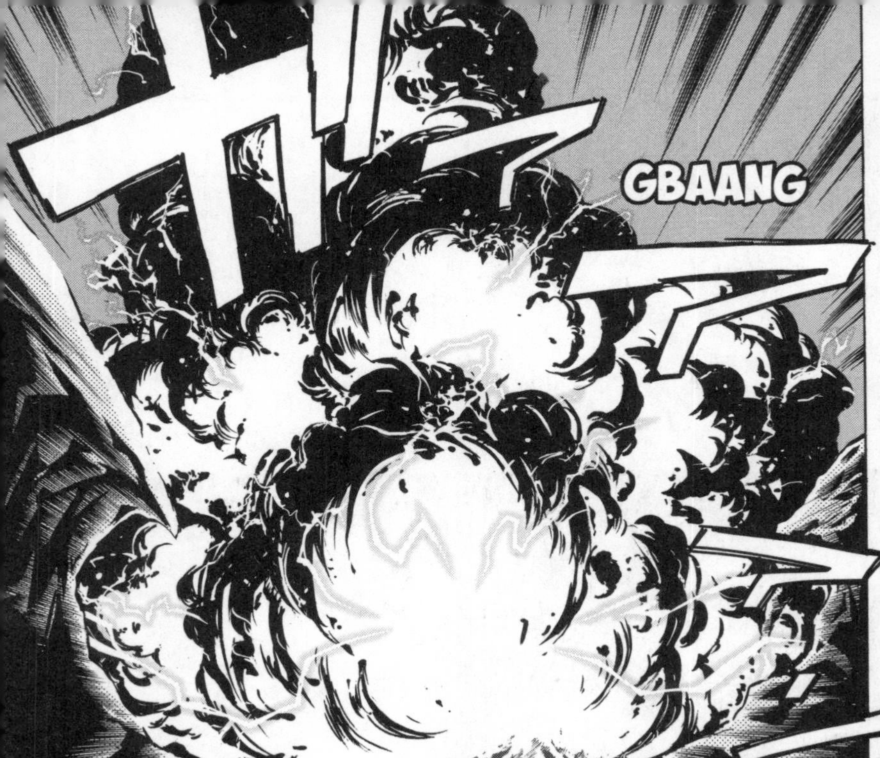
GBAANG
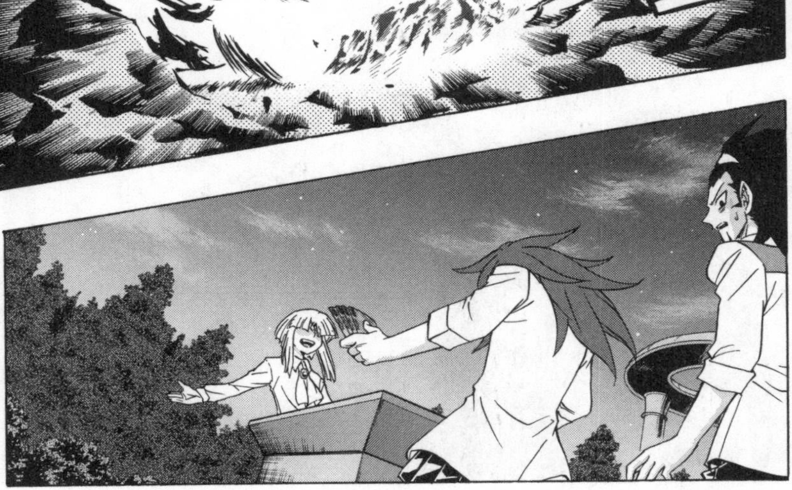

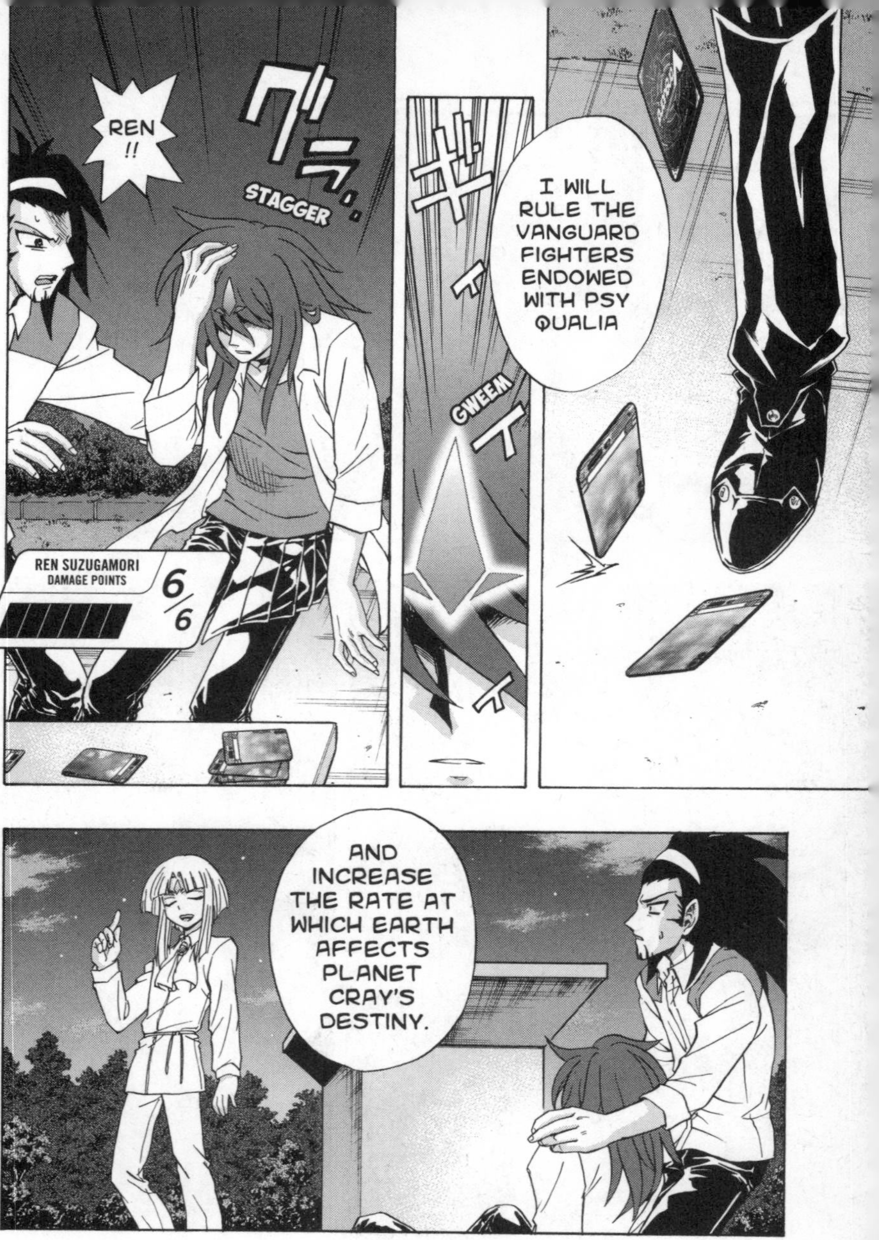
I WILL RULE THE VANGUARD FIGHTERS ENDOWED WITH PSY QUALIA
GWEEM
STAGGER
REN !!
REN SUZUGAMORI
DAMAGE POINTS
6/6
AND INCREASE THE RATE AT WHICH EARTH AFFECTS PLANET CRAY'S DESTINY.

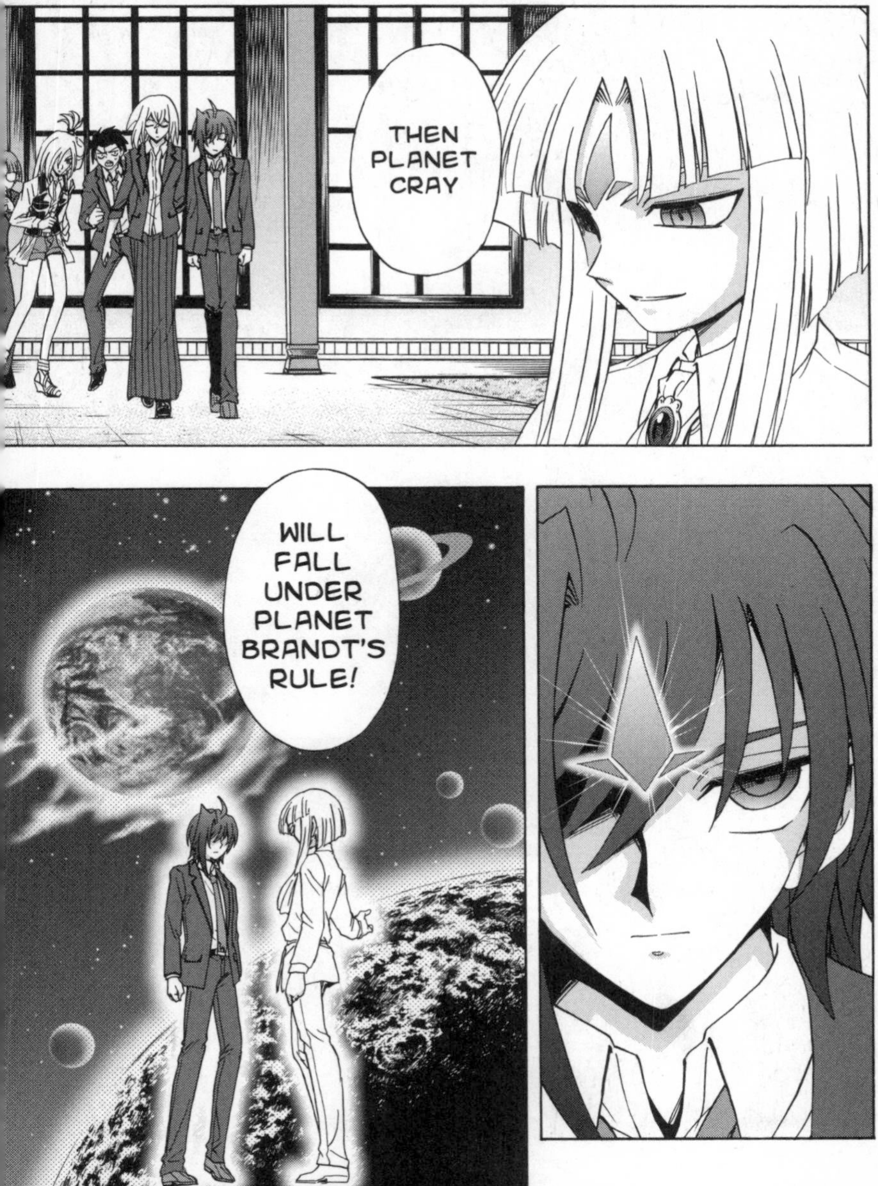
THEN PLANET CRAY
WILL FALL UNDER PLANET BRANDT'S RULE!

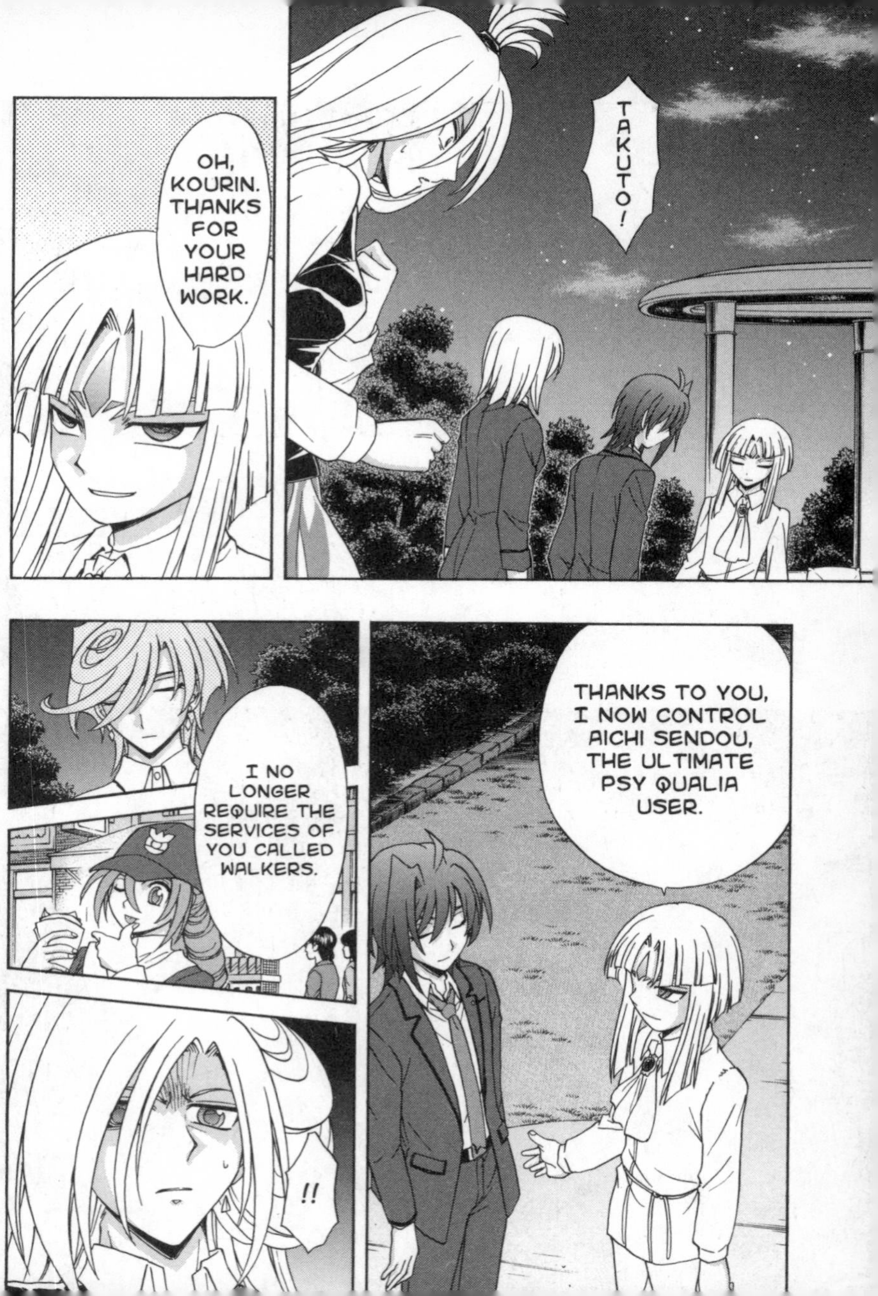
TAKUTO!
OH, KOURIN. THANKS FOR YOUR HARD WORK.
THANKS TO YOU, I NOW CONTROL AICHI SENDOU, THE ULTIMATE PSY QUALIA USER.
I NO LONGER REQUIRE THE SERVICES OF YOU CALLED WALKERS.
!!

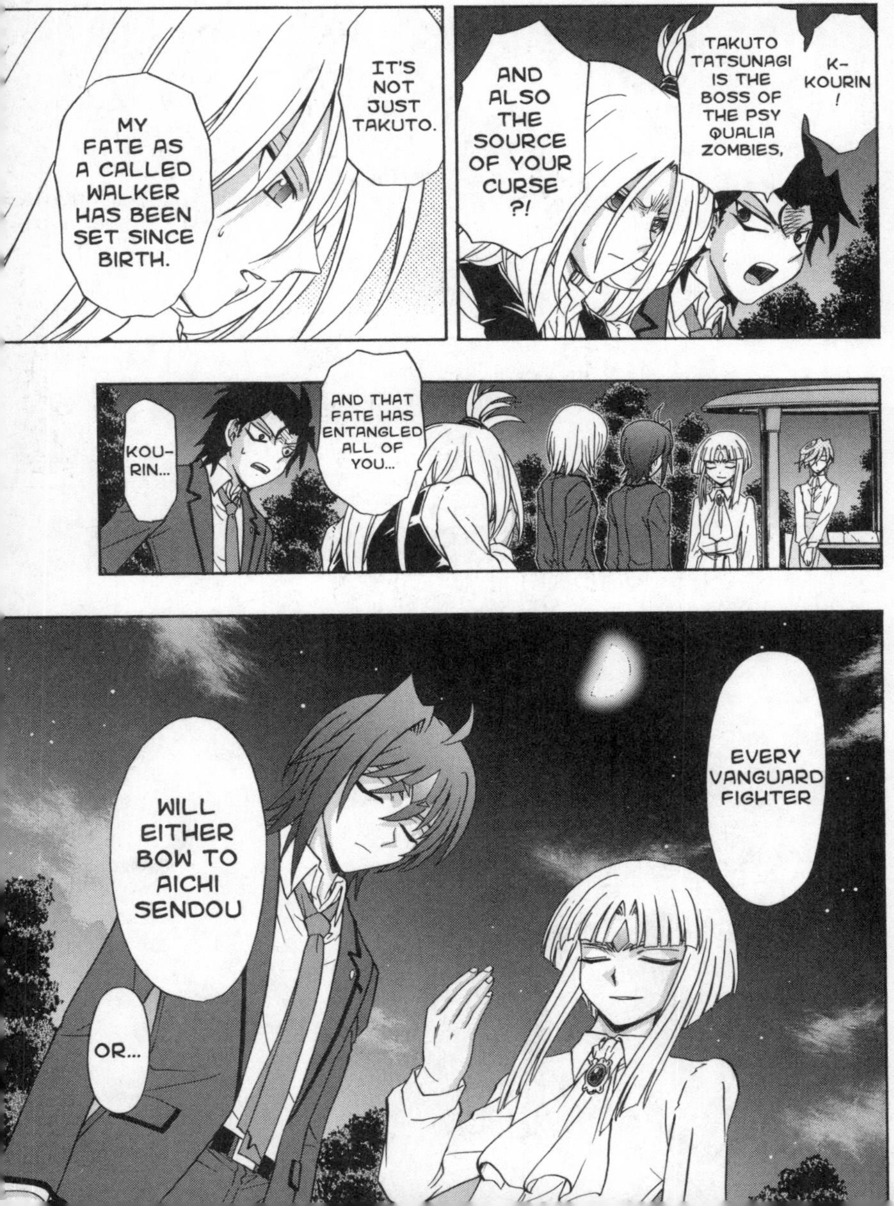

K-KOURIN!
TAKUTO TATSUNAGI IS THE BOSS OF THE PSY QUALIA ZOMBIES,
AND ALSO THE SOURCE OF YOUR CURSE?!
IT'S NOT JUST TAKUTO.
MY FATE AS A CALLED WALKER HAS BEEN SET SINCE BIRTH.
AND THAT FATE HAS ENTANGLED ALL OF YOU...
KOU-RIN...
EVERY VANGUARD FIGHTER
WILL EITHER BOW TO AICHI SENDOU
OR...

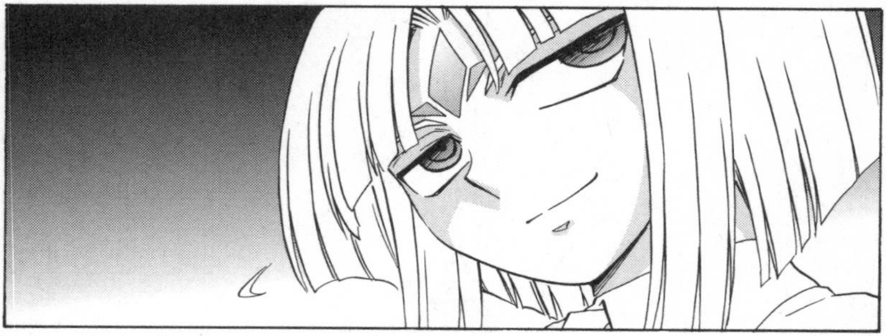

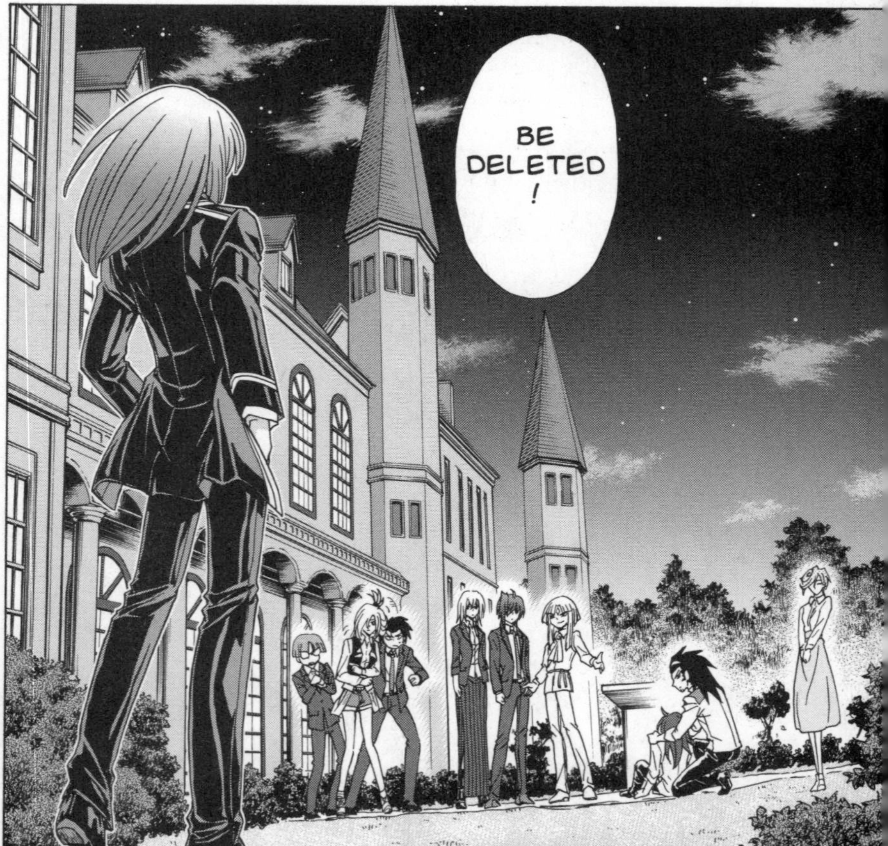
BE DELETED !

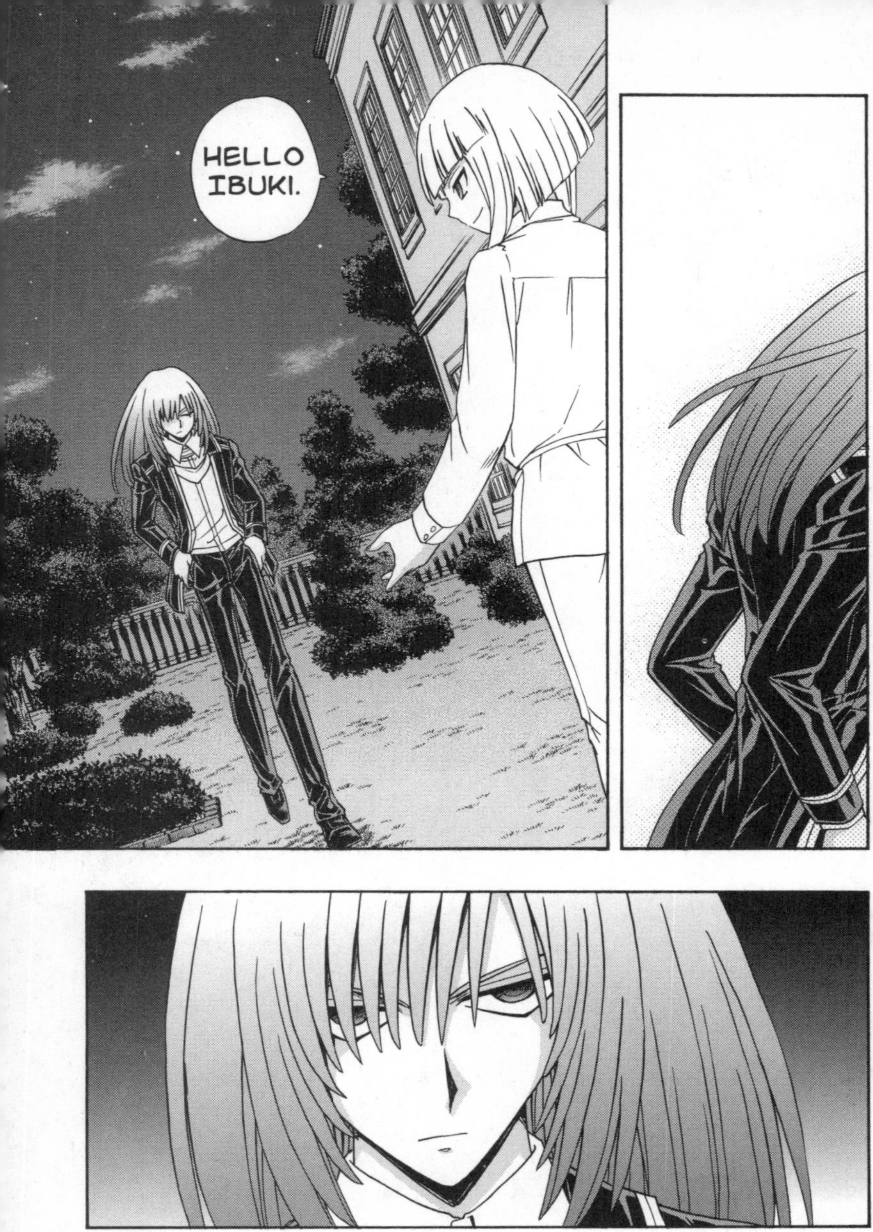
HELLO
IBUKI.

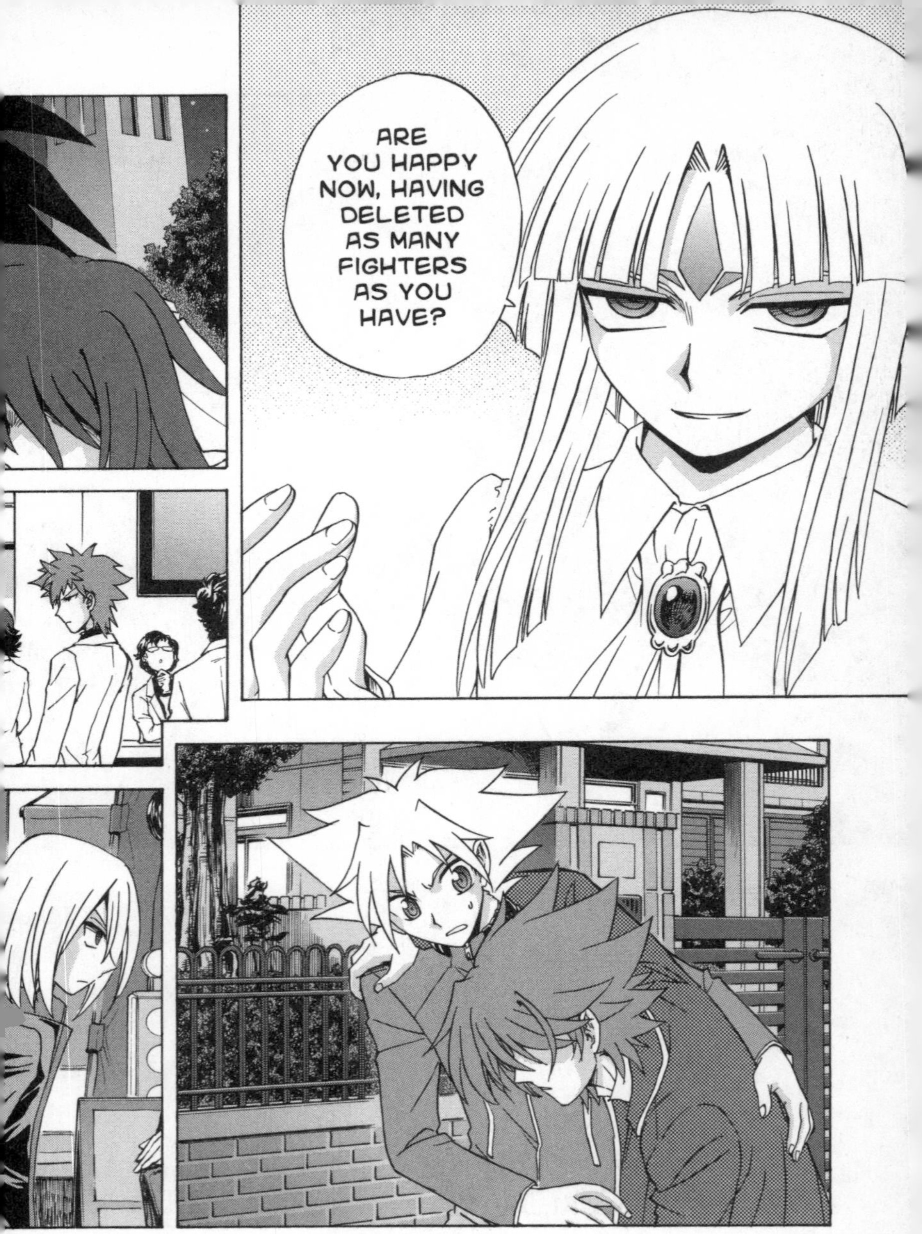
ARE YOU HAPPY NOW, HAVING DELETED AS MANY FIGHTERS AS YOU HAVE?

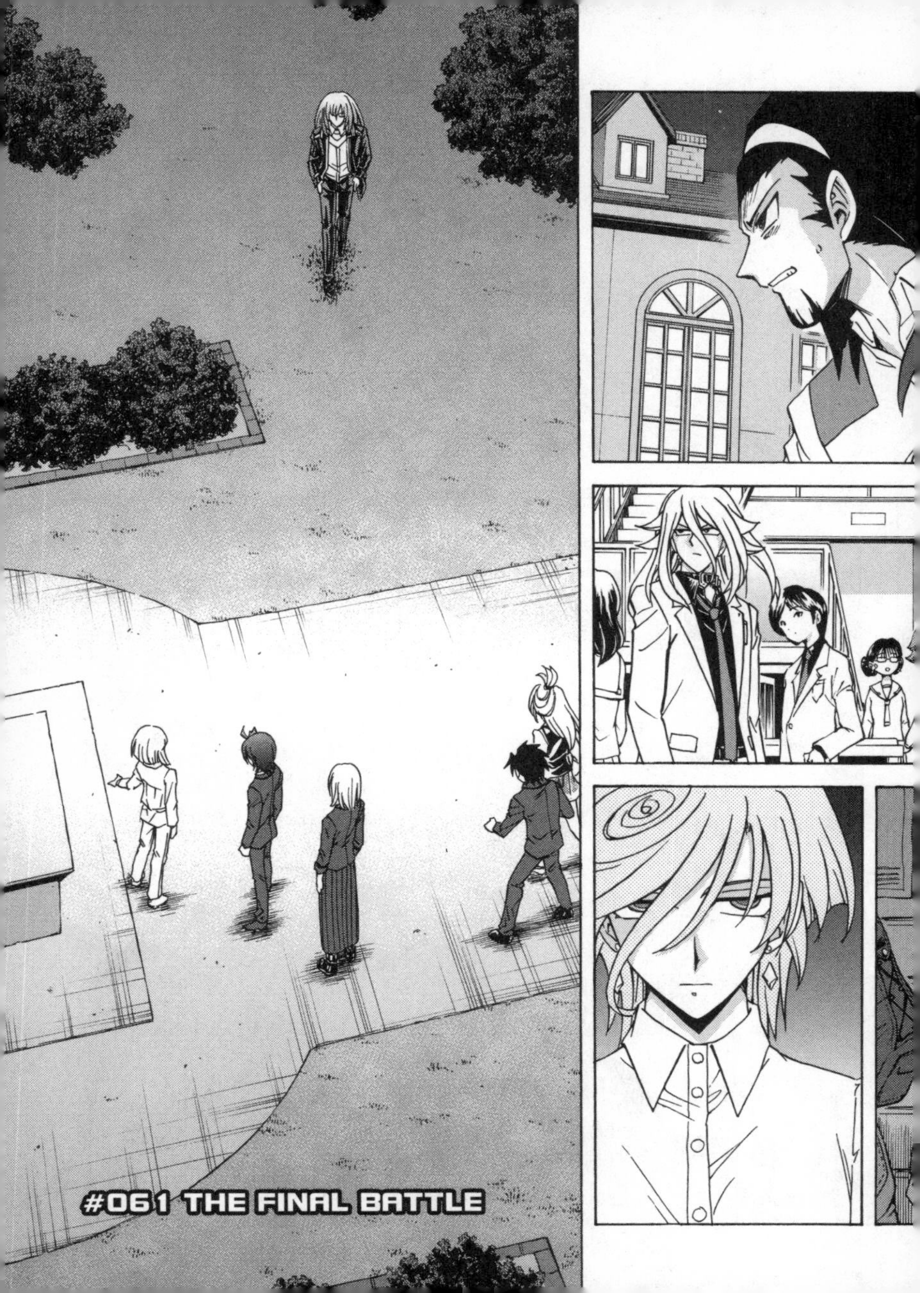
#061 THE FINAL BATTLE

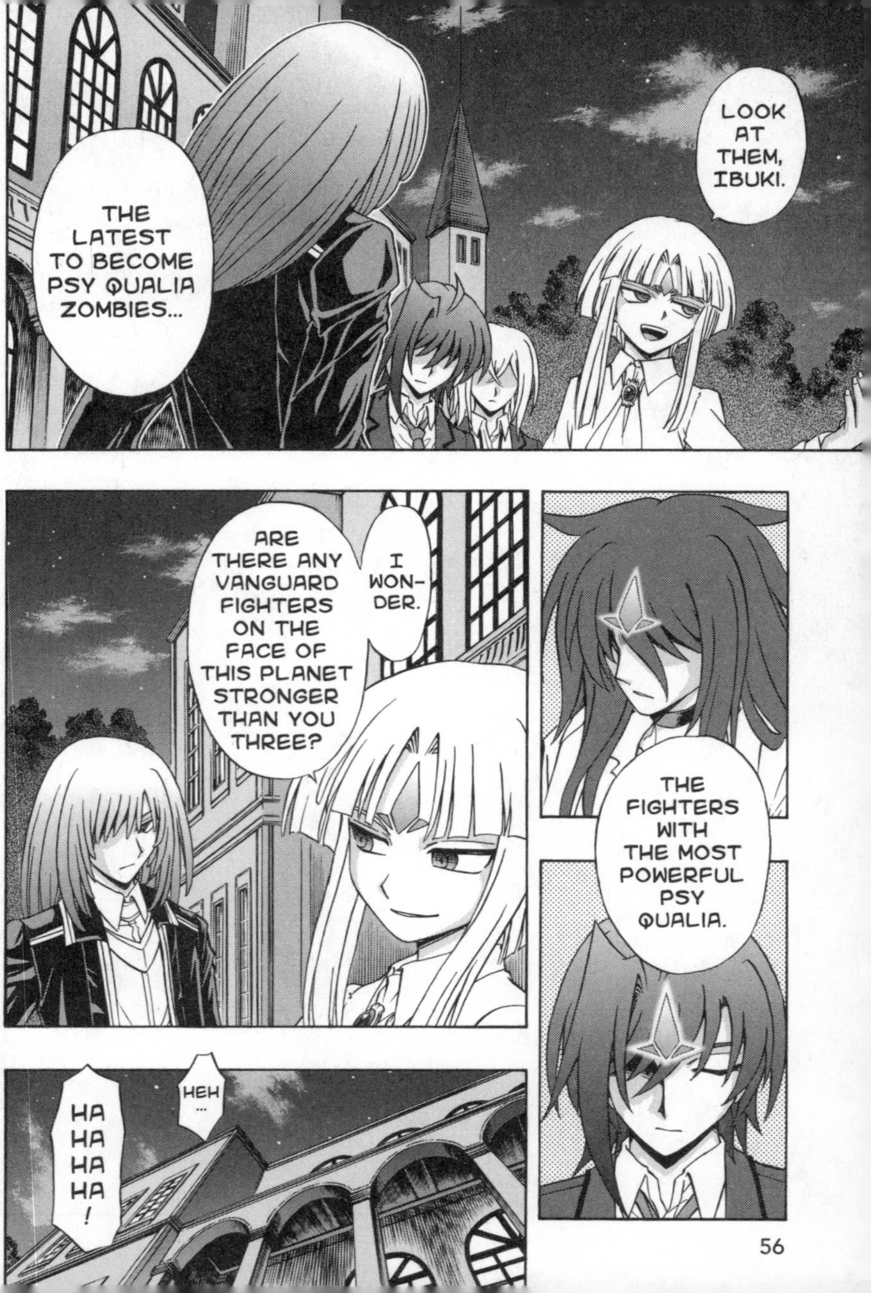
LOOK AT THEM, IBUKI.
THE LATEST TO BECOME PSY QUALIA ZOMBIES...
I WON-DER.
ARE THERE ANY VANGUARD FIGHTERS ON THE FACE OF THIS PLANET STRONGER THAN YOU THREE?
THE FIGHTERS WITH THE MOST POWERFUL PSY QUALIA.
HEH ...
HA HA HA HA HA !

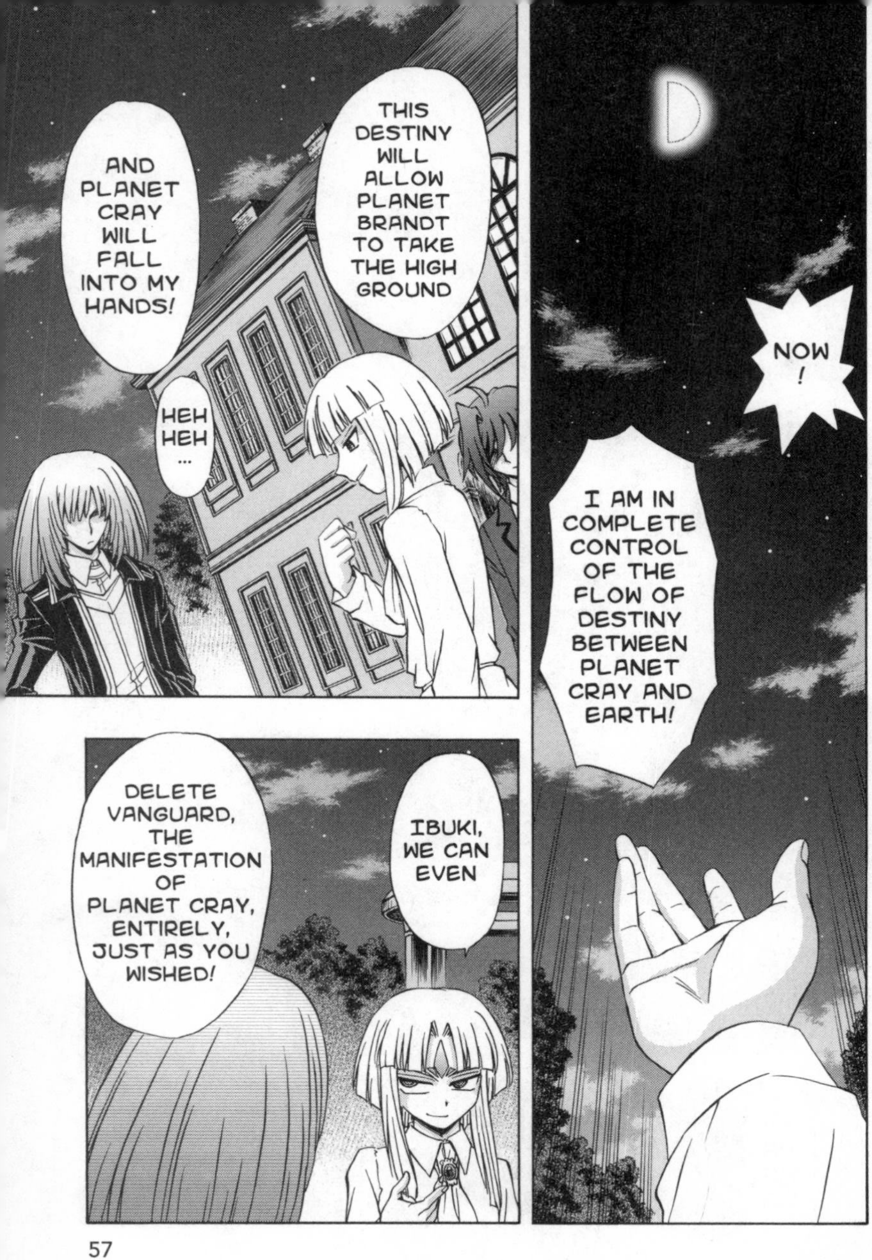
NOW!
I AM IN COMPLETE CONTROL OF THE FLOW OF DESTINY BETWEEN PLANET CRAY AND EARTH!
THIS DESTINY WILL ALLOW PLANET BRANDT TO TAKE THE HIGH GROUND
AND PLANET CRAY WILL FALL INTO MY HANDS!
HEH HEH ...
IBUKI, WE CAN EVEN
DELETE VANGUARD, THE MANIFESTATION OF PLANET CRAY, ENTIRELY, JUST AS YOU WISHED!

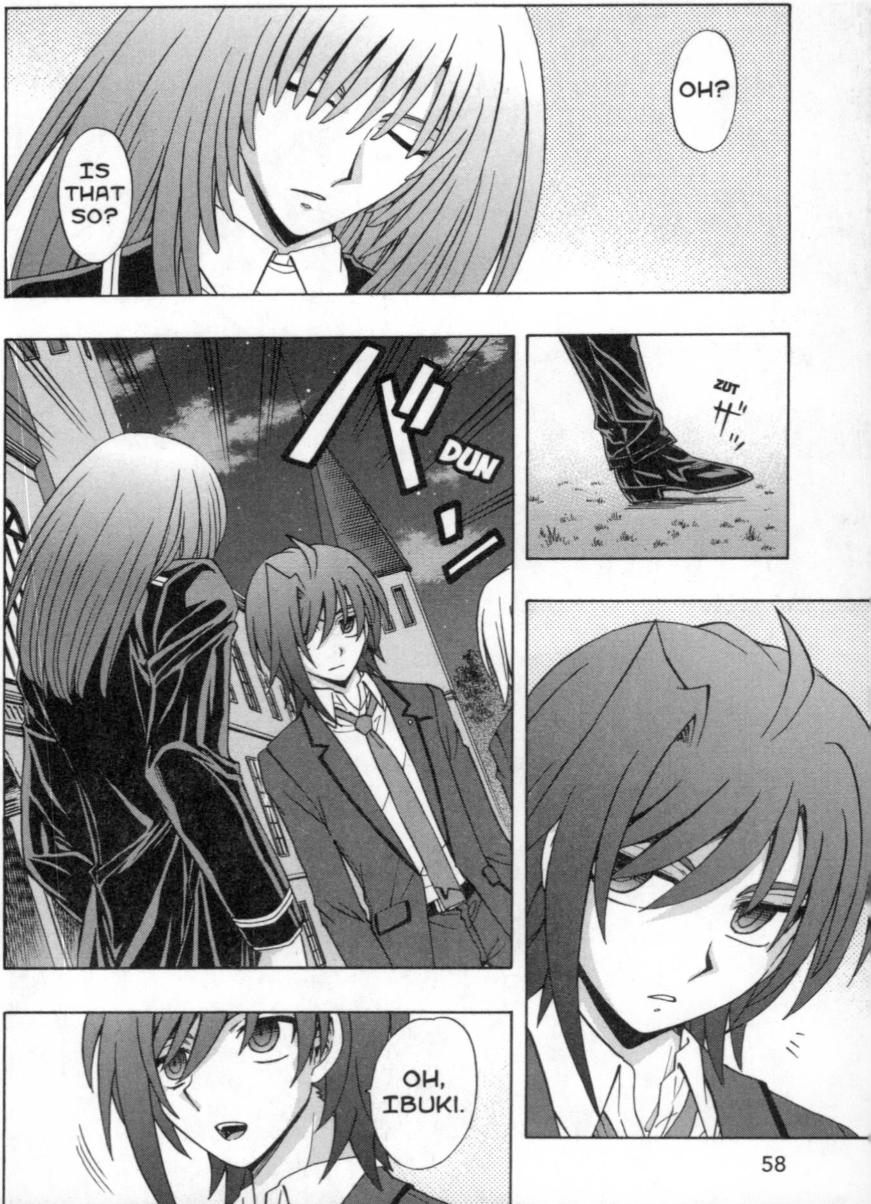
OH?
IS THAT SO?
ZUT
ザッ
DUN
OH, IBUKI.

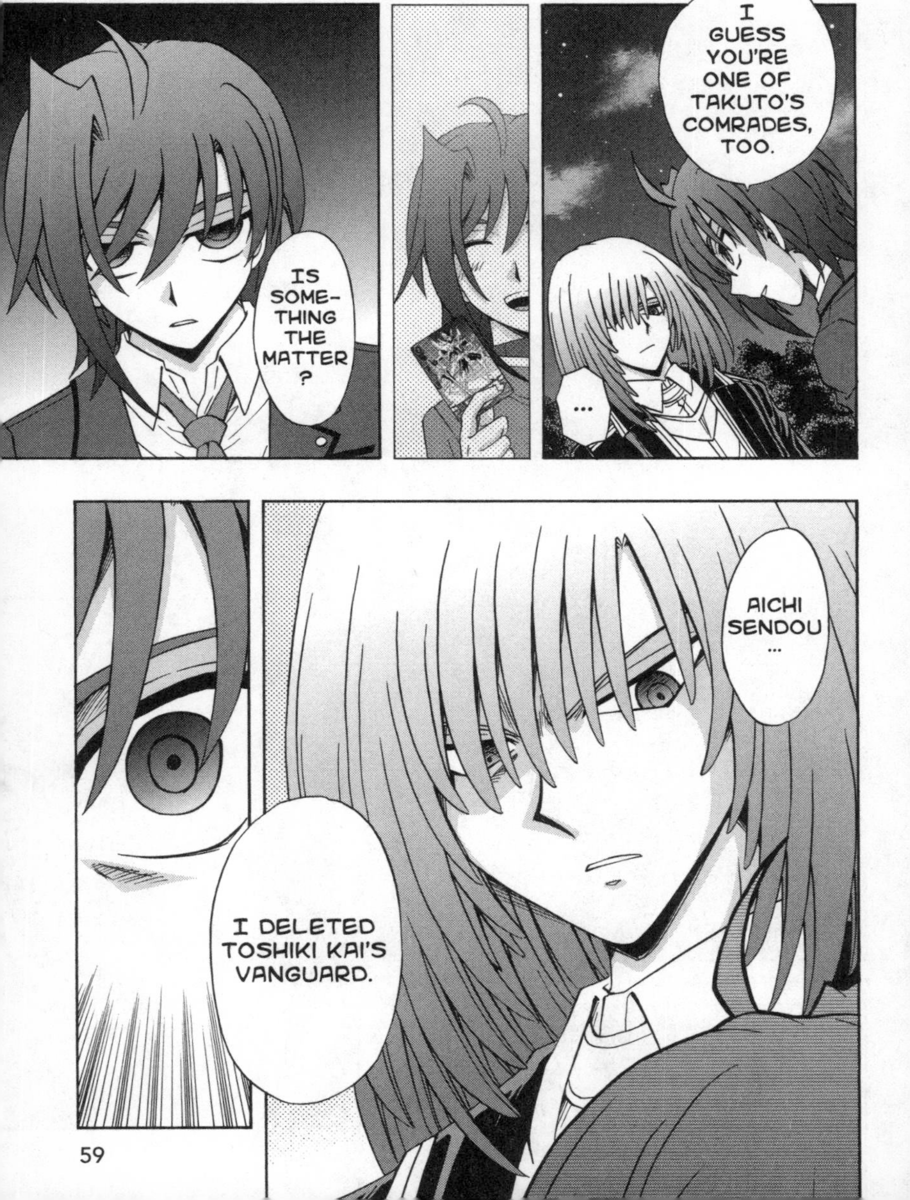
I GUESS YOU'RE ONE OF TAKUTO'S COMRADES, TOO.
...
IS SOME-THING THE MATTER?
AICHI SENDOU...
I DELETED TOSHIKI KAI'S VANGUARD.

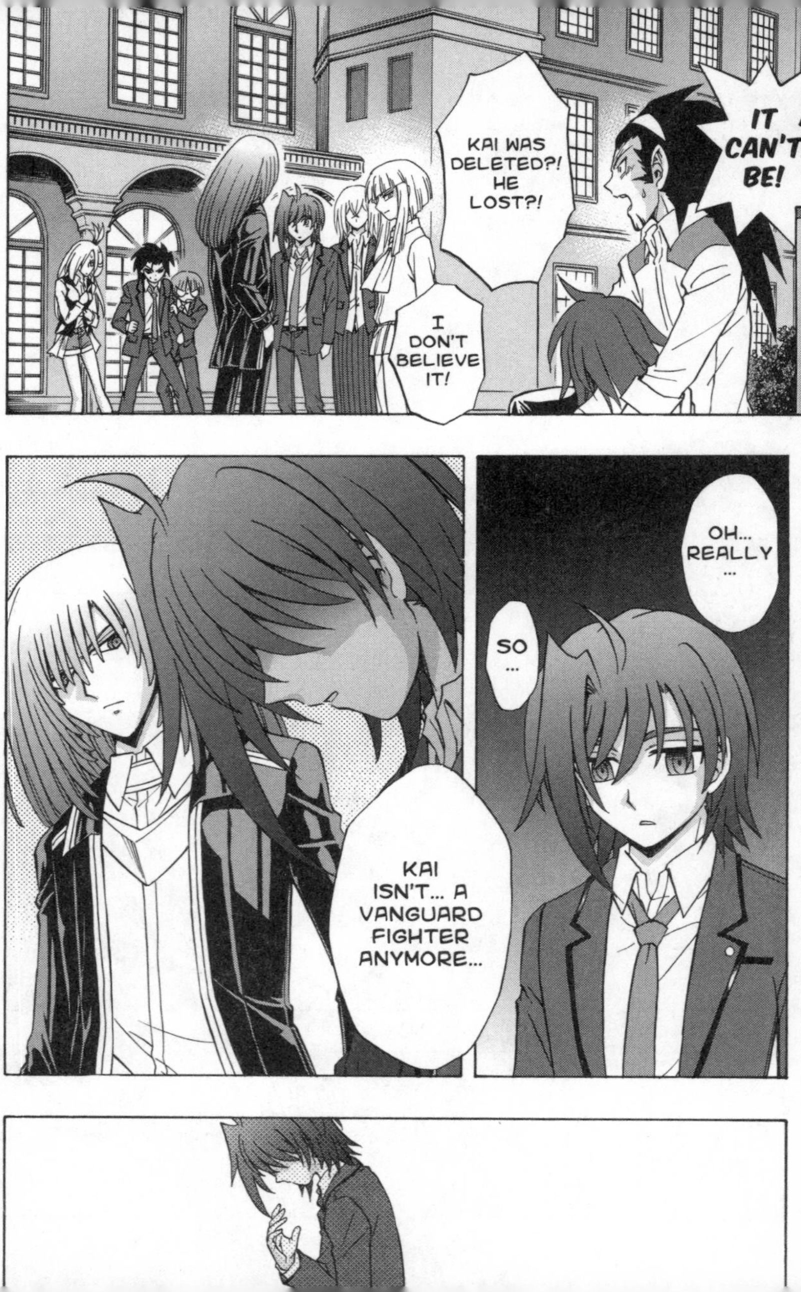
IT CAN'T BE!
KAI WAS DELETED?! HE LOST?!
I DON'T BELIEVE IT!
OH... REALLY ...
SO ...
KAI ISN'T... A VANGUARD FIGHTER ANYMORE...

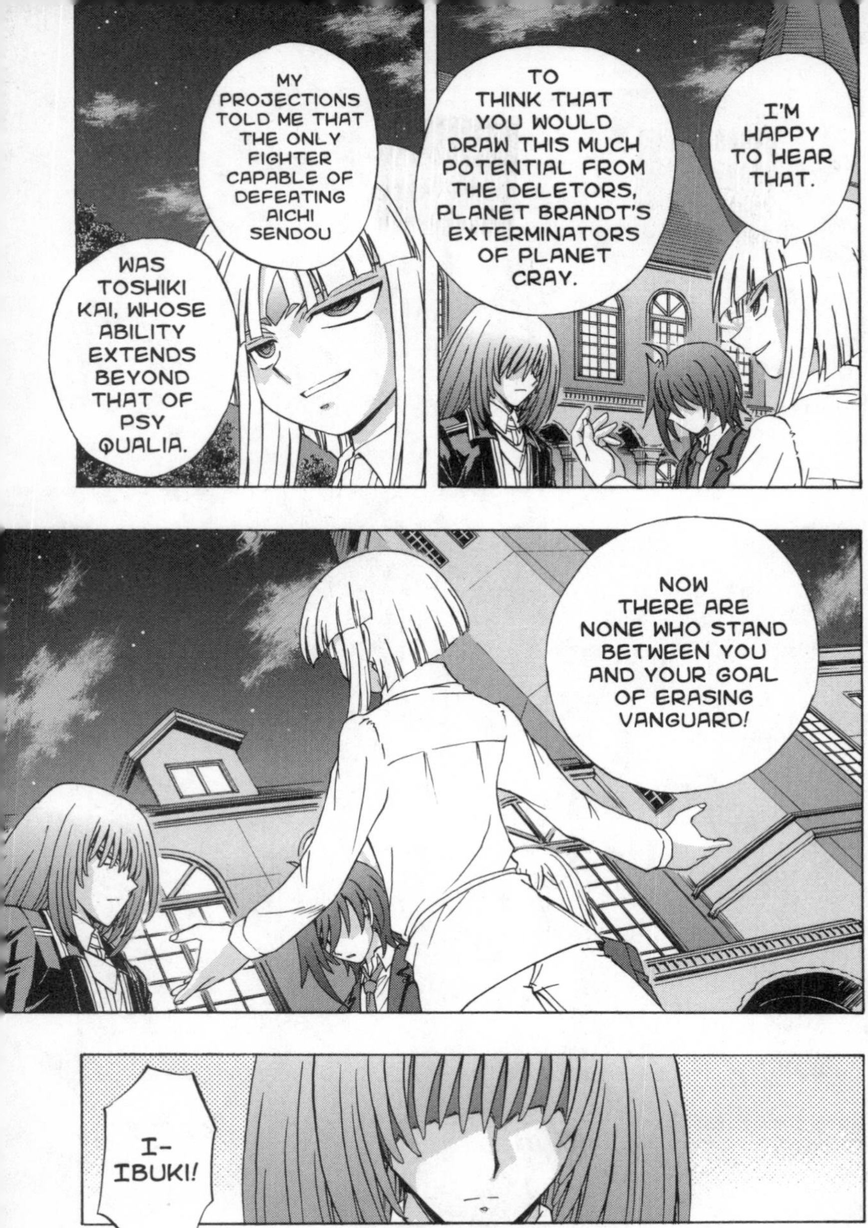
TO THINK THAT YOU WOULD DRAW THIS MUCH POTENTIAL FROM THE DELETORS, PLANET BRANDT'S EXTERMINATORS OF PLANET CRAY.
I'M HAPPY TO HEAR THAT.
MY PROJECTIONS TOLD ME THAT THE ONLY FIGHTER CAPABLE OF DEFEATING AICHI SENDOU
WAS TOSHIKI KAI, WHOSE ABILITY EXTENDS BEYOND THAT OF PSY QUALIA.
NOW THERE ARE NONE WHO STAND BETWEEN YOU AND YOUR GOAL OF ERASING VANGUARD!
I- IBUKI!

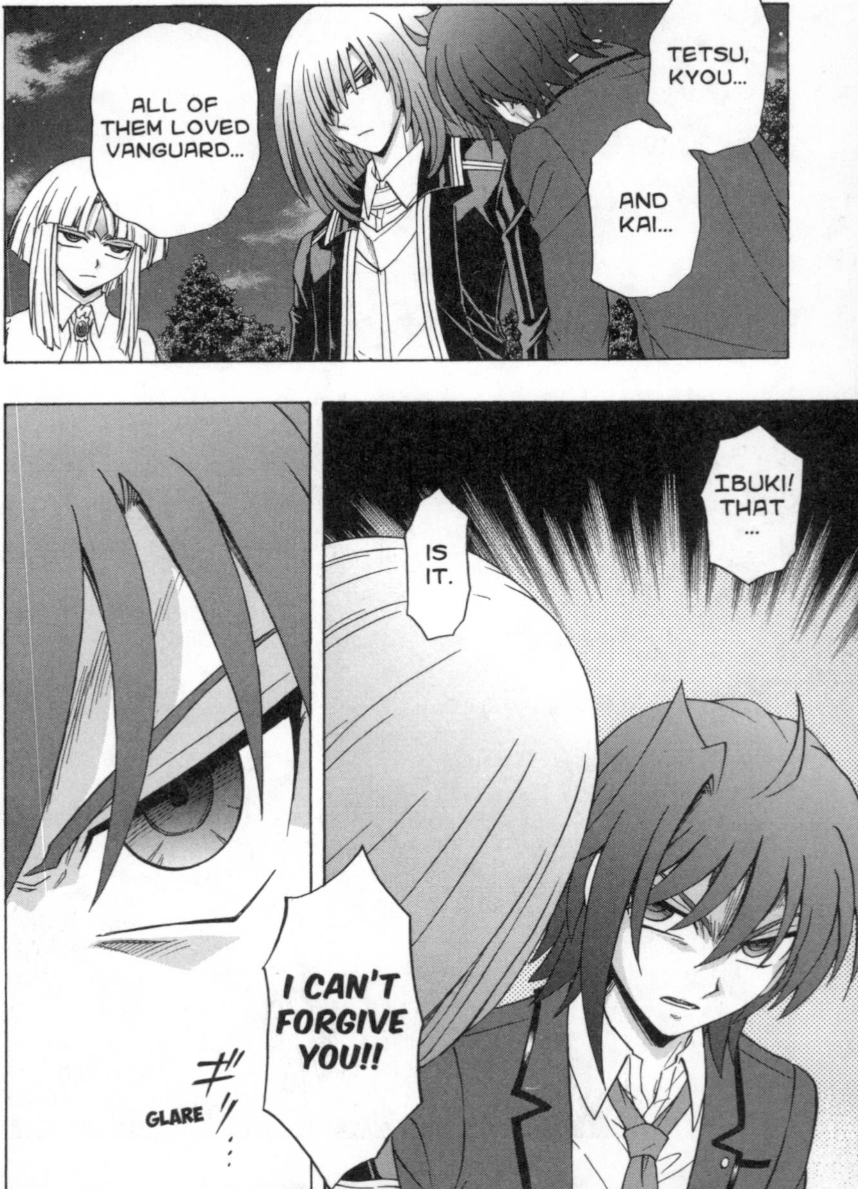
TETSU, KYOU...
AND KAI...
ALL OF THEM LOVED VANGUARD...
IBUKI! THAT ...
IS IT.
I CAN'T FORGIVE YOU!!
GLARE

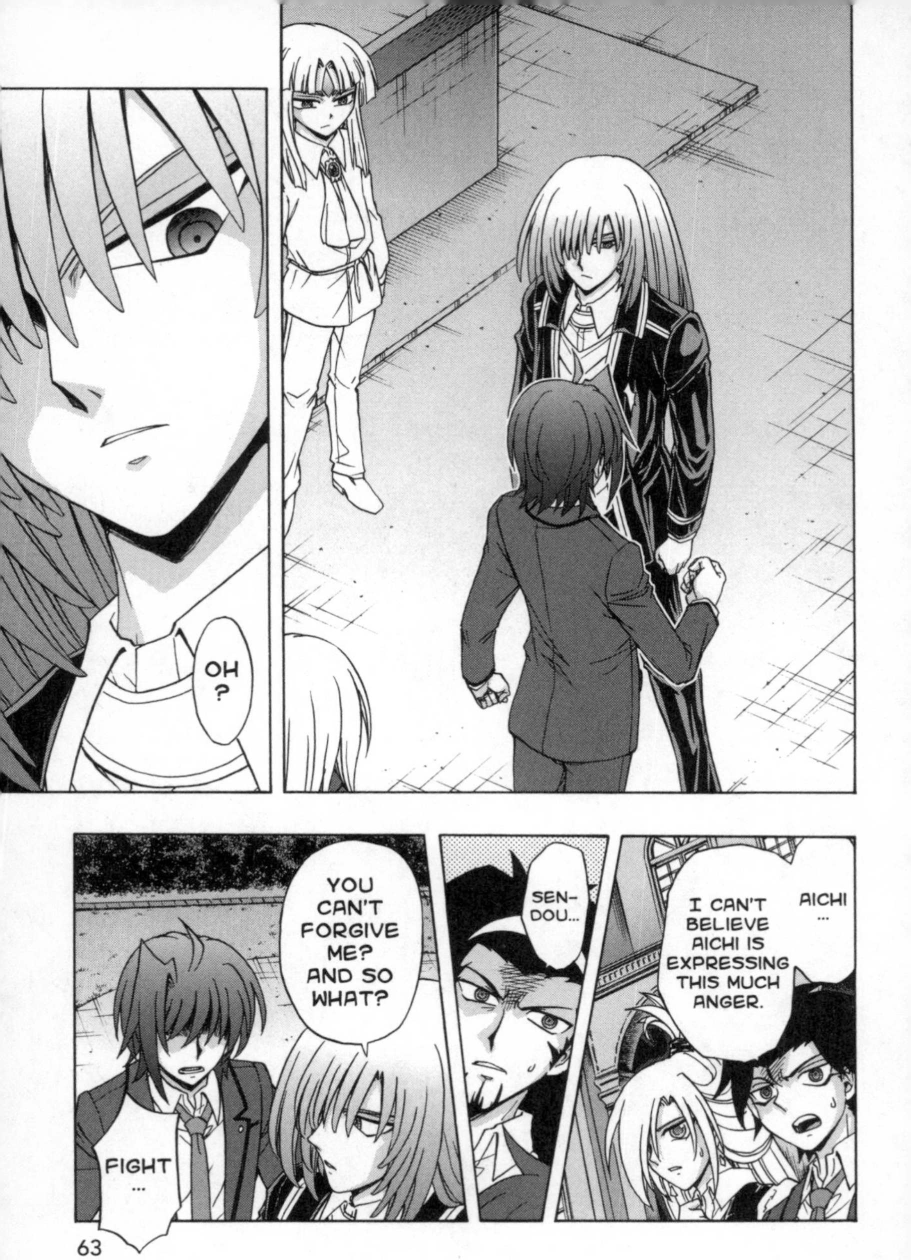
OH ?
AICHI ...
I CAN'T BELIEVE AICHI IS EXPRESSING THIS MUCH ANGER.
SEN-DOU...
YOU CAN'T FORGIVE ME? AND SO WHAT?
FIGHT ...

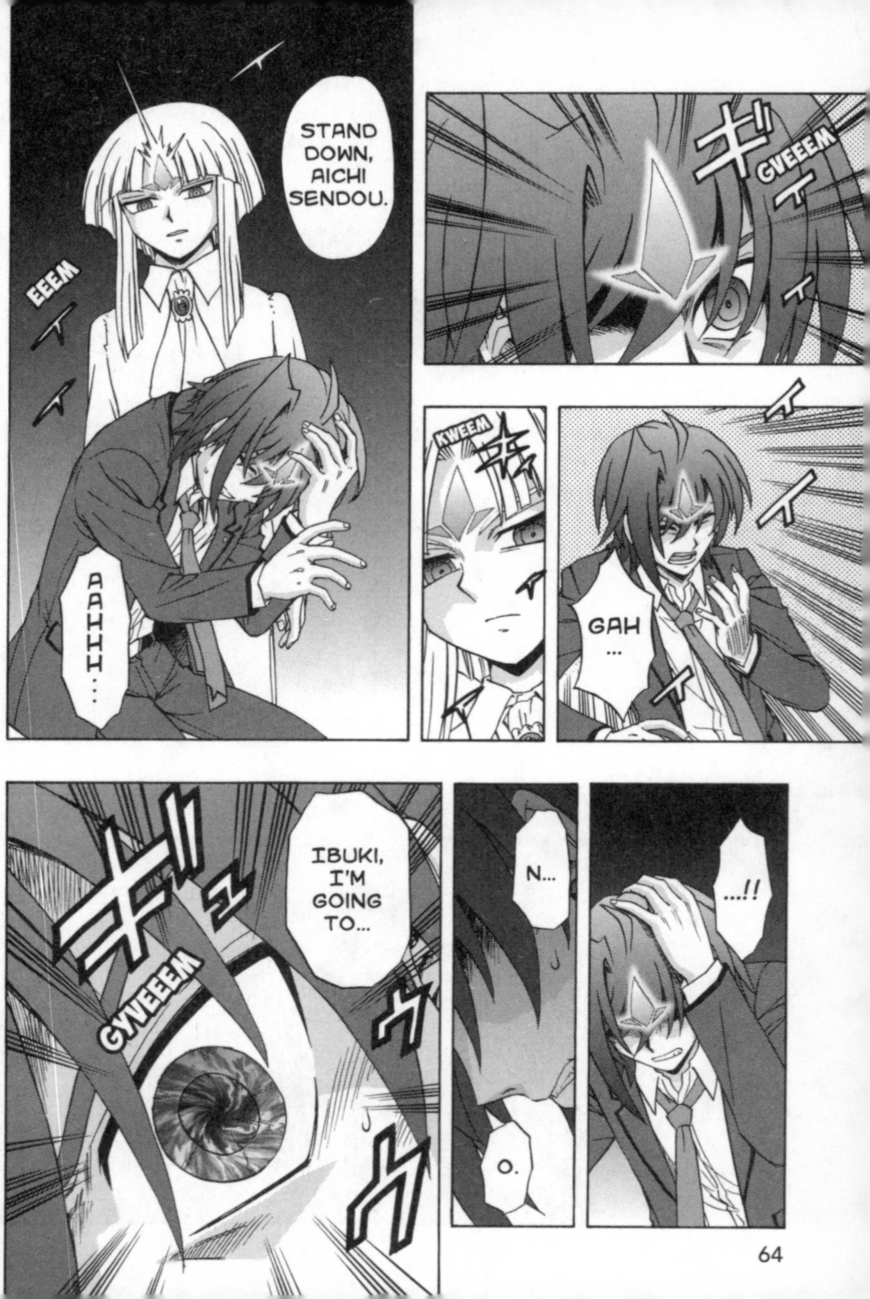
GVEEEM
GAH ...
KWEEM
STAND DOWN, AICHI SENDOU.
EEEM
AAHHH...
...!!
N...
O.
IBUKI, I'M GOING TO...
GYVEEEM

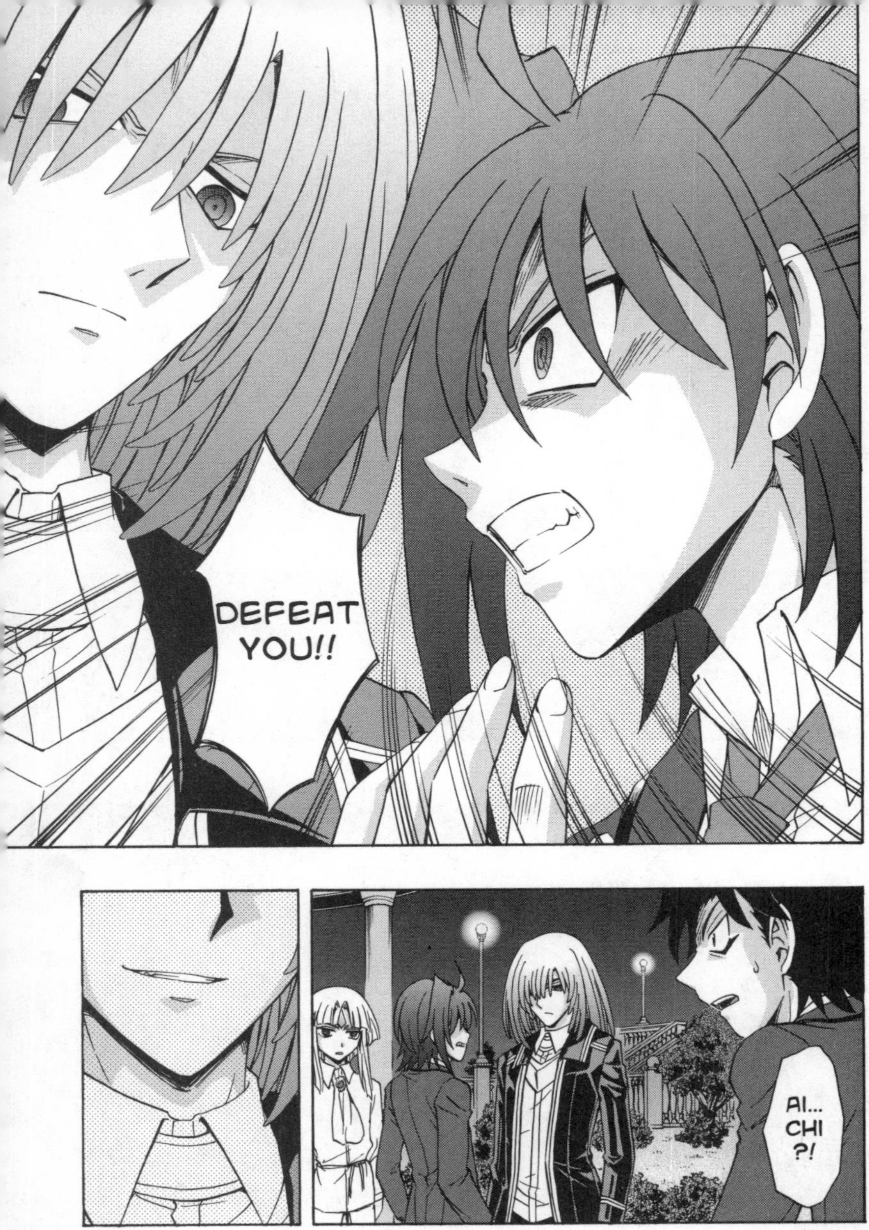
DEFEAT YOU!!
AI... CHI ?!

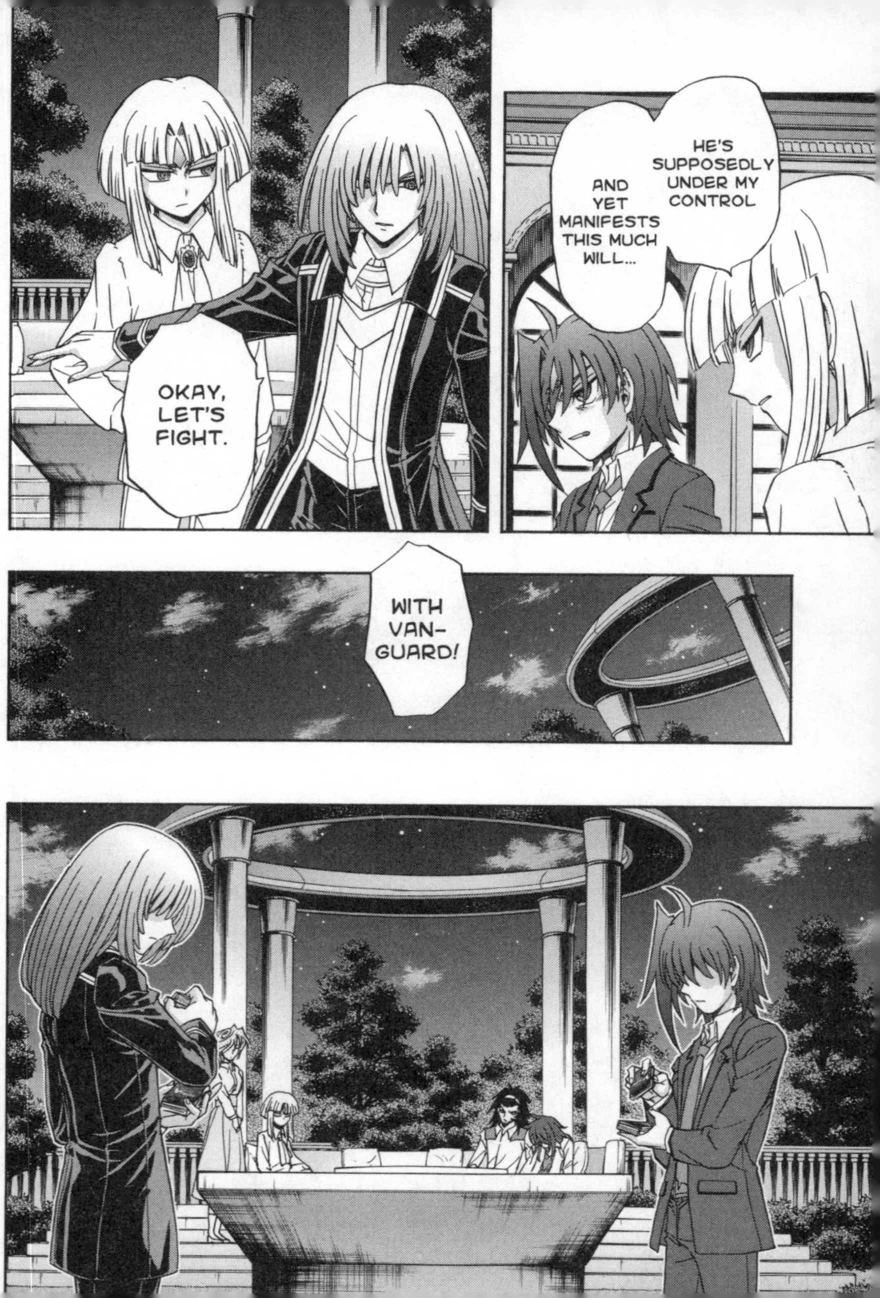
HE'S SUPPOSEDLY UNDER MY CONTROL
AND YET MANIFESTS THIS MUCH WILL...
OKAY, LET'S FIGHT.
WITH VAN-GUARD!

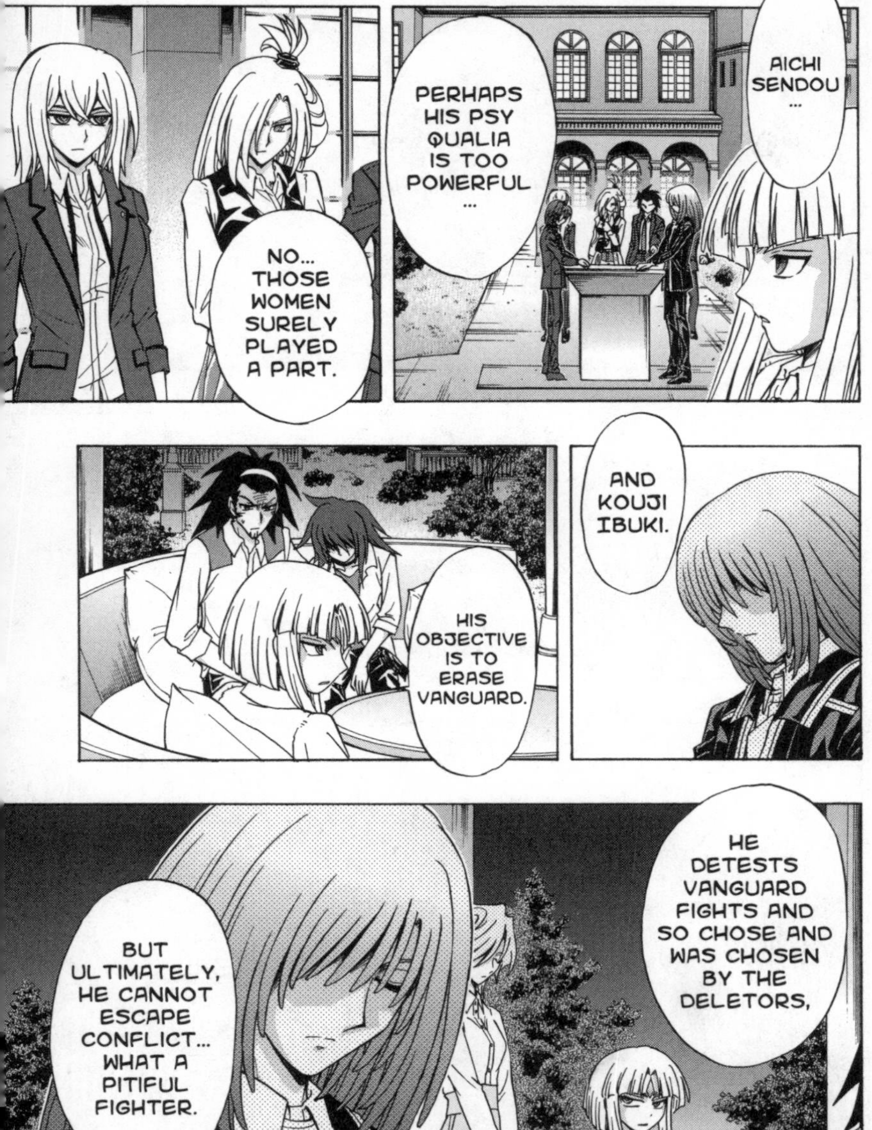
AICHI SENDOU...
PERHAPS HIS PSY QUALIA IS TOO POWERFUL...
NO... THOSE WOMEN SURELY PLAYED A PART.
AND KOUJI IBUKI.
HIS OBJECTIVE IS TO ERASE VANGUARD.
HE DETESTS VANGUARD FIGHTS AND SO CHOSE AND WAS CHOSEN BY THE DELETORS,
BUT ULTIMATELY, HE CANNOT ESCAPE CONFLICT... WHAT A PITIFUL FIGHTER.

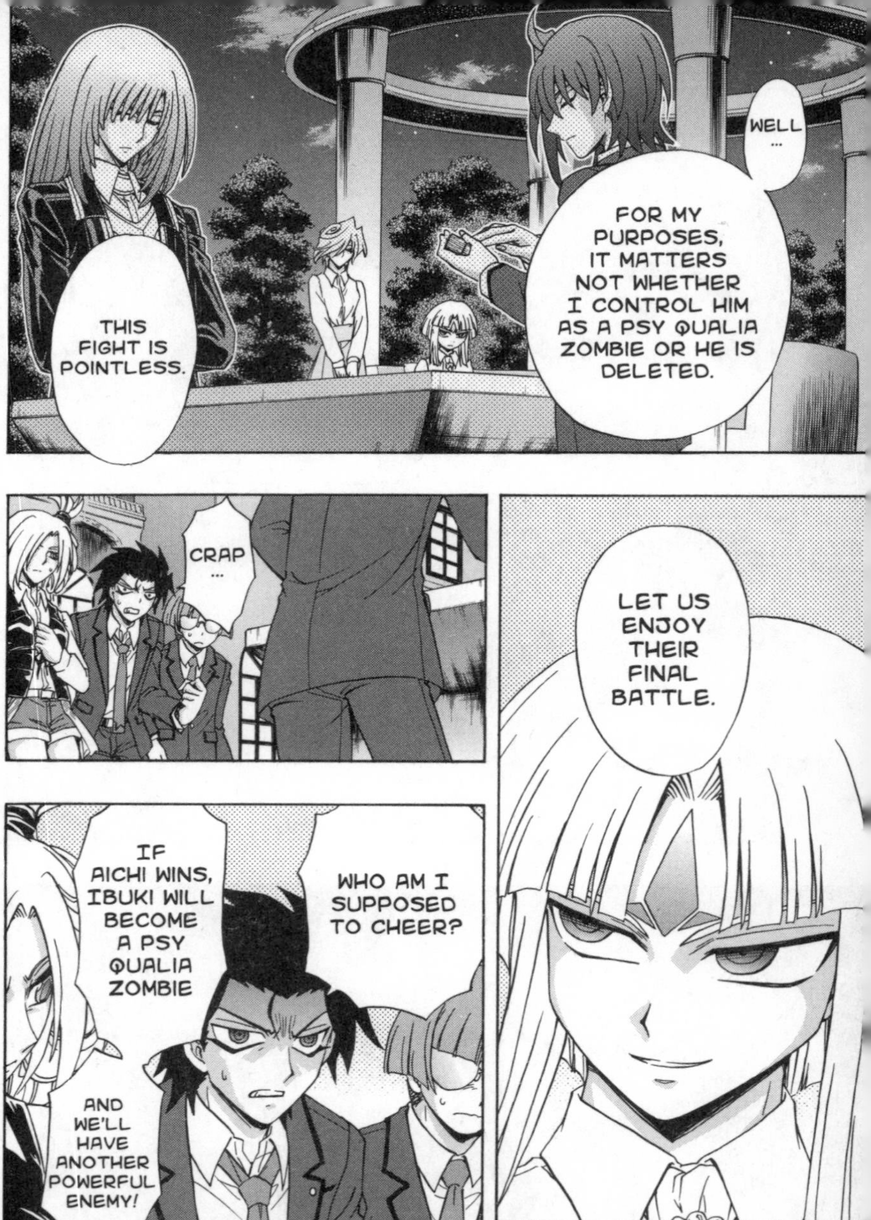
THIS FIGHT IS POINTLESS.
WELL ...
FOR MY PURPOSES, IT MATTERS NOT WHETHER I CONTROL HIM AS A PSY QUALIA ZOMBIE OR HE IS DELETED.
LET US ENJOY THEIR FINAL BATTLE.
CRAP ...
WHO AM I SUPPOSED TO CHEER?
IF AICHI WINS, IBUKI WILL BECOME A PSY QUALIA ZOMBIE
AND WE'LL HAVE ANOTHER POWERFUL ENEMY!

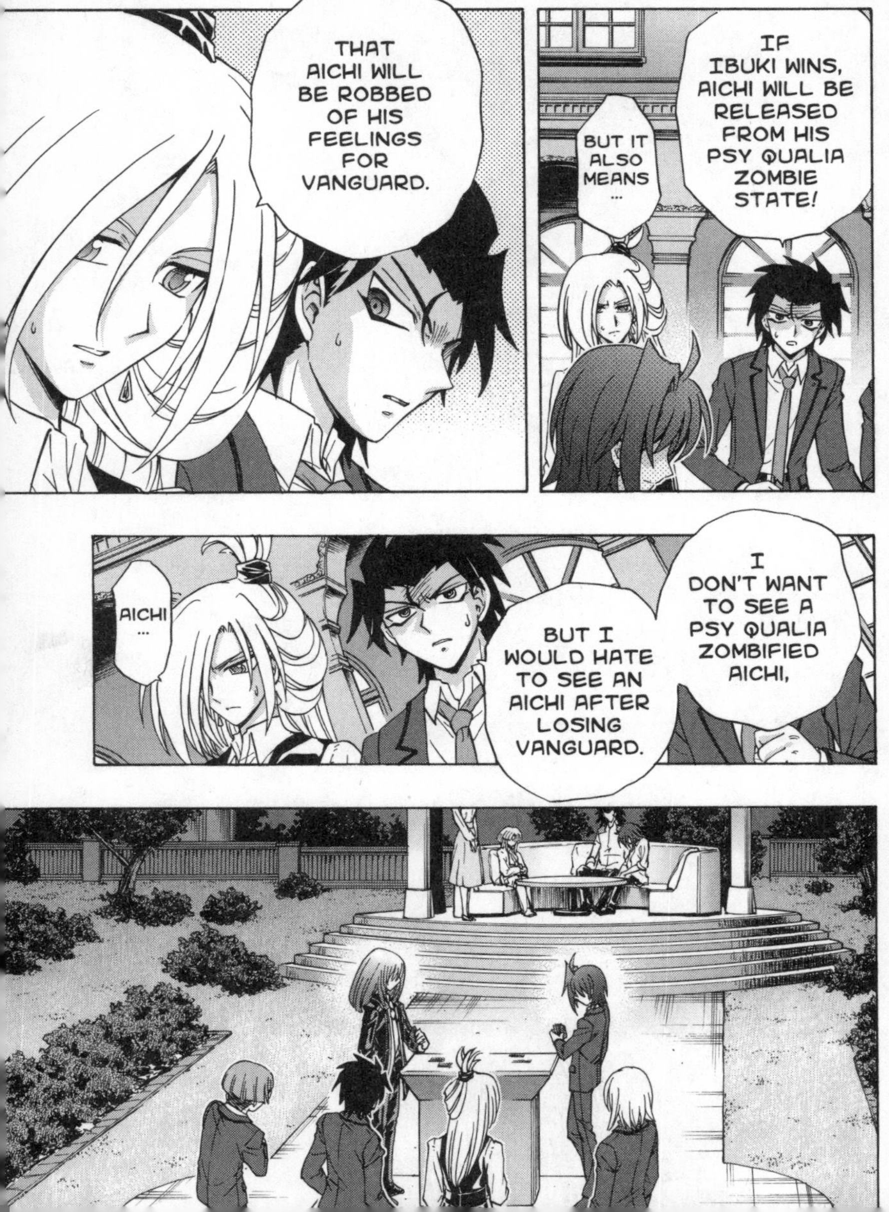
IF IBUKI WINS, AICHI WILL BE RELEASED FROM HIS PSY QUALIA ZOMBIE STATE!
BUT IT ALSO MEANS ...
THAT AICHI WILL BE ROBBED OF HIS FEELINGS FOR VANGUARD.
I DON'T WANT TO SEE A PSY QUALIA ZOMBIFIED AICHI,
BUT I WOULD HATE TO SEE AN AICHI AFTER LOSING VANGUARD.
AICHI ...

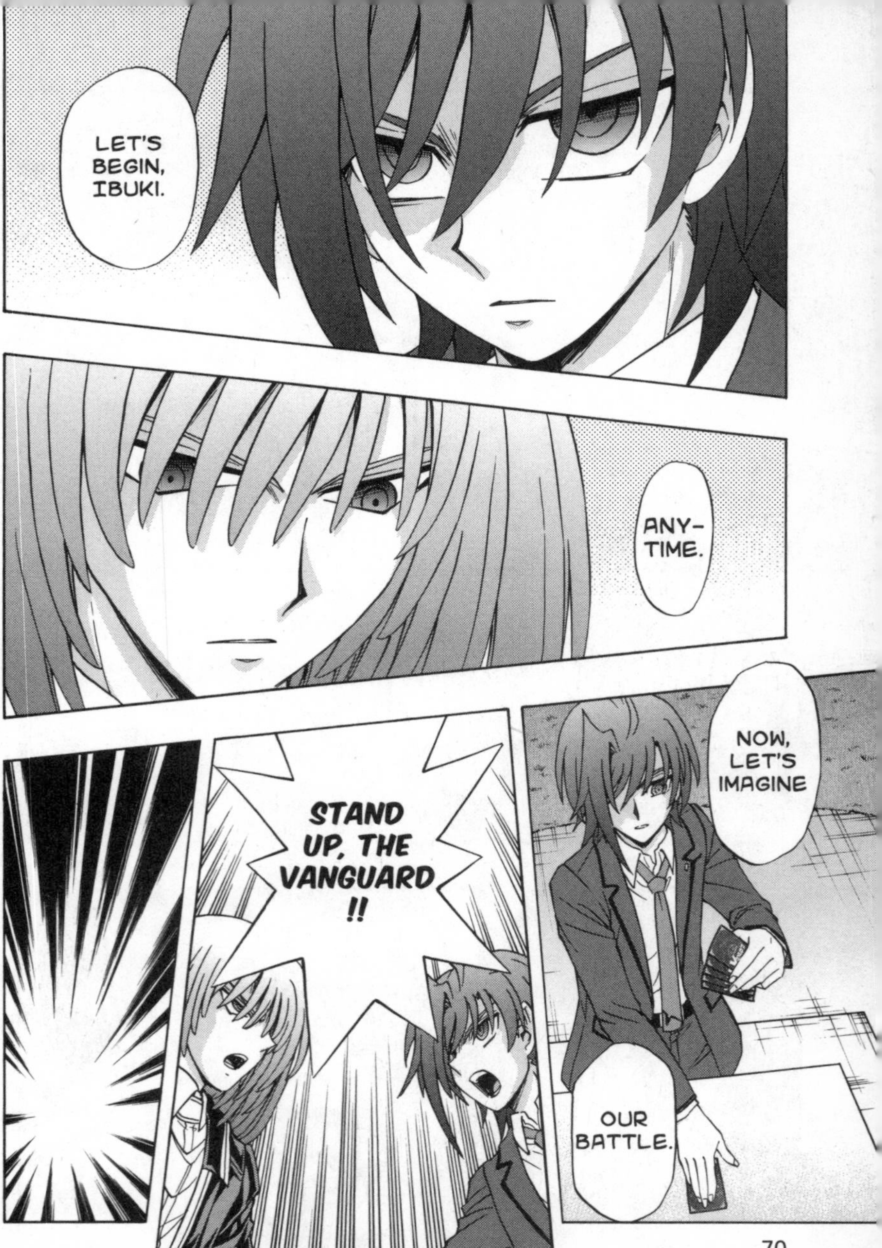
LET'S BEGIN, IBUKI.
ANY-TIME.
NOW, LET'S IMAGINE
OUR BATTLE.
STAND UP, THE VANGUARD !!

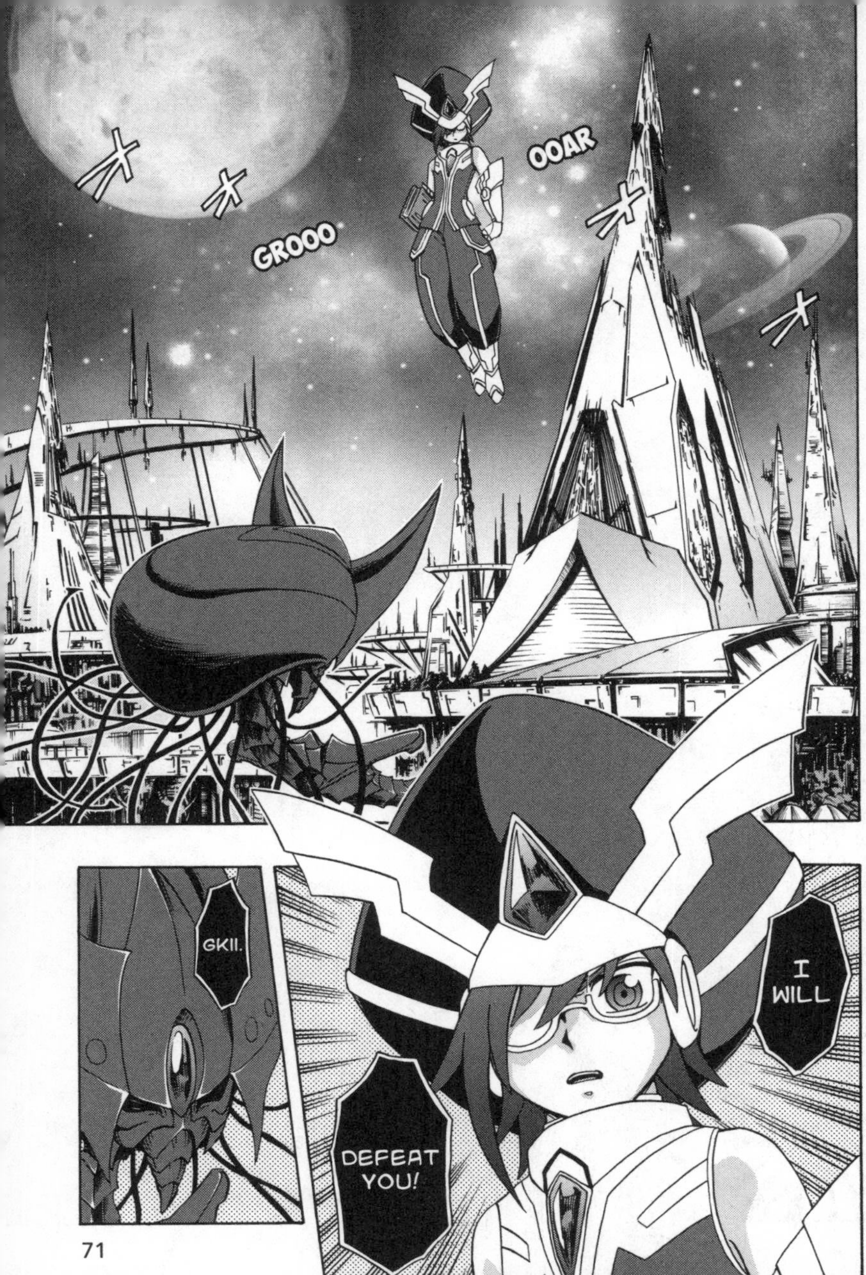
OOAR
GROOO
I WILL
DEFEAT YOU!
GKII.

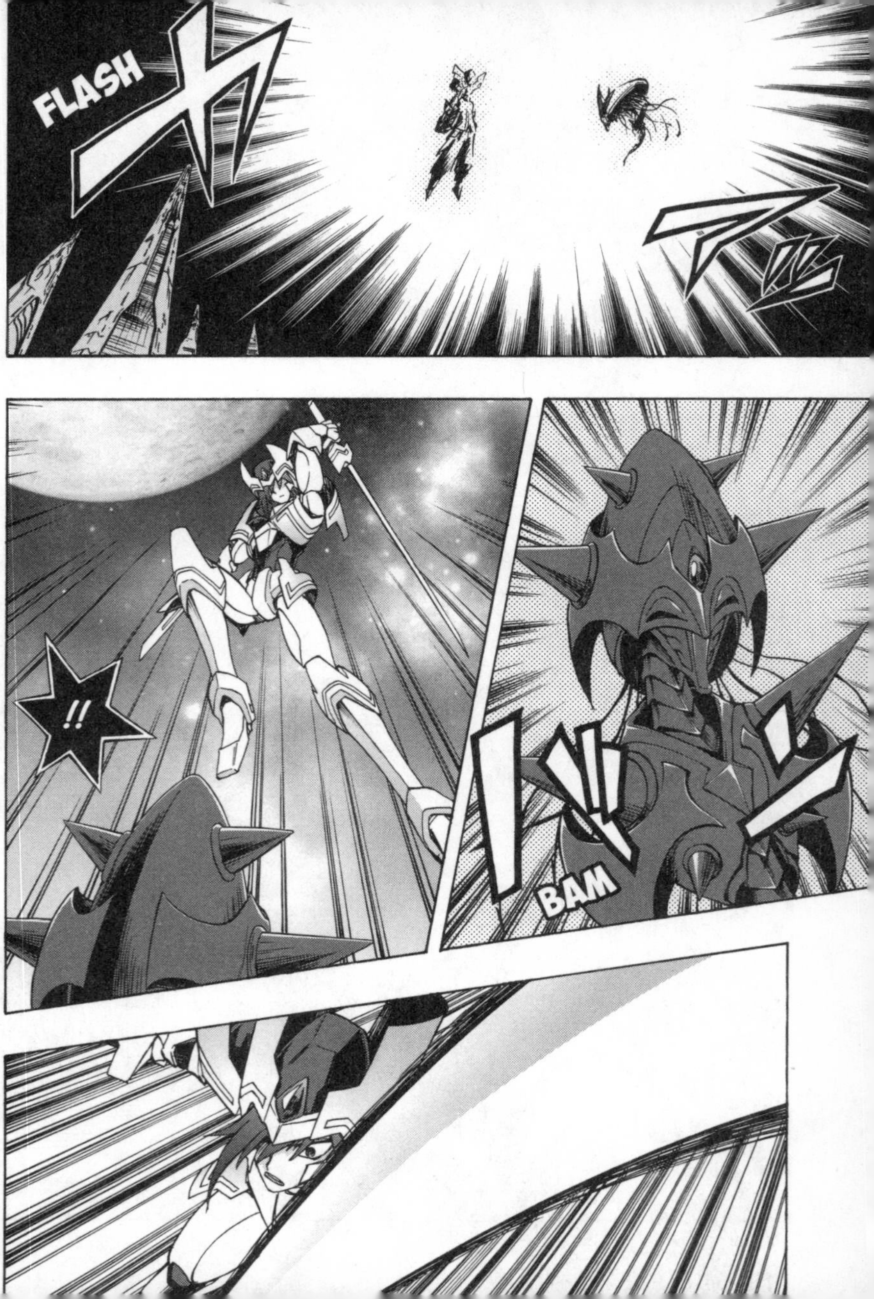
FLASH
!!
BAM

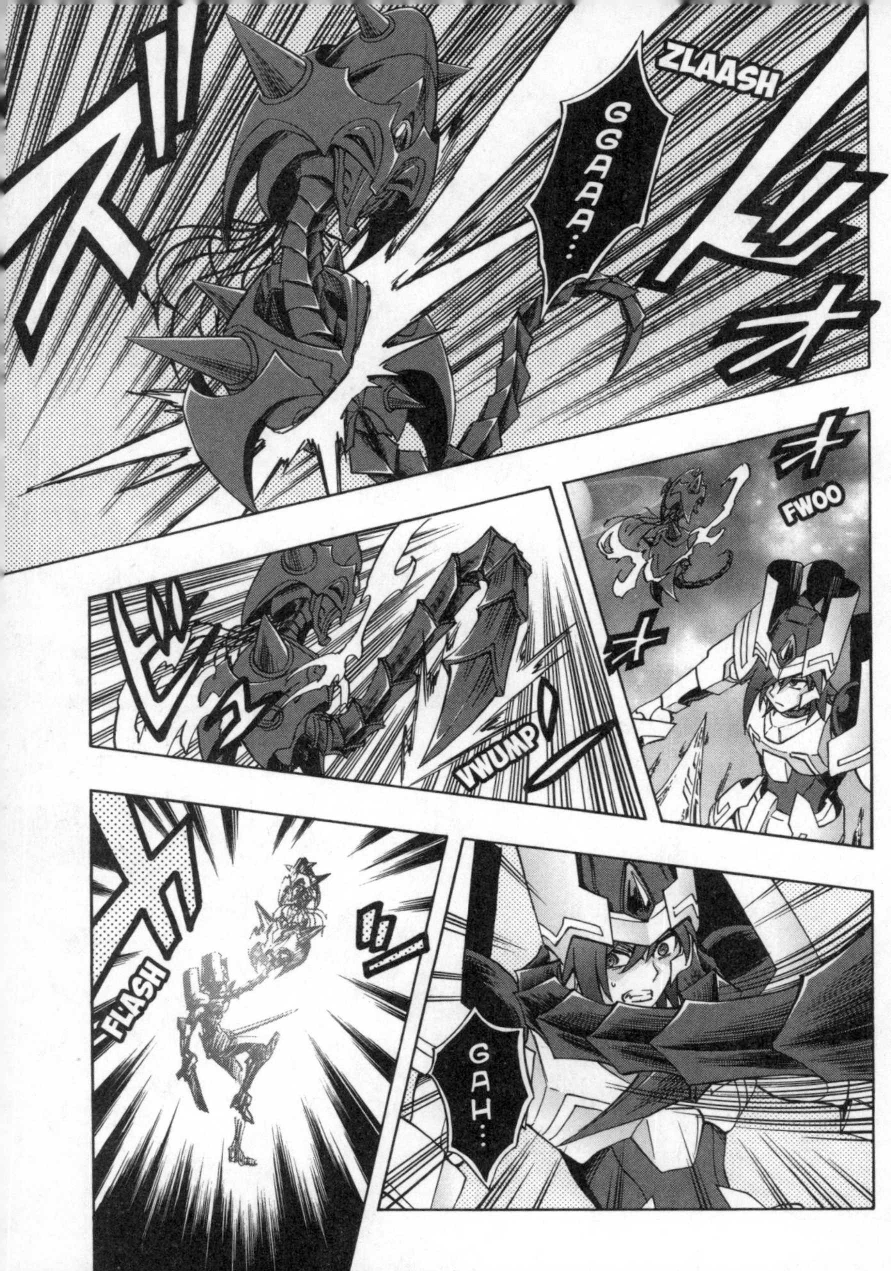
ZLAASH
GGAAAA...
FWOO
VWUMP
GAH...
FLASH

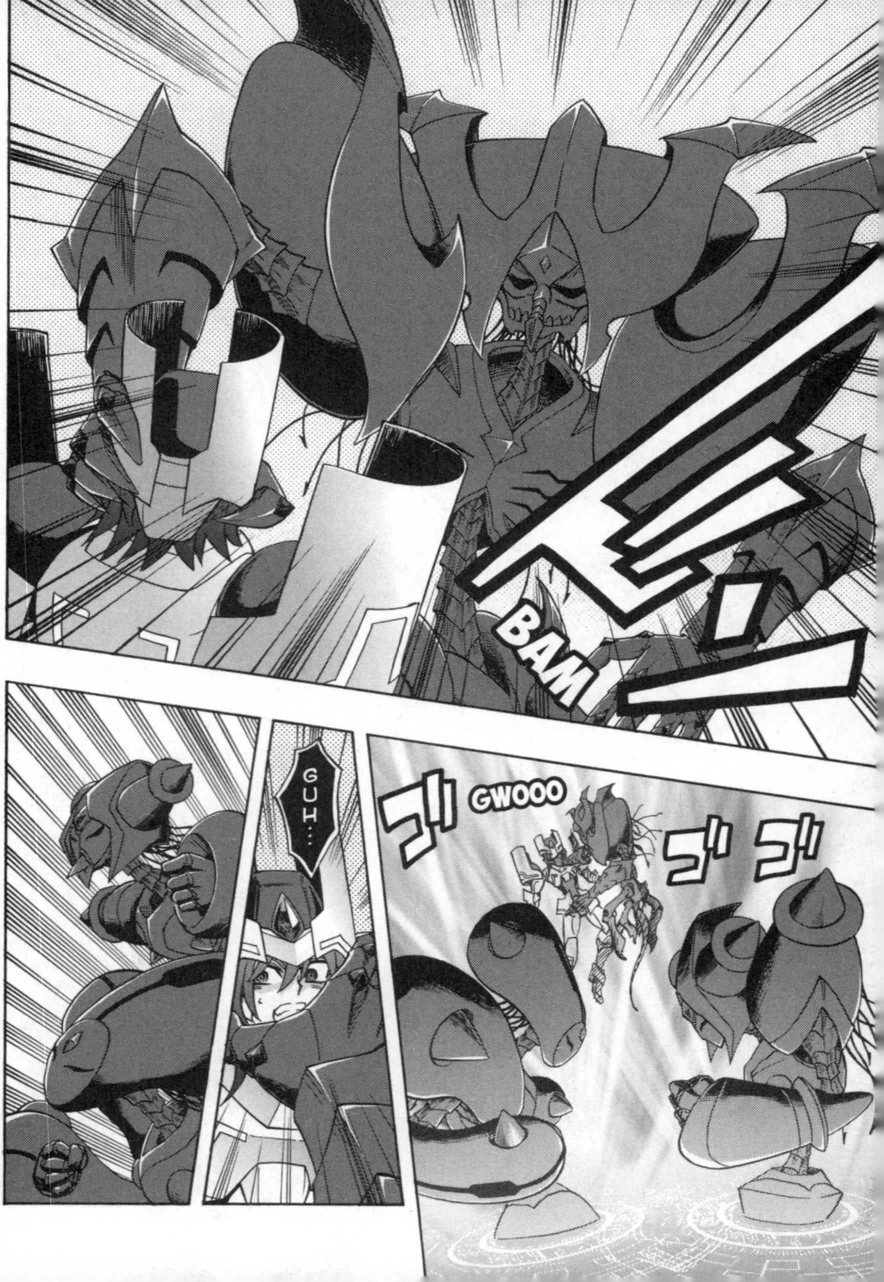
BAM
ゴ
GWOOO
ゴゴ
GUH...

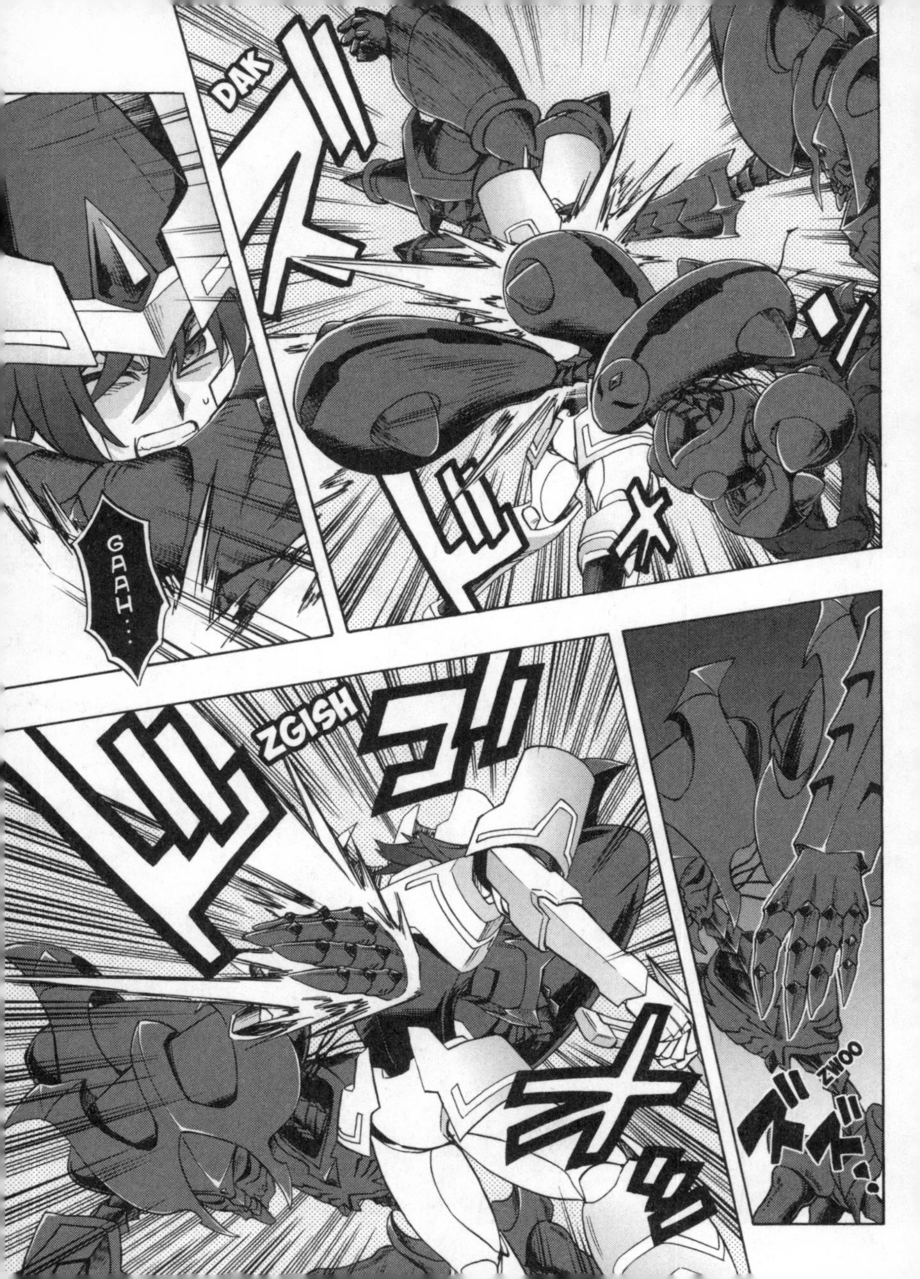
DAK
GAAAH...
ZWOO
ZGISH

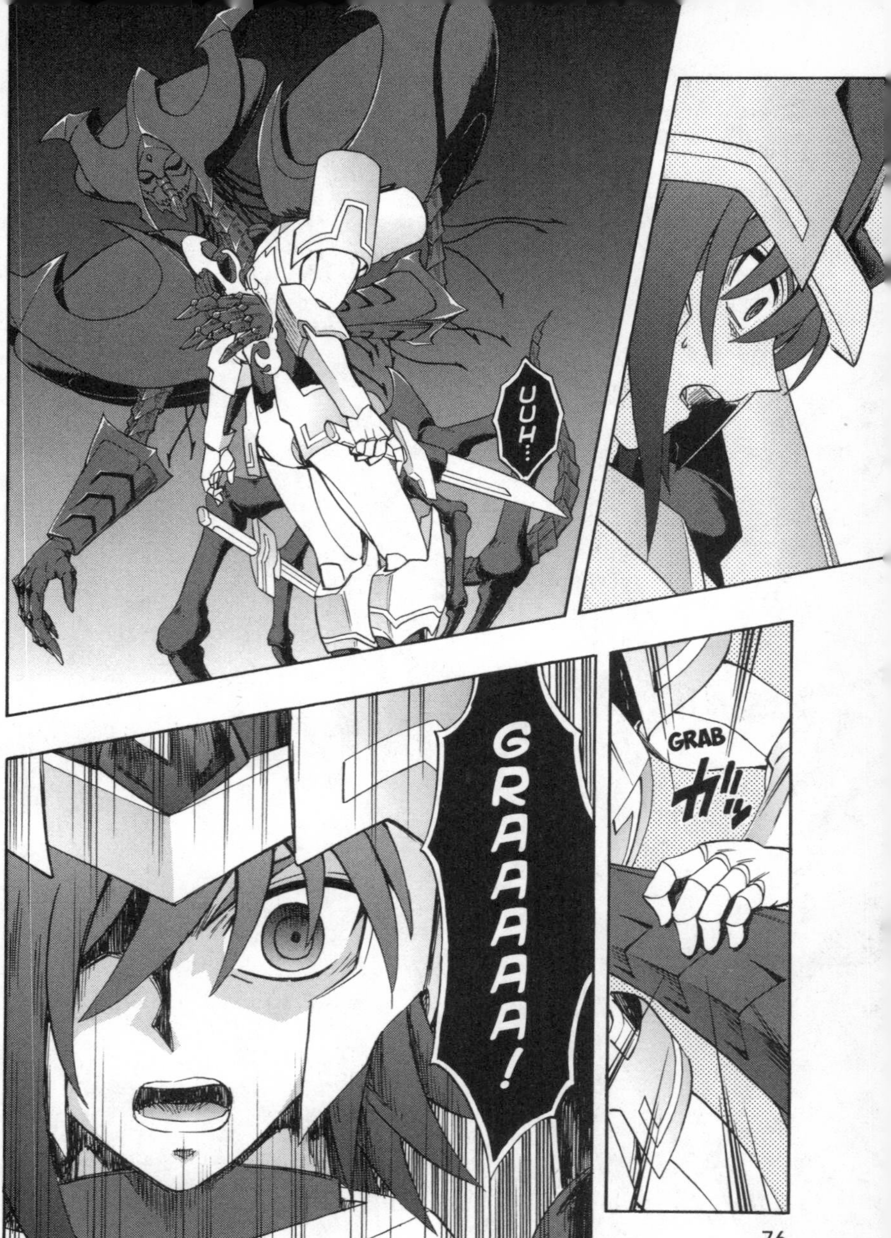
UUH...
GRAB
ガッ
GRAAAAAAA!

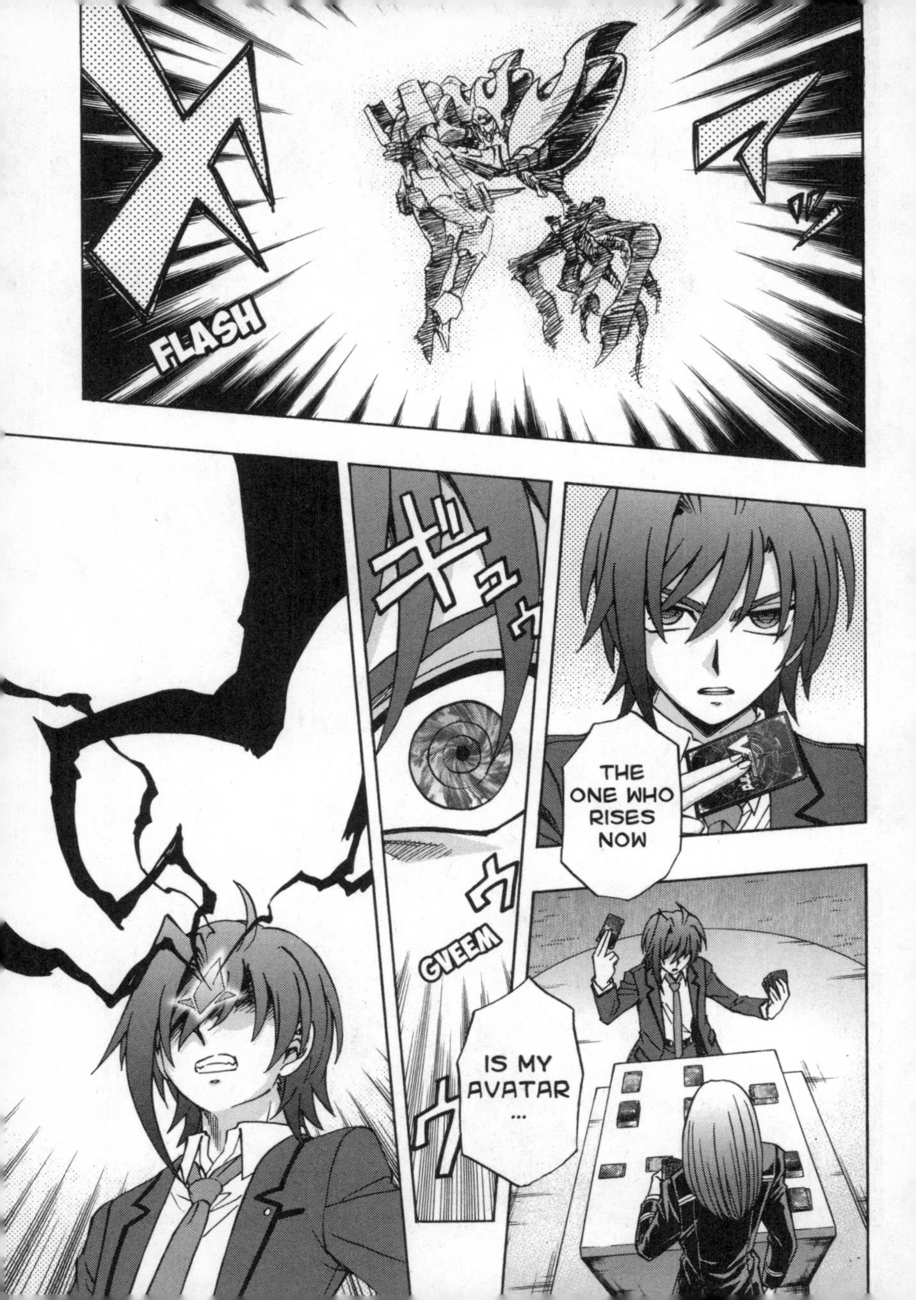
FLASH
THE ONE WHO RISES NOW
GVEEM
IS MY AVATAR ...

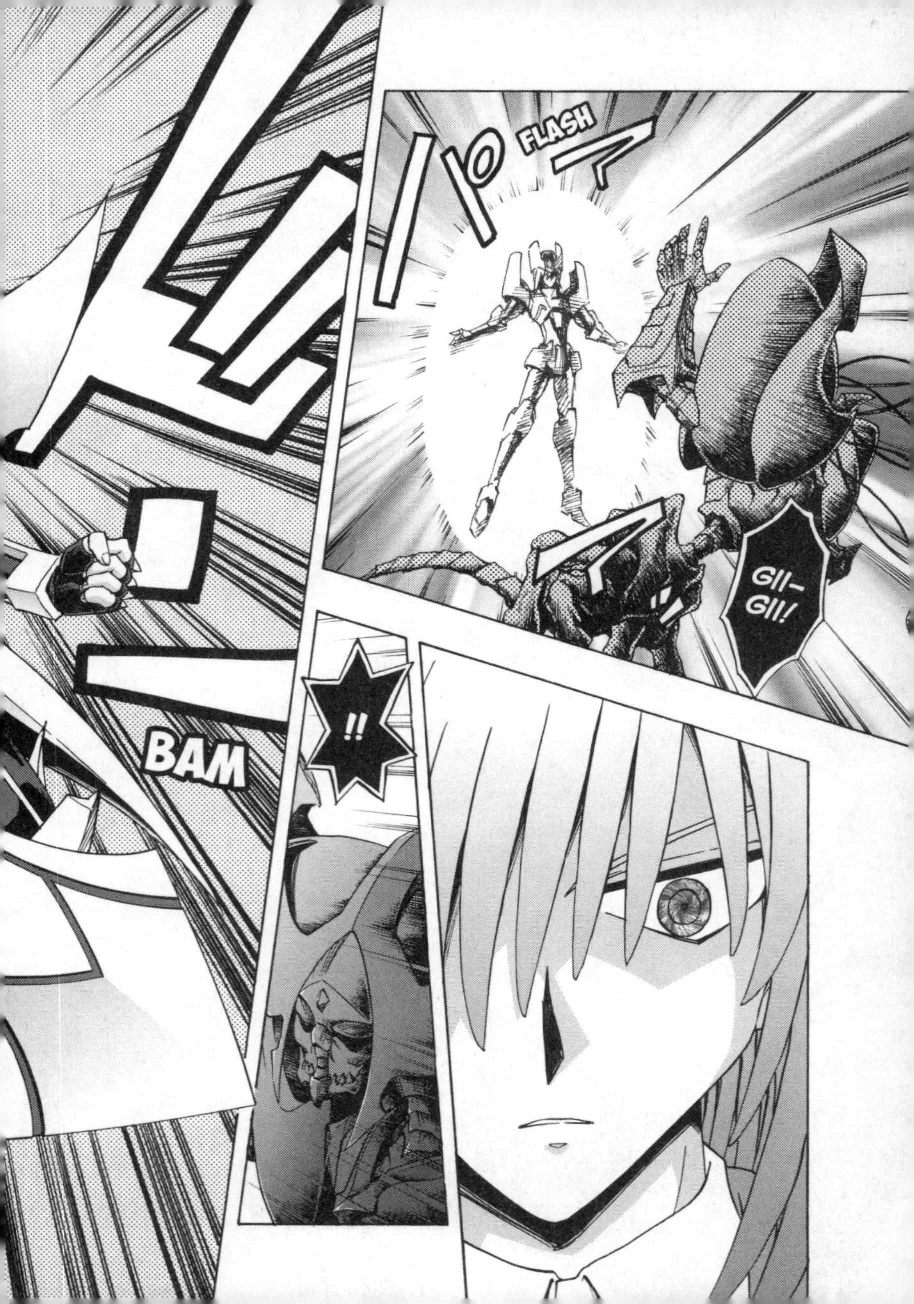
FLASH
GII-GII!
BAM
!!

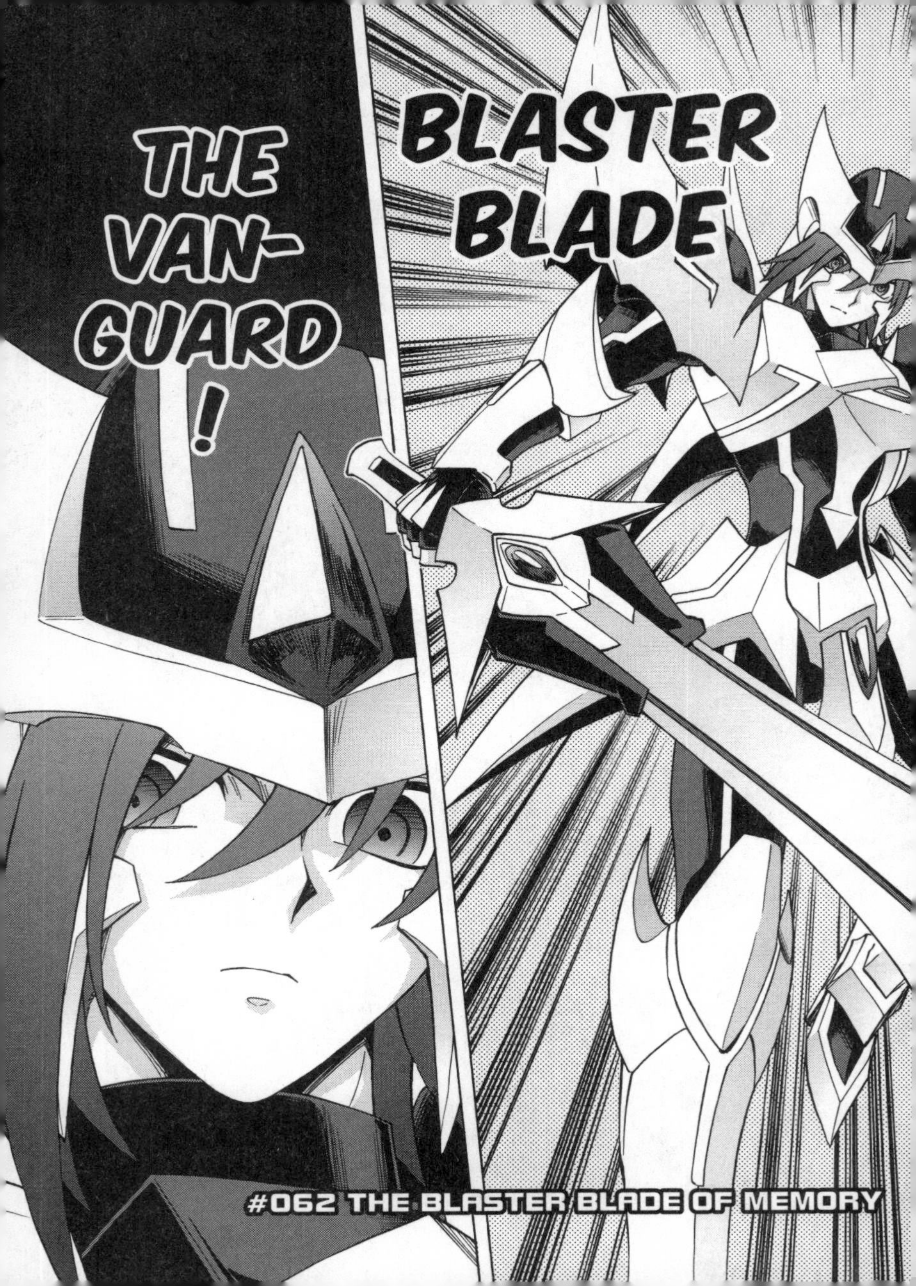
BLASTER BLADE
THE VAN-GUARD!
#062 THE BLASTER BLADE OF MEMORY

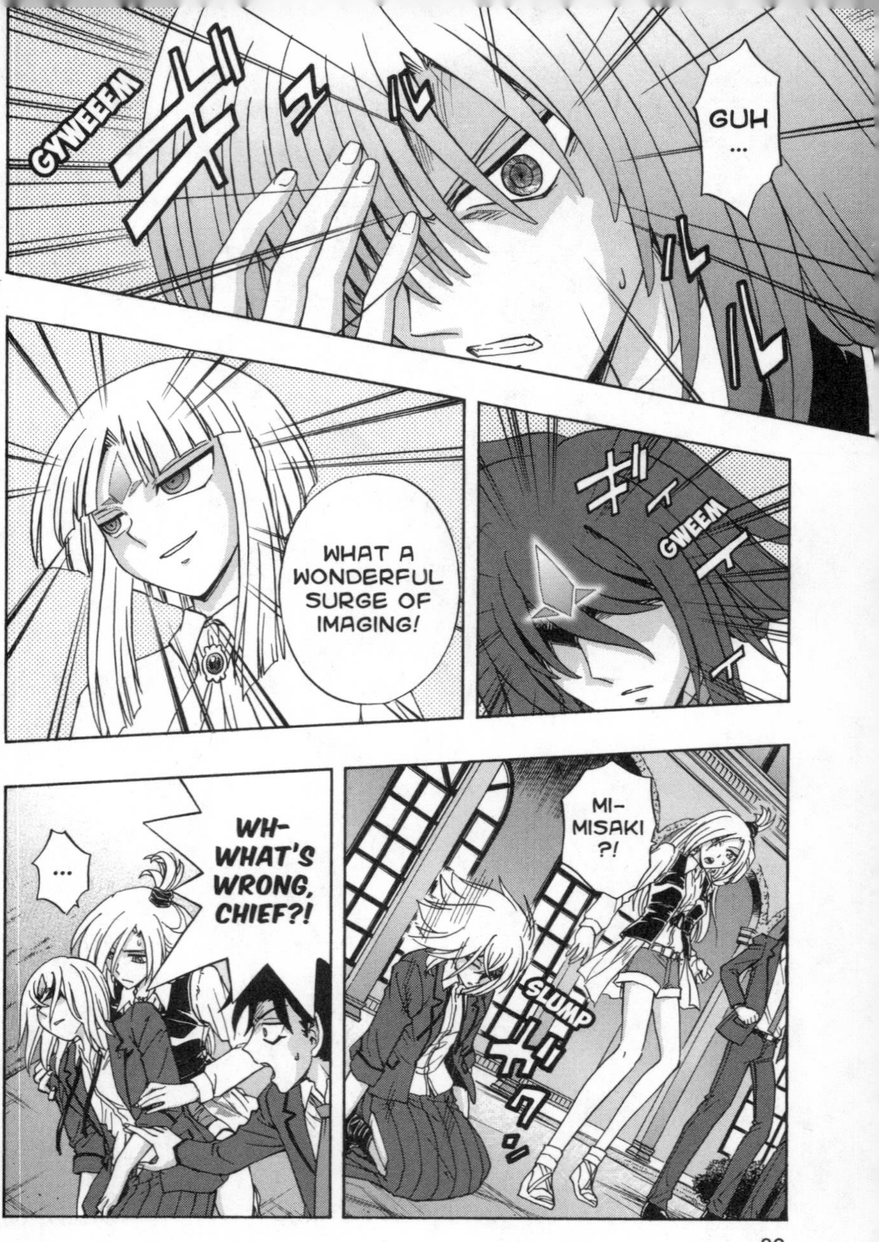
GYWEEEM
GUH ...
GWEEM
WHAT A WONDERFUL SURGE OF IMAGING!
MI-MISAKI ?!
SLUMP
WH-WHAT'S WRONG, CHIEF?!
...

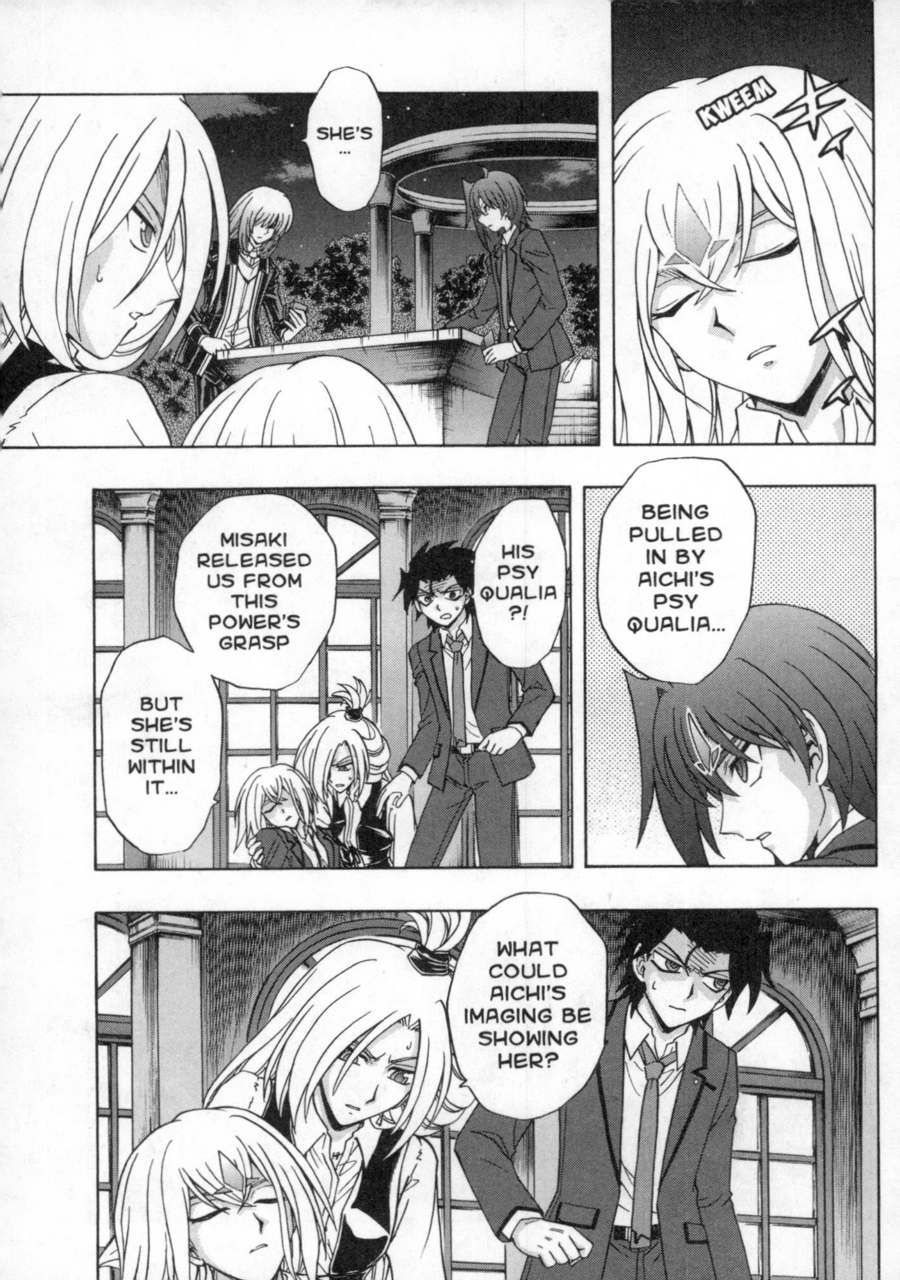
KWEEM
SHE'S ...
BEING PULLED IN BY AICHI'S PSY QUALIA...
HIS PSY QUALIA ?!
MISAKI RELEASED US FROM THIS POWER'S GRASP
BUT SHE'S STILL WITHIN IT...
WHAT COULD AICHI'S IMAGING BE SHOWING HER?

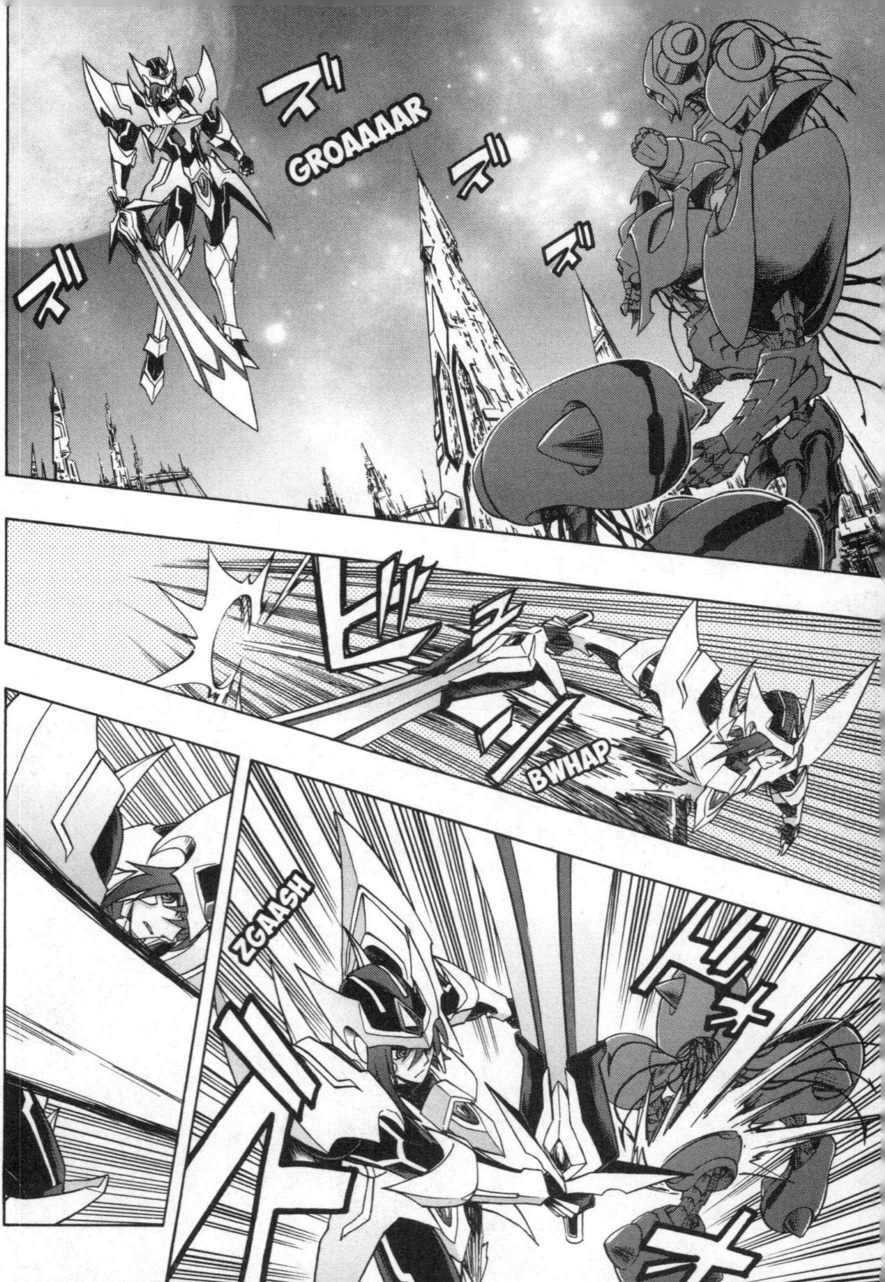
GROAAAAR
BWHAP
ZGAASH

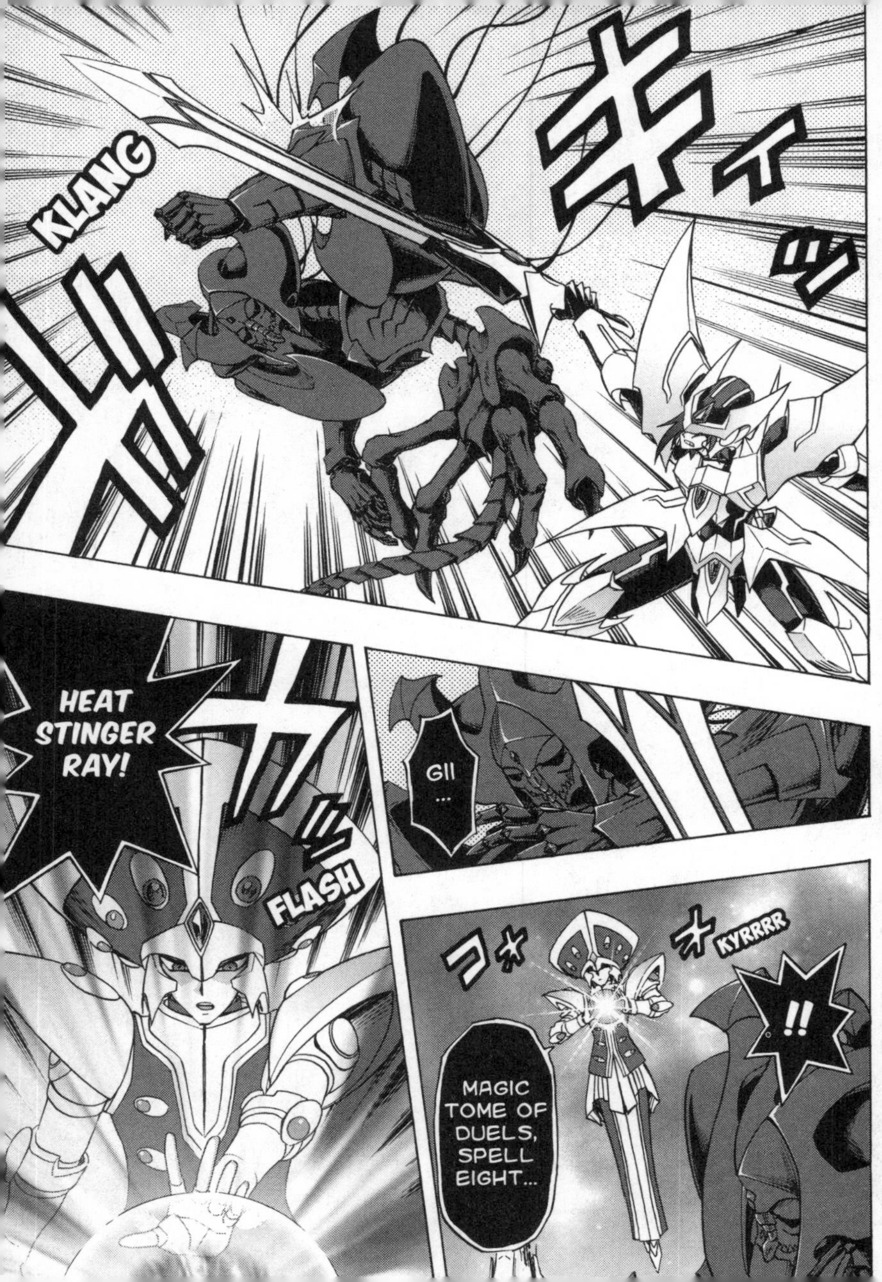
KLANG
GII ...
HEAT STINGER RAY!
FLASH
KYRRRR
!!
MAGIC TOME OF DUELS, SPELL EIGHT...

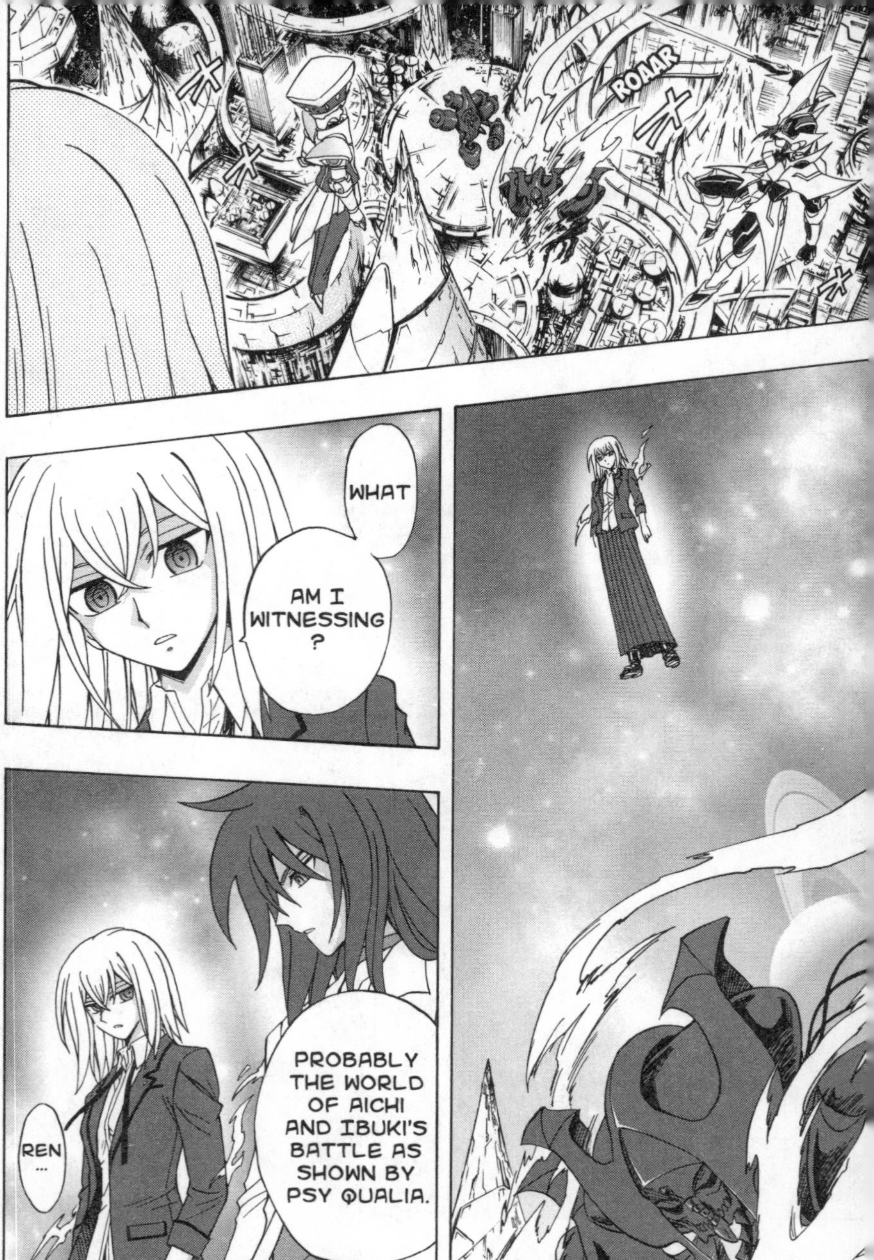
ROAAR
WHAT
AM I WITNESSING ?
PROBABLY THE WORLD OF AICHI AND IBUKI'S BATTLE AS SHOWN BY PSY QUALIA.
REN ...

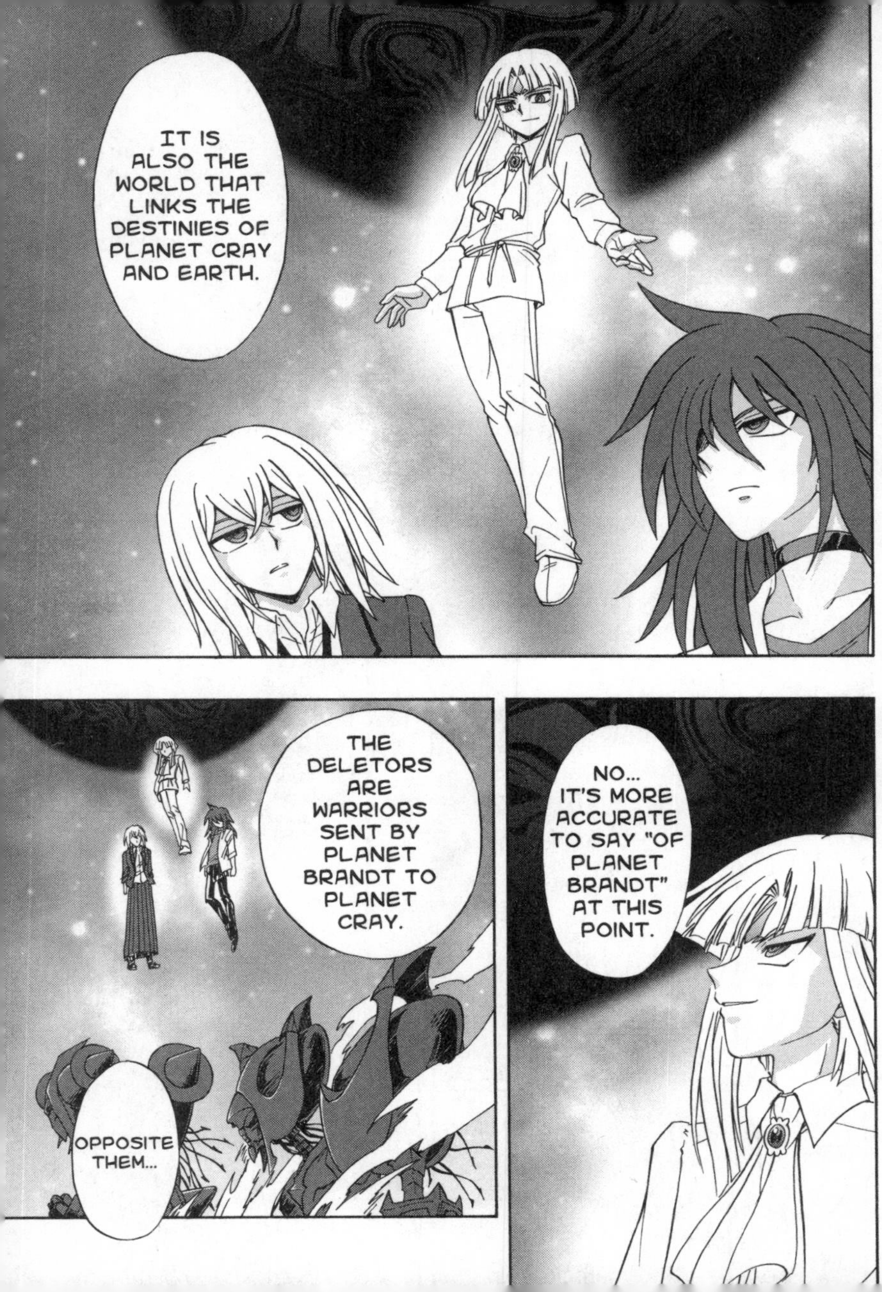
IT IS ALSO THE WORLD THAT LINKS THE DESTINIES OF PLANET CRAY AND EARTH.
NO... IT'S MORE ACCURATE TO SAY "OF PLANET BRANDT" AT THIS POINT.
THE DELETORS ARE WARRIORS SENT BY PLANET BRANDT TO PLANET CRAY.
OPPOSITE THEM...

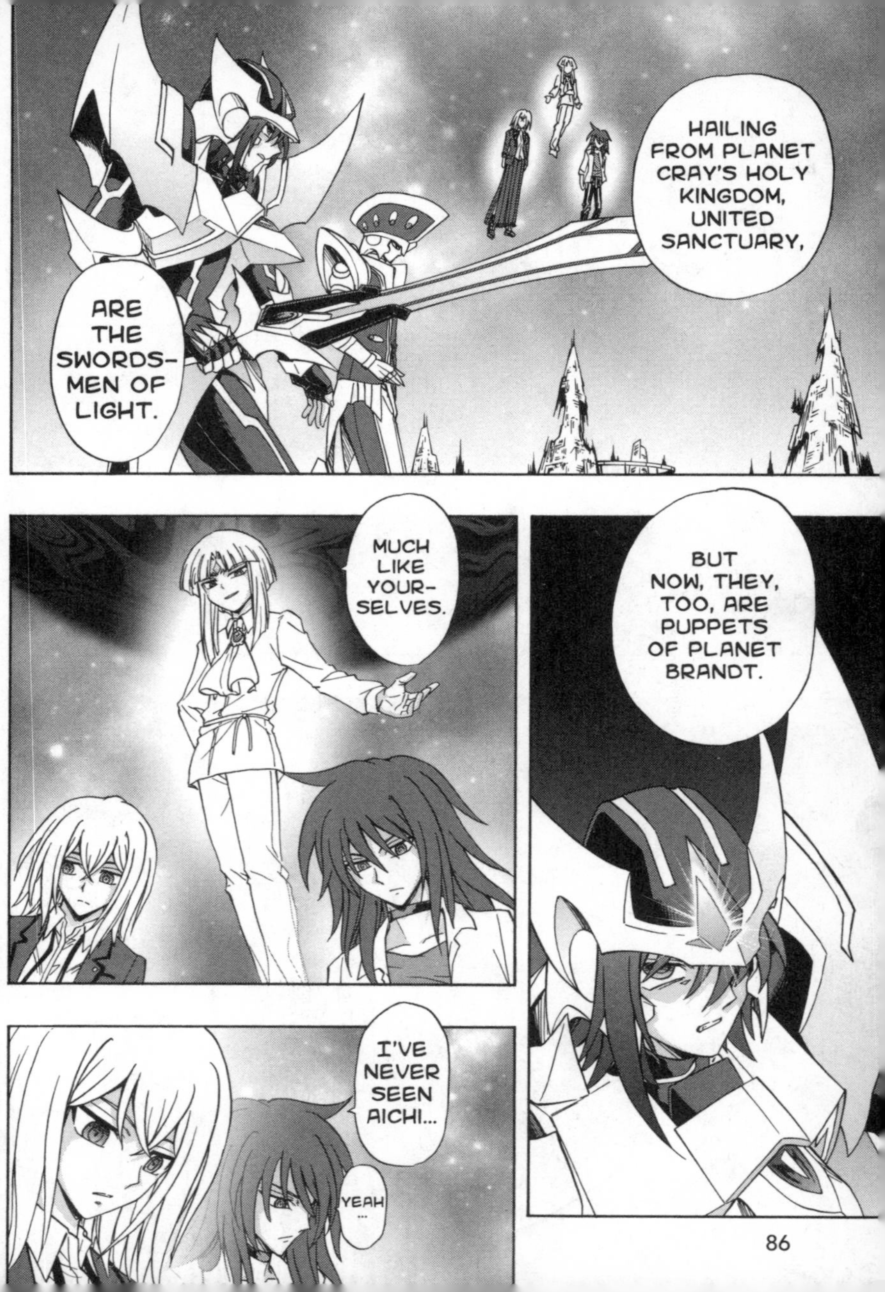
HAILING FROM PLANET CRAY'S HOLY KINGDOM, UNITED SANCTUARY,
ARE THE SWORDS-MEN OF LIGHT.
BUT NOW, THEY, TOO, ARE PUPPETS OF PLANET BRANDT.
MUCH LIKE YOUR-SELVES.
I'VE NEVER SEEN AICHI...
YEAH ...

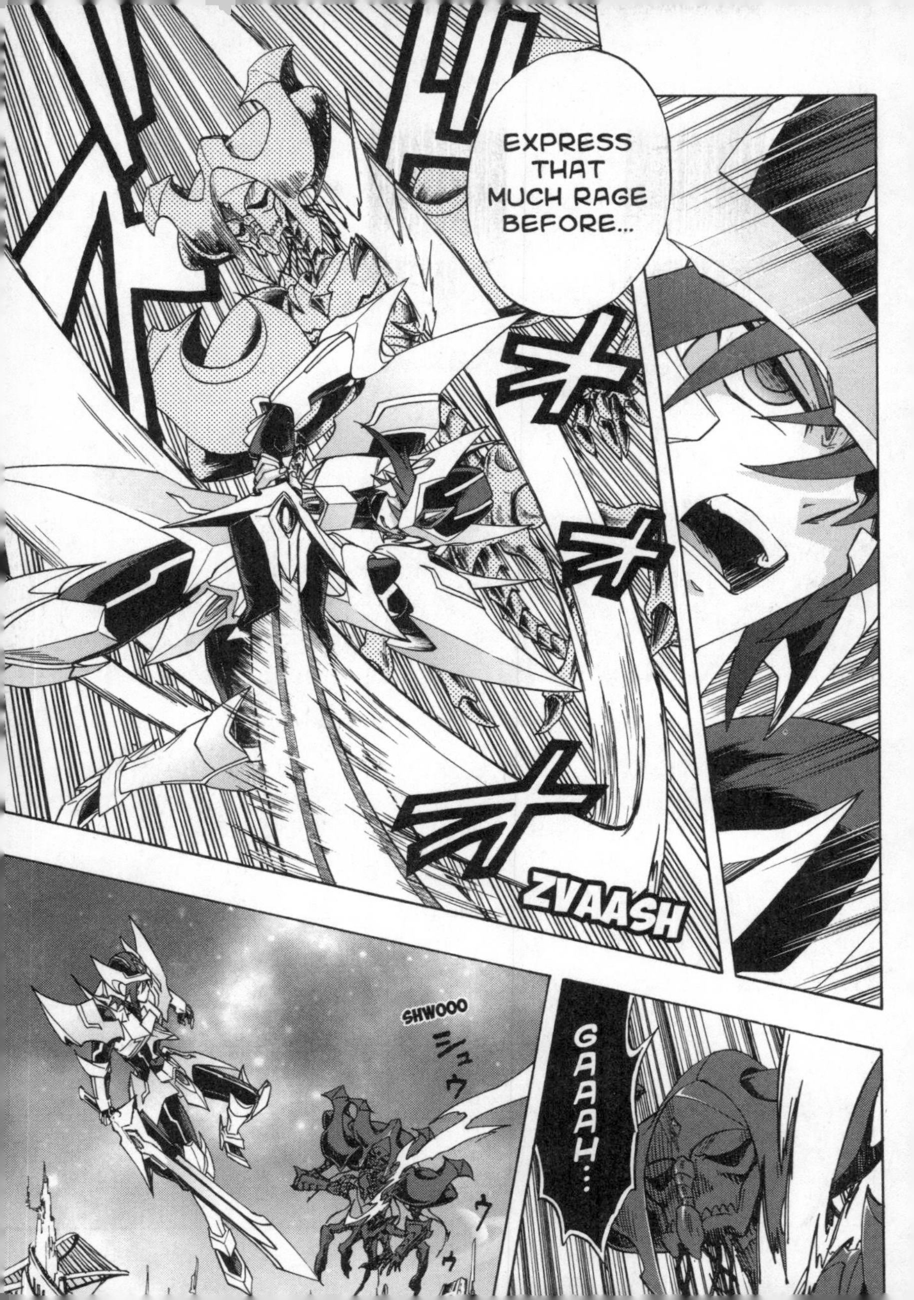
EXPRESS THAT MUCH RAGE BEFORE...
ZVAASH
GAAAAH...
SHWOOO

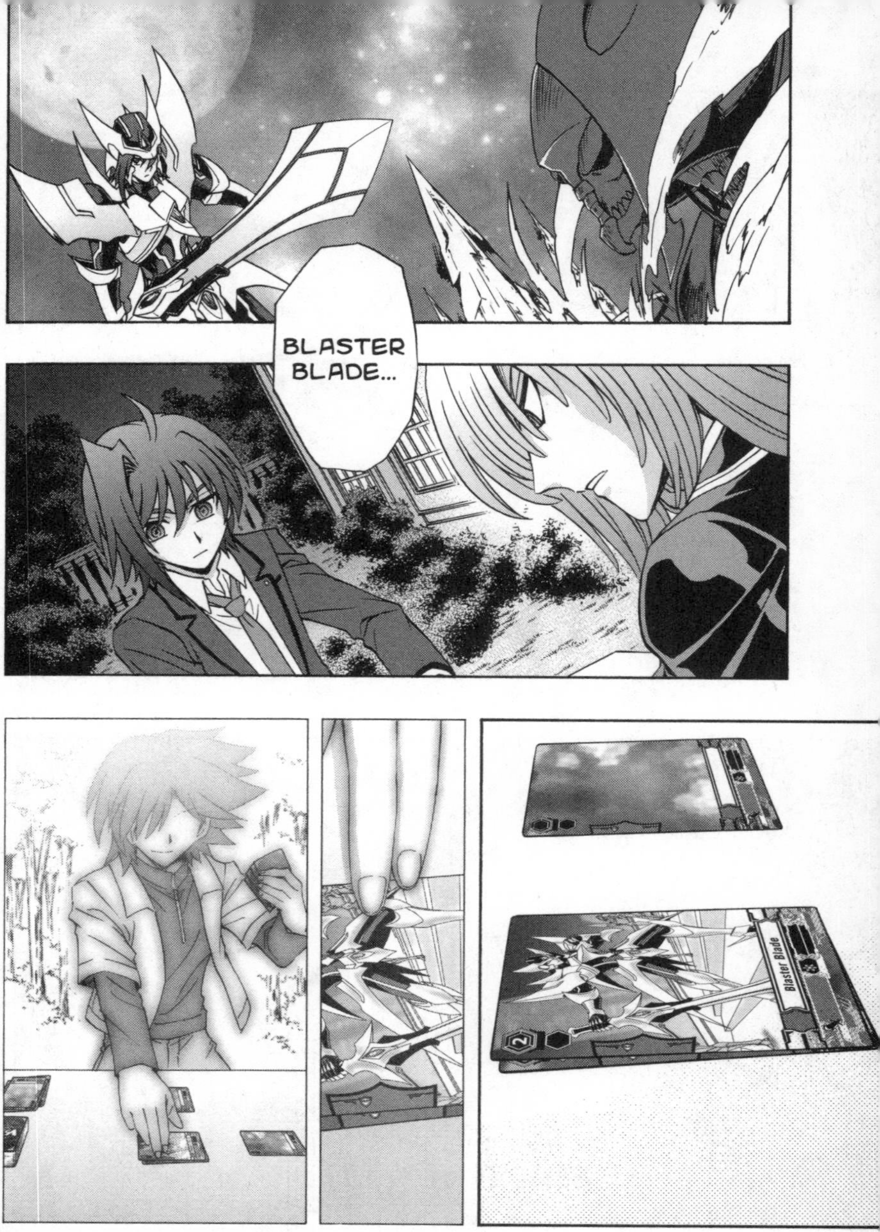
BLASTER BLADE...
Blaster Blade

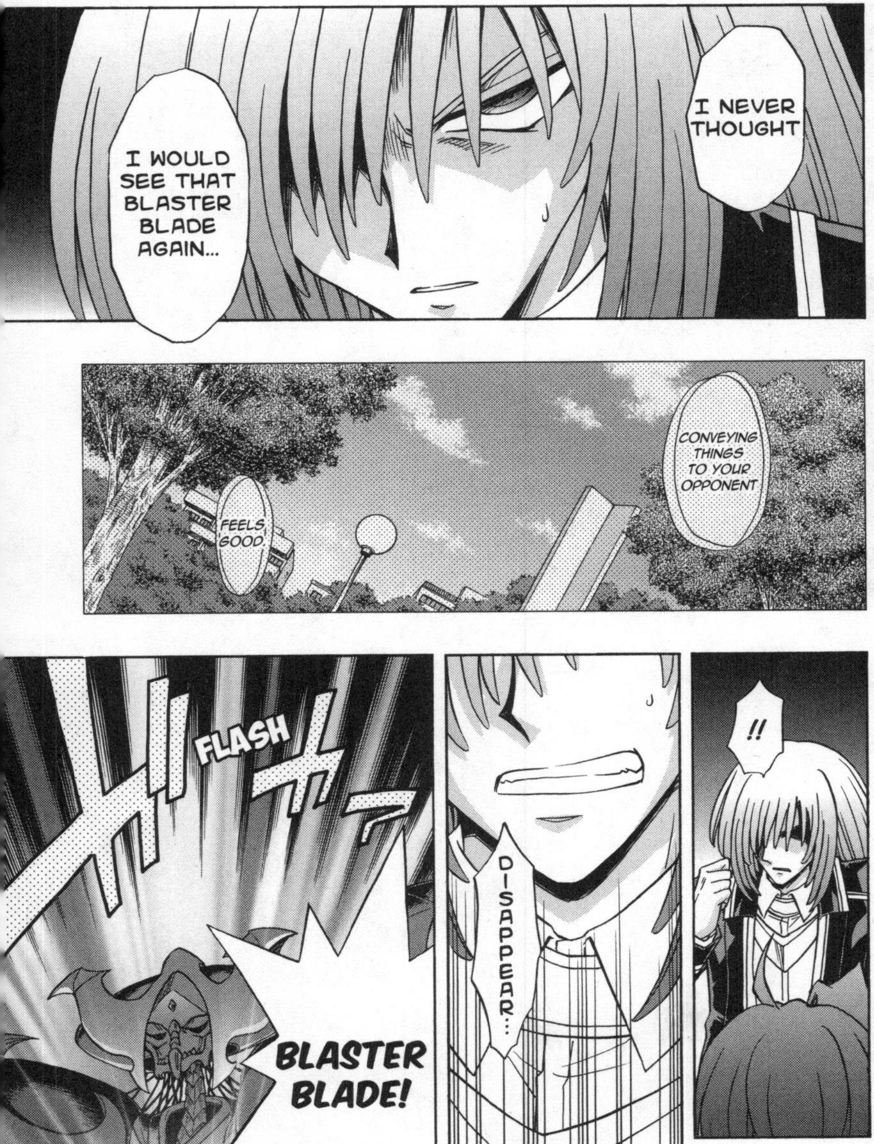
I NEVER THOUGHT
I WOULD SEE THAT BLASTER BLADE AGAIN...
CONVEYING THINGS TO YOUR OPPONENT
FEELS GOOD.
!!
DISAPPEAR...
FLASH
BLASTER BLADE!

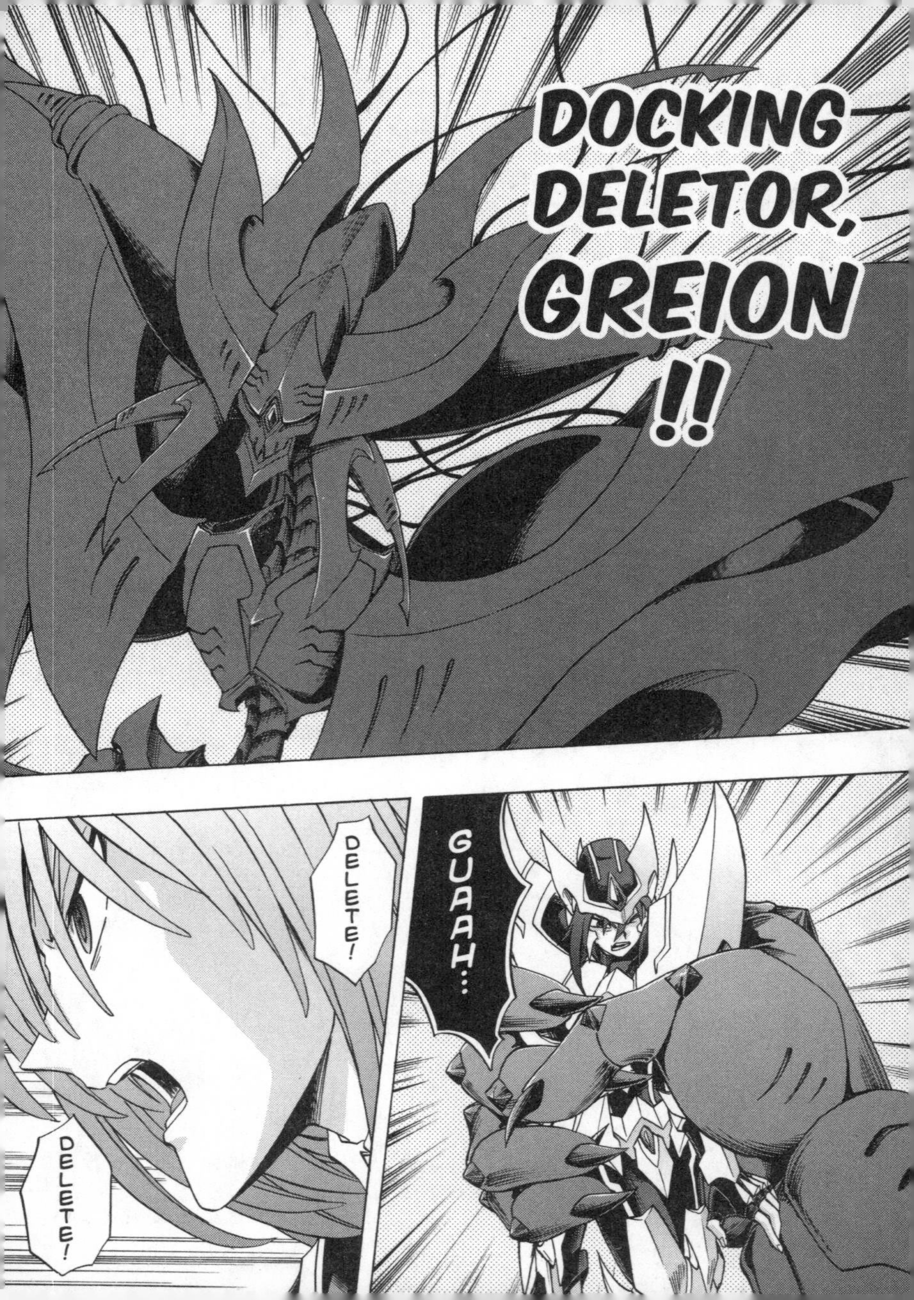
DOCKING DELETOR, GREION!!
GUAAH...
DELETE!
DELETE!

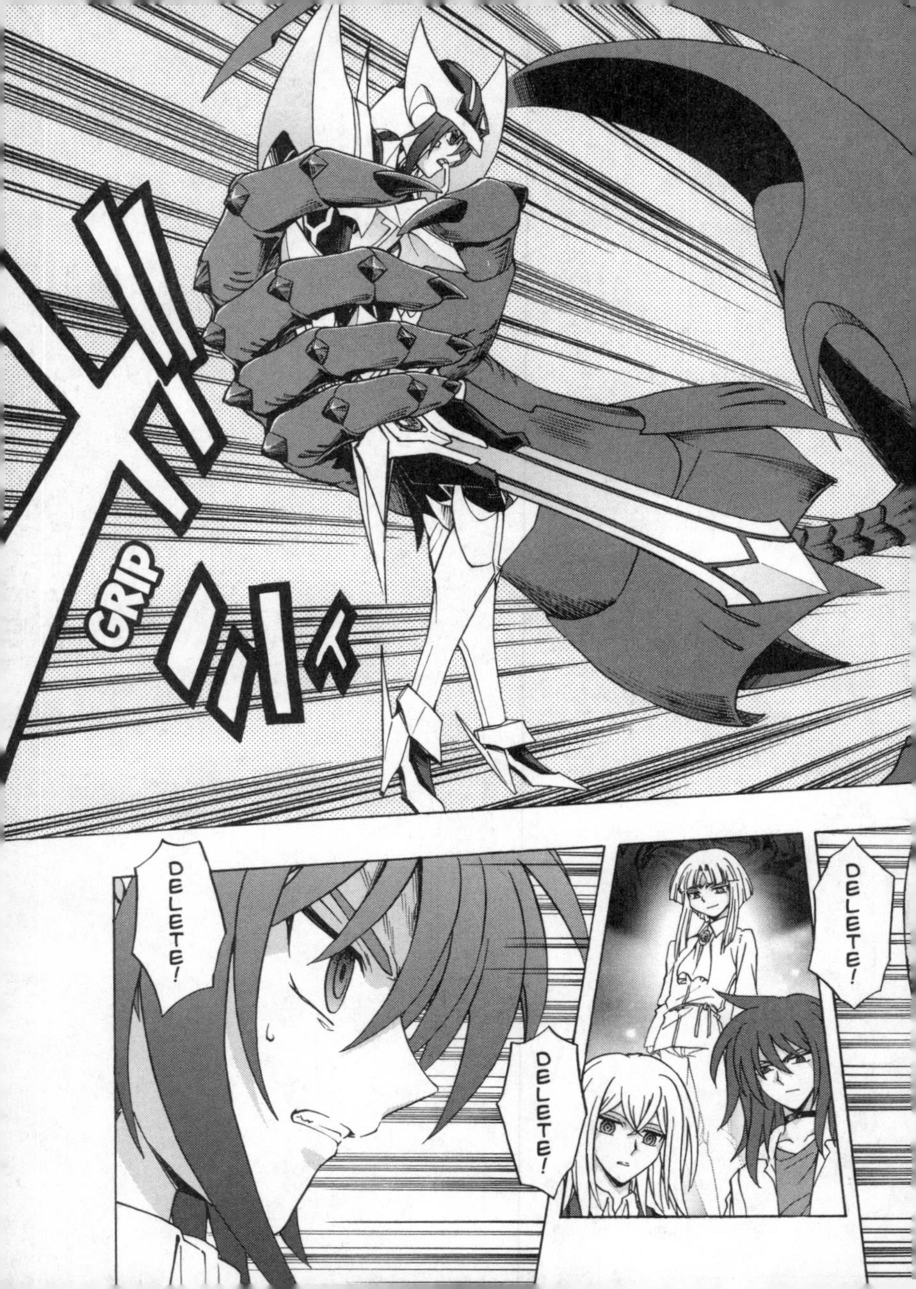
GRIP
DELETE!
DELETE!
DELETE!

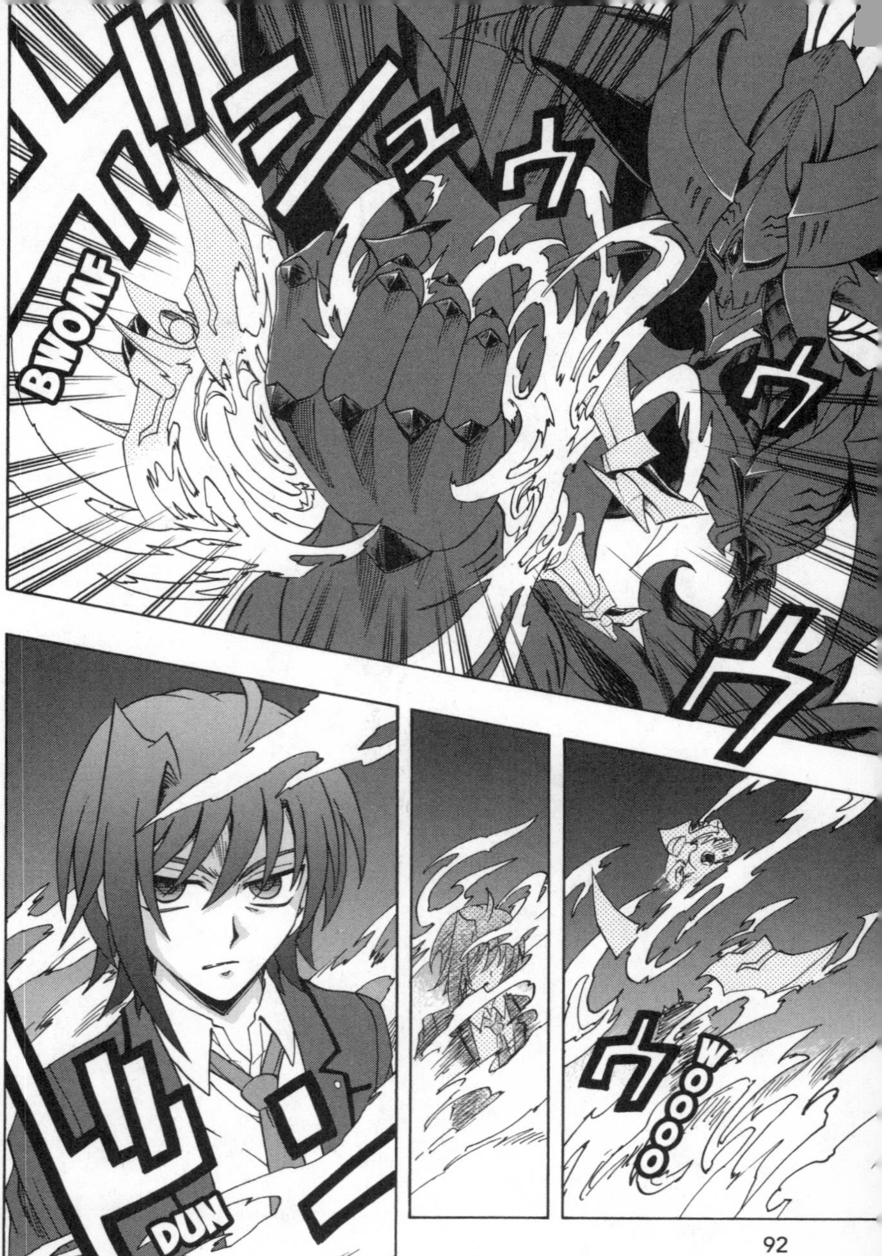
BWOMF
WOOOOO
DUN

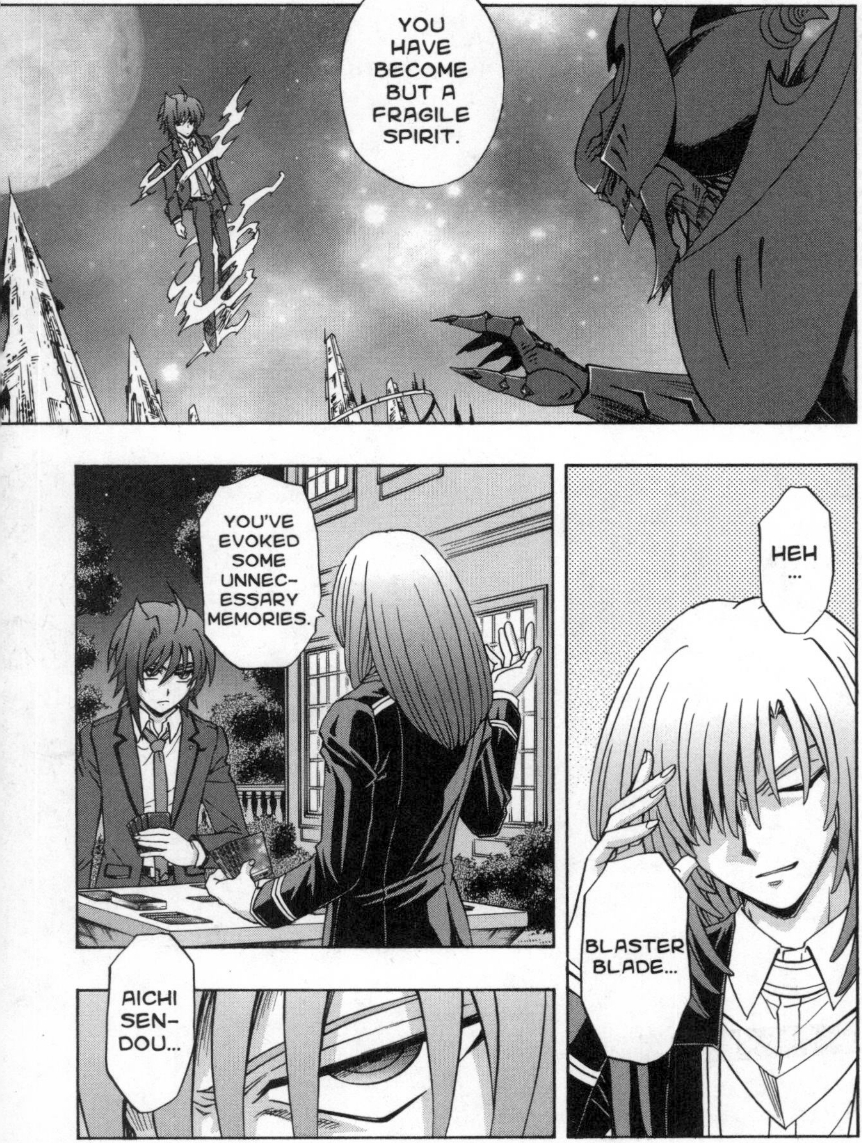
YOU HAVE BECOME BUT A FRAGILE SPIRIT.
HEH...
BLASTER BLADE...
YOU'VE EVOKED SOME UNNEC-ESSARY MEMORIES.
AICHI SEN-DOU...

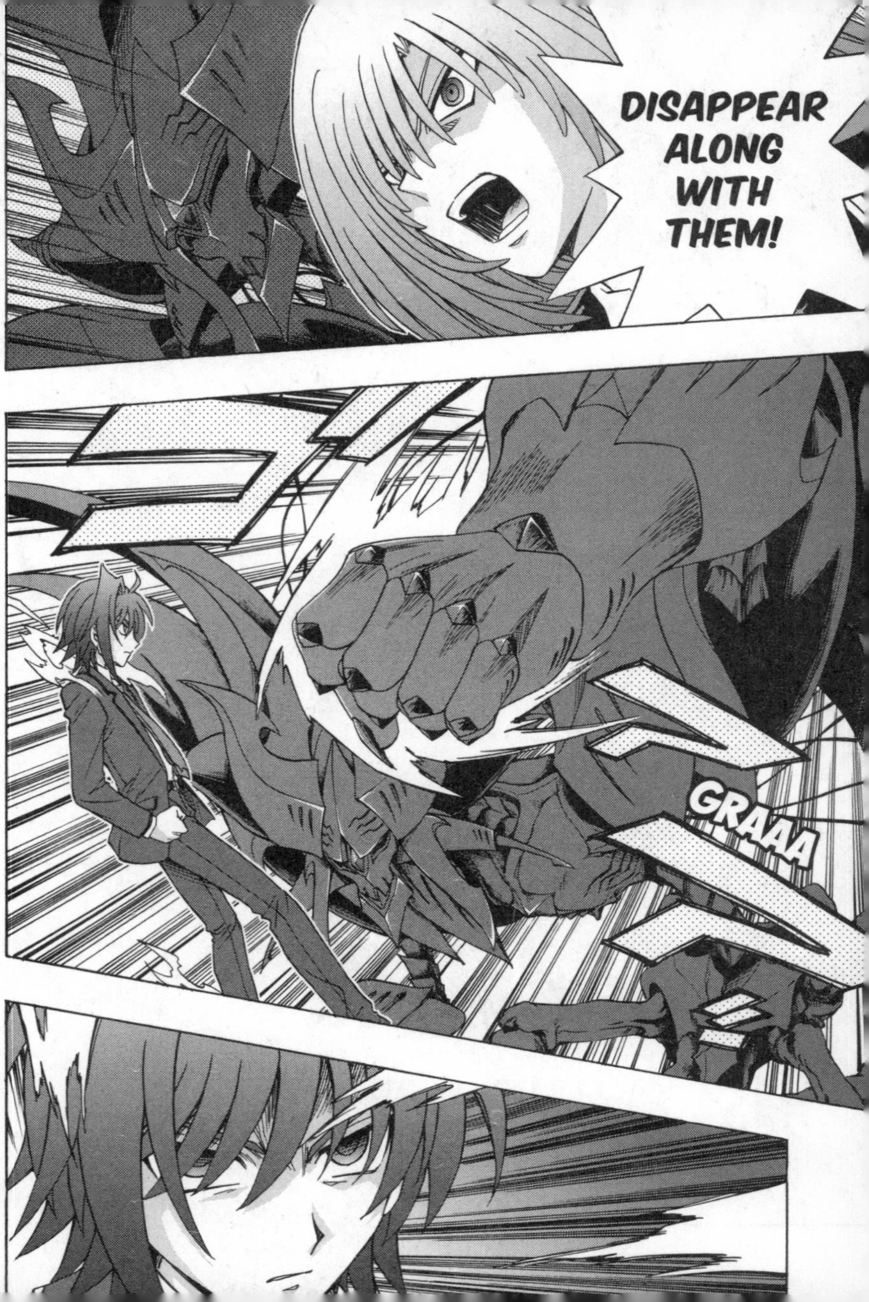
DISAPPEAR ALONG WITH THEM!
GRAAA

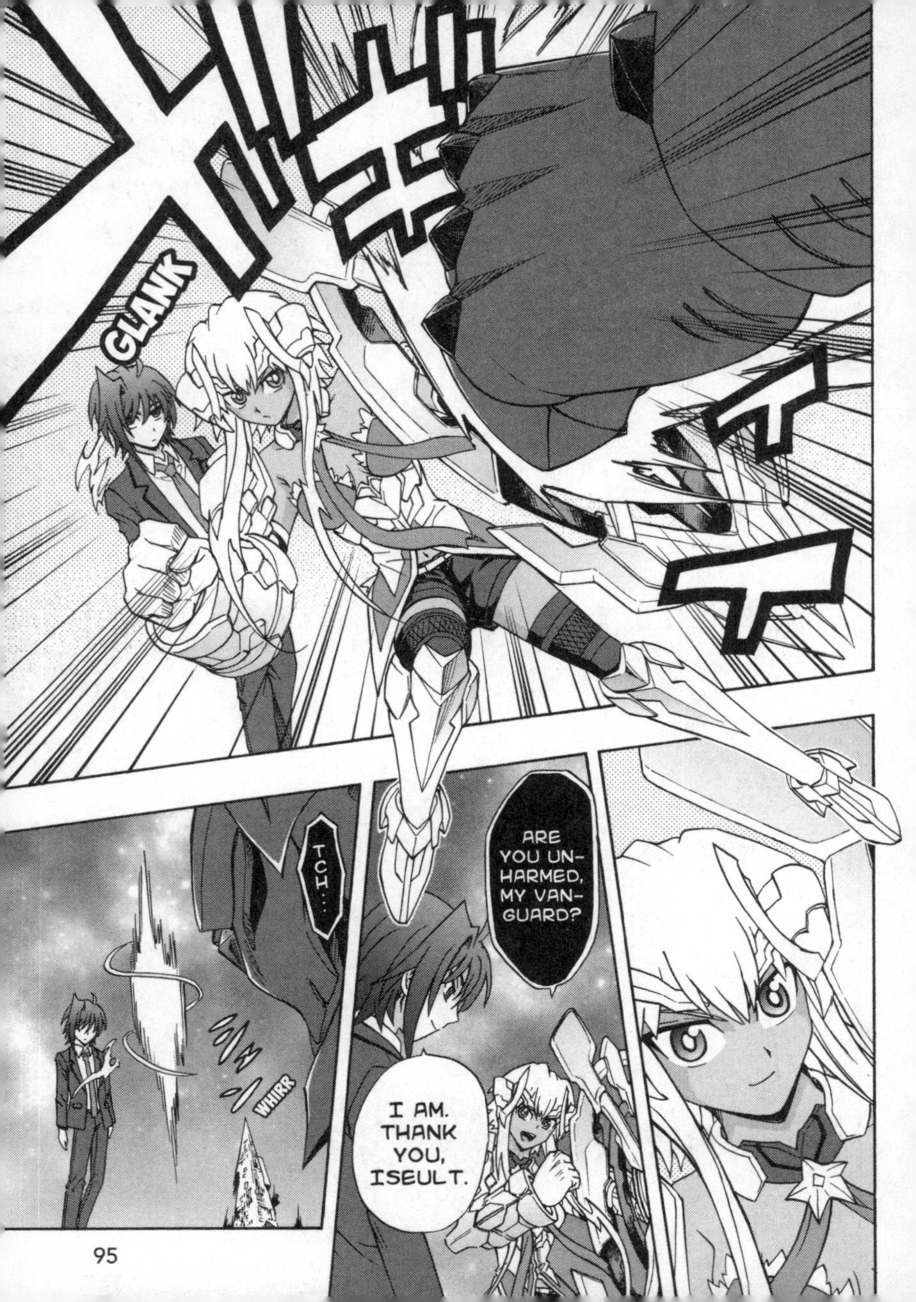
GLANK
ARE YOU UN-HARMED, MY VAN-GUARD?
TCH...
I AM. THANK YOU, ISEULT.
WHIRR

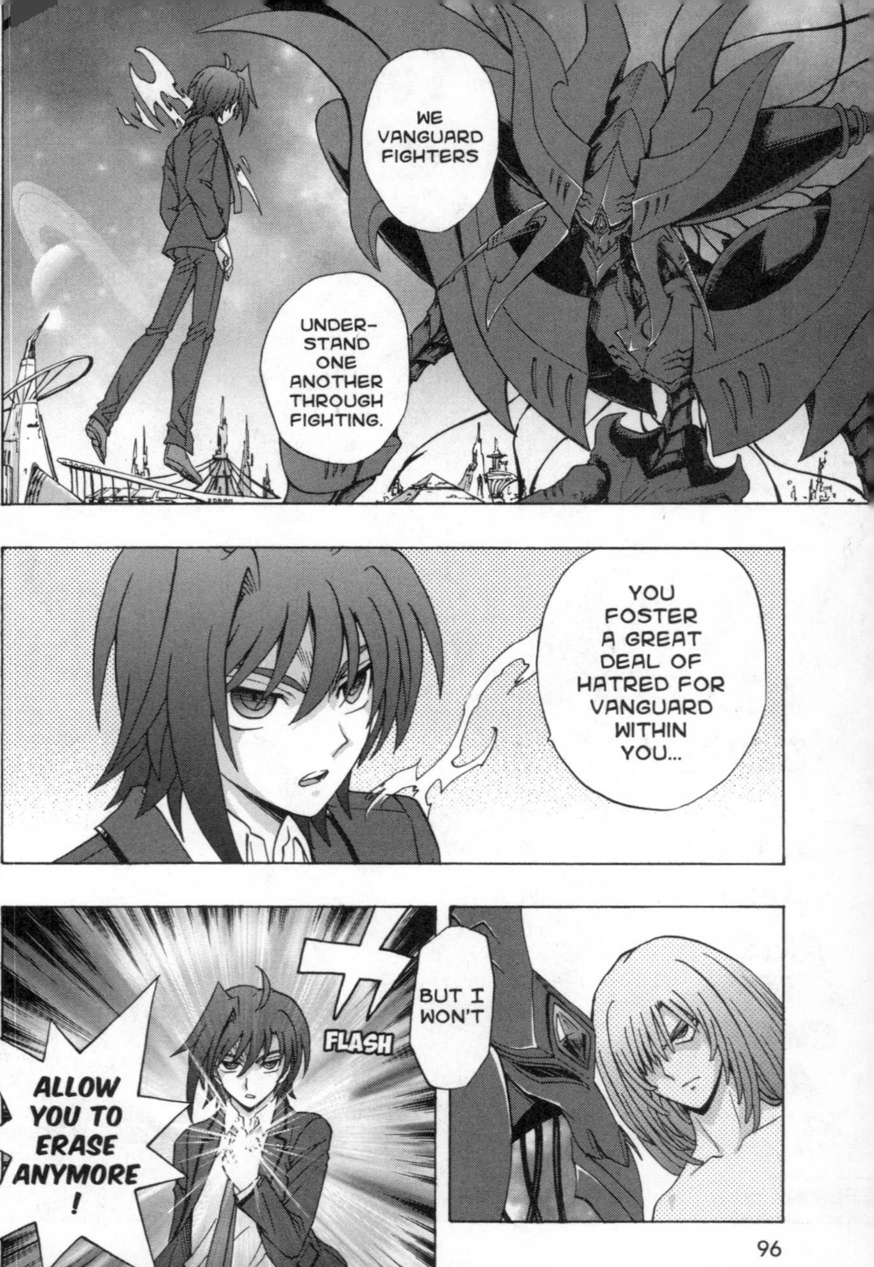
WE VANGUARD FIGHTERS
UNDER-STAND ONE ANOTHER THROUGH FIGHTING.
YOU FOSTER A GREAT DEAL OF HATRED FOR VANGUARD WITHIN YOU...
BUT I WON'T
FLASH
ALLOW YOU TO ERASE ANYMORE!

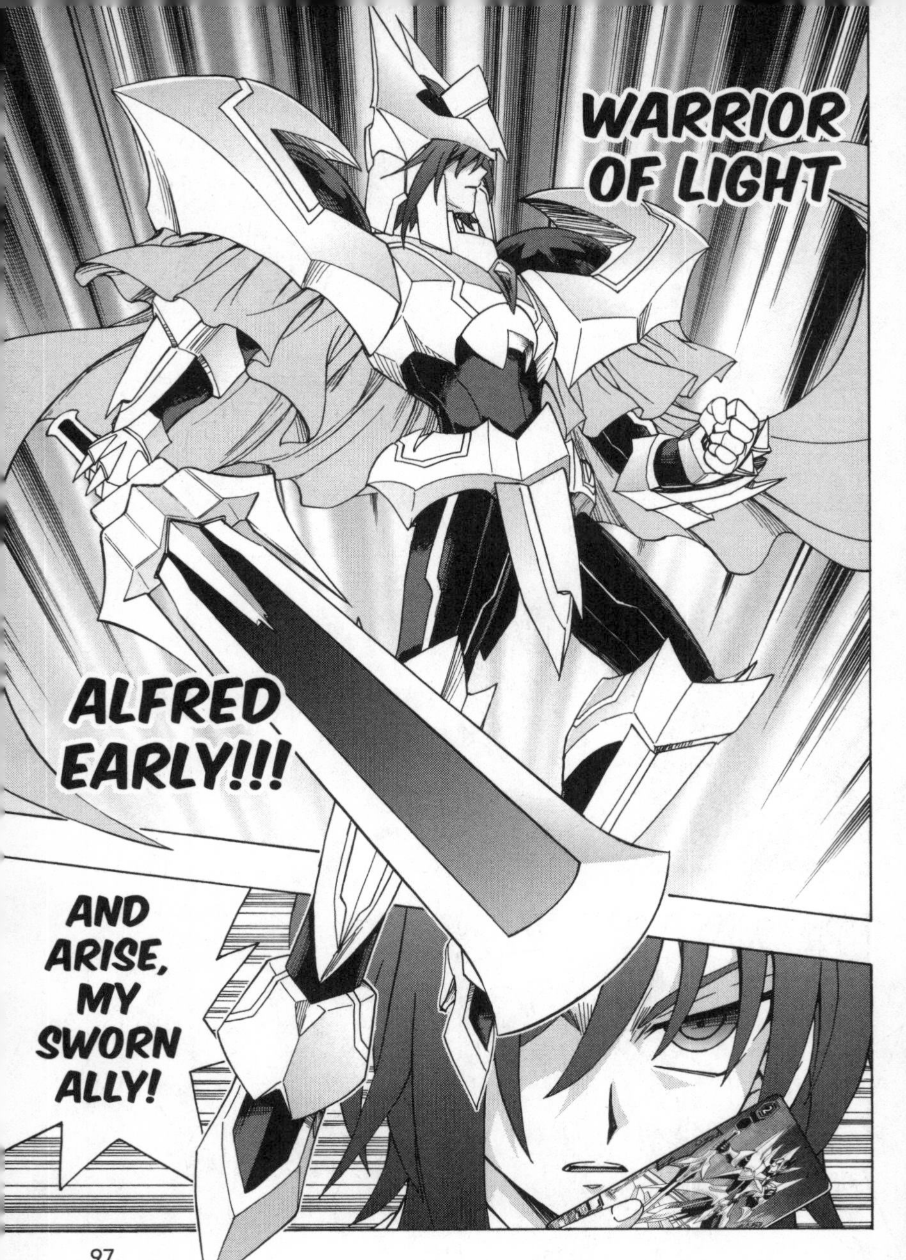
WARRIOR OF LIGHT
ALFRED EARLY!!!
AND ARISE, MY SWORN ALLY!

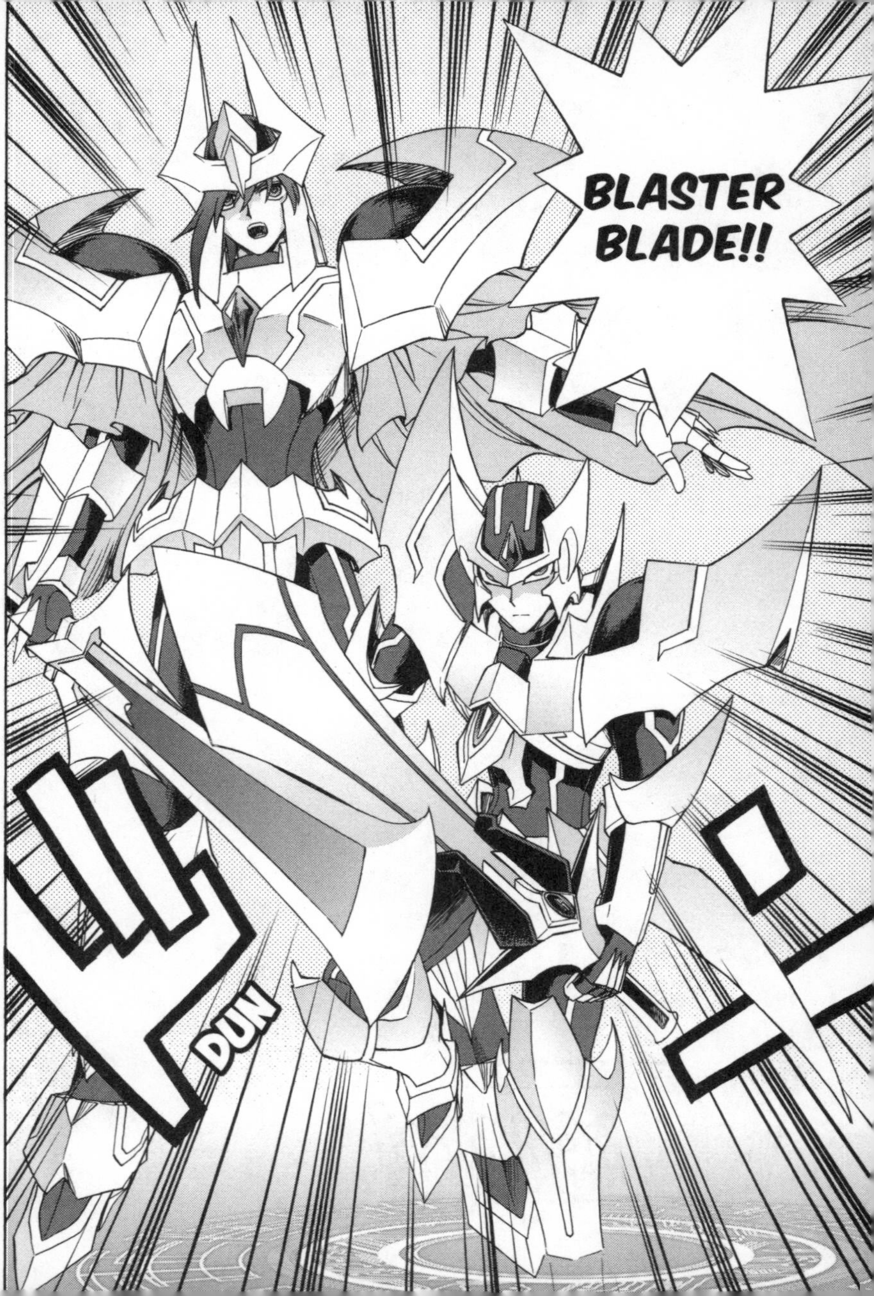
BLASTER BLADE!!
DUN

CARDFIGHT!! Vanguard

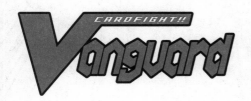

BONUS! CARDFIGHT!! Vanguard

NEVER-BEFORE-SEEN IMAGE BOARDS

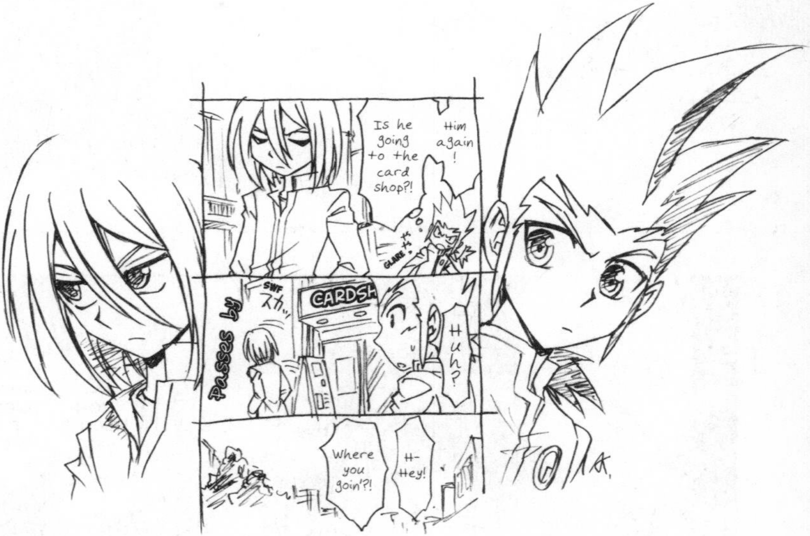

Him again!
Is he going to the card shop?!
GLARE
Huh?
CARDSH
SWF
Passes by
H-Hey!
Where you goin'?!

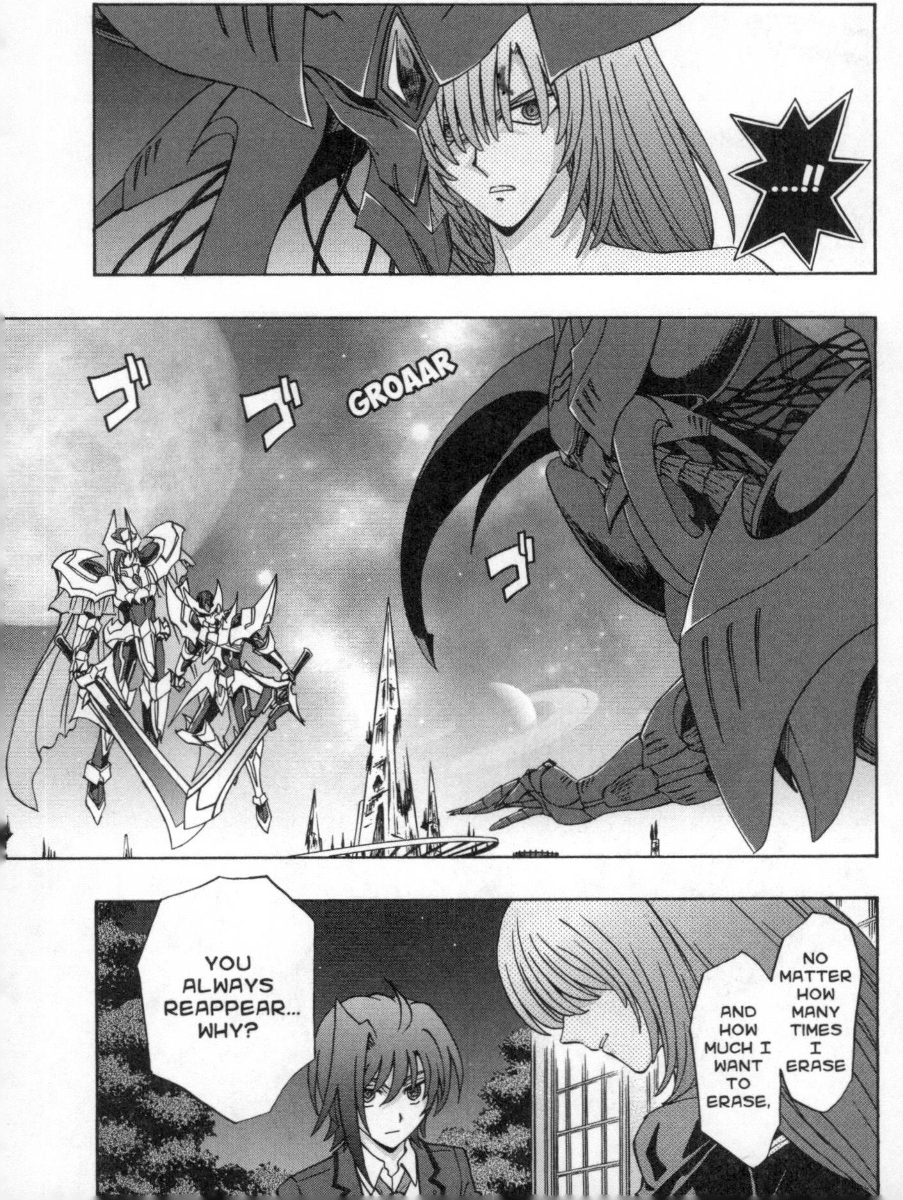
...!!
GROAAR
ゴ
ゴ
ゴ
NO MATTER HOW MANY TIMES I ERASE
AND HOW MUCH I WANT TO ERASE,
YOU ALWAYS REAPPEAR... WHY?

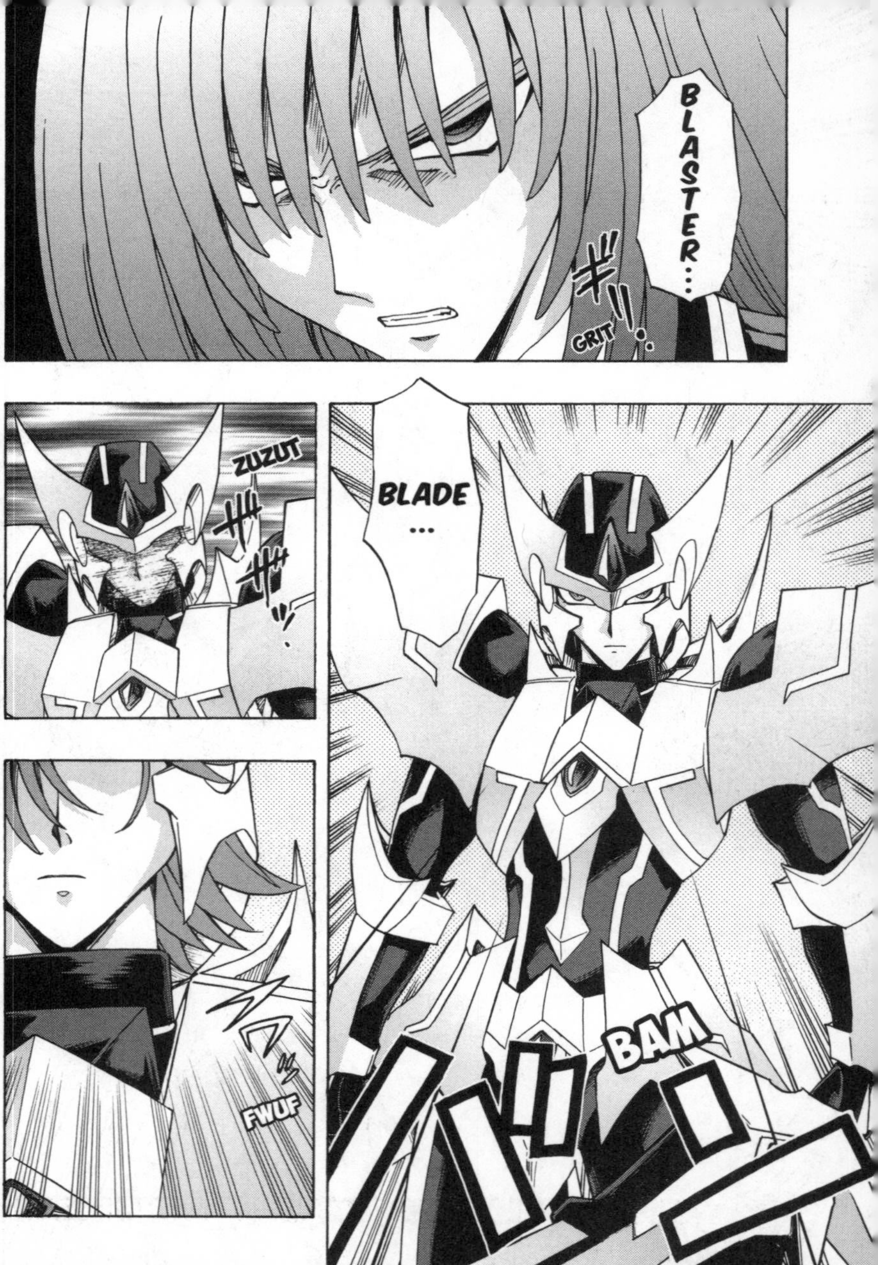
BLASTER...
GRIT
BLADE ...
BAM
ZUZUT
FWUF

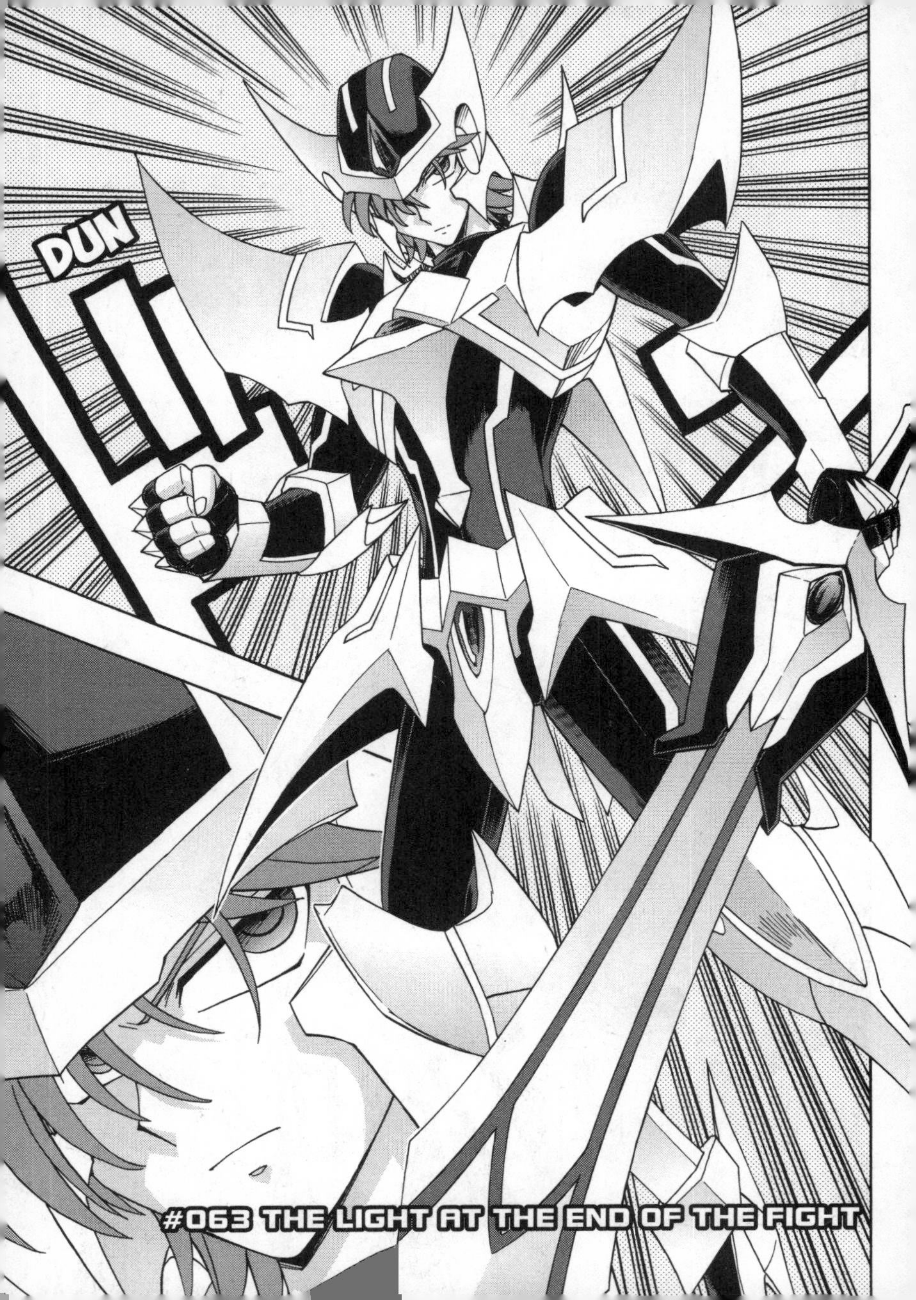
DUN
#063 THE LIGHT AT THE END OF THE FIGHT

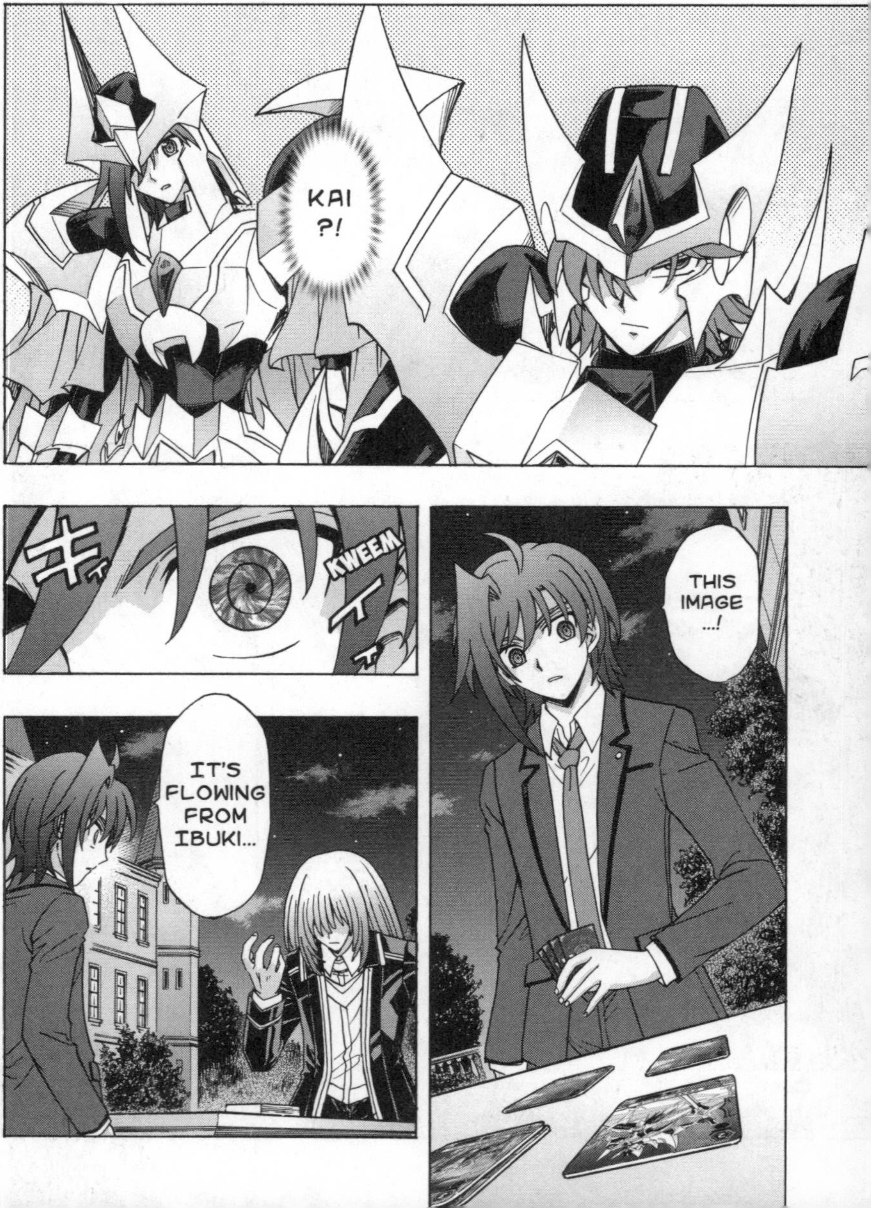
KAI ?!
THIS IMAGE ...!
KWEEM
IT'S FLOWING FROM IBUKI...

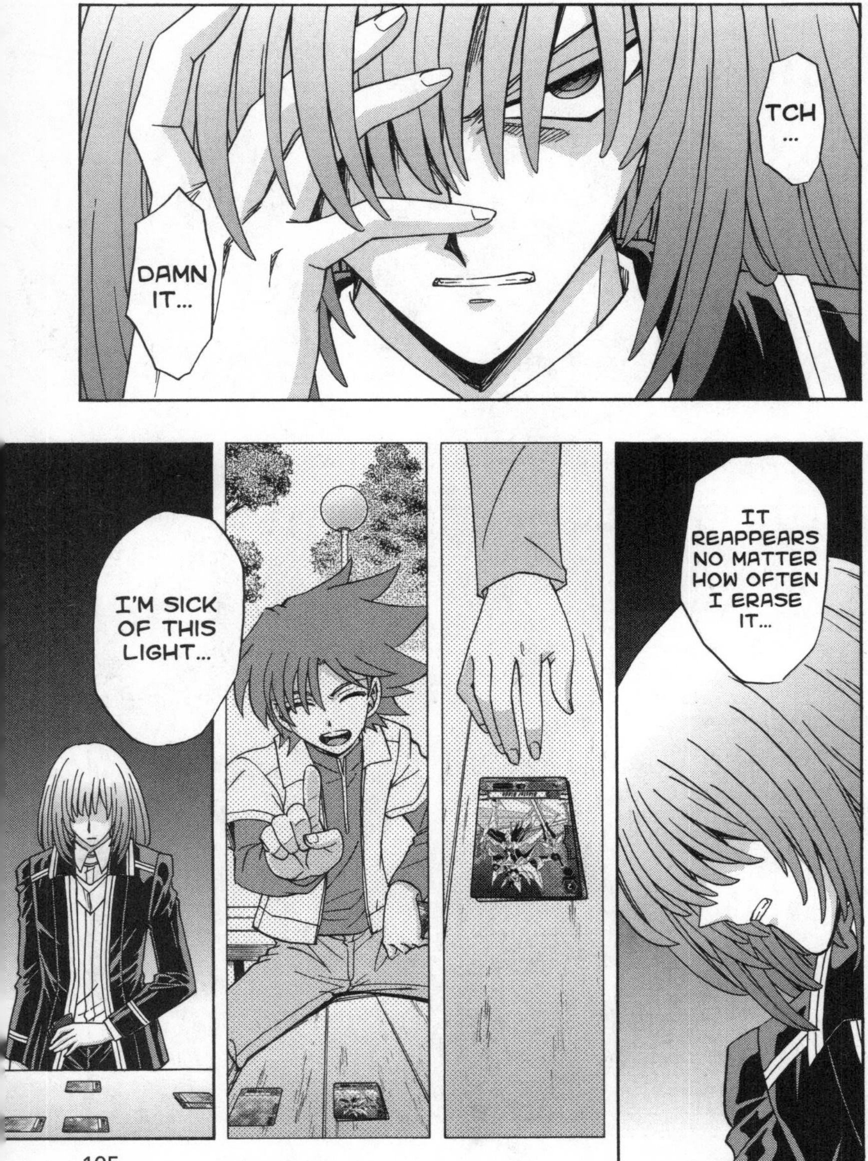
TCH ...
DAMN IT...
IT REAPPEARS NO MATTER HOW OFTEN I ERASE IT...
I'M SICK OF THIS LIGHT...

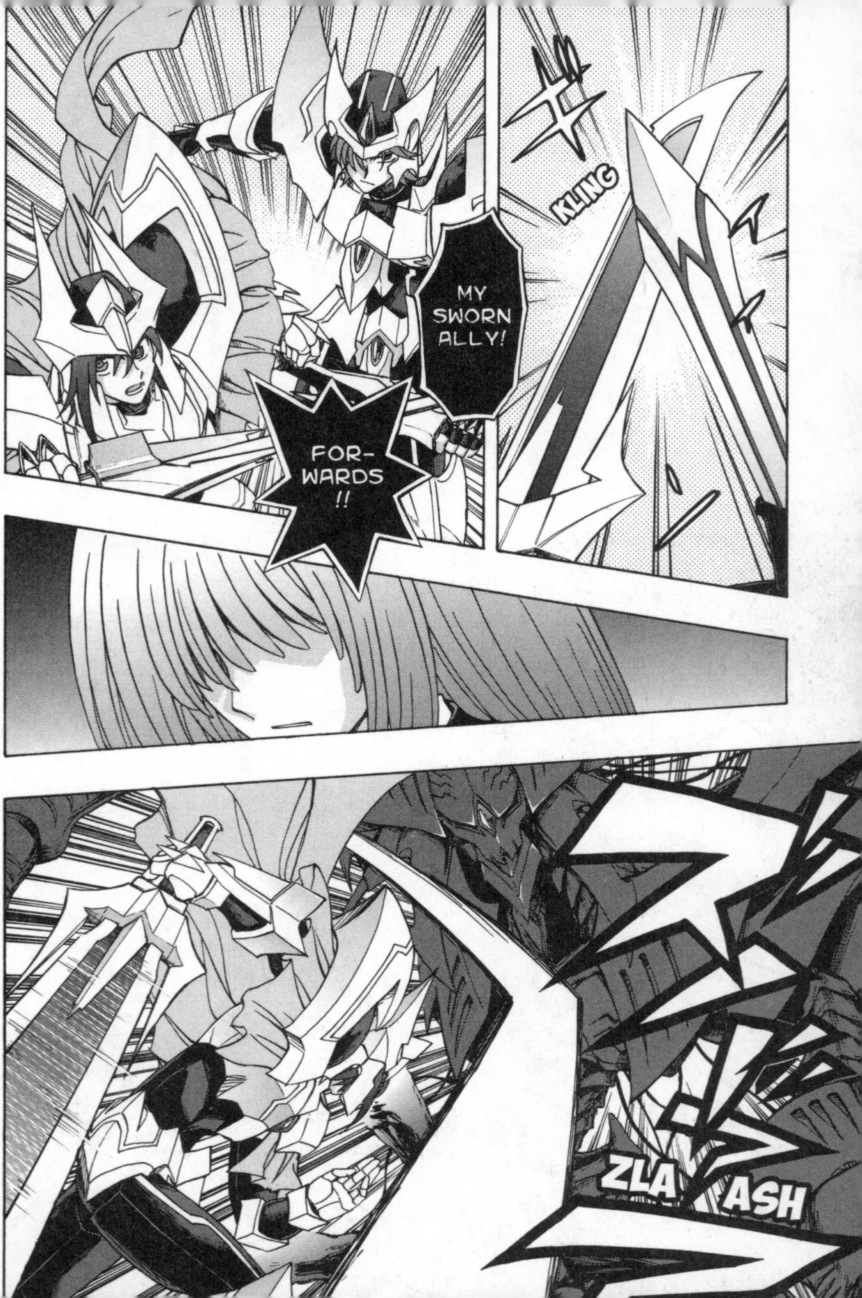
KLING
MY SWORN ALLY!
FOR-WARDS!!
ZLA ASH

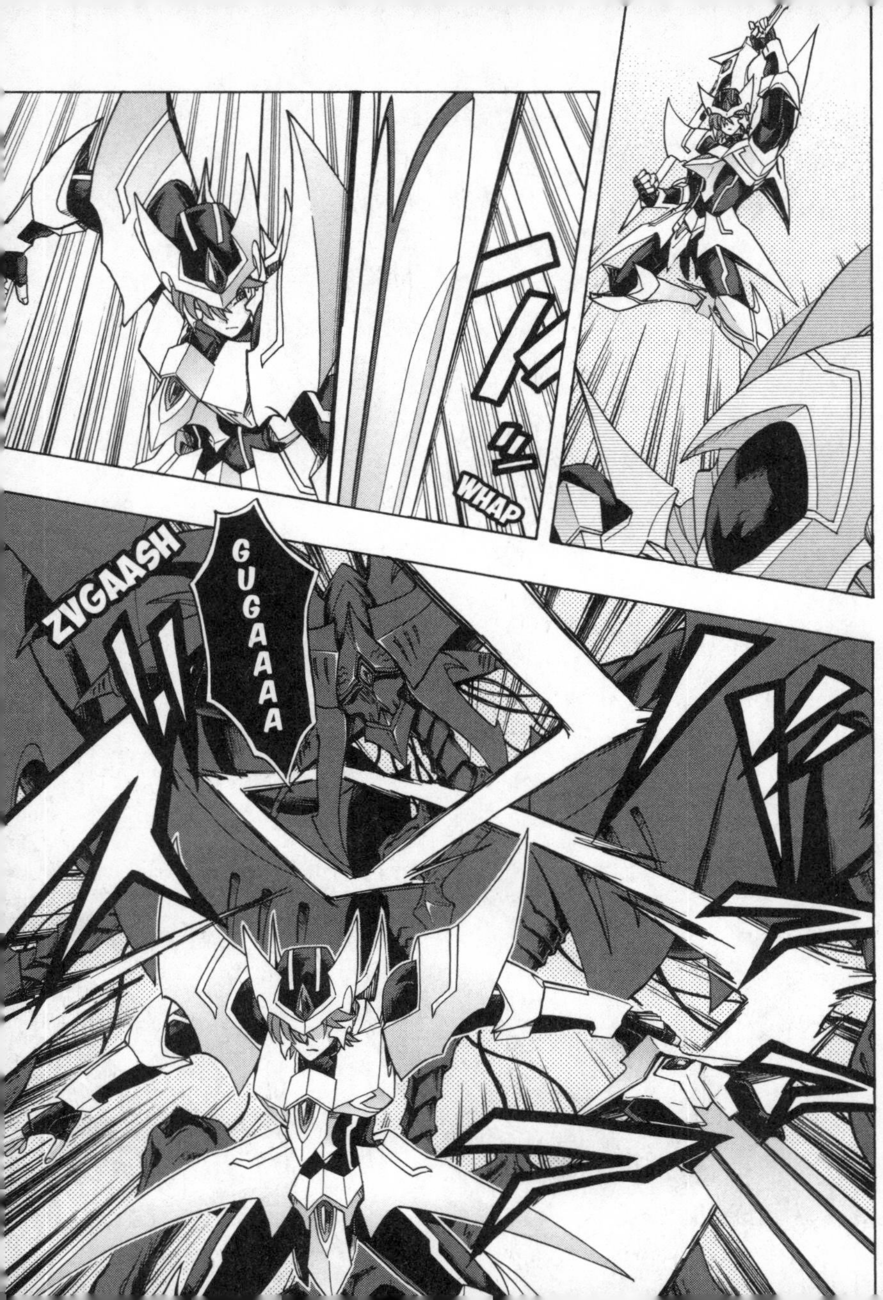
WHAP
ZVGAASH
GUGAAAA

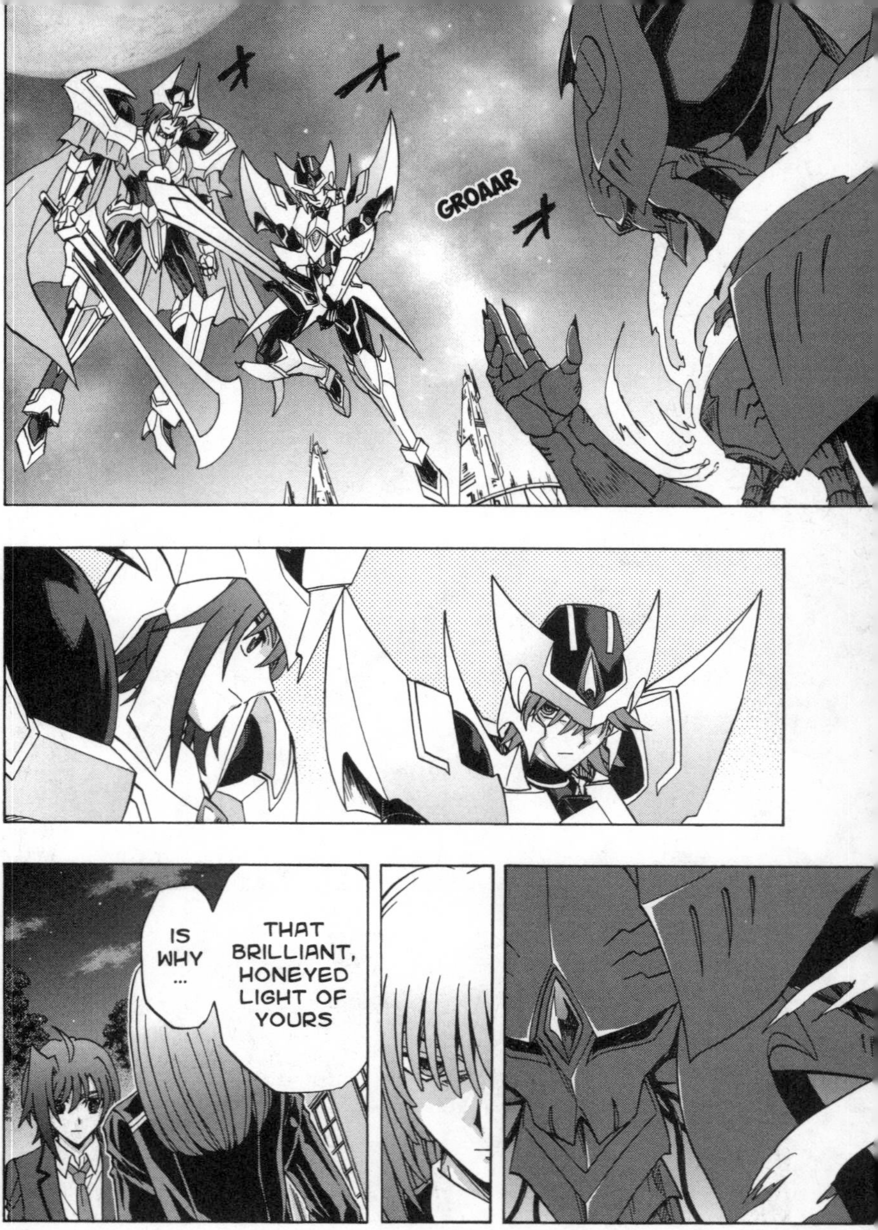
GROAAR
THAT BRILLIANT, HONEYED LIGHT OF YOURS
IS WHY ...

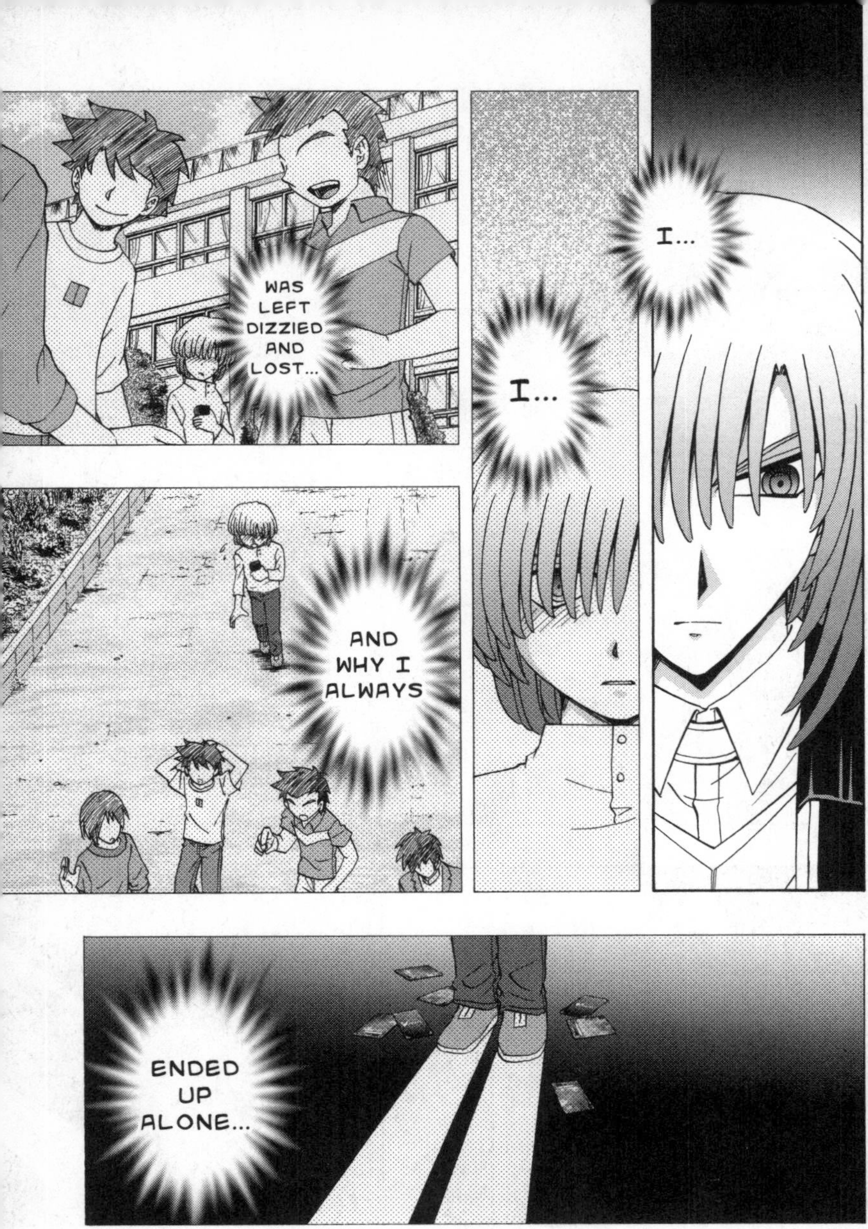
I...
I...
WAS LEFT DIZZIED AND LOST...
AND WHY I ALWAYS
ENDED UP ALONE...

KAI...

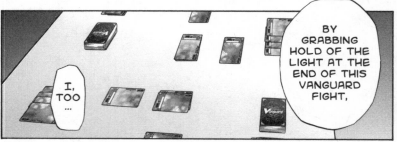

I, TOO...

BY GRABBING HOLD OF THE LIGHT AT THE END OF THIS VANGUARD FIGHT,

BUT...

WOULD OBTAIN WHAT YOU HAD.

THAT MIGHT BE WHAT I HAD HOPED.

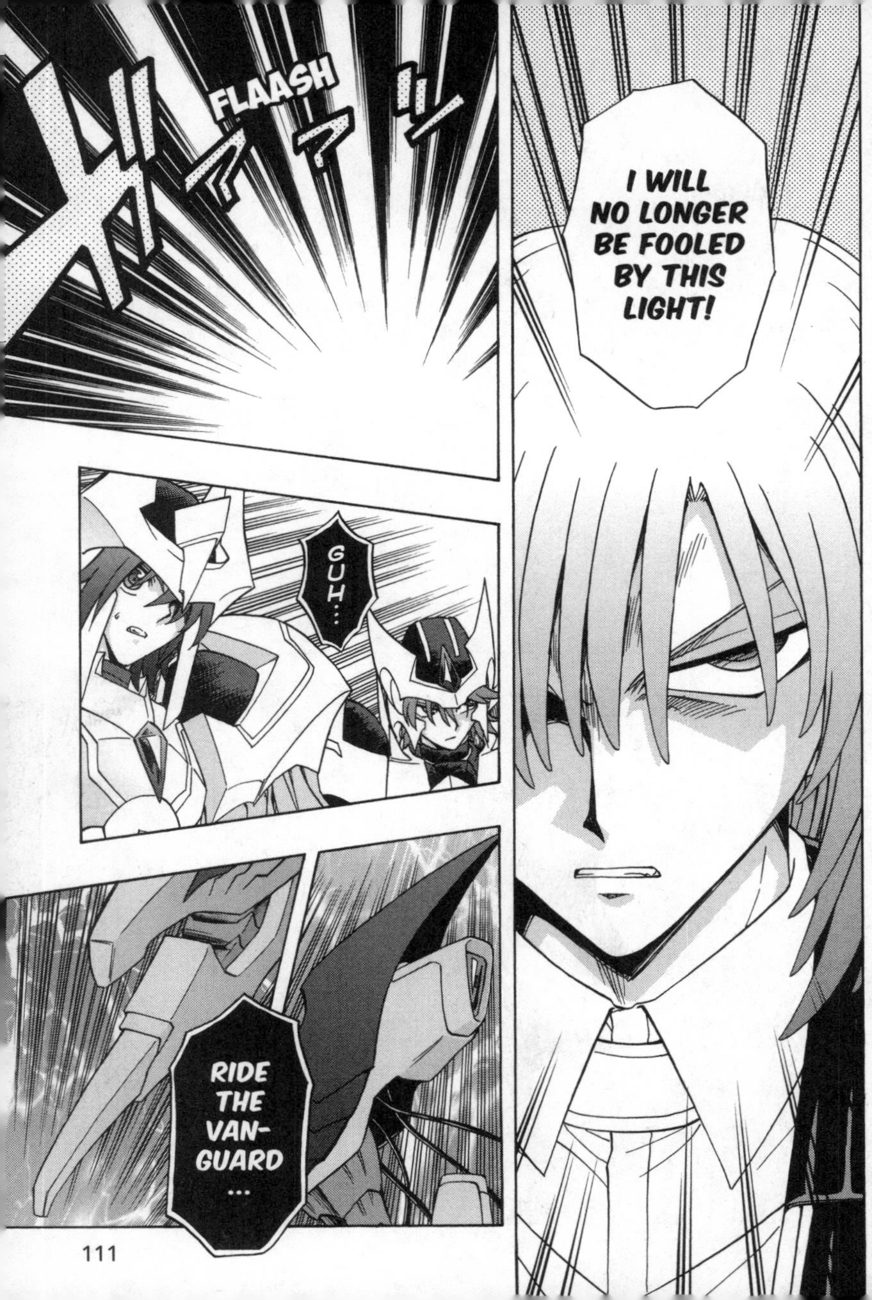
I WILL NO LONGER BE FOOLED BY THIS LIGHT!
FLAASH
GUH...
RIDE THE VAN-GUARD ...

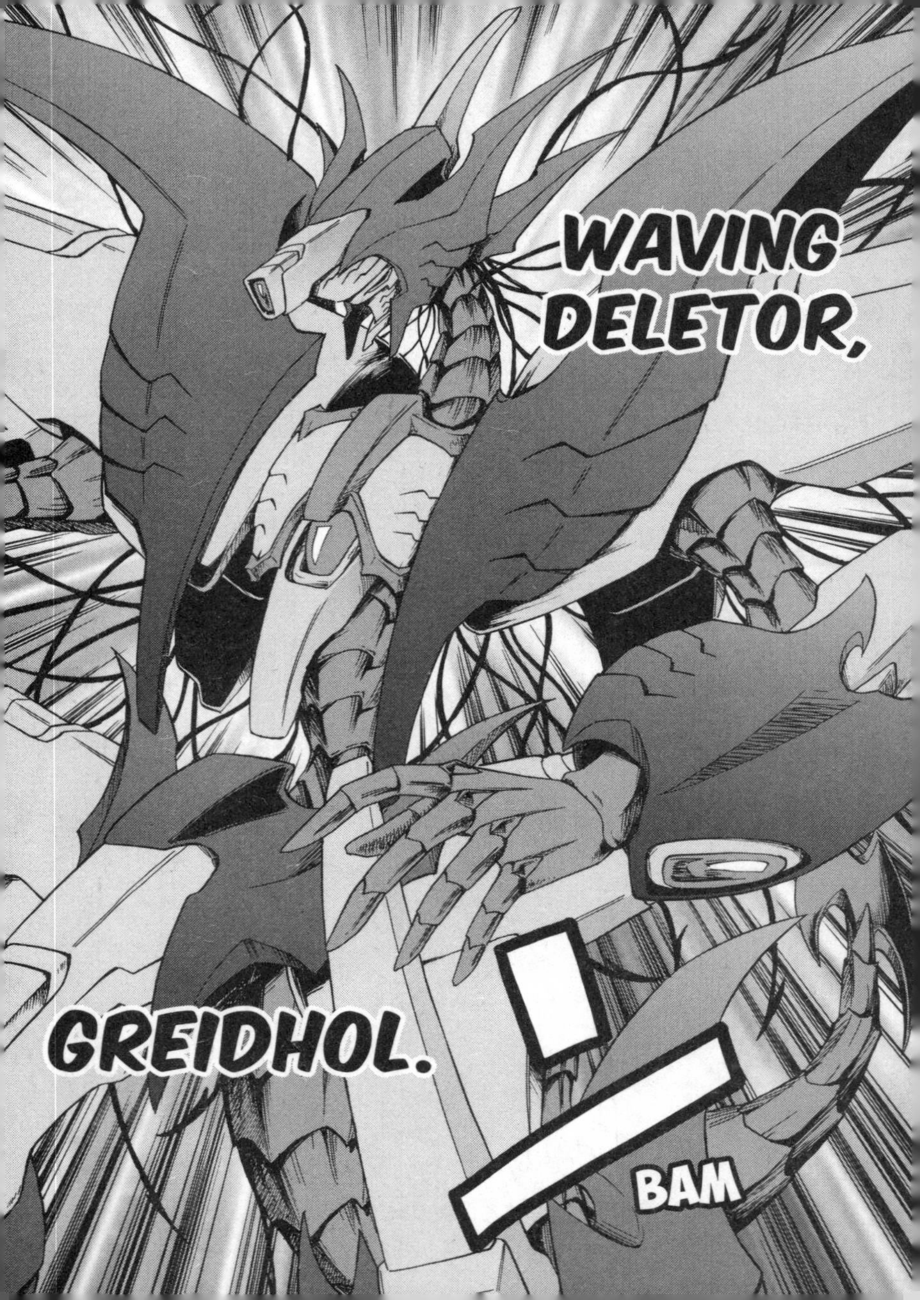
WAVING DELETOR,
GREIDHOL.
BAM

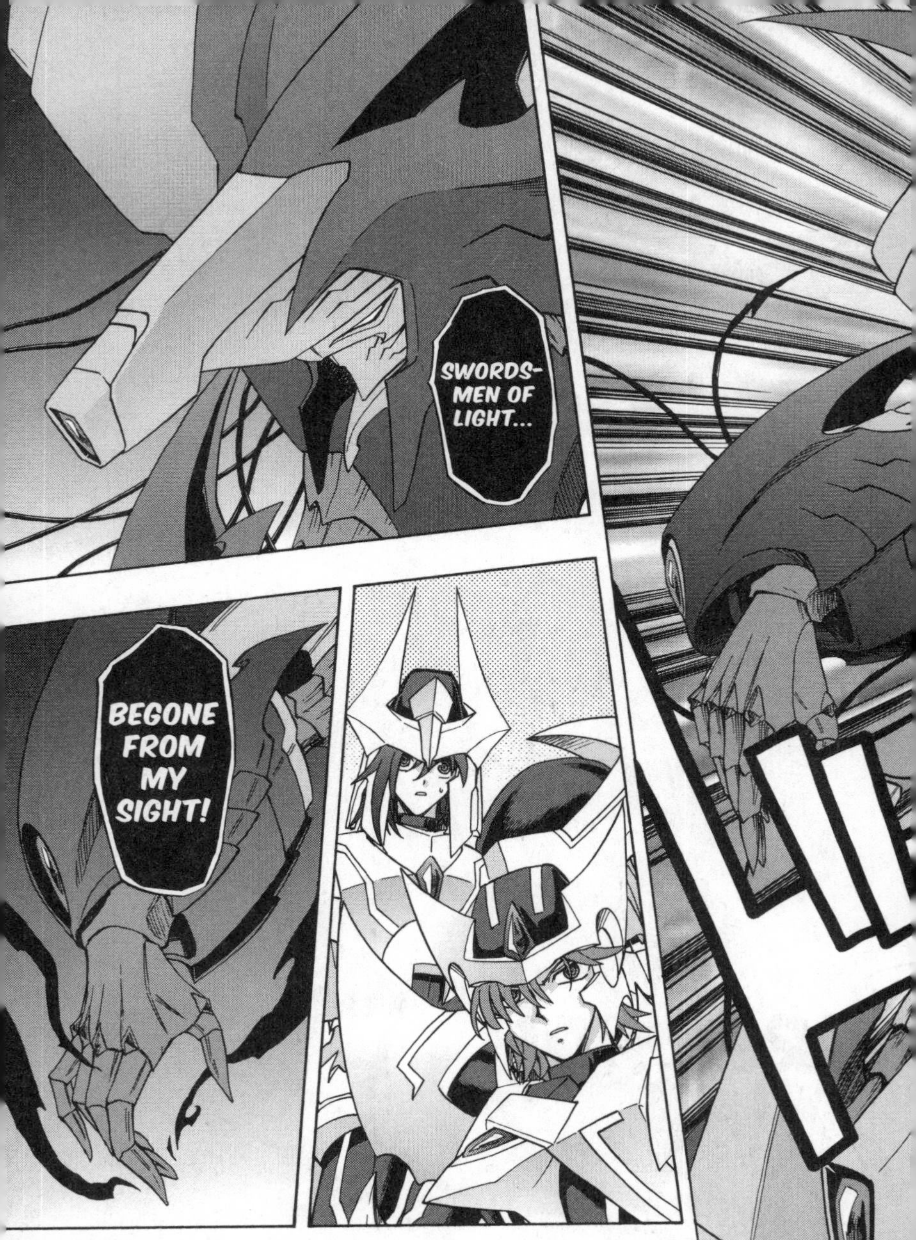
SWORDS-MEN OF LIGHT...
BEGONE FROM MY SIGHT!

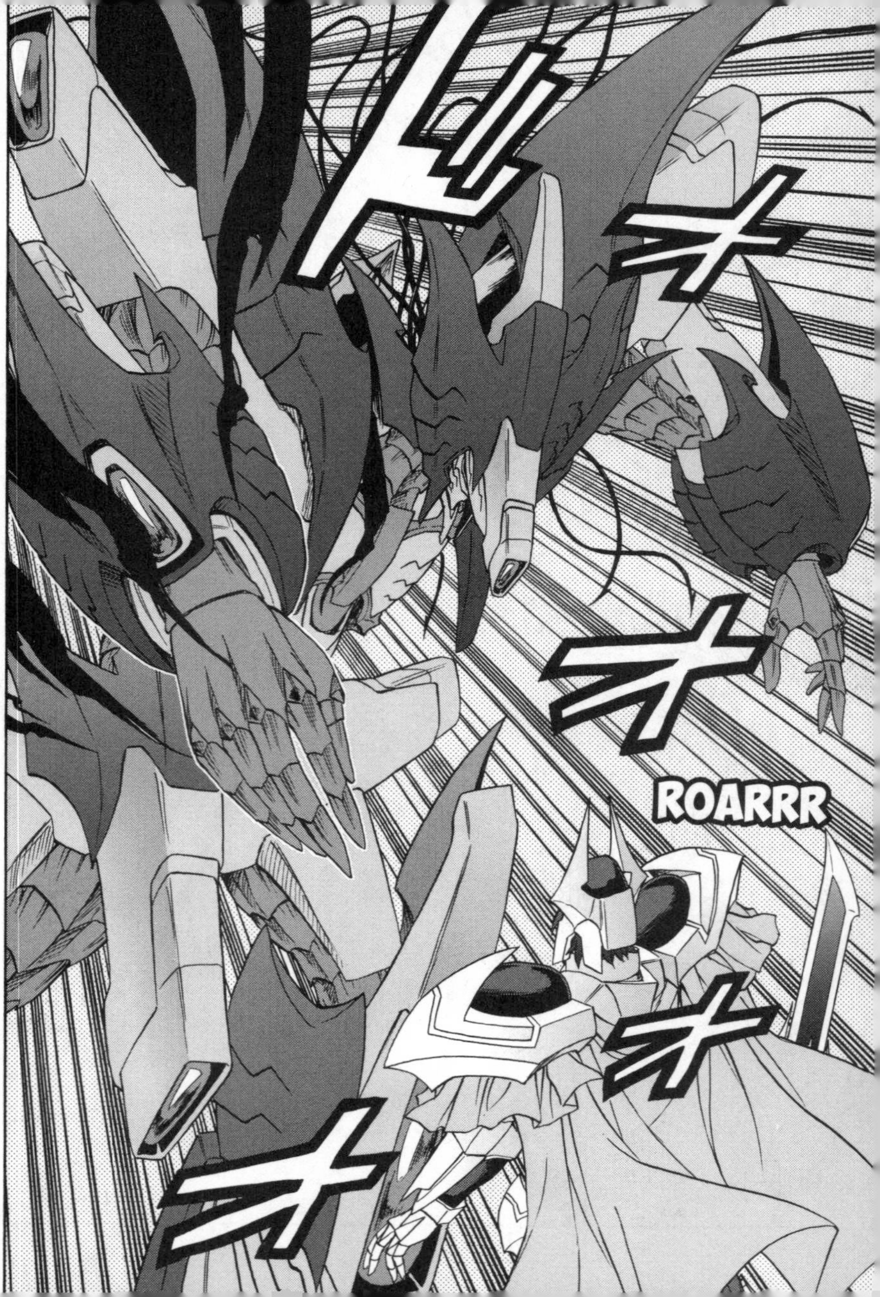
ドオオオオ
ROARRR

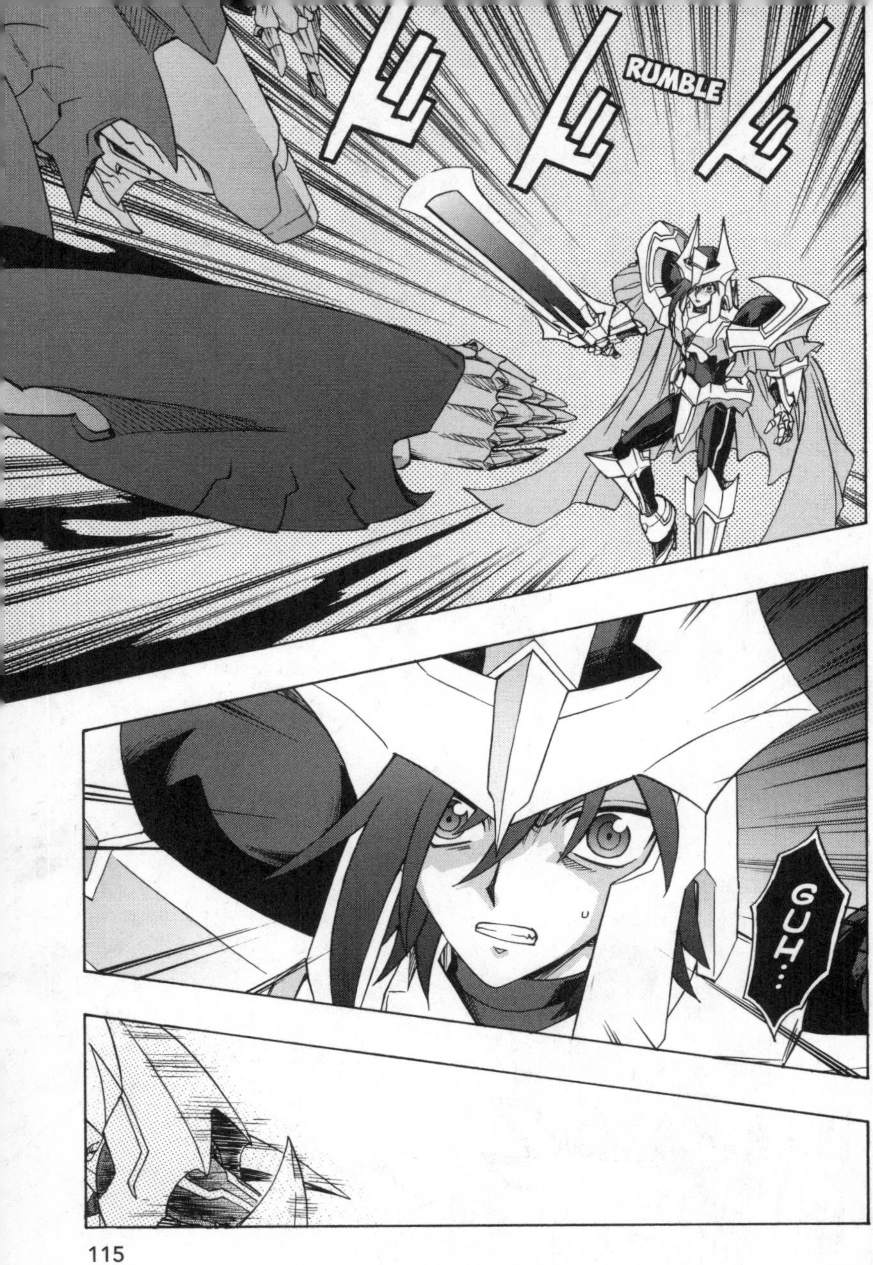
RUMBLE
GUH...

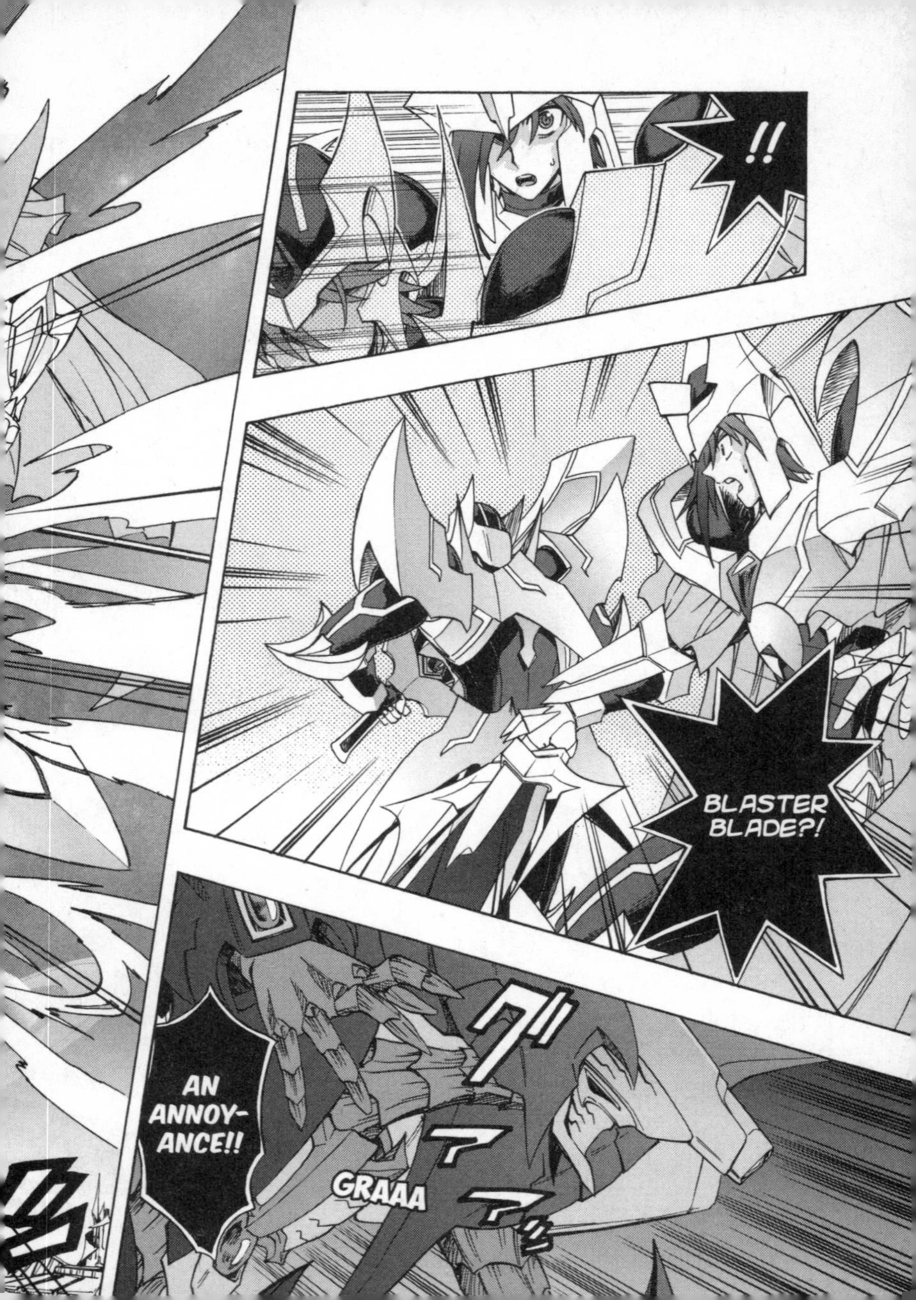
!!
BLASTER BLADE?!
AN ANNOY-ANCE!!
GRAAA

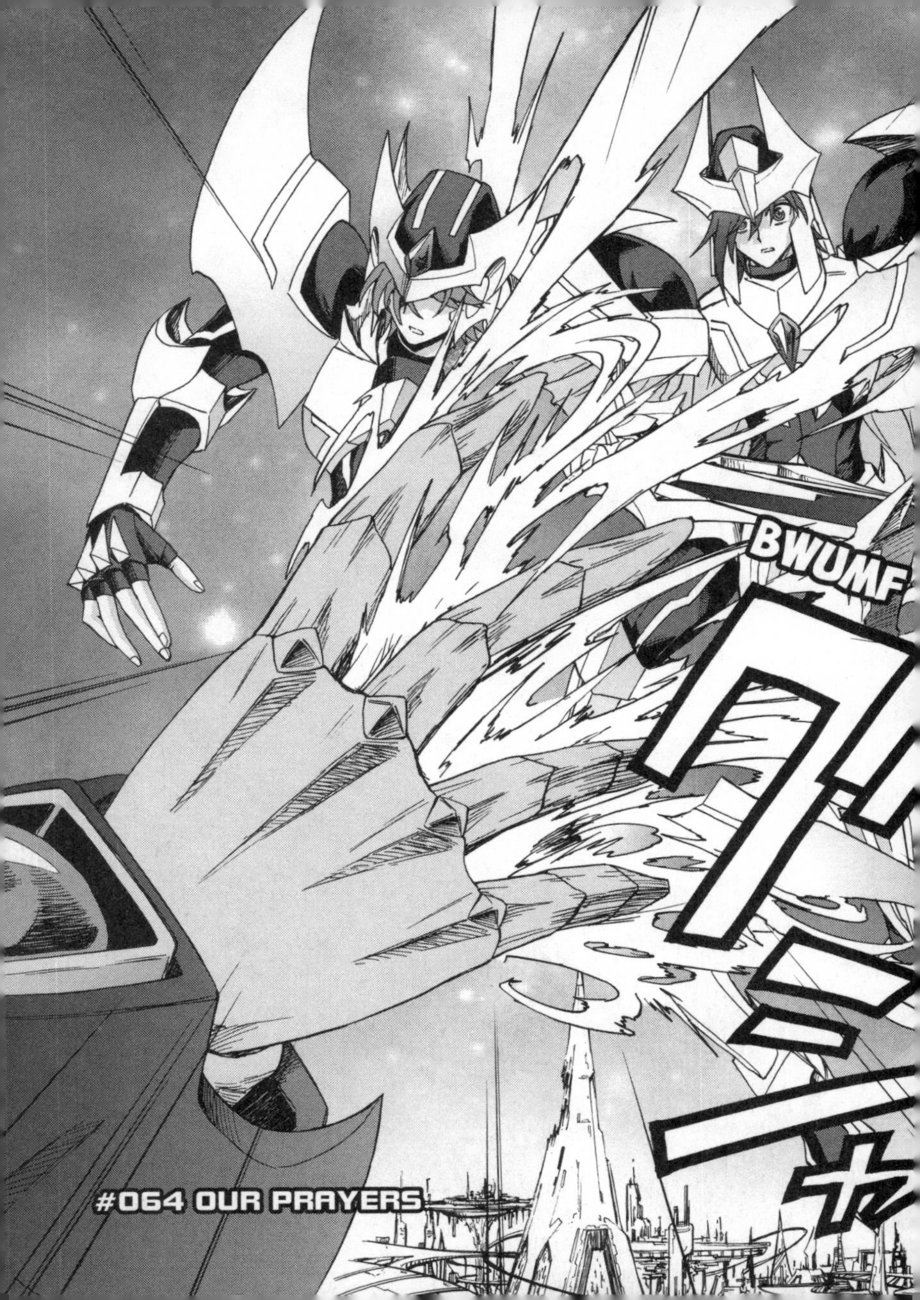
BWUMF
#064 OUR PRAYERS

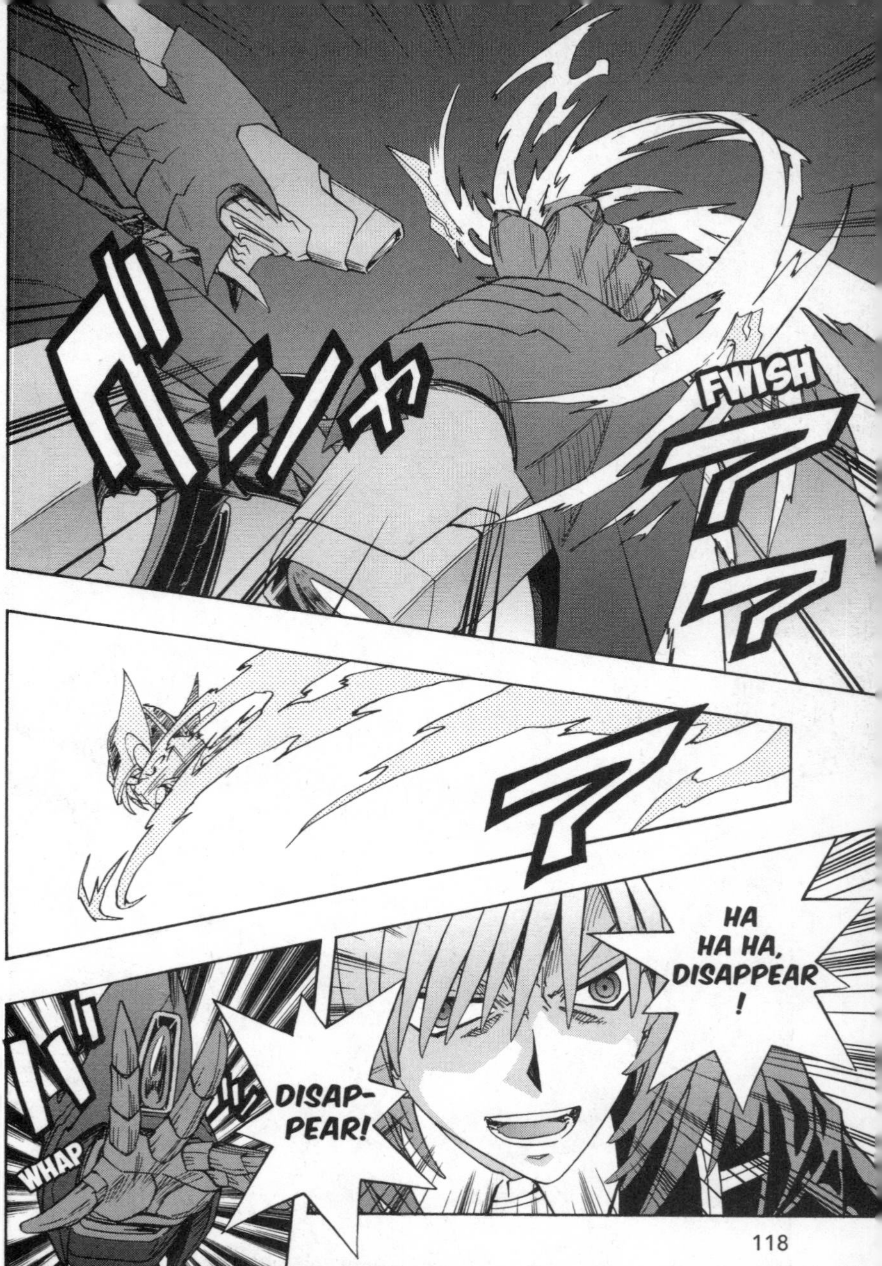
FWISH
HA HA HA, DISAPPEAR!
DISAP-PEAR!
WHAP

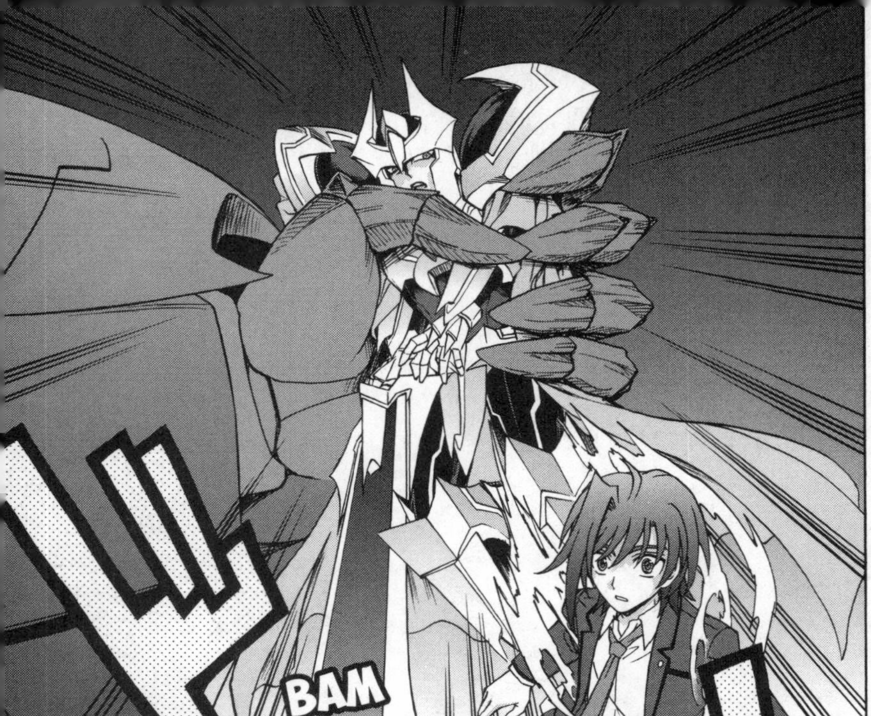
BAM

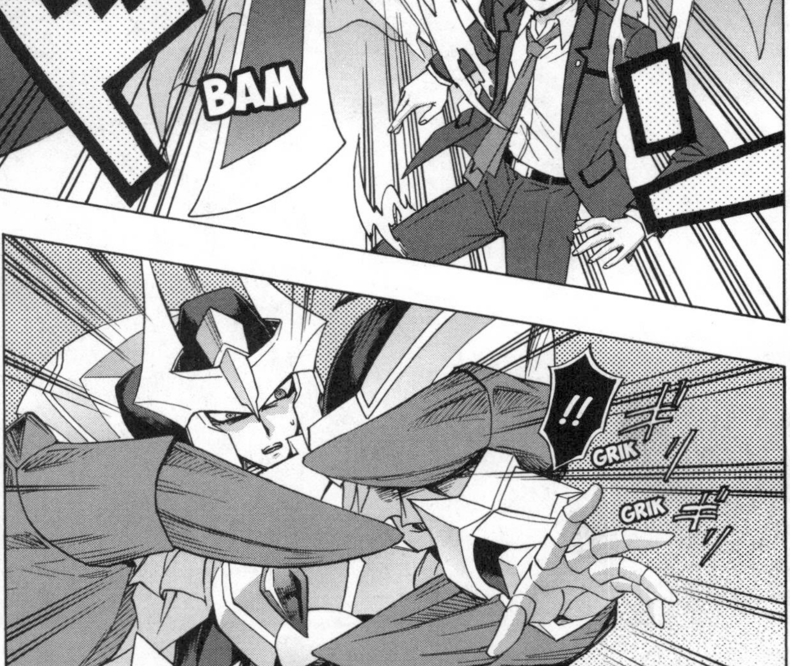
!!
ギリ
GRIK
ギリ
GRIK

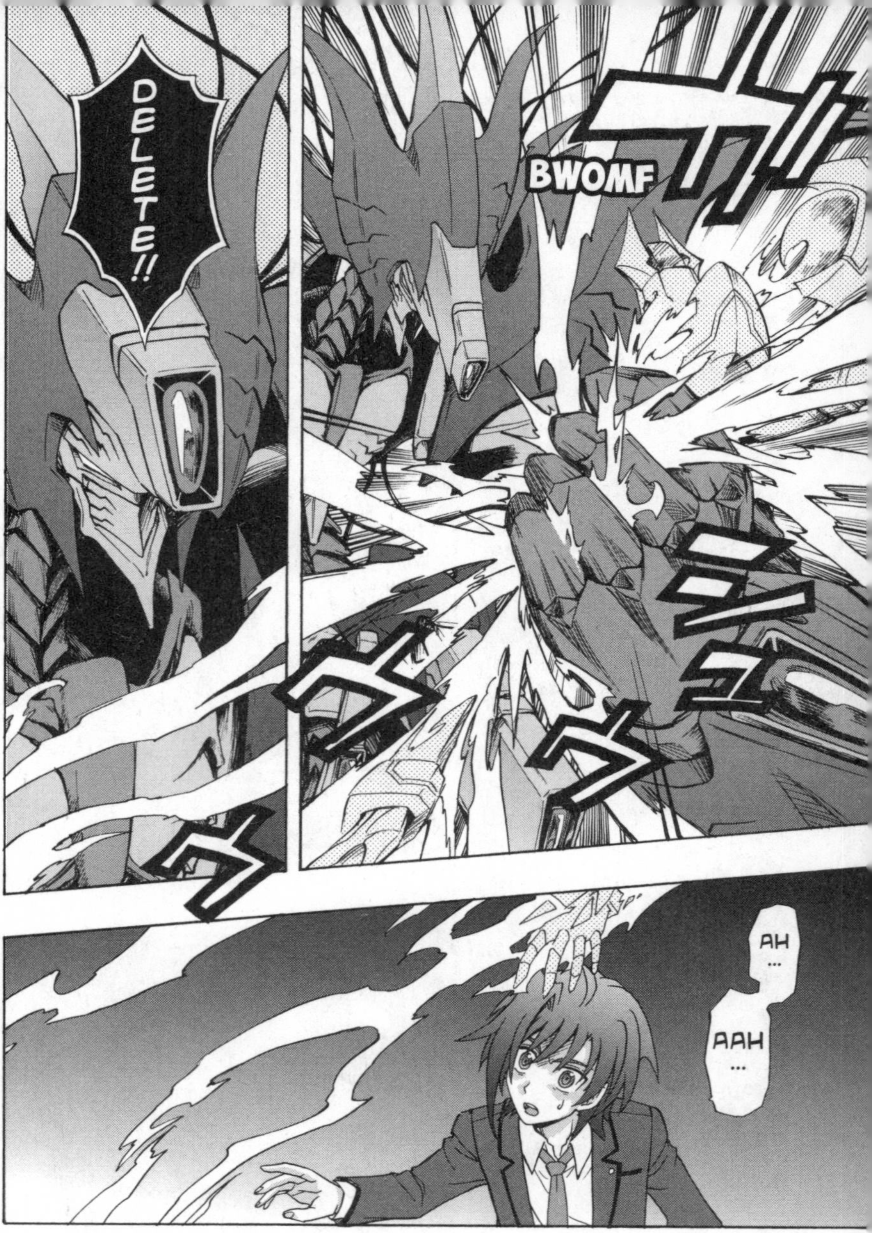
BWOMF
DELETE!!
AH...
AAH...

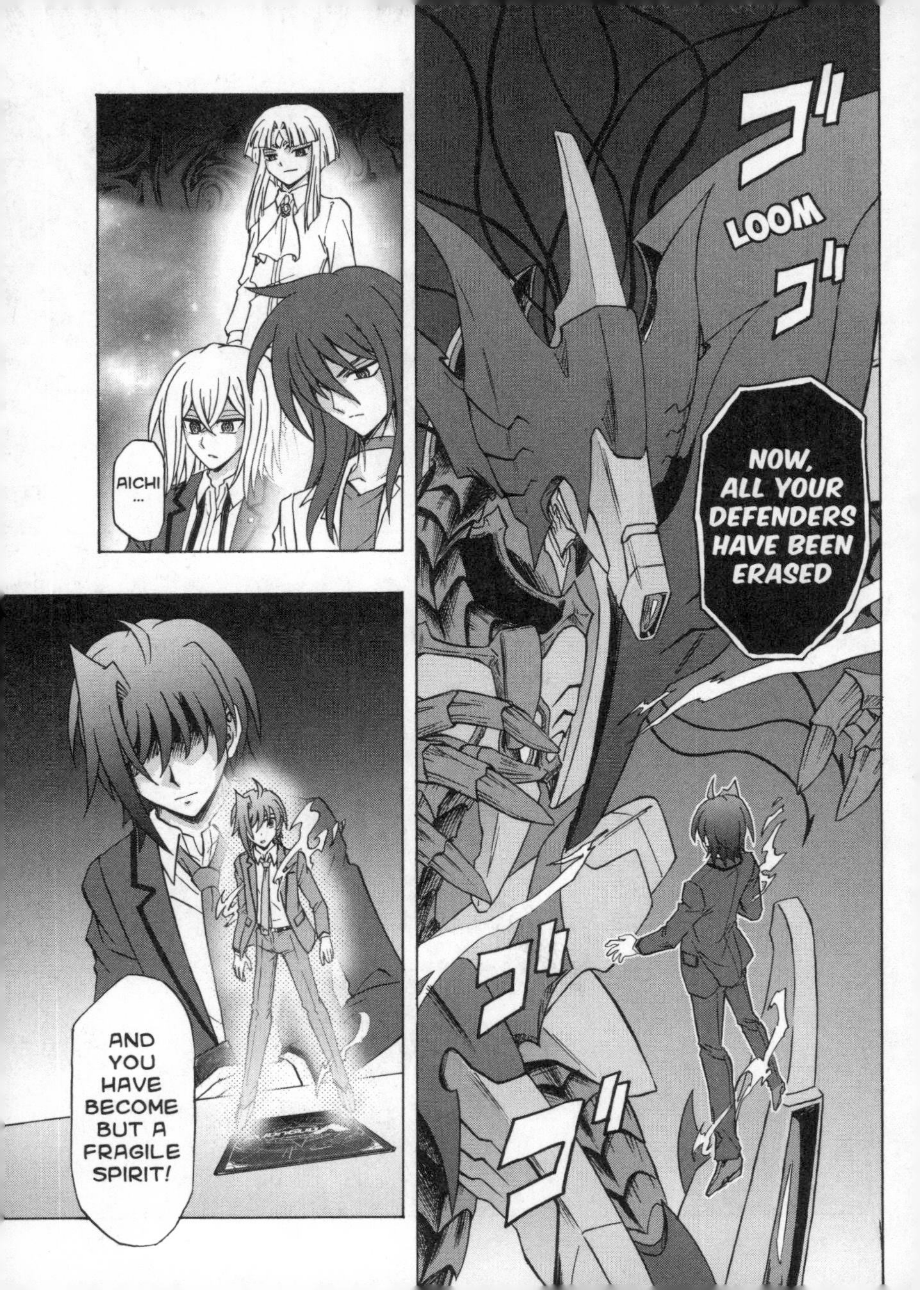
ゴ
LOOM
ゴ
NOW, ALL YOUR DEFENDERS HAVE BEEN ERASED
ゴ
ゴ
AICHI ...
AND YOU HAVE BECOME BUT A FRAGILE SPIRIT!

SEN- DOU...

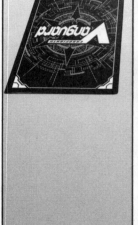

CRAP, HIS VANGUARD IS DEFENSE- LESS...

AICHI ...

OH NO ...

I DELETED KAI'S VANGUARD TOO...

HA HA ...

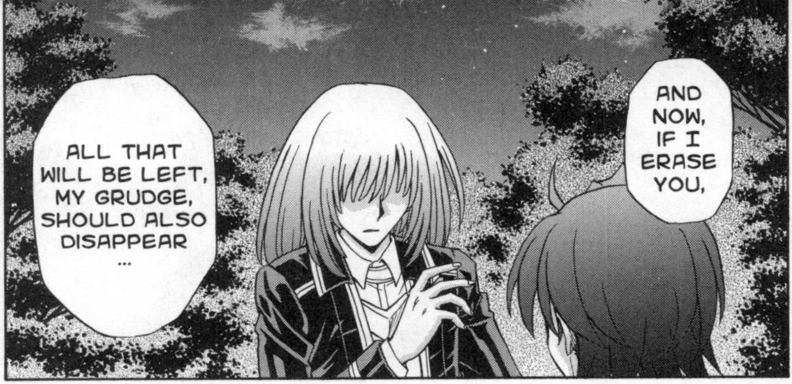
AND NOW, IF I ERASE YOU,
ALL THAT WILL BE LEFT, MY GRUDGE, SHOULD ALSO DISAPPEAR ...

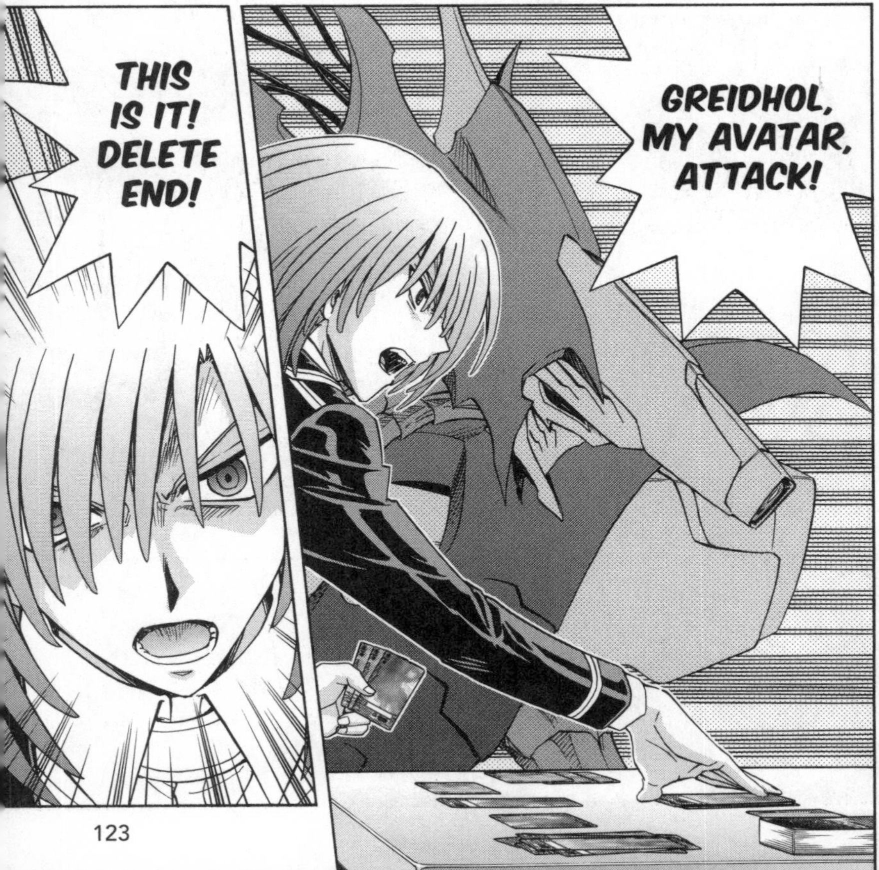
GREIDHOL, MY AVATAR, ATTACK!
THIS IS IT! DELETE END!

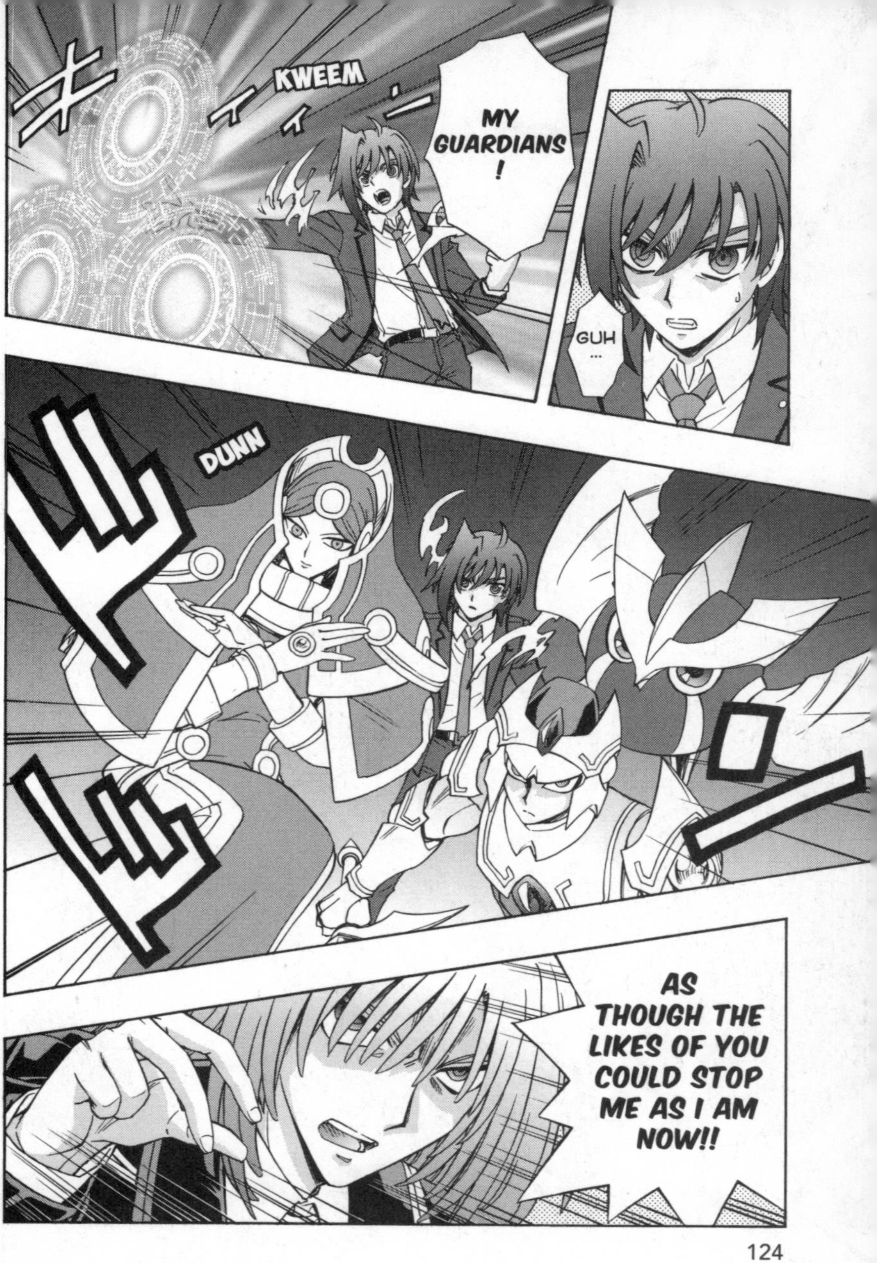

MY GUARDIANS!
KWEEM
GUH...
DUNN
AS THOUGH THE LIKES OF YOU COULD STOP ME AS I AM NOW!!

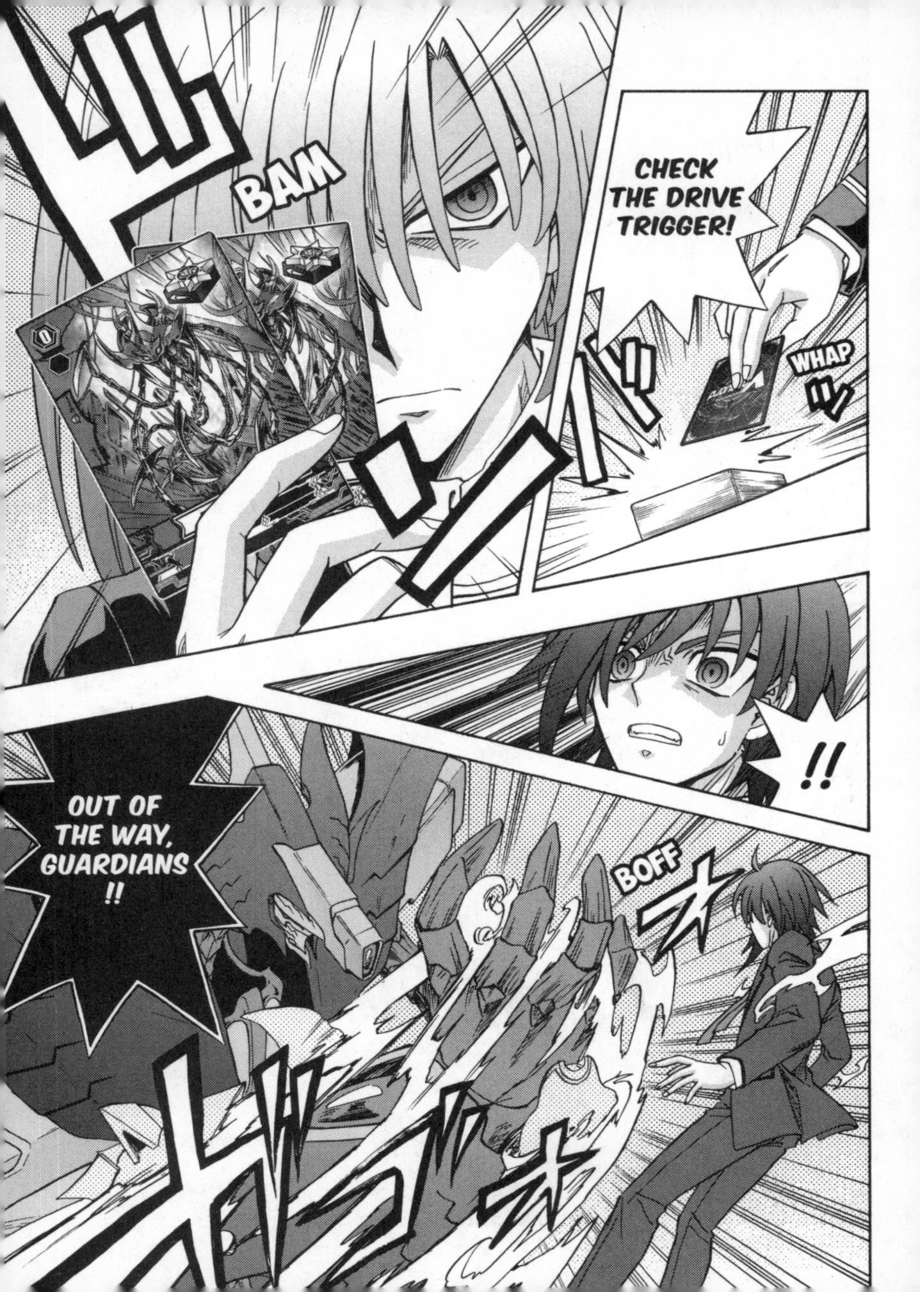
CHECK THE DRIVE TRIGGER!
WHAP
BAM
!!
BOFF
OUT OF THE WAY, GUARDIANS !!

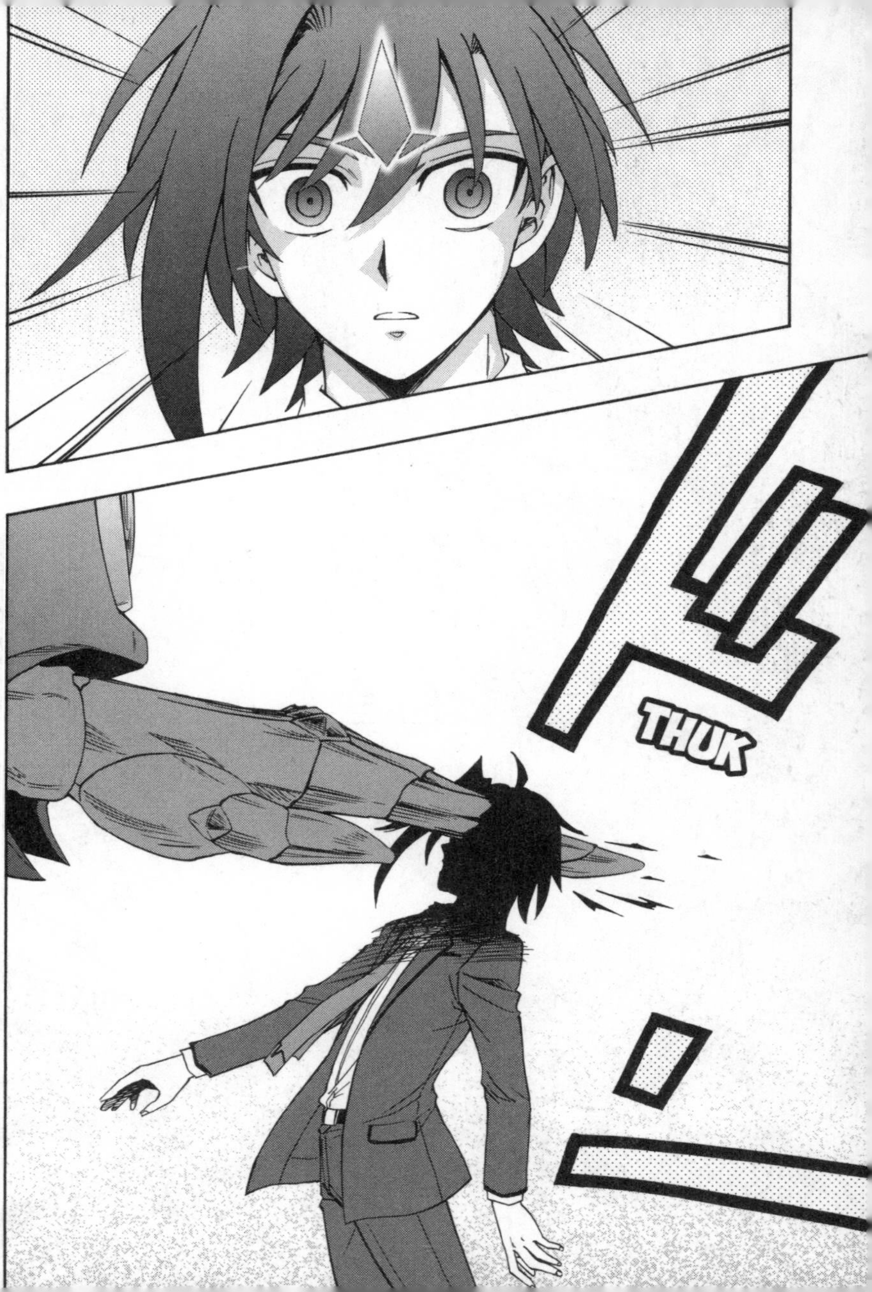
THUK

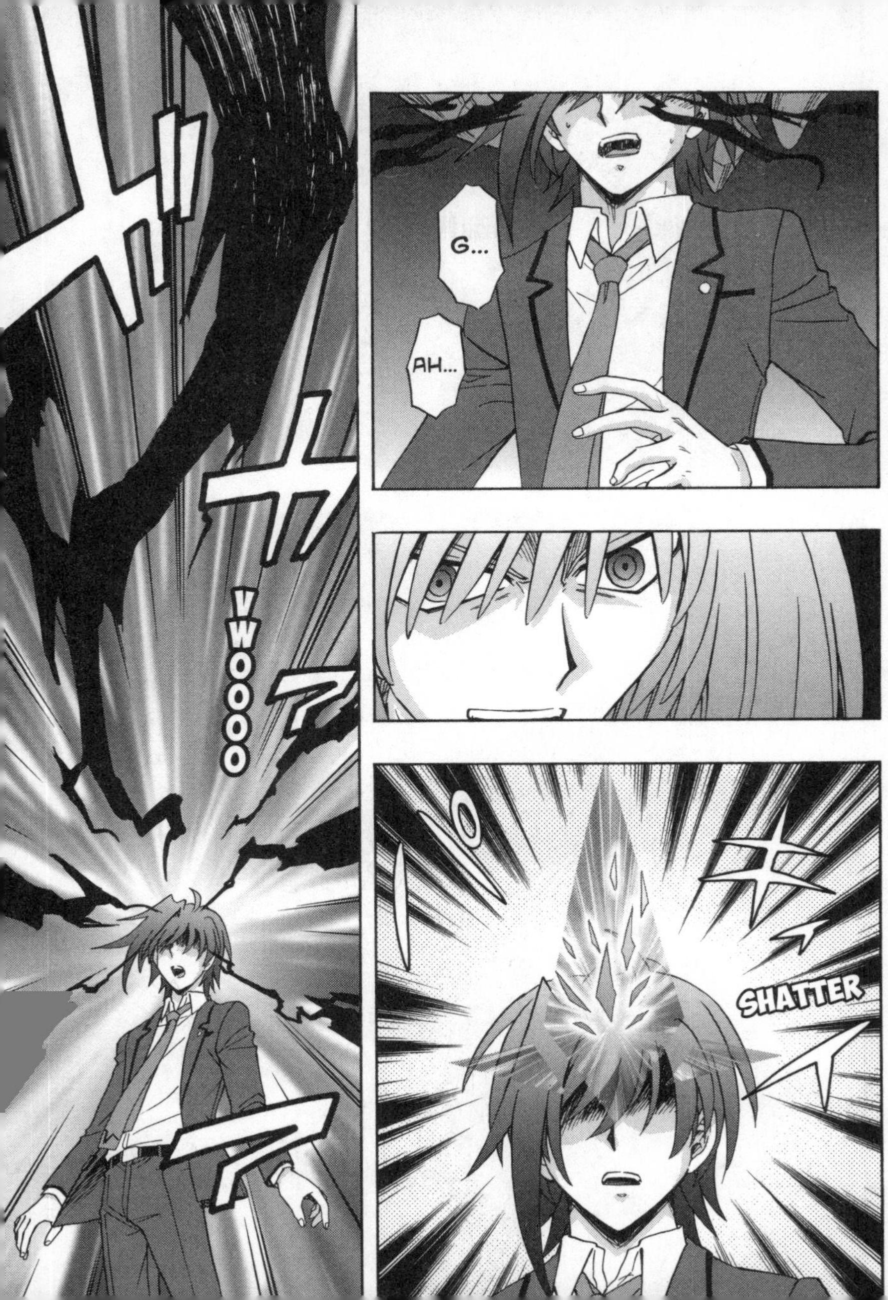
G...
AH...
SHATTER
VWOOOO

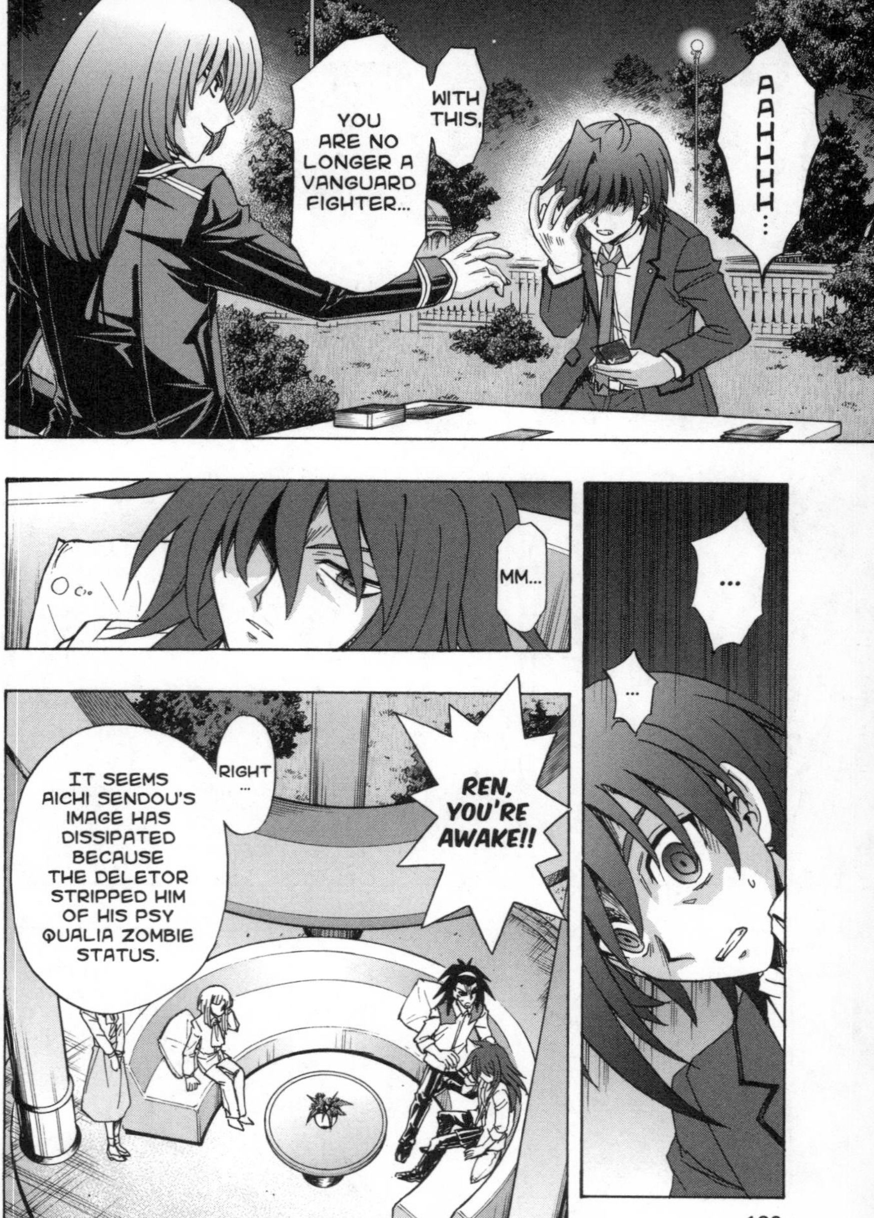
WITH THIS,
YOU ARE NO LONGER A VANGUARD FIGHTER...
AAHHHH...
...
...
MM...
REN, YOU'RE AWAKE!!
RIGHT...
IT SEEMS AICHI SENDOU'S IMAGE HAS DISSIPATED BECAUSE THE DELETOR STRIPPED HIM OF HIS PSY QUALIA ZOMBIE STATUS.

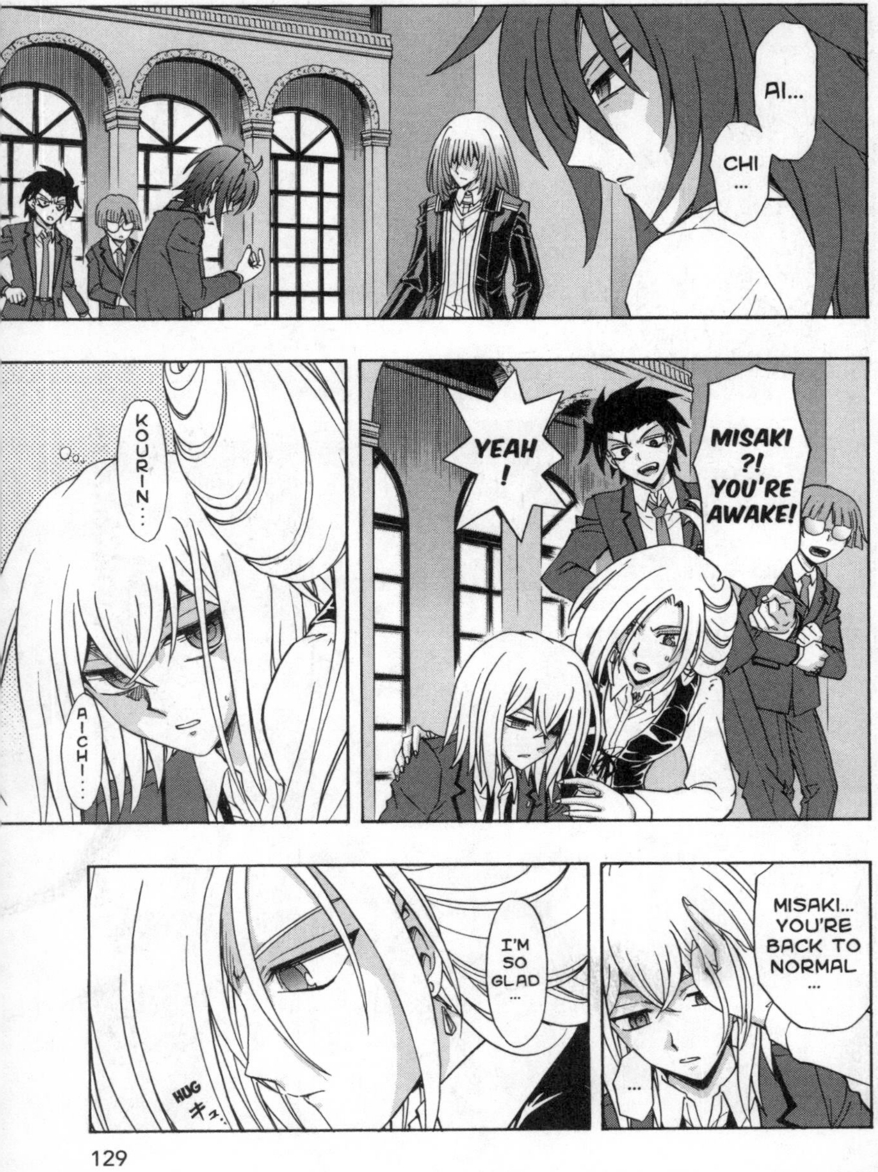
AI...
CHI ...
MISAKI ?! YOU'RE AWAKE!
YEAH !
KOURIN...
AICHI...
MISAKI... YOU'RE BACK TO NORMAL ...
...
I'M SO GLAD ...
HUG キュ...

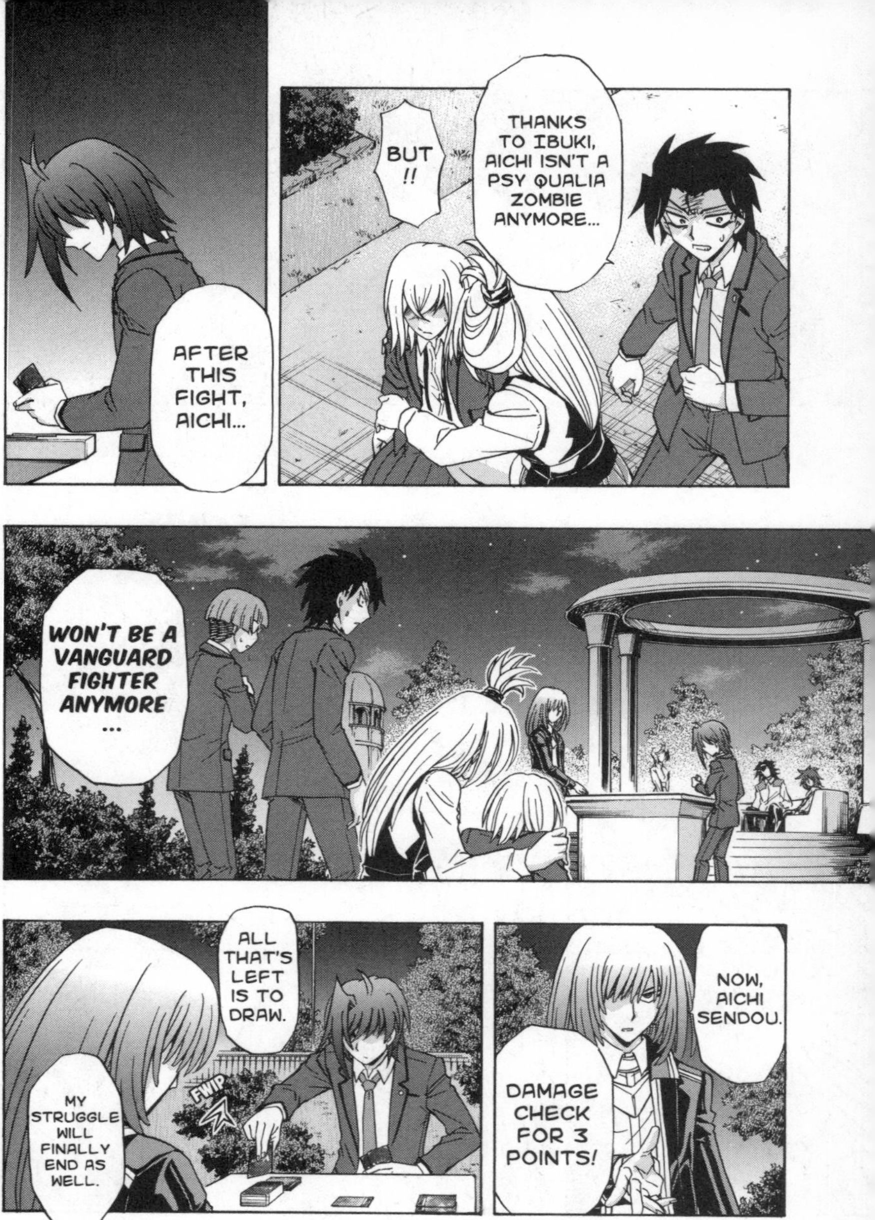
THANKS TO IBUKI, AICHI ISN'T A PSY QUALIA ZOMBIE ANYMORE...
BUT !!
AFTER THIS FIGHT, AICHI...
WON'T BE A VANGUARD FIGHTER ANYMORE ...
NOW, AICHI SENDOU.
DAMAGE CHECK FOR 3 POINTS!
ALL THAT'S LEFT IS TO DRAW.
FWIP
MY STRUGGLE WILL FINALLY END AS WELL.

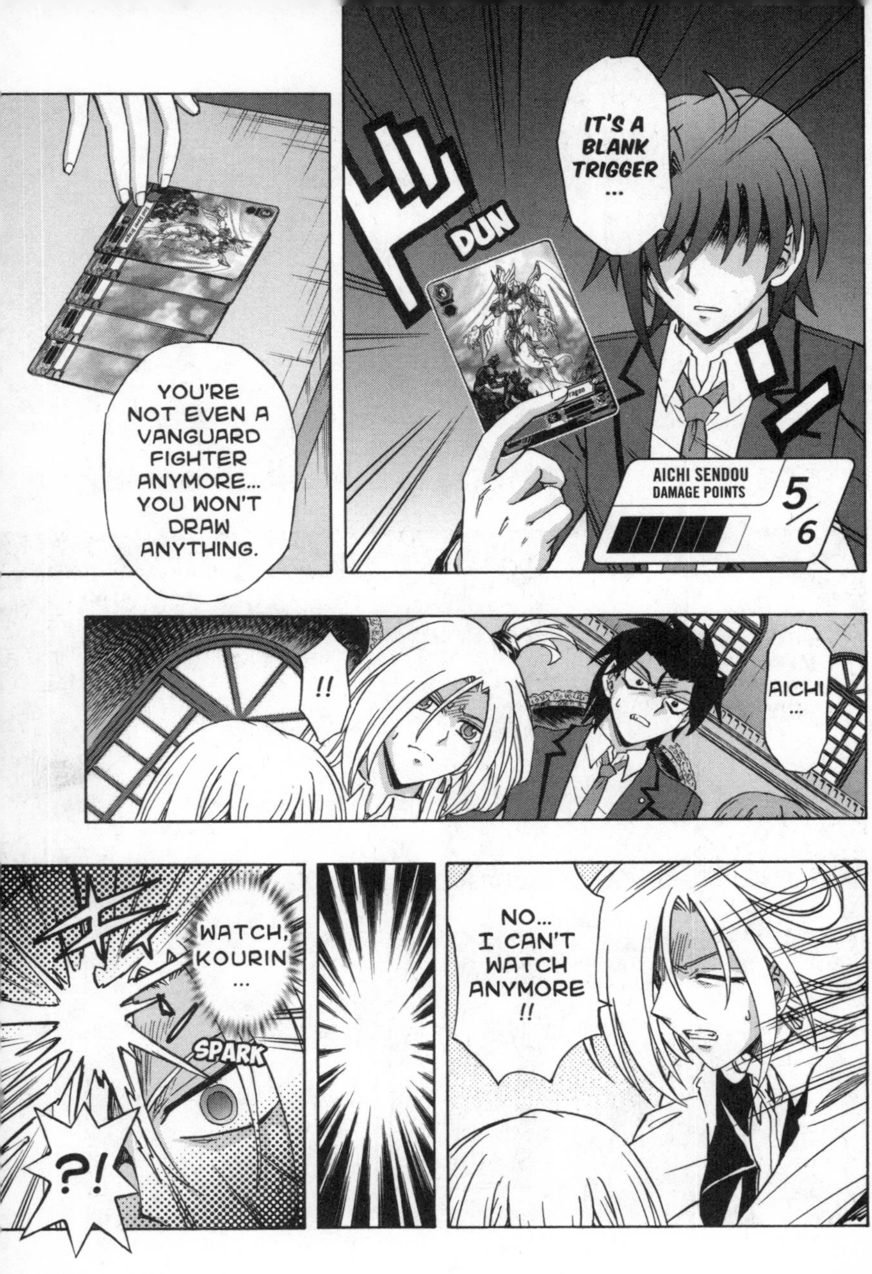
IT'S A BLANK TRIGGER ...
DUN
AICHI SENDOU DAMAGE POINTS
5/6
YOU'RE NOT EVEN A VANGUARD FIGHTER ANYMORE... YOU WON'T DRAW ANYTHING.
AICHI ...
!!
NO... I CAN'T WATCH ANYMORE !!
WATCH, KOURIN ...
SPARK
?!

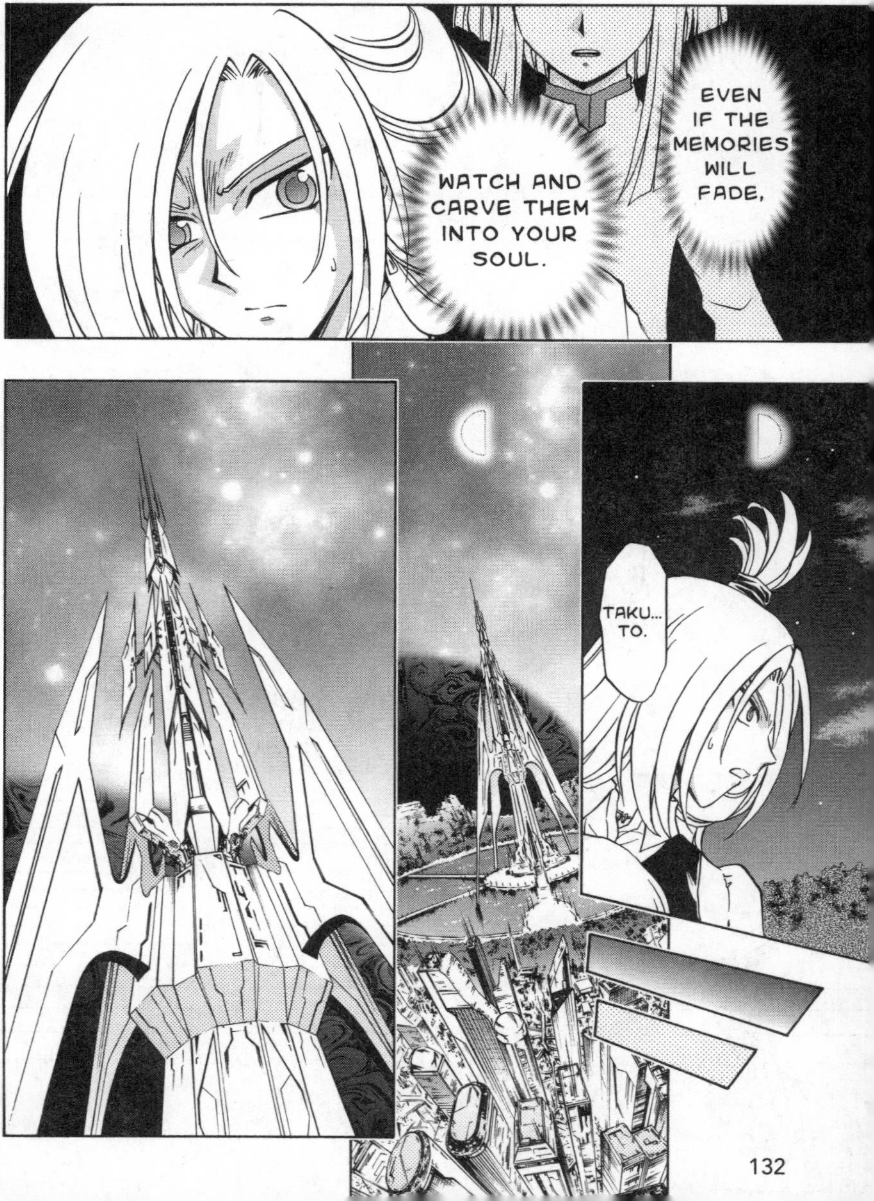
EVEN IF THE MEMORIES WILL FADE,
WATCH AND CARVE THEM INTO YOUR SOUL.
TAKU... TO.

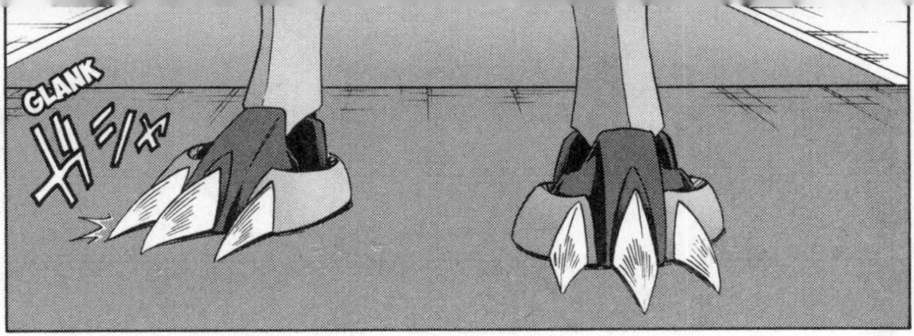
GLANK
ギシャ
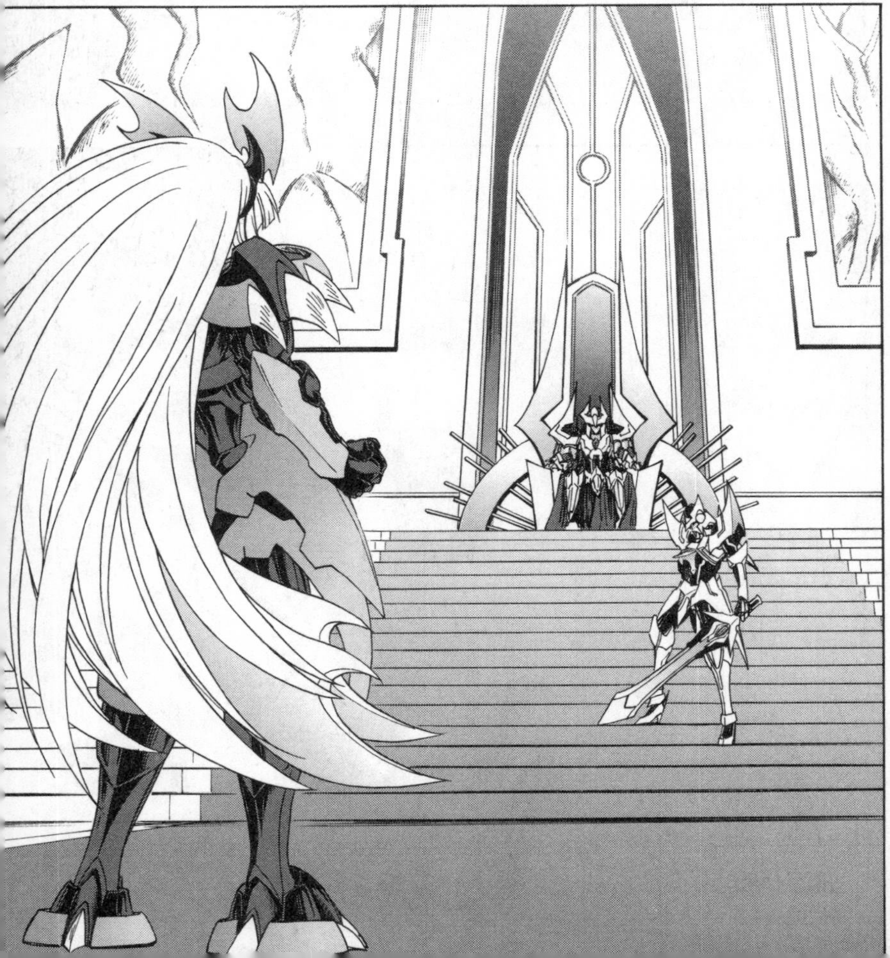

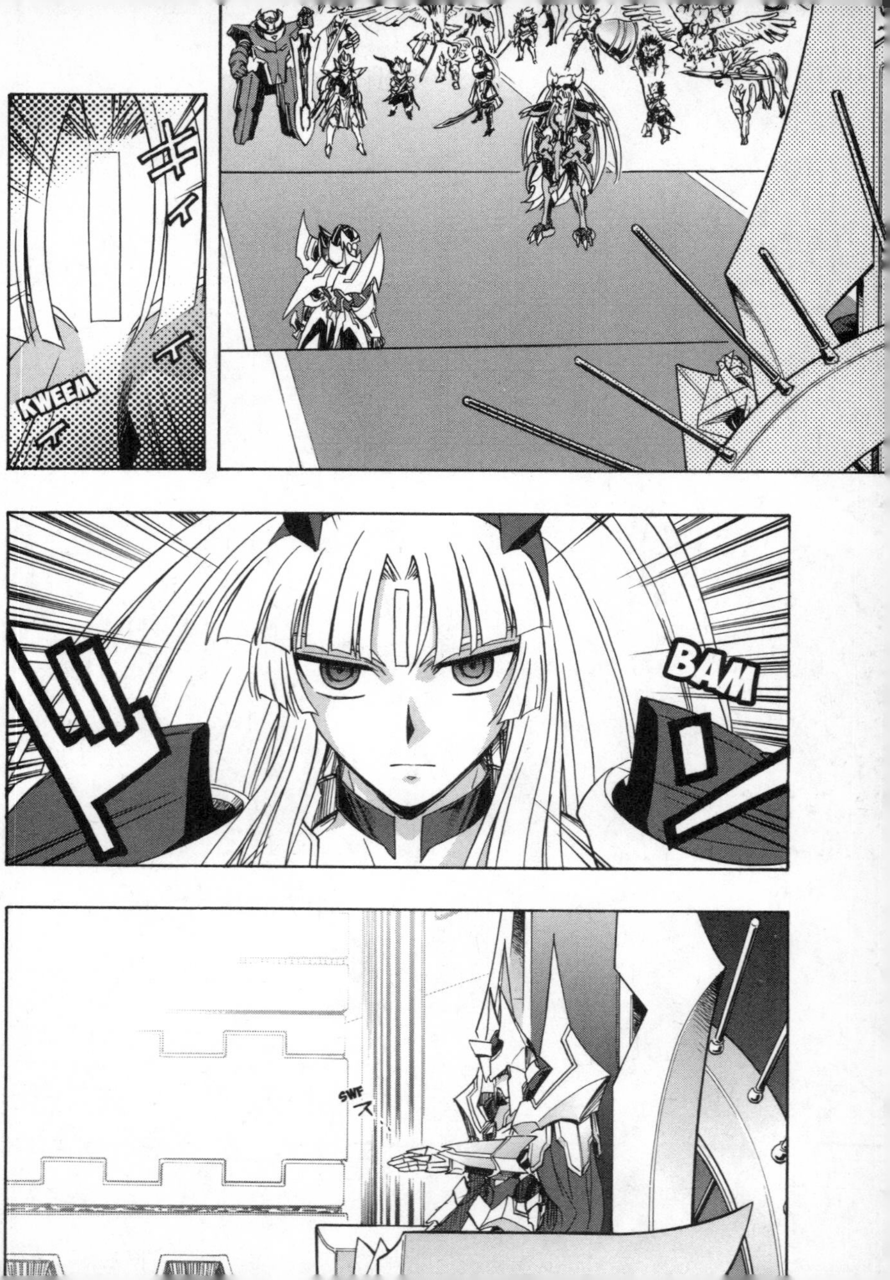
KWEEM
BAM
SWF

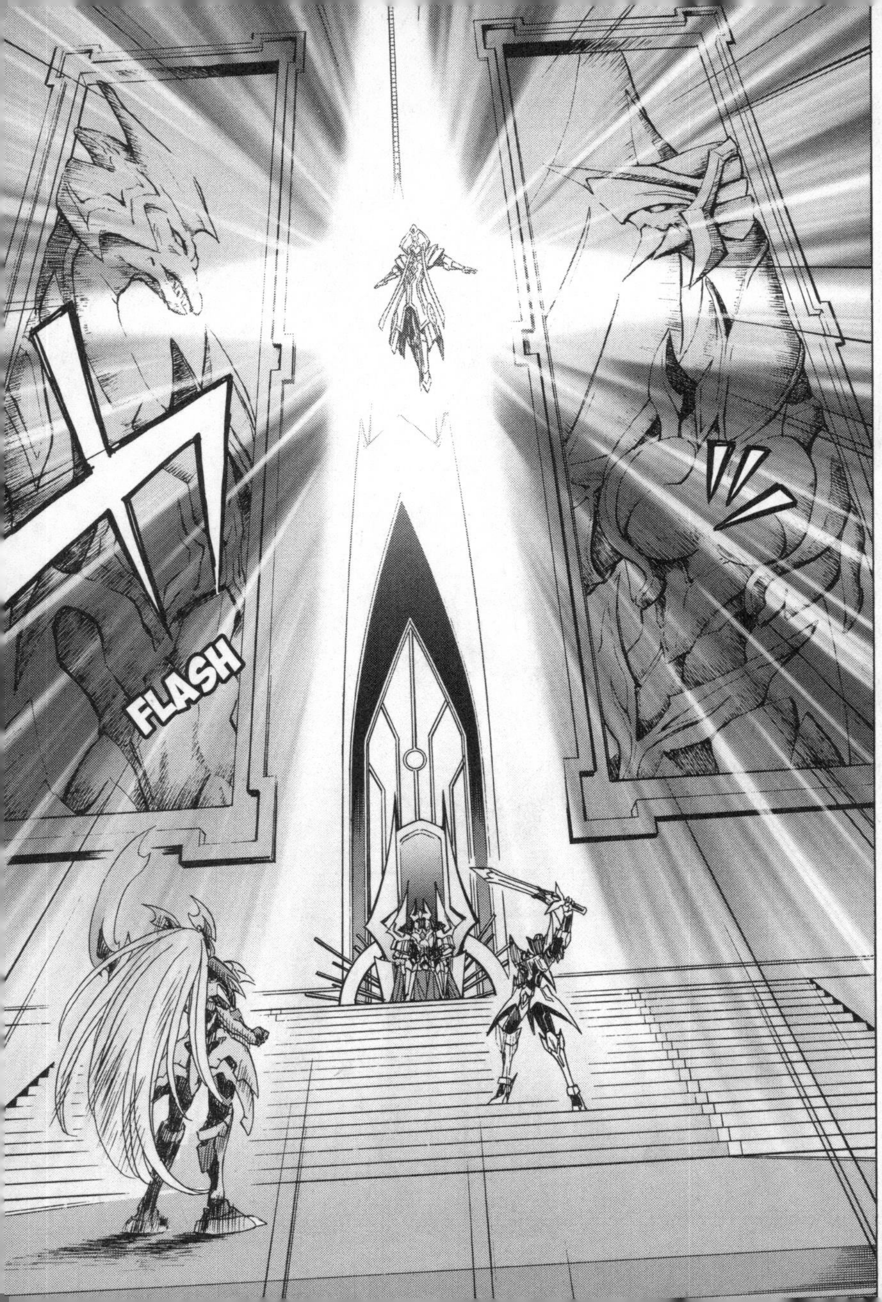
FLASH

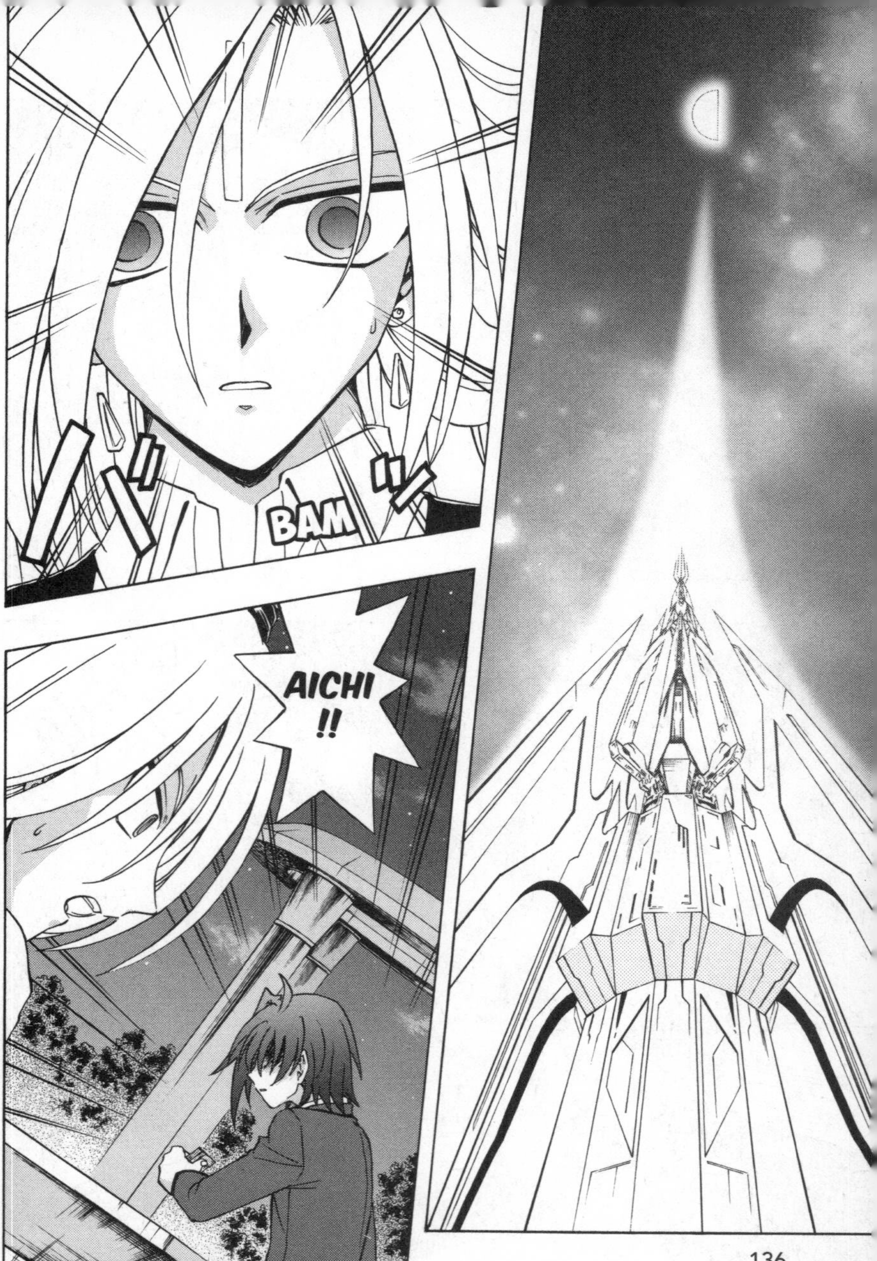
BAM
AICHI!!

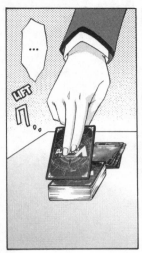

...

LIFT

SECOND DAMAGE CHECK...

DUN

WHUP

Elaine

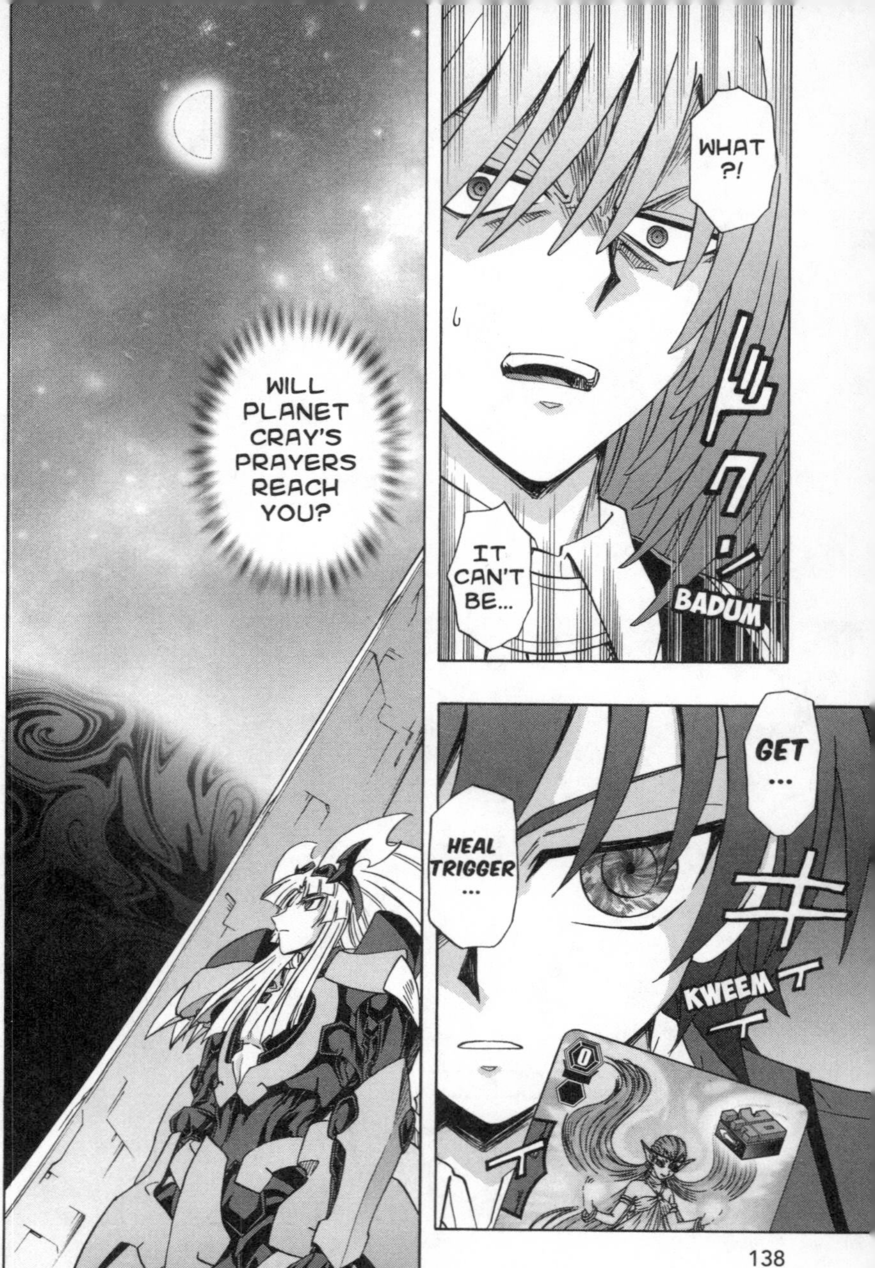
WHAT ?!
IT CAN'T BE...
BADUM
GET ...
HEAL TRIGGER ...
KWEEM
WILL PLANET CRAY'S PRAYERS REACH YOU?

CARDFIGHT!!
Vanguard

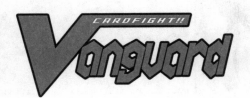

BONUS!

CARDFIGHT!! Vanguard

NEVER-BEFORE-SEEN IMAGE BOARDS

カード

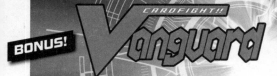

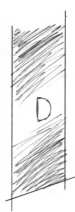

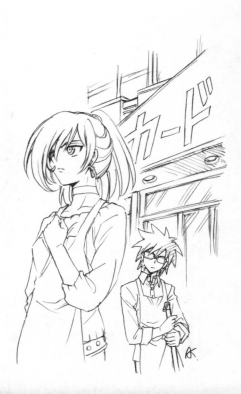

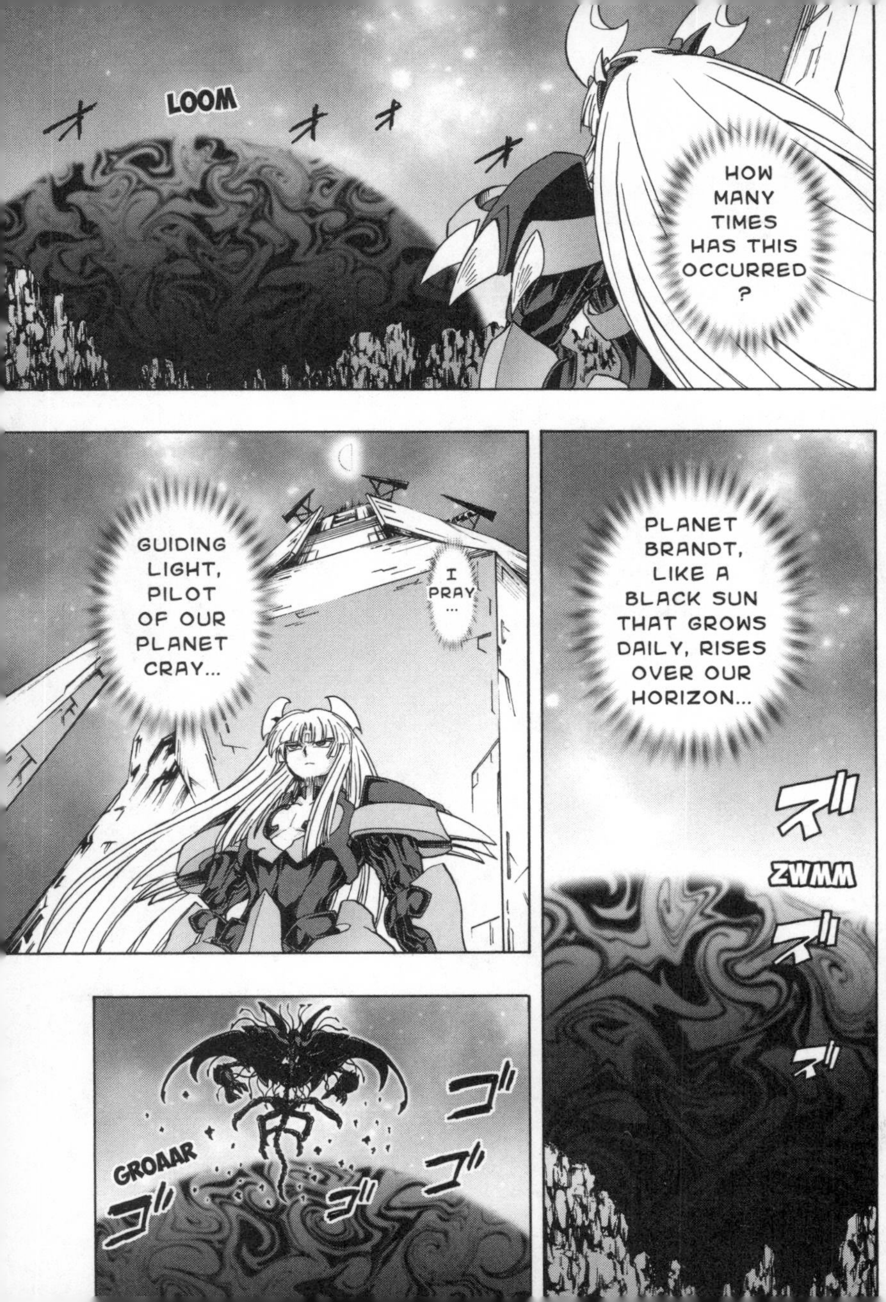

LOOM
オ オ オ オ
HOW MANY TIMES HAS THIS OCCURRED ?
PLANET BRANDT, LIKE A BLACK SUN THAT GROWS DAILY, RISES OVER OUR HORIZON...
ズ
ZWMM
ズ
ズ
GUIDING LIGHT, PILOT OF OUR PLANET CRAY...
I PRAY ...
ゴ
GROAAR
ゴ
ゴ
ゴ

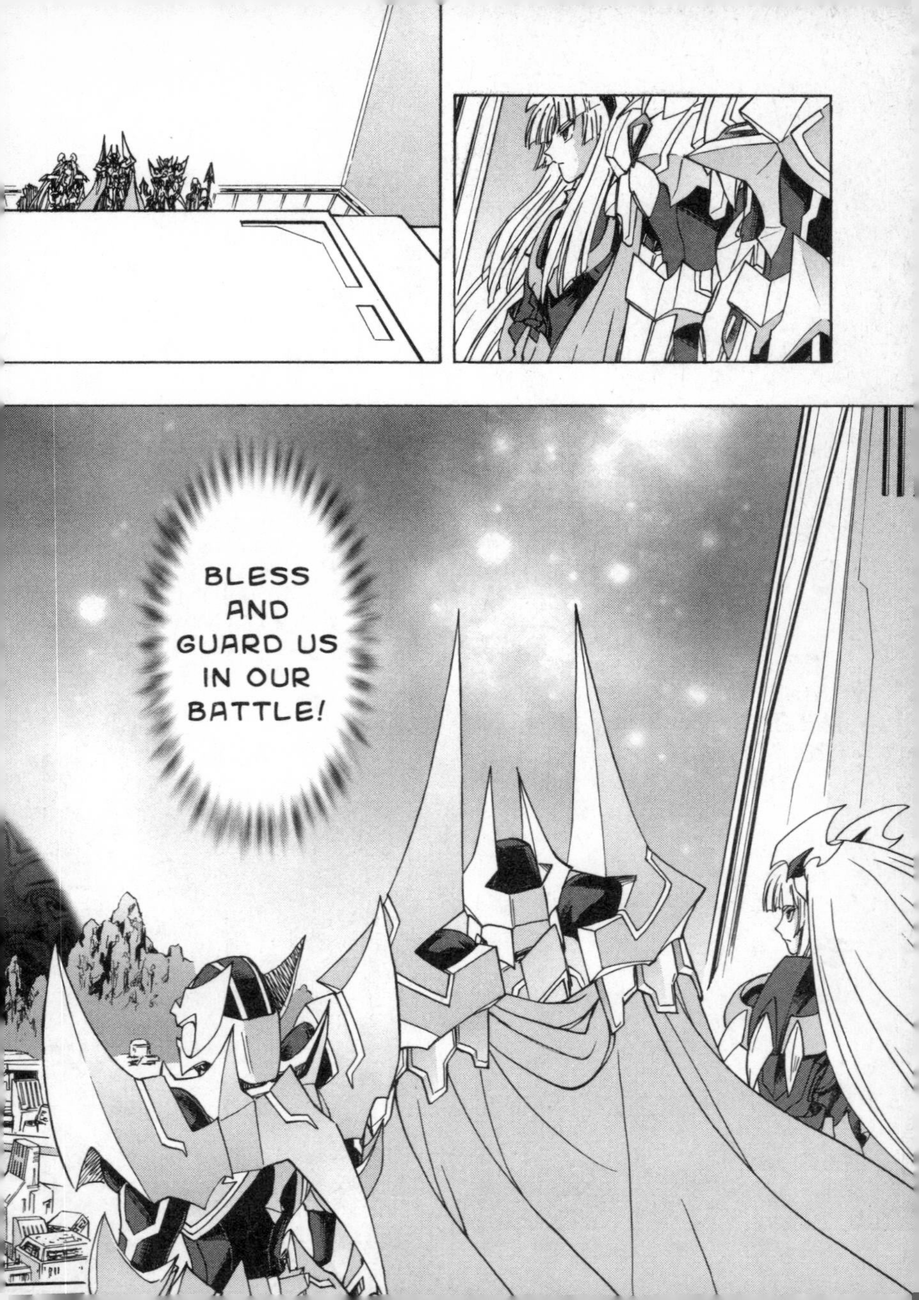
BLESS AND GUARD US IN OUR BATTLE!

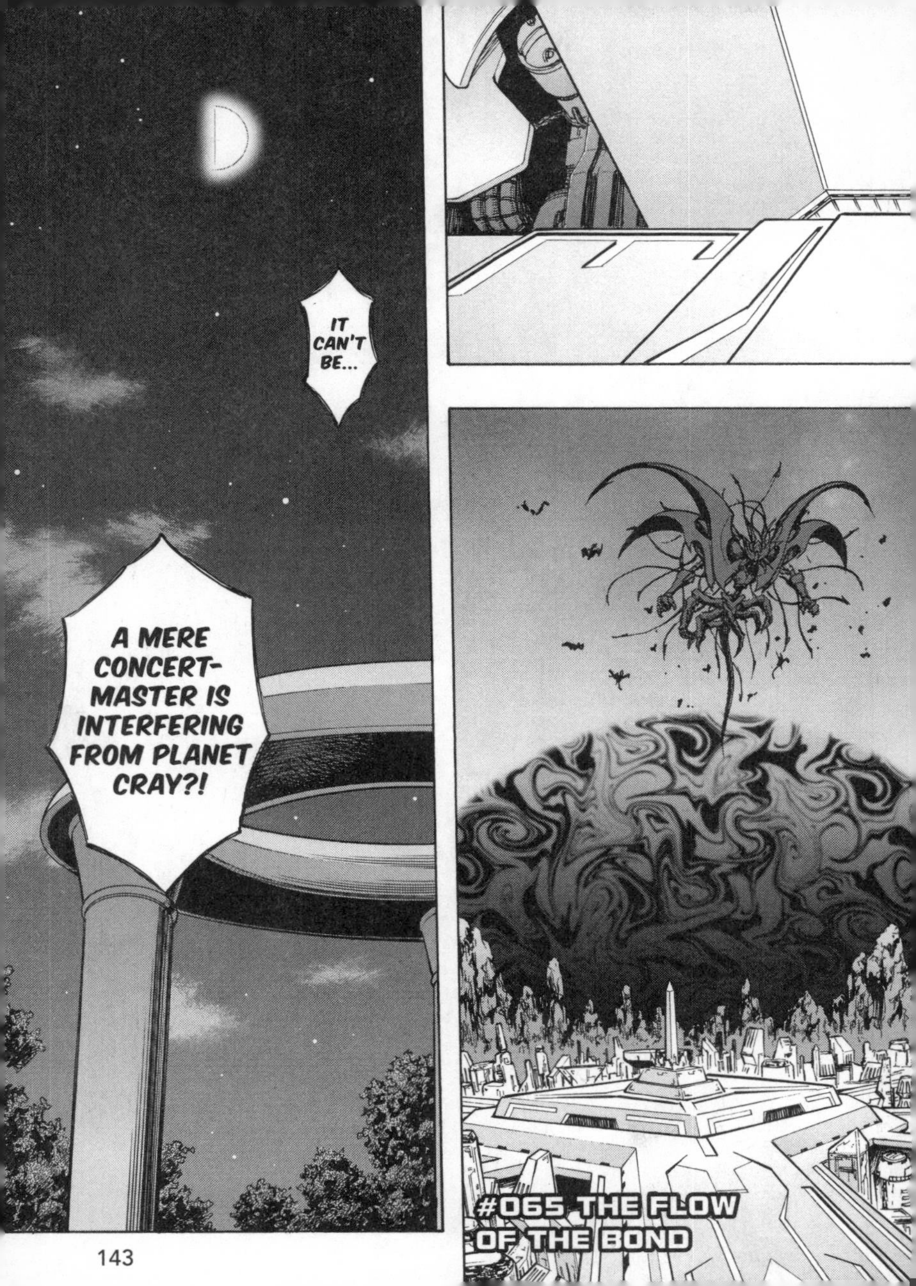
#065 THE FLOW OF THE BOND
IT CAN'T BE...
A MERE CONCERT-MASTER IS INTERFERING FROM PLANET CRAY?!

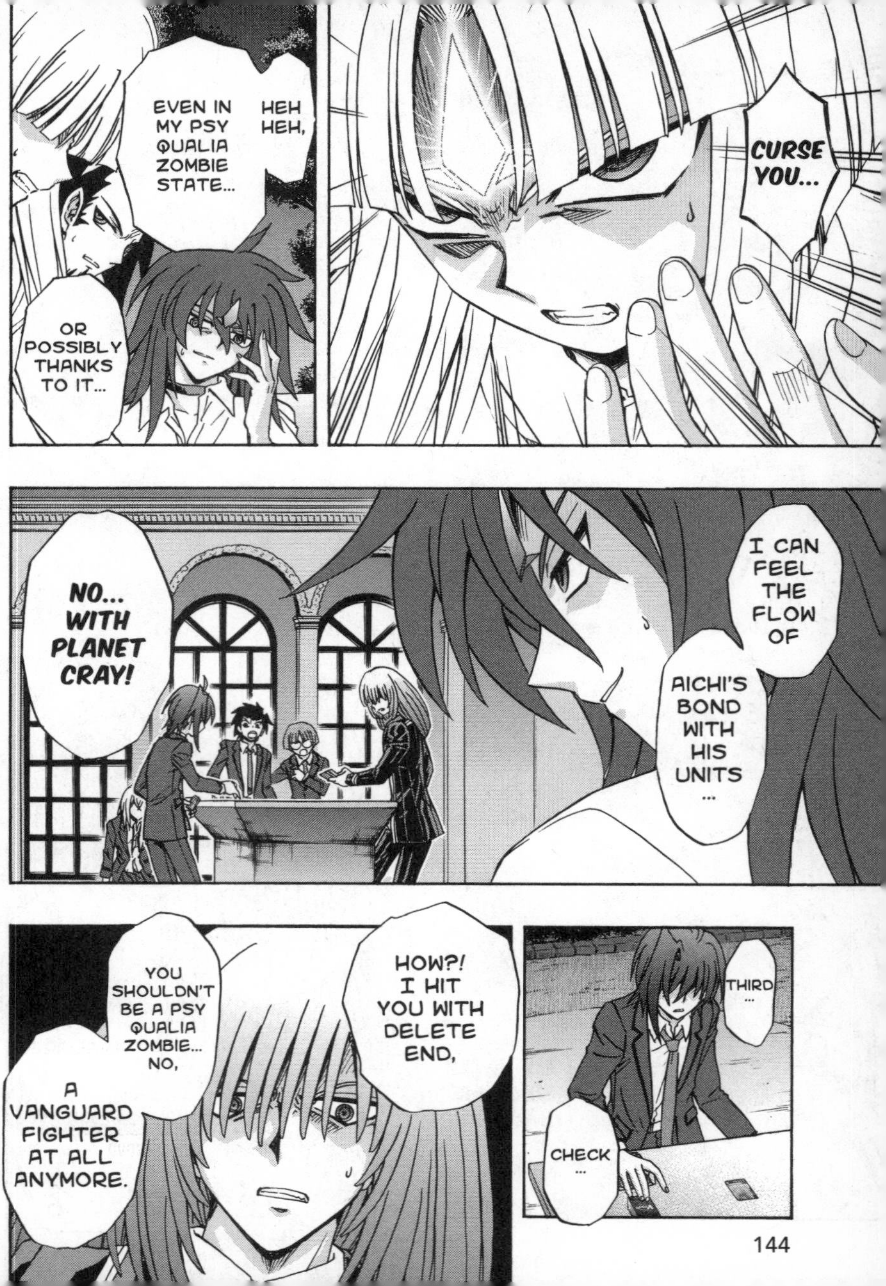
CURSE YOU...
HEH HEH,
EVEN IN MY PSY QUALIA ZOMBIE STATE...
OR POSSIBLY THANKS TO IT...
I CAN FEEL THE FLOW OF
AICHI'S BOND WITH HIS UNITS ...
NO... WITH PLANET CRAY!
THIRD ...
CHECK ...
HOW?! I HIT YOU WITH DELETE END,
YOU SHOULDN'T BE A PSY QUALIA ZOMBIE... NO,
A VANGUARD FIGHTER AT ALL ANYMORE.

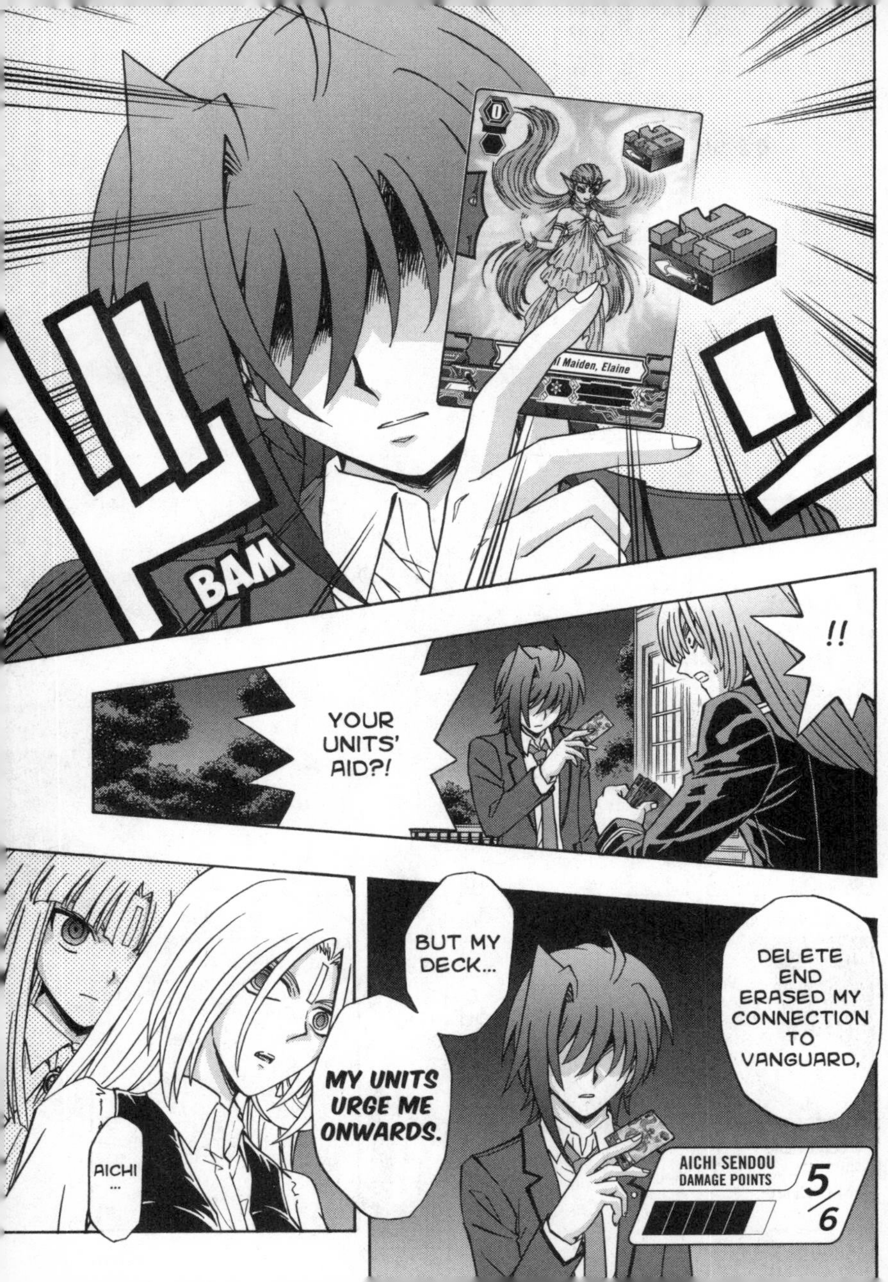

Maiden, Elaine
BAM
!!
YOUR UNITS' AID?!
DELETE END ERASED MY CONNECTION TO VANGUARD,
BUT MY DECK...
MY UNITS URGE ME ONWARDS.
AICHI SENDOU DAMAGE POINTS
5/6
AICHI ...

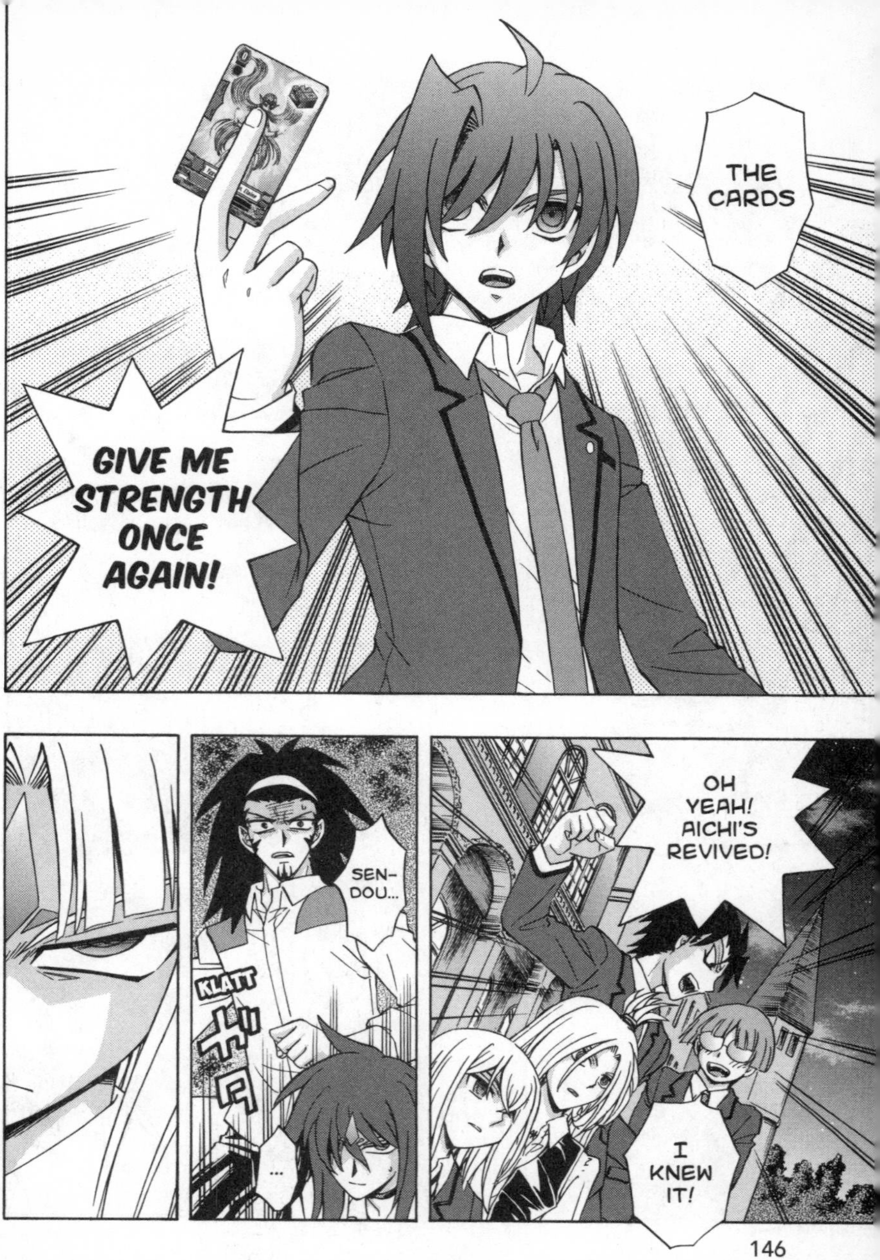
THE CARDS
GIVE ME STRENGTH ONCE AGAIN!
OH YEAH! AICHI'S REVIVED!
I KNEW IT!
SEN-DOU...
KLATT
...

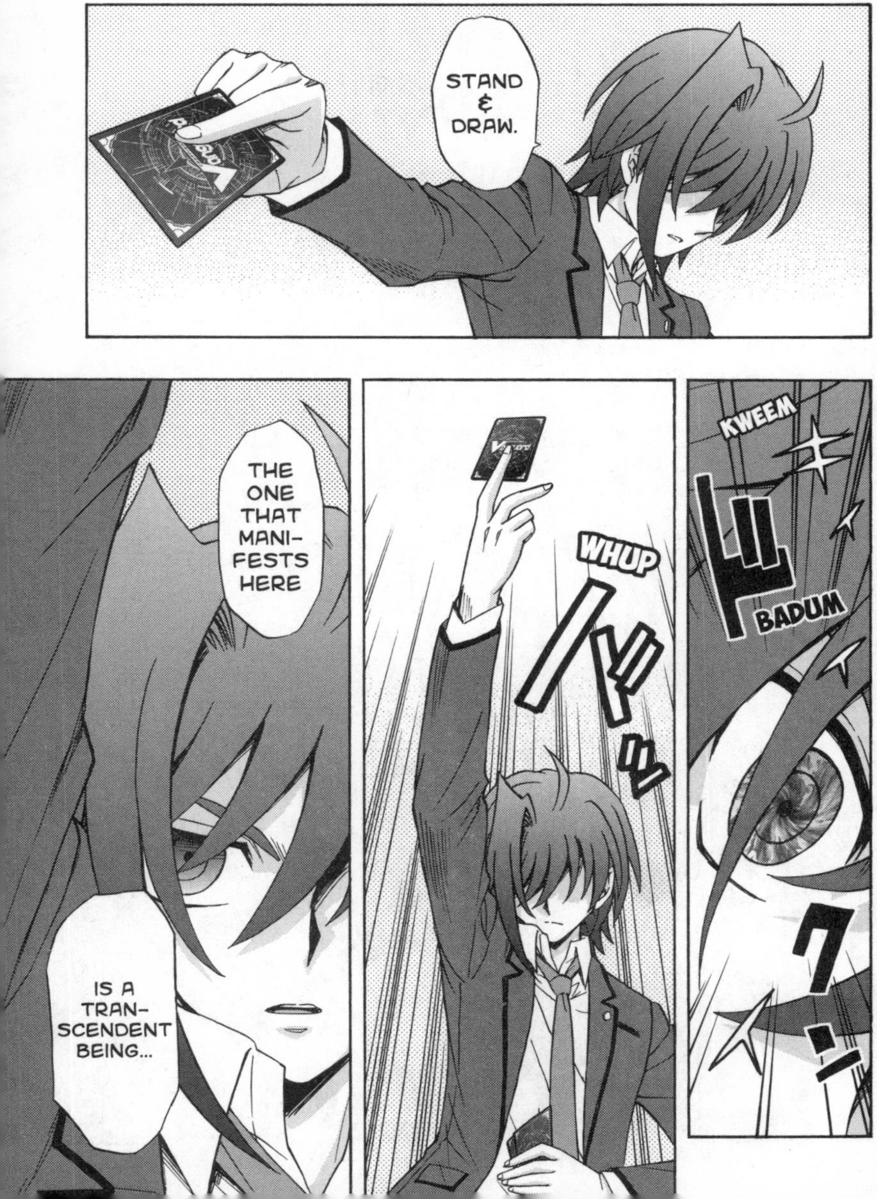
STAND & DRAW.
KWEEM
BADUM
WHUP
THE ONE THAT MANI-FESTS HERE
IS A TRAN-SCENDENT BEING...

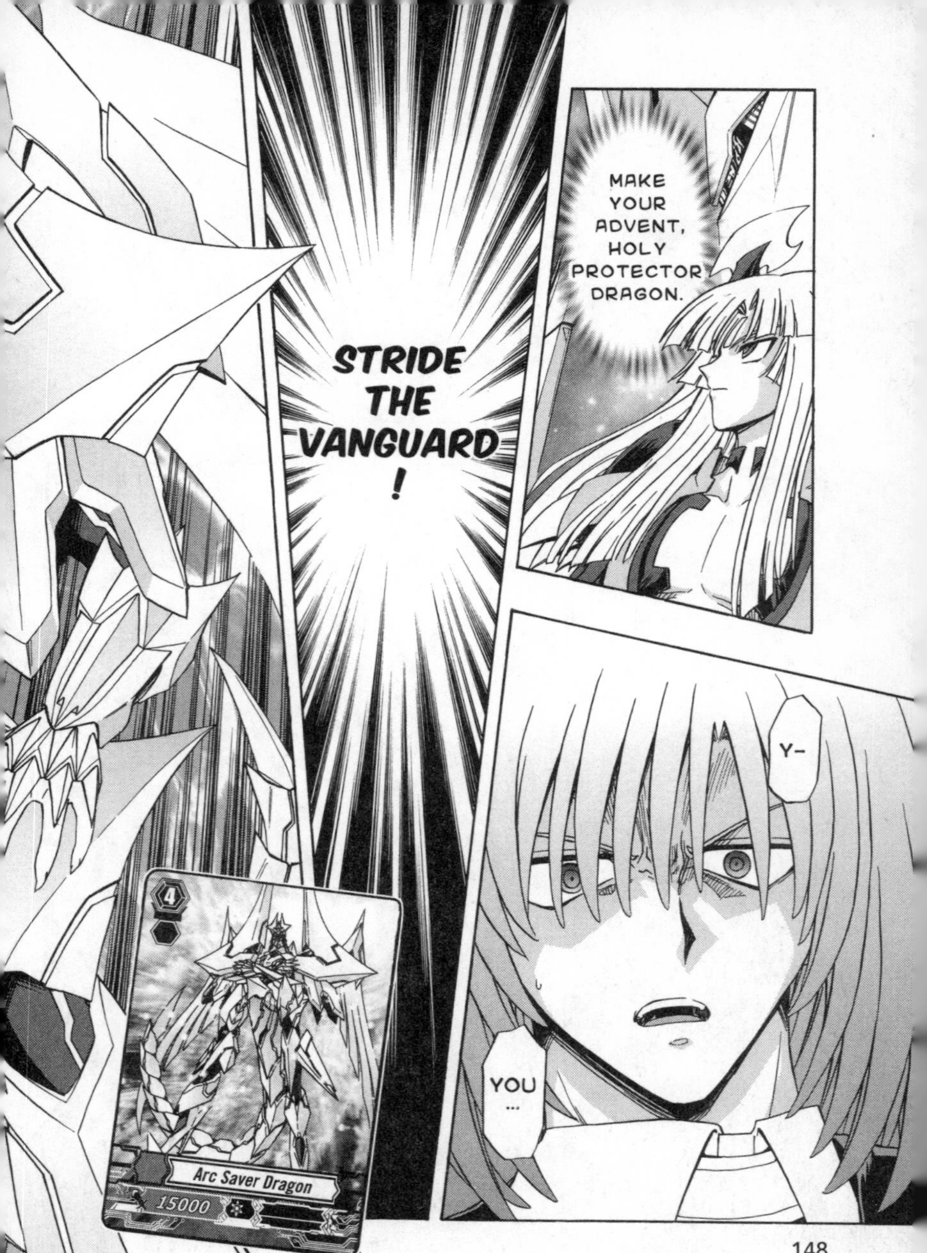
MAKE YOUR ADVENT, HOLY PROTECTOR DRAGON.
Y-
YOU ...
STRIDE THE VANGUARD!
4
Arc Saver Dragon
15000

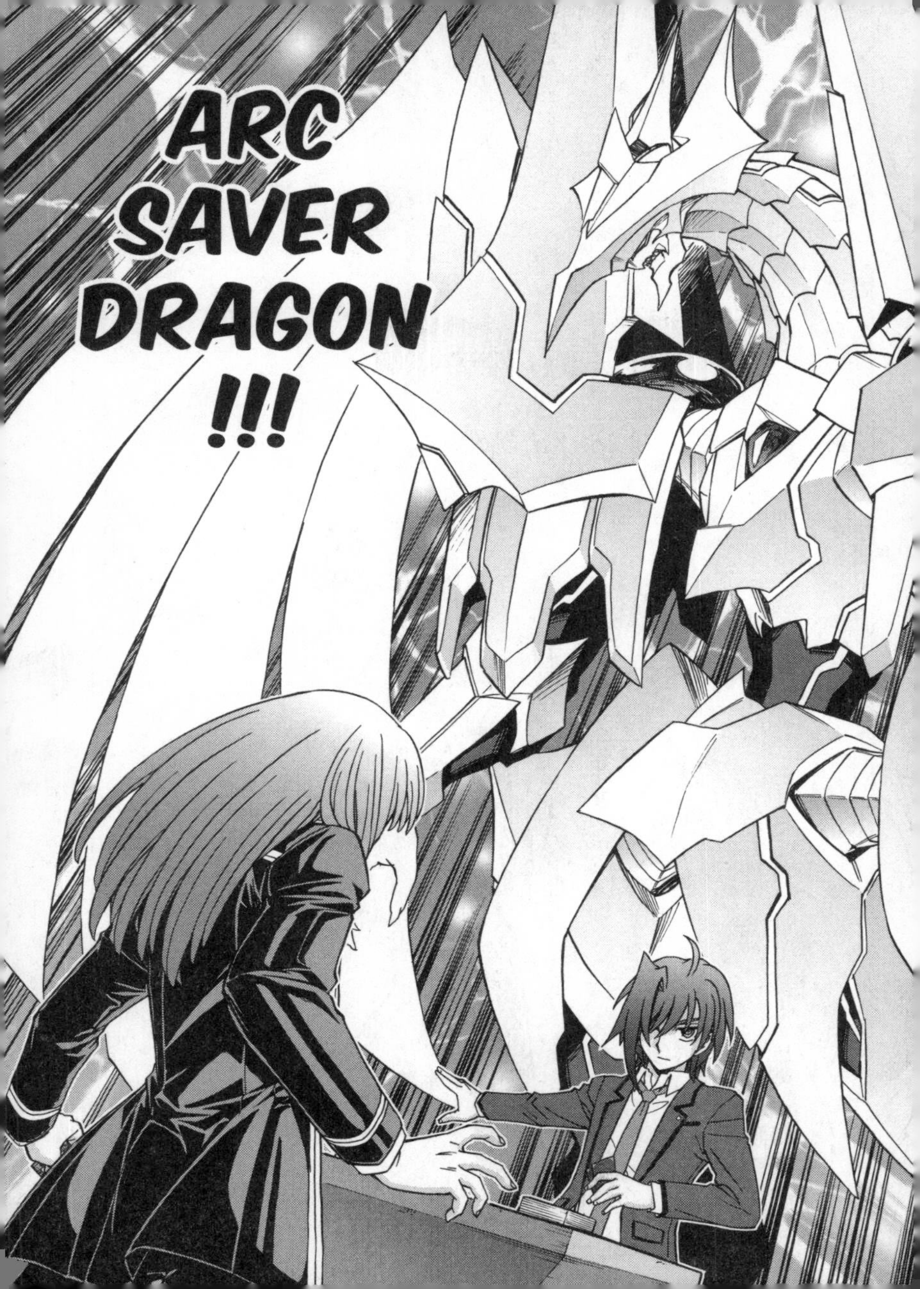
ARC SAVER DRAGON !!!

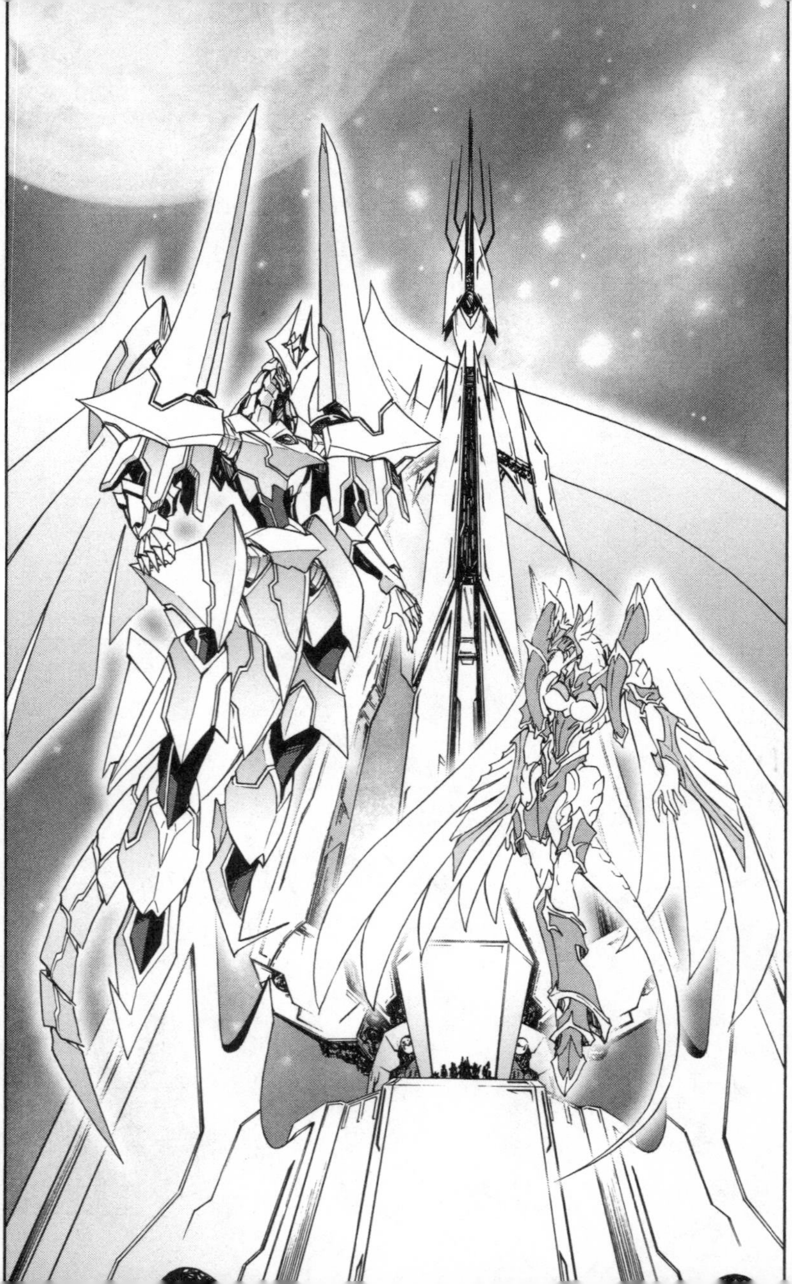

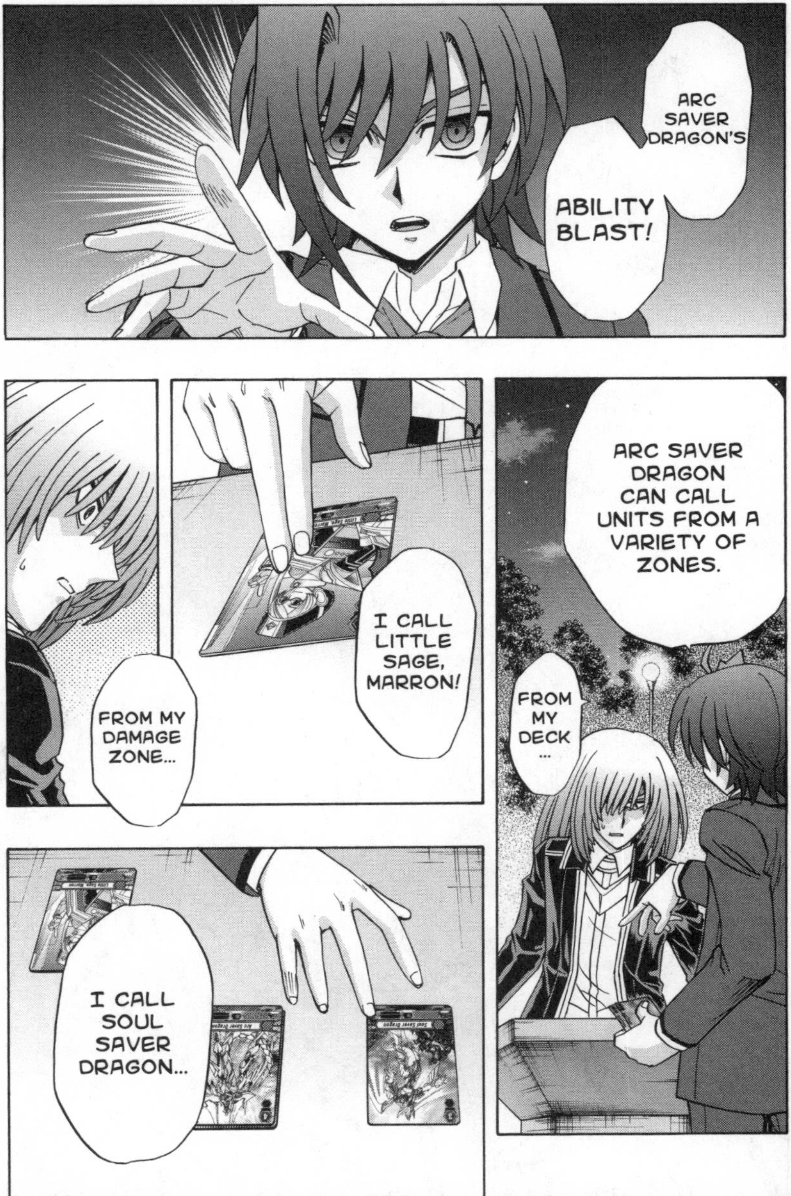
ARC SAVER DRAGON'S
ABILITY BLAST!
ARC SAVER DRAGON CAN CALL UNITS FROM A VARIETY OF ZONES.
FROM MY DECK ...
I CALL LITTLE SAGE, MARRON!
FROM MY DAMAGE ZONE...
I CALL SOUL SAVER DRAGON...

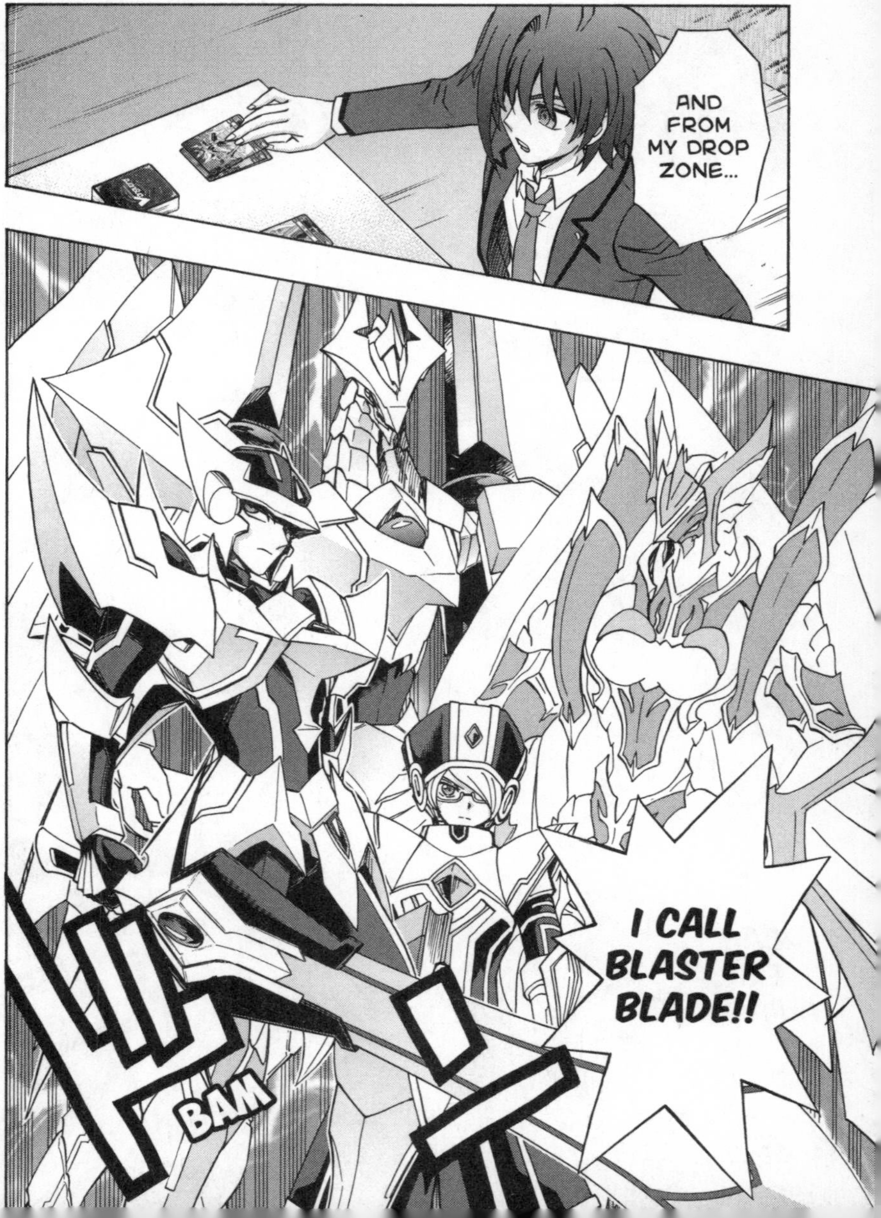
AND FROM MY DROP ZONE...
I CALL BLASTER BLADE!!
BAM

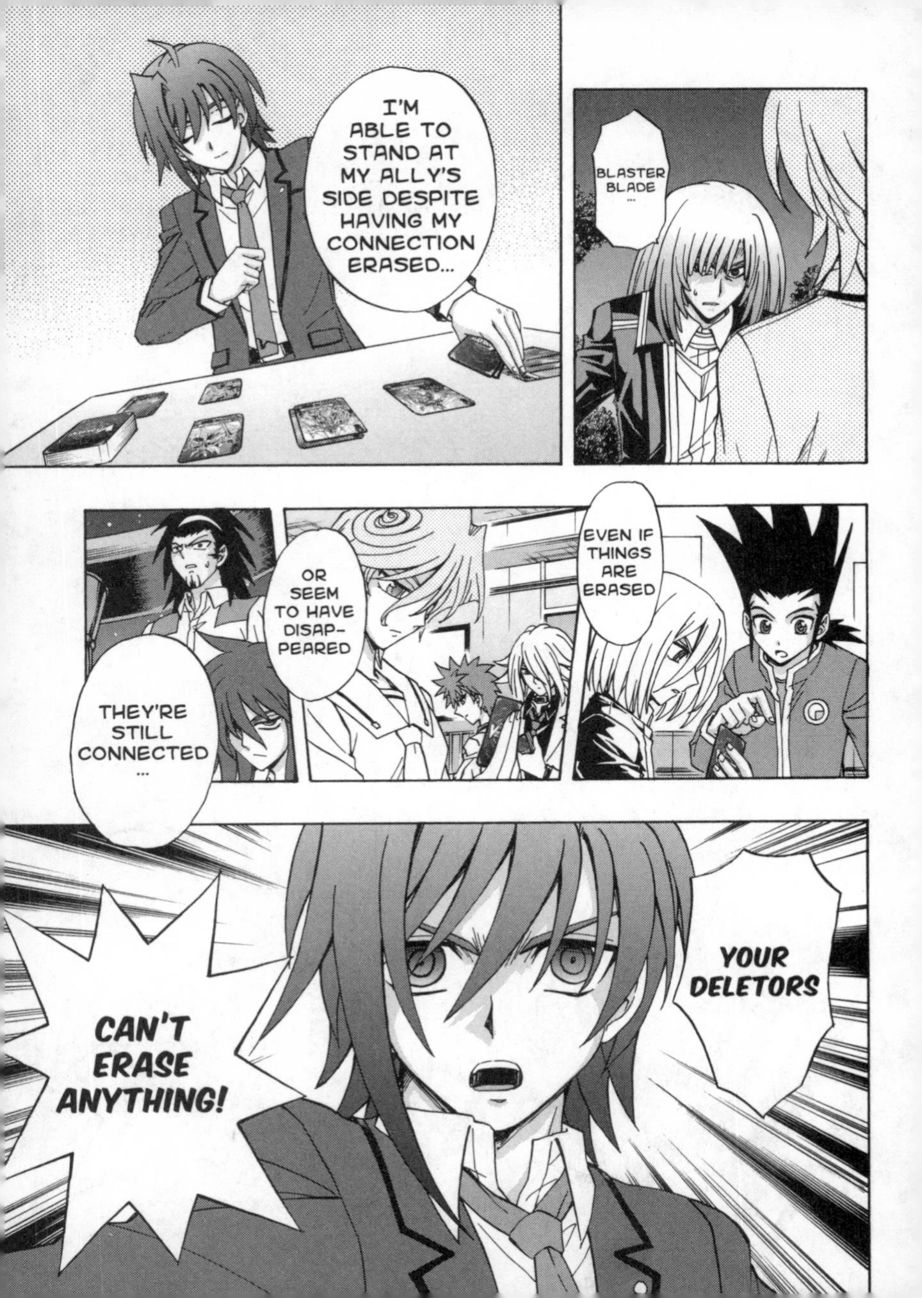
BLASTER BLADE ...
I'M ABLE TO STAND AT MY ALLY'S SIDE DESPITE HAVING MY CONNECTION ERASED...
EVEN IF THINGS ARE ERASED
OR SEEM TO HAVE DISAP-PEARED
THEY'RE STILL CONNECTED ...
YOUR DELETORS
CAN'T ERASE ANYTHING!

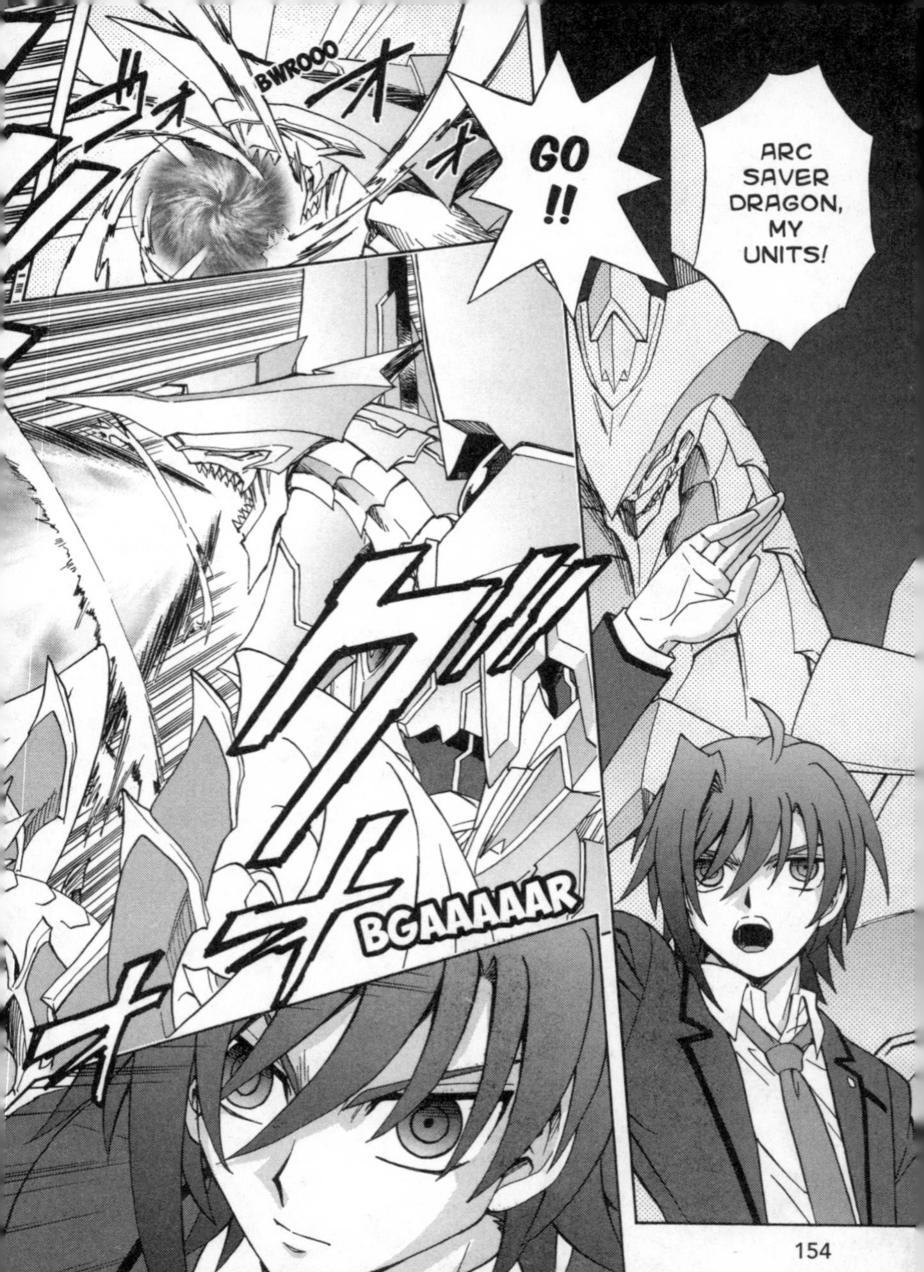
ARC SAVER DRAGON, MY UNITS!
GO !!
BWROOO
BGAAAAAR

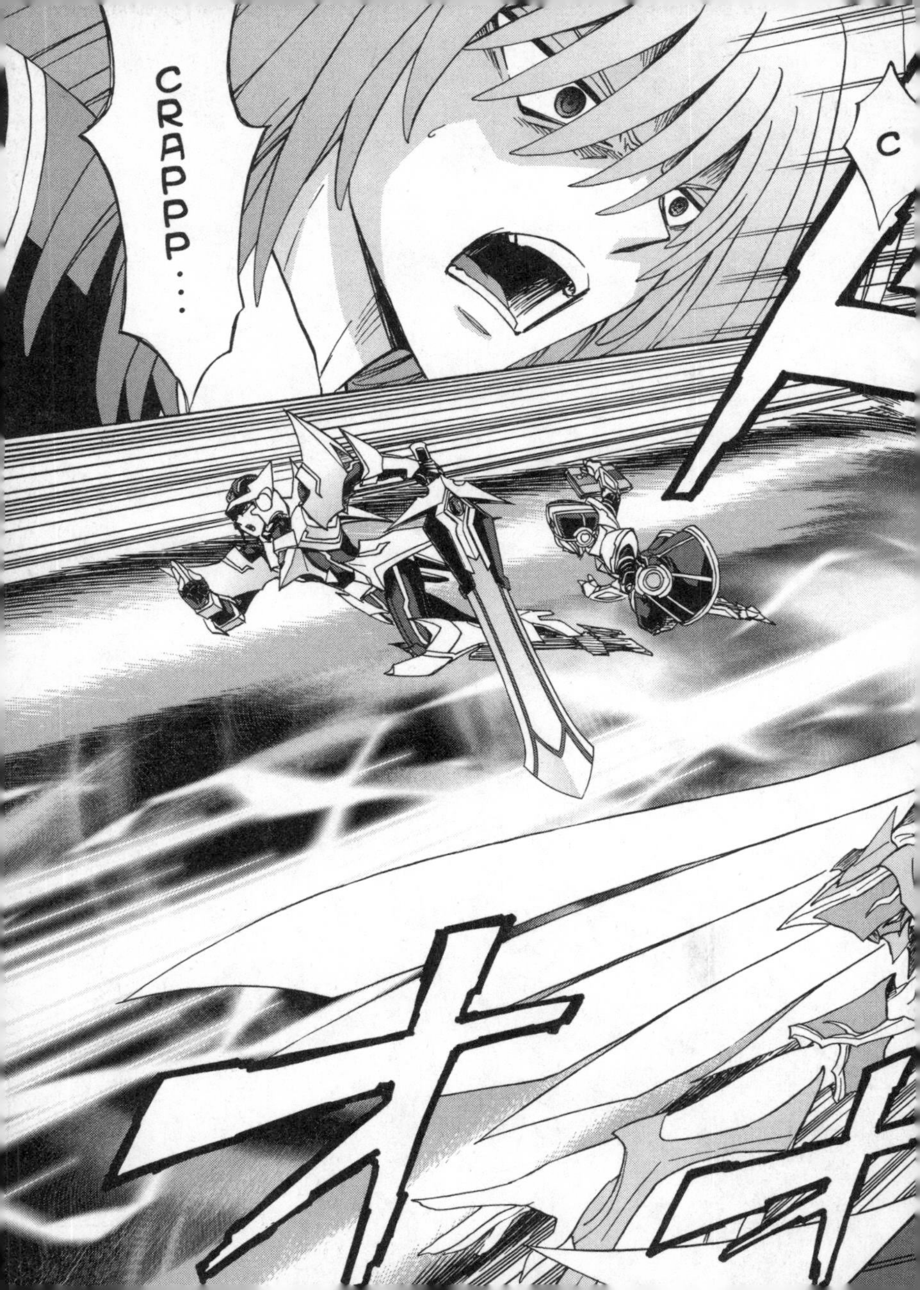
C
CRAPPP...

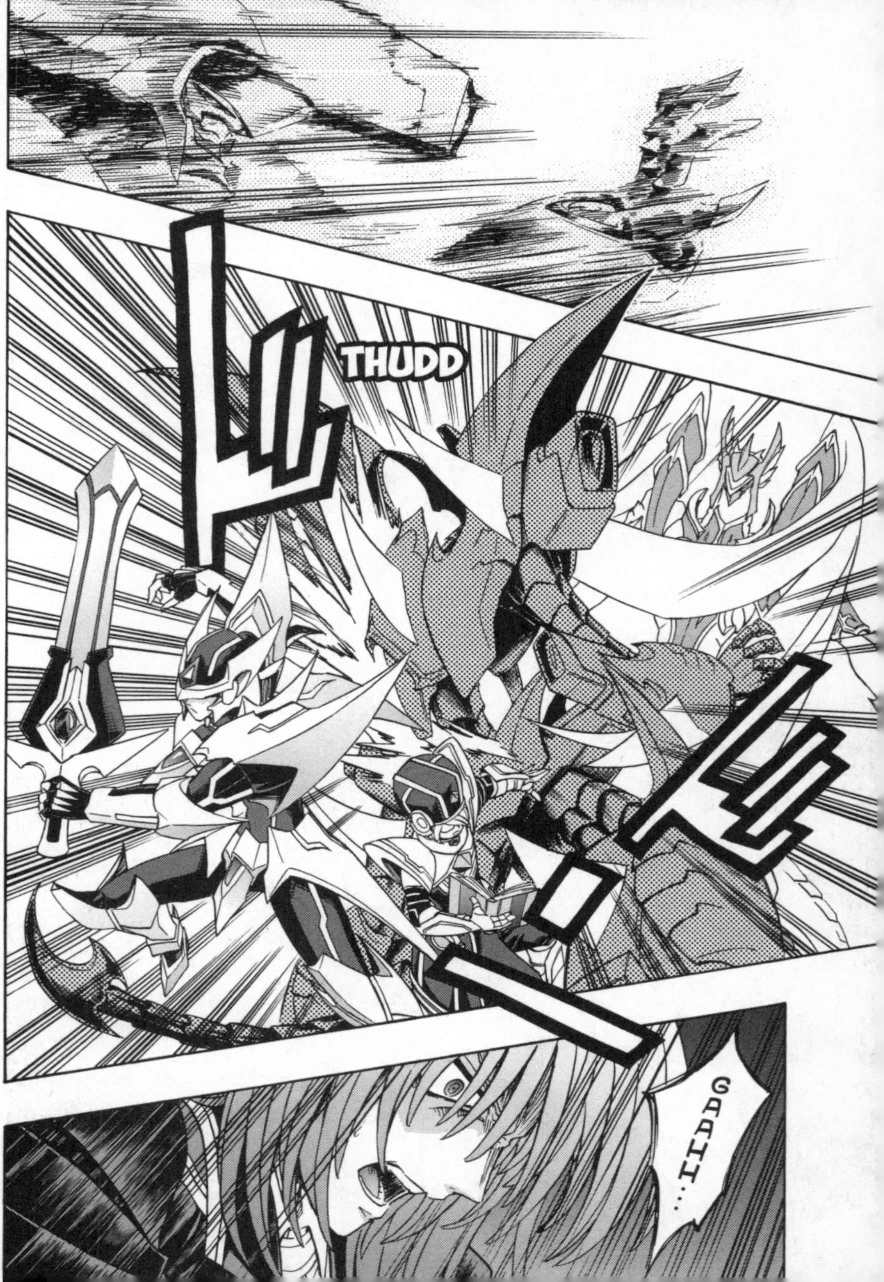
THUDD
GAAHH...

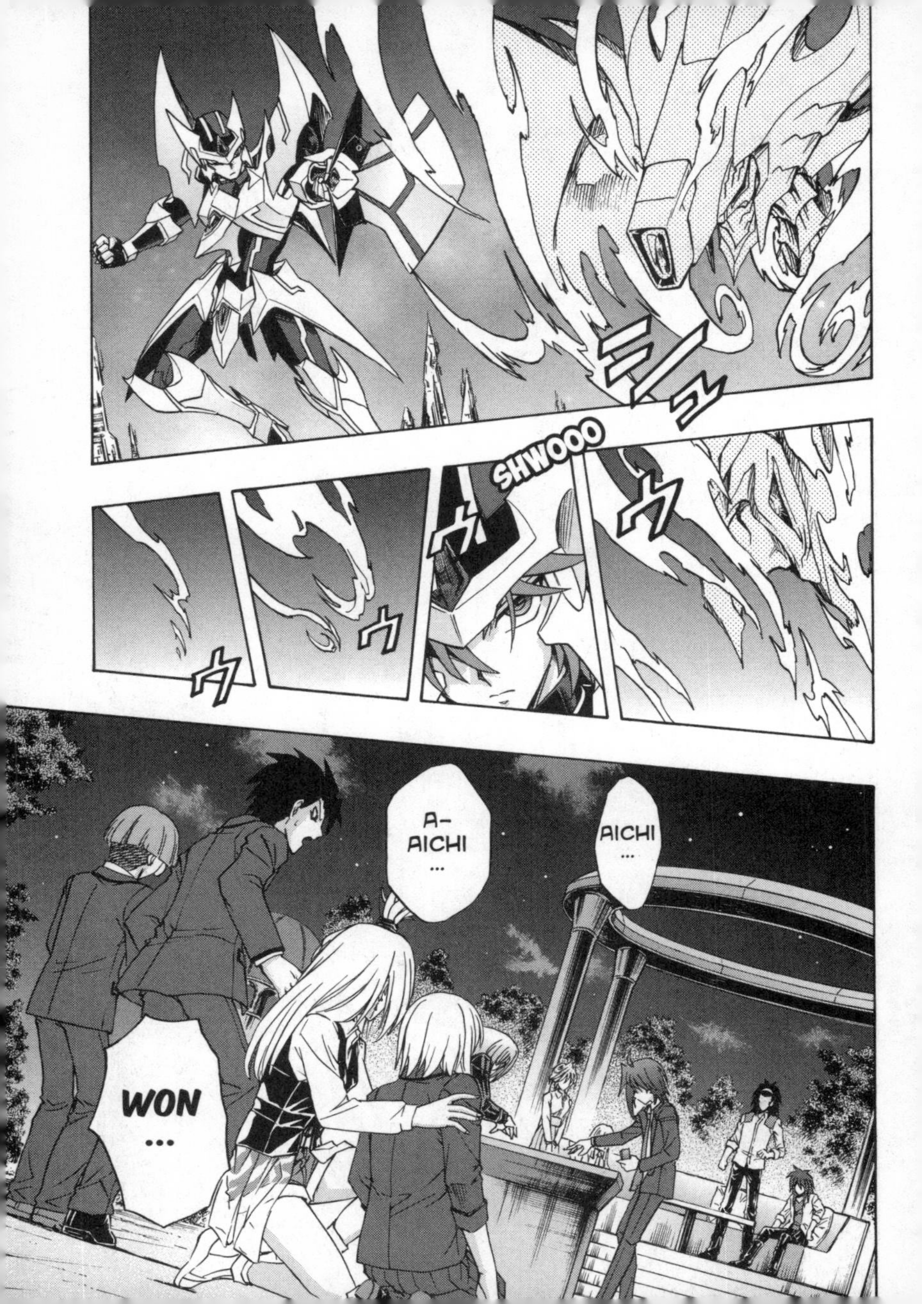
SHWOOO
AICHI ...
A- AICHI ...
WON ...

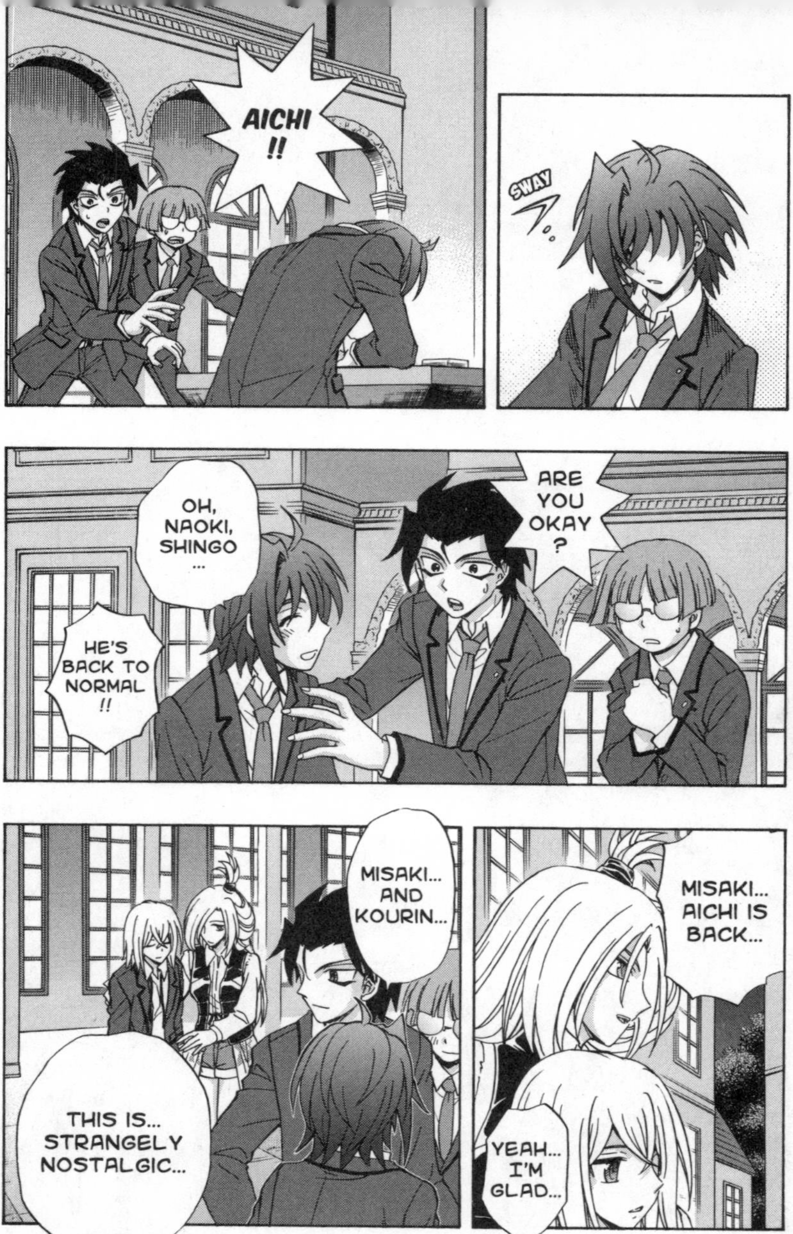
SWAY
AICHI !!
ARE YOU OKAY ?
OH, NAOKI, SHINGO ...
HE'S BACK TO NORMAL !!
MISAKI... AICHI IS BACK...
YEAH... I'M GLAD...
MISAKI... AND KOURIN...
THIS IS... STRANGELY NOSTALGIC...

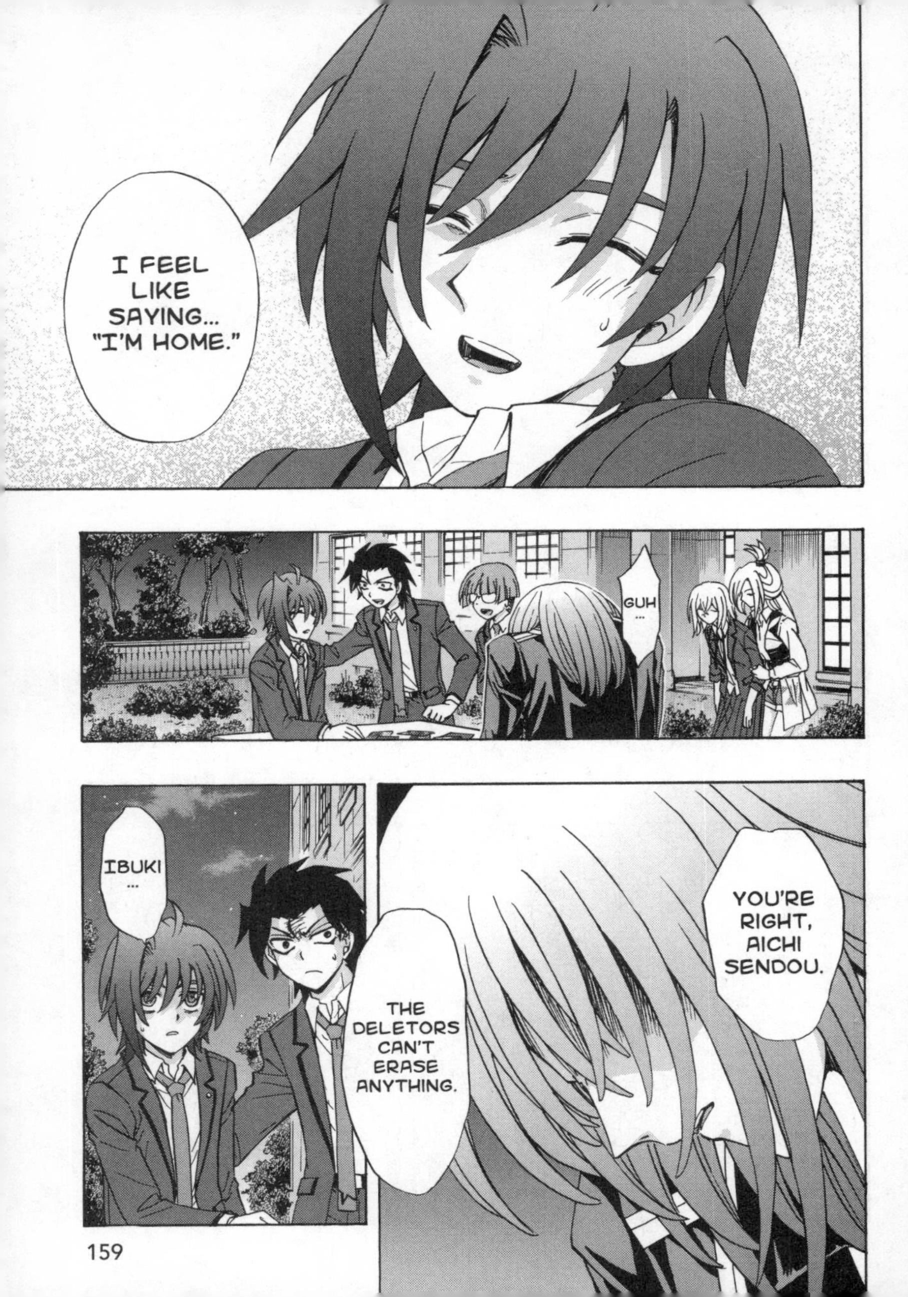
I FEEL LIKE SAYING... "I'M HOME."
GUH ...
YOU'RE RIGHT, AICHI SENDOU.
THE DELETORS CAN'T ERASE ANYTHING.
IBUKI ...

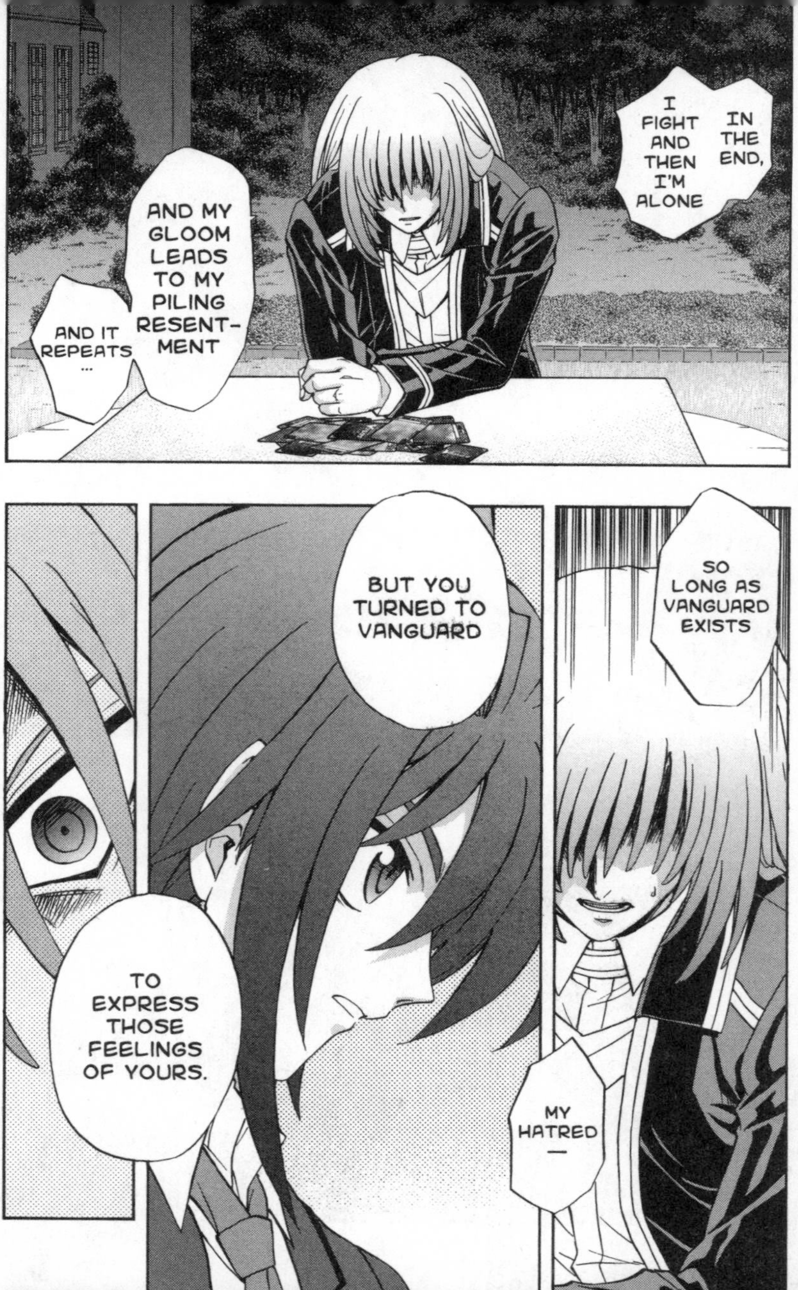
IN THE END,
I FIGHT AND THEN I'M ALONE
AND MY GLOOM LEADS TO MY PILING RESENTMENT
AND IT REPEATS ...
SO LONG AS VANGUARD EXISTS
MY HATRED —
BUT YOU TURNED TO VANGUARD
TO EXPRESS THOSE FEELINGS OF YOURS.

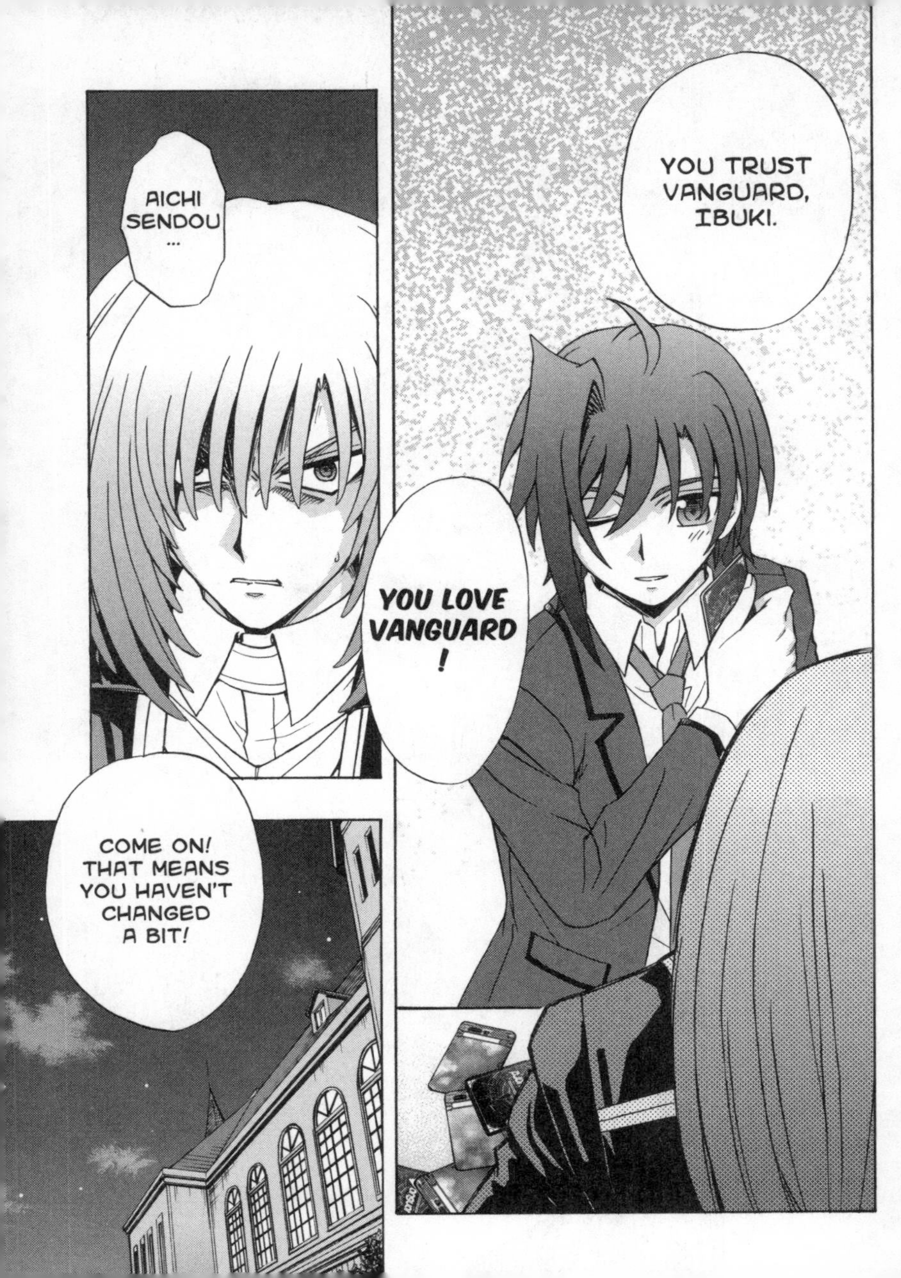
YOU TRUST VANGUARD, IBUKI.
YOU LOVE VANGUARD!
AICHI SENDOU ...
COME ON! THAT MEANS YOU HAVEN'T CHANGED A BIT!

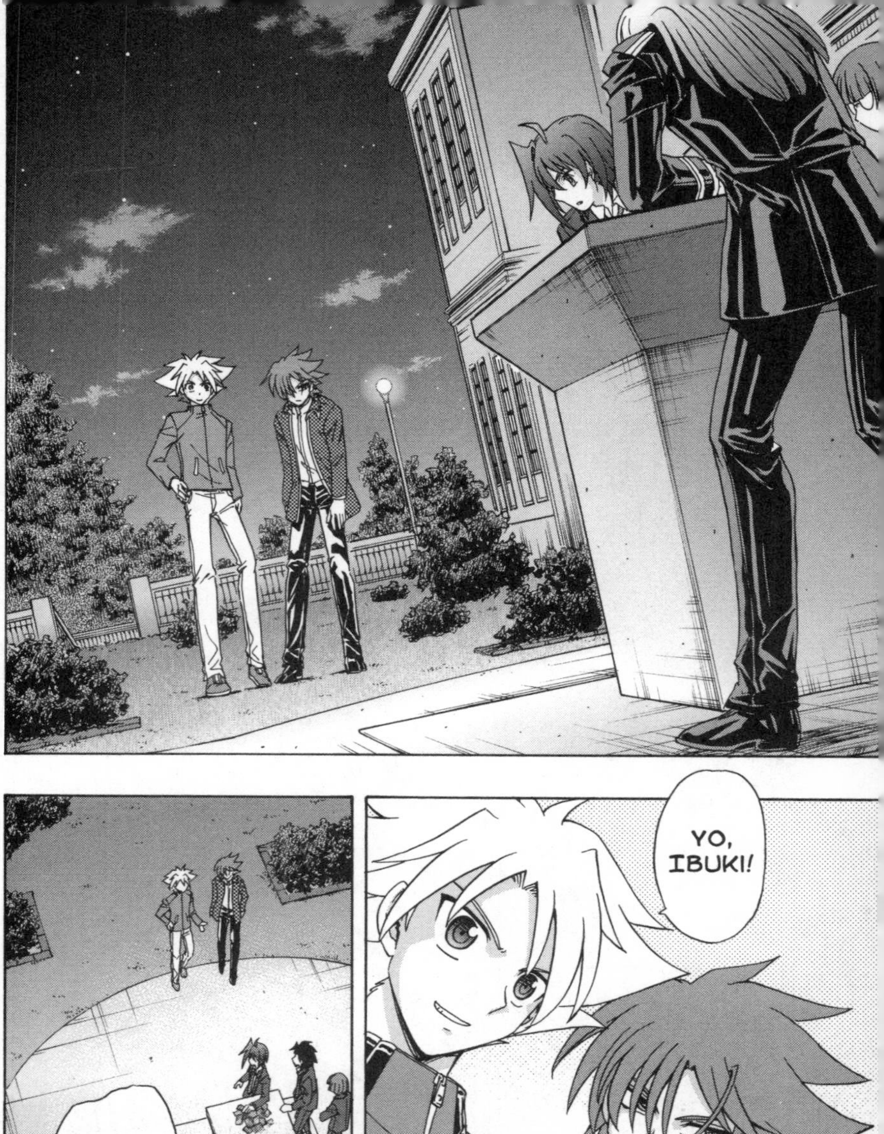
YO, IBUKI!
MIWA... KAI...

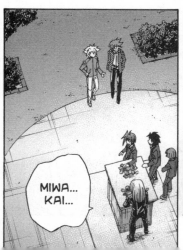

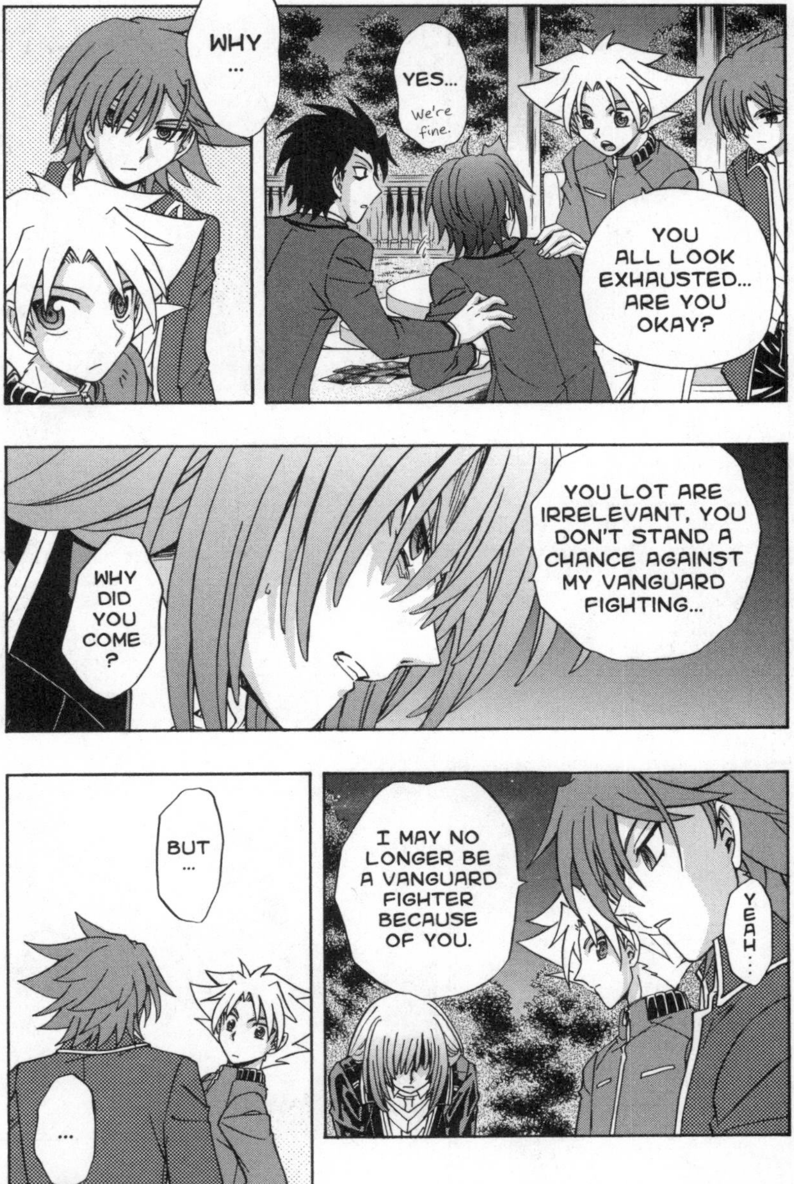
YOU ALL LOOK EXHAUSTED... ARE YOU OKAY?
YES...
We're fine.
WHY ...
YOU LOT ARE IRRELEVANT, YOU DON'T STAND A CHANCE AGAINST MY VANGUARD FIGHTING...
WHY DID YOU COME ?
YEAH...
I MAY NO LONGER BE A VANGUARD FIGHTER BECAUSE OF YOU.
BUT ...
...

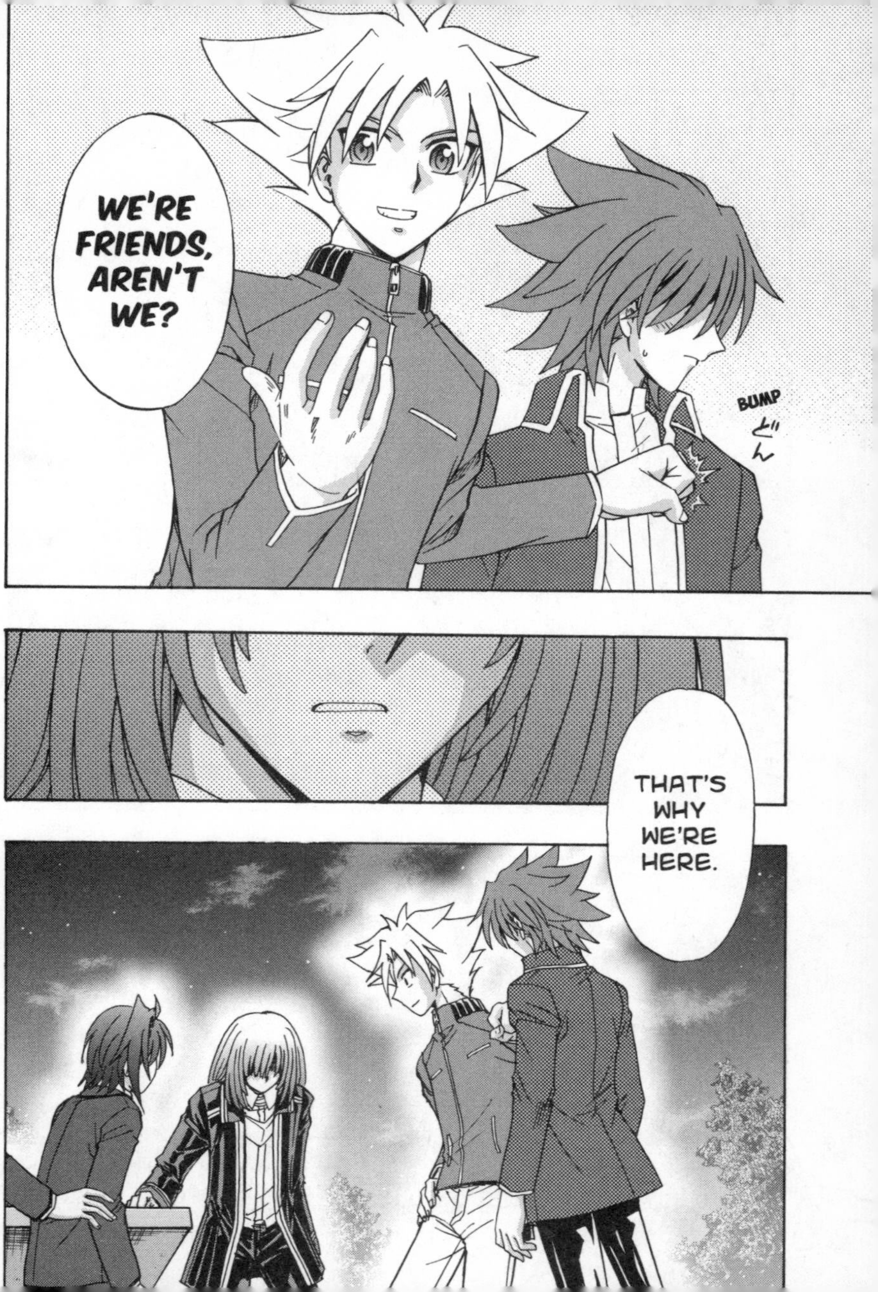
WE'RE FRIENDS, AREN'T WE?
BUMP
どん
THAT'S WHY WE'RE HERE.

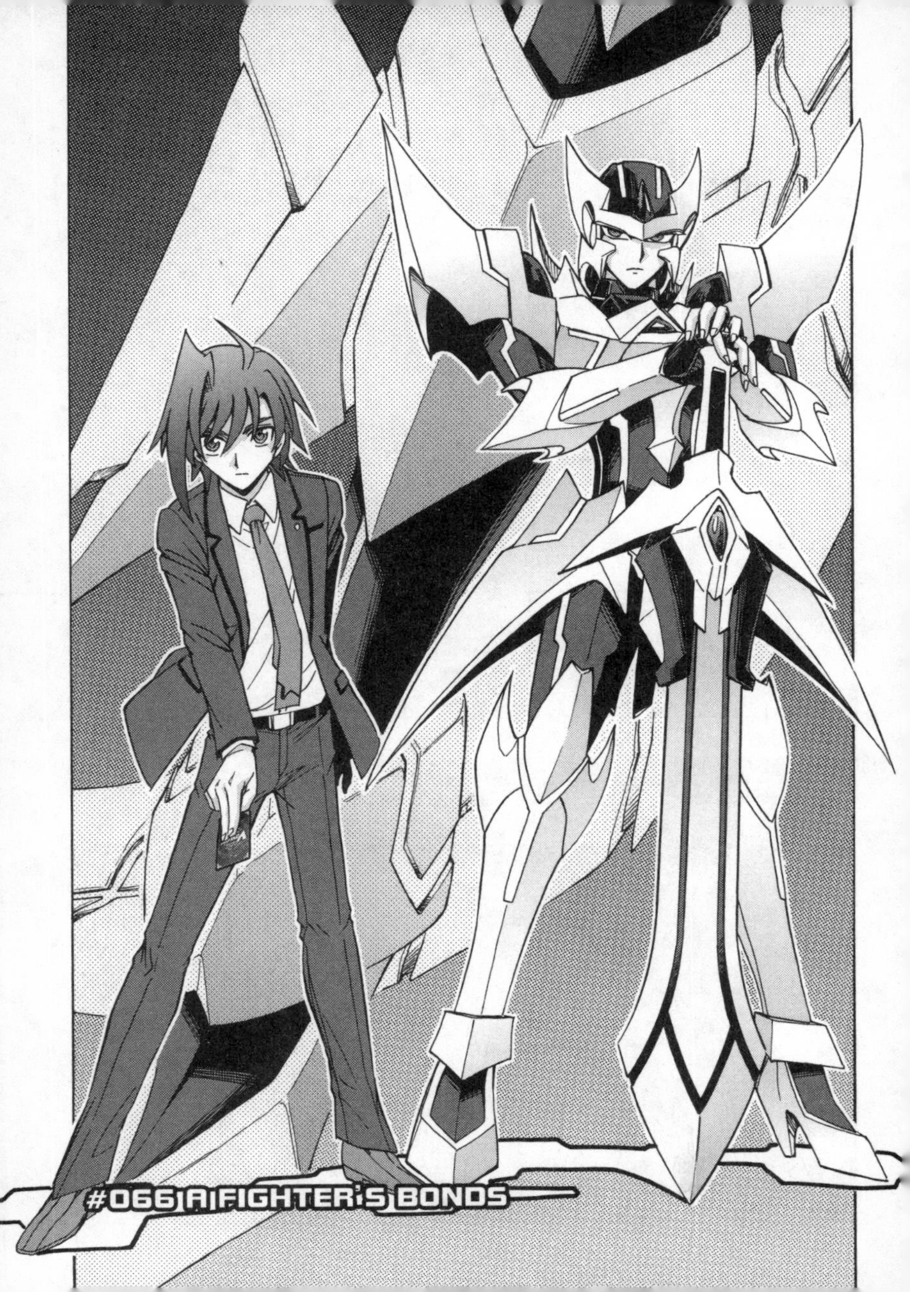
#066 A FIGHTER'S BONDS

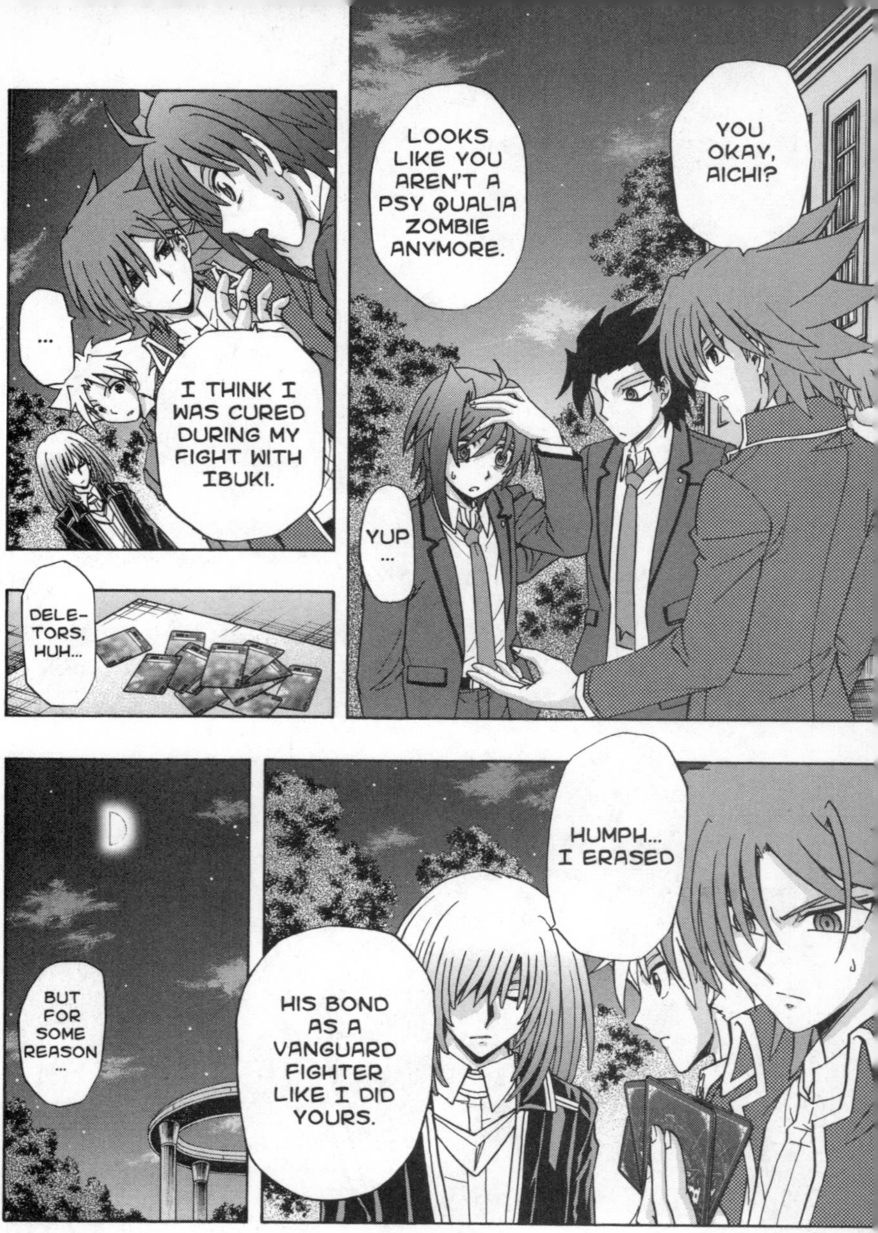
YOU OKAY, AICHI?
LOOKS LIKE YOU AREN'T A PSY QUALIA ZOMBIE ANYMORE.
YUP ...
...
I THINK I WAS CURED DURING MY FIGHT WITH IBUKI.
DELE- TORS, HUH...
HUMPH... I ERASED
HIS BOND AS A VANGUARD FIGHTER LIKE I DID YOURS.
BUT FOR SOME REASON ...

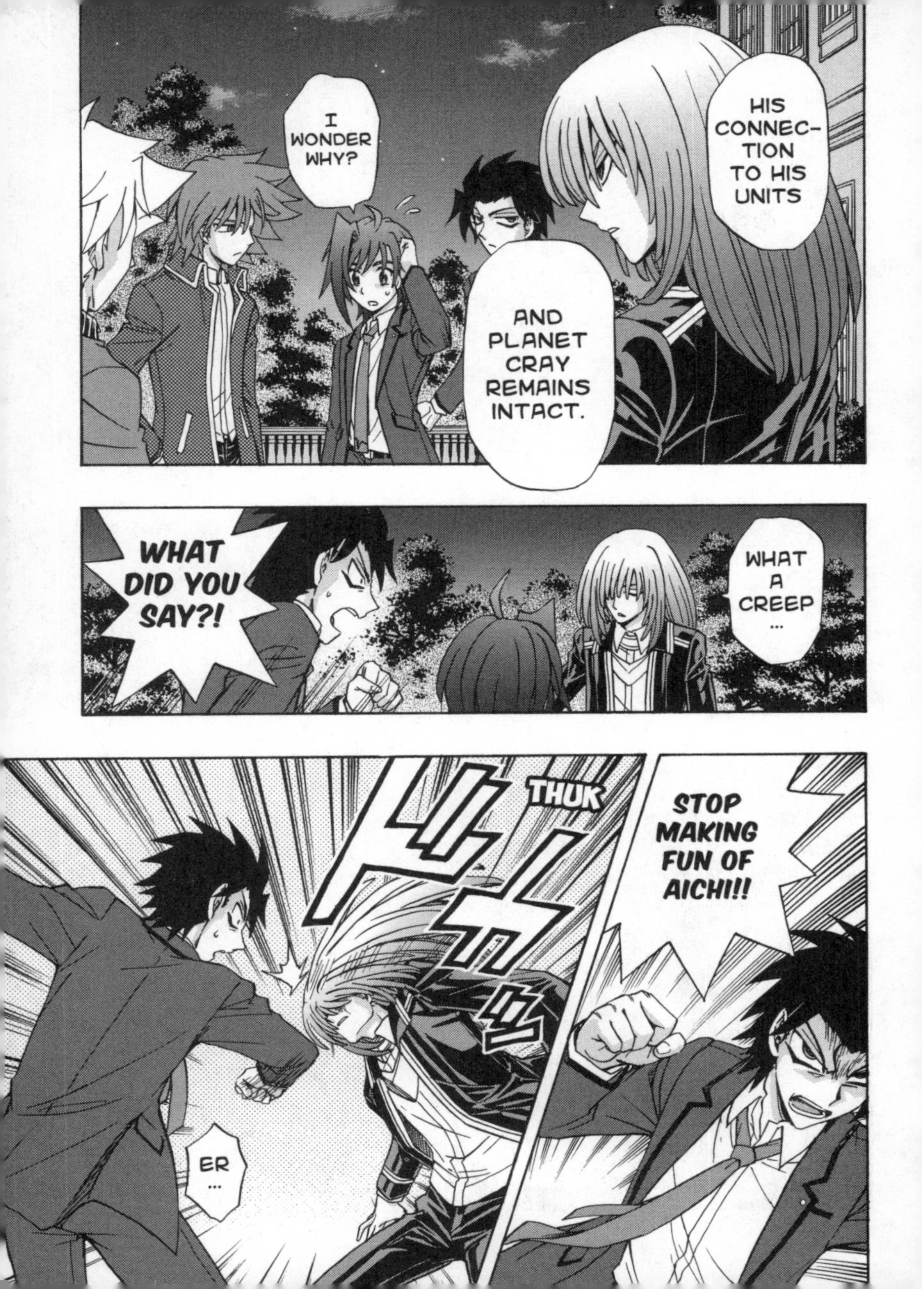
HIS CONNEC-TION TO HIS UNITS
AND PLANET CRAY REMAINS INTACT.
I WONDER WHY?
WHAT A CREEP ...
WHAT DID YOU SAY?!
STOP MAKING FUN OF AICHI!!
THUK
ER ...

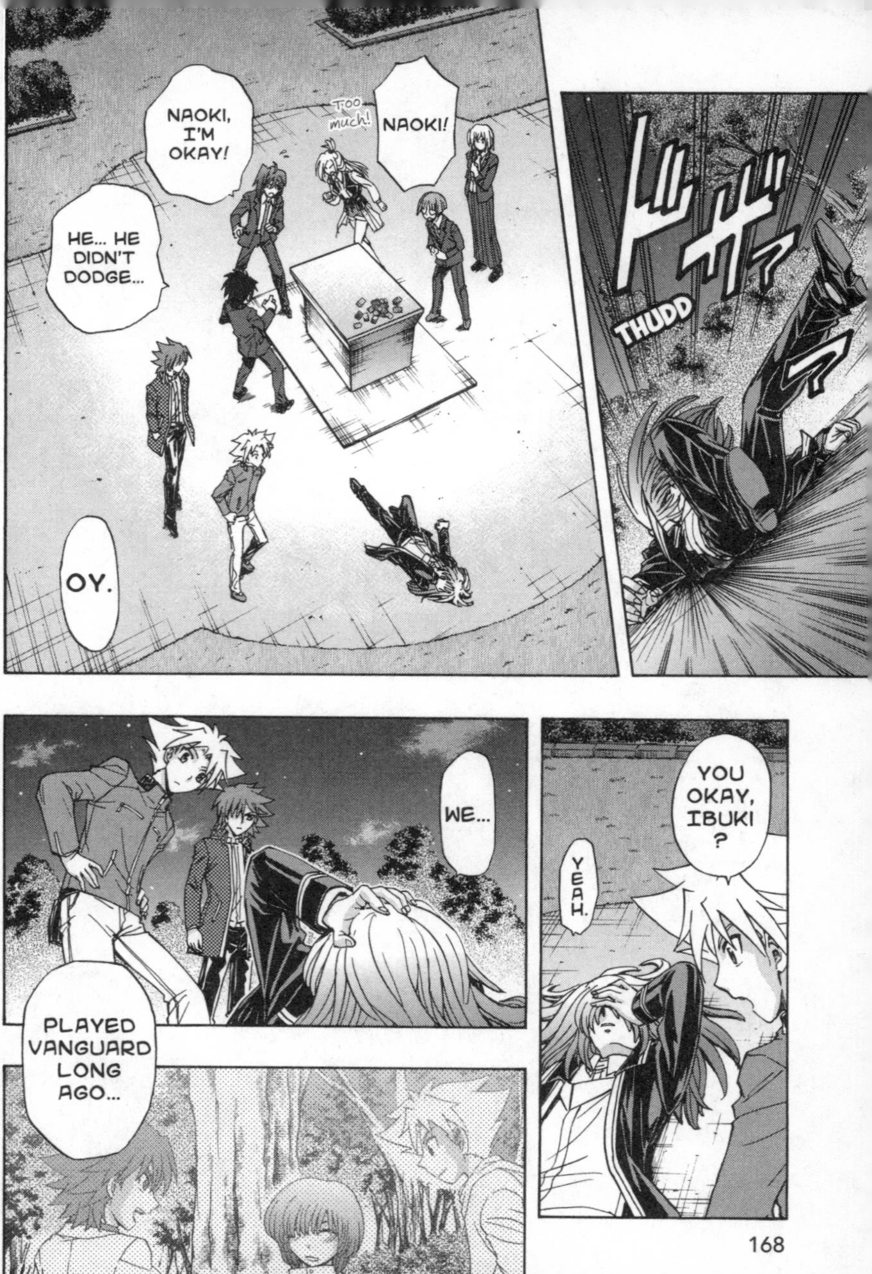
THUDD
NAOKI!
Too much!
NAOKI, I'M OKAY!
HE... HE DIDN'T DODGE...
OY.
YOU OKAY, IBUKI?
YEAH.
WE...
PLAYED VANGUARD LONG AGO...

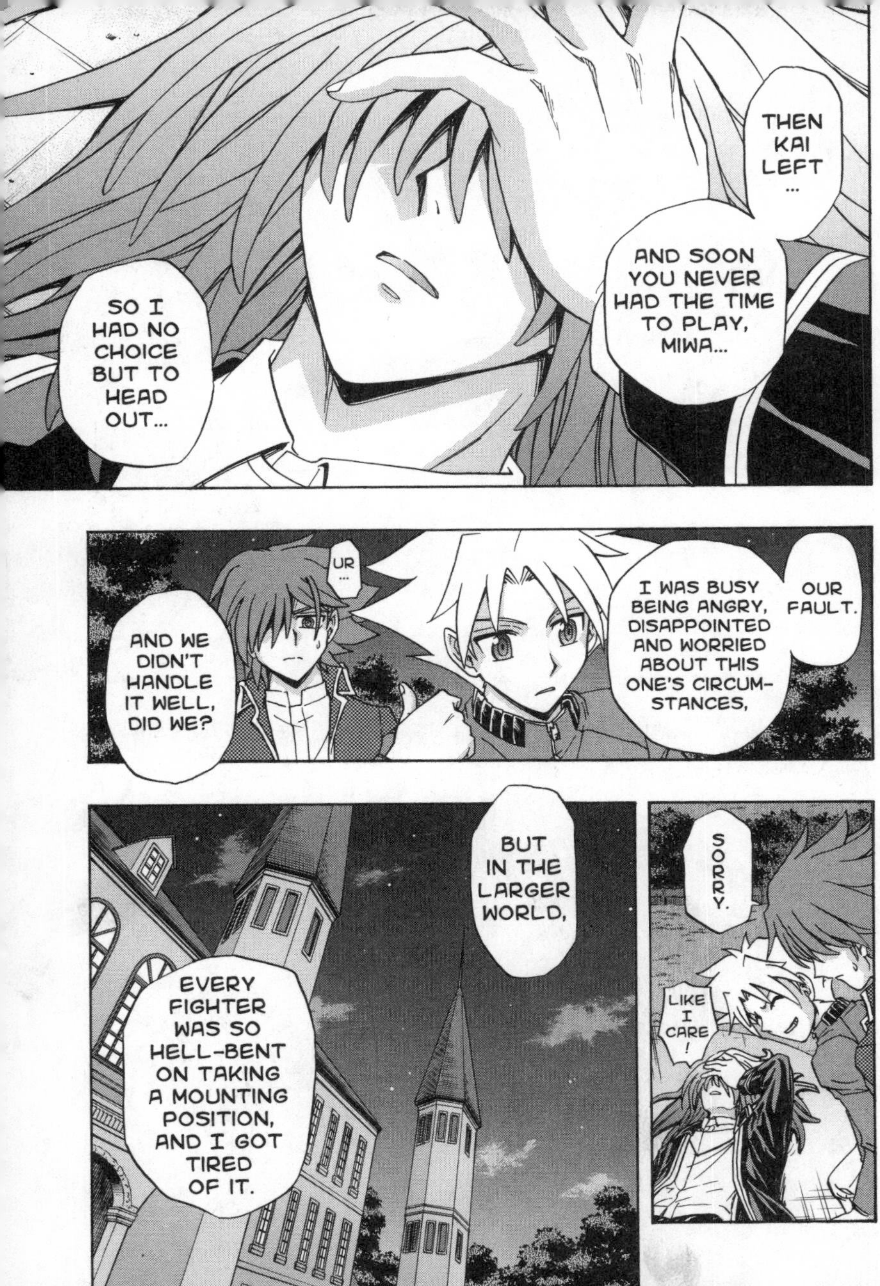
THEN KAI LEFT ...
AND SOON YOU NEVER HAD THE TIME TO PLAY, MIWA...
SO I HAD NO CHOICE BUT TO HEAD OUT...
OUR FAULT.
I WAS BUSY BEING ANGRY, DISAPPOINTED AND WORRIED ABOUT THIS ONE'S CIRCUM-STANCES,
UR ...
AND WE DIDN'T HANDLE IT WELL, DID WE?
SORRY.
LIKE I CARE!
BUT IN THE LARGER WORLD,
EVERY FIGHTER WAS SO HELL-BENT ON TAKING A MOUNTING POSITION, AND I GOT TIRED OF IT.

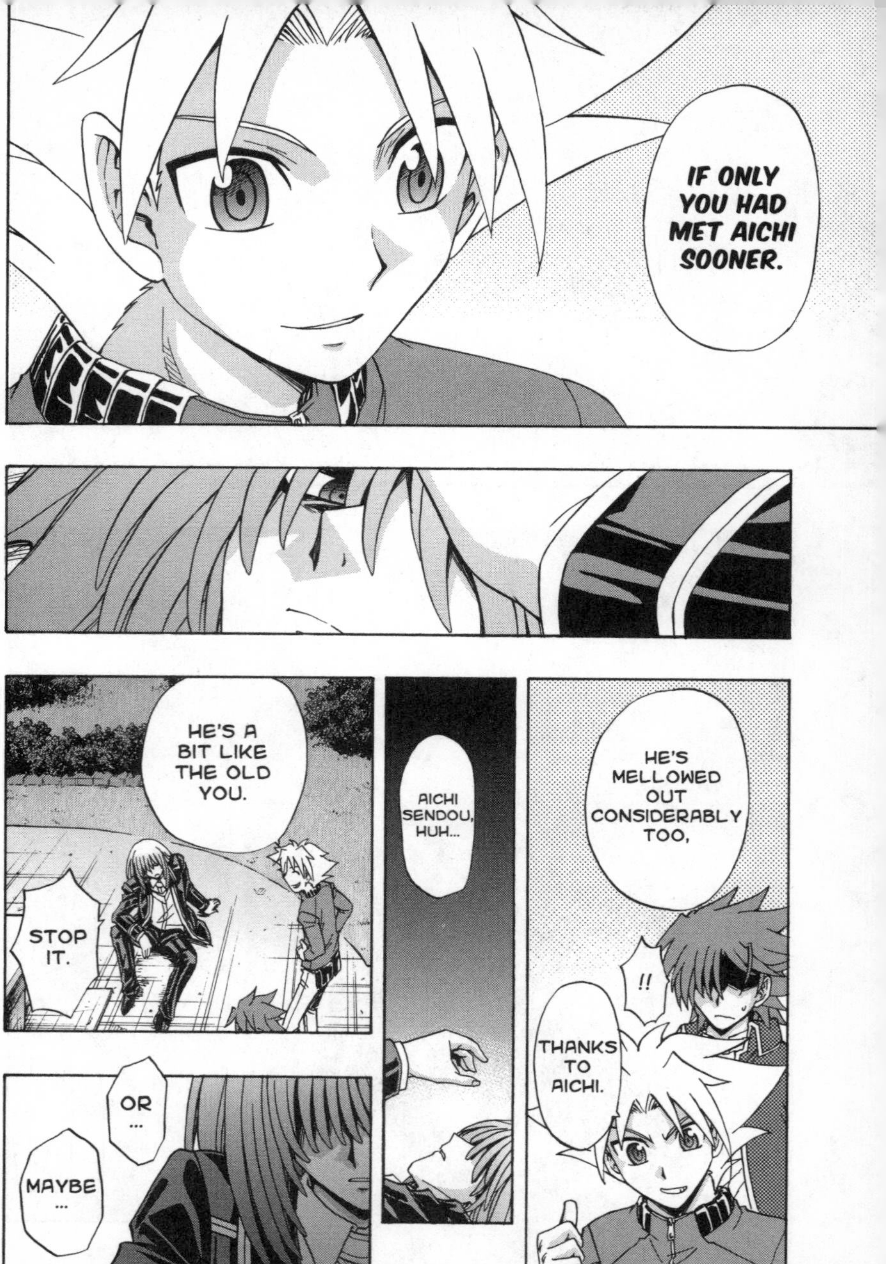
IF ONLY YOU HAD MET AICHI SOONER.
HE'S MELLOWED OUT CONSIDERABLY TOO,
!!
THANKS TO AICHI.
AICHI SENDOU, HUH...
HE'S A BIT LIKE THE OLD YOU.
STOP IT.
OR ...
MAYBE ...

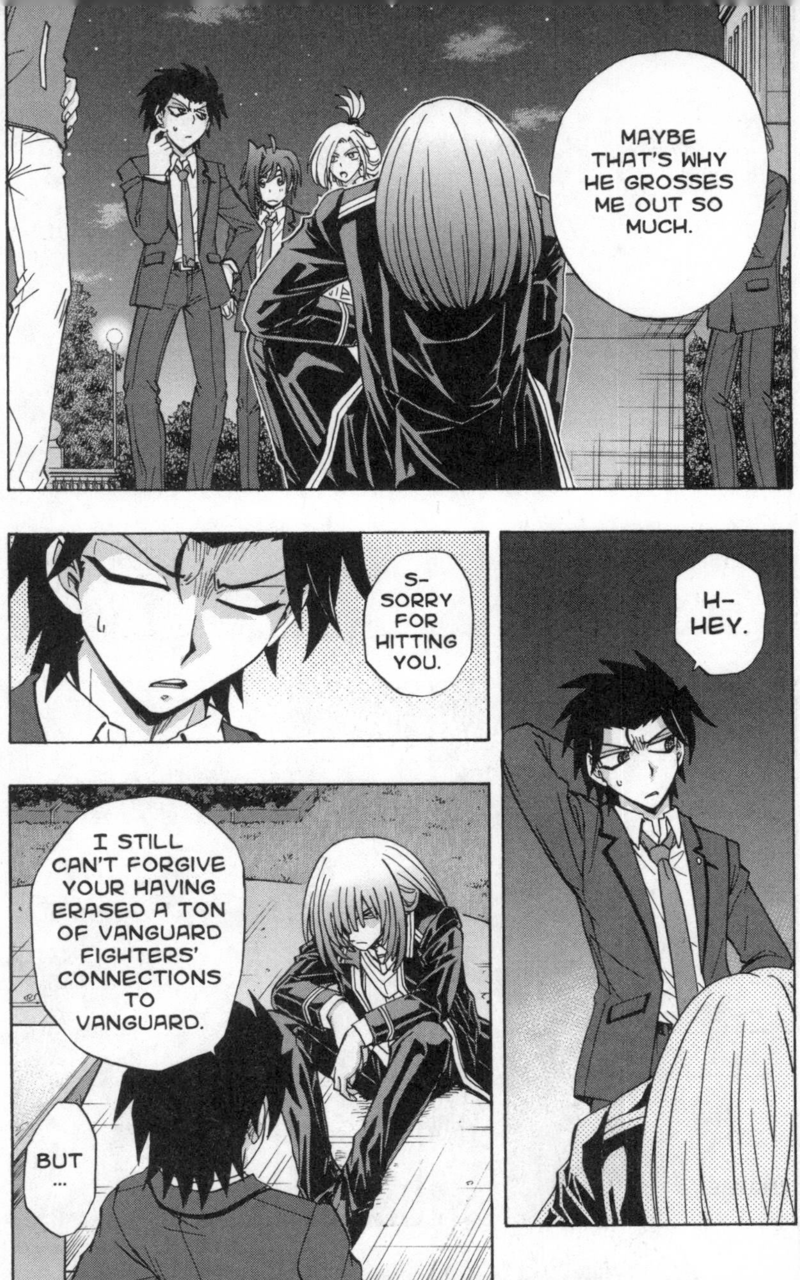
MAYBE THAT'S WHY HE GROSSES ME OUT SO MUCH.
H- HEY.
S- SORRY FOR HITTING YOU.
I STILL CAN'T FORGIVE YOUR HAVING ERASED A TON OF VANGUARD FIGHTERS' CONNECTIONS TO VANGUARD.
BUT ...

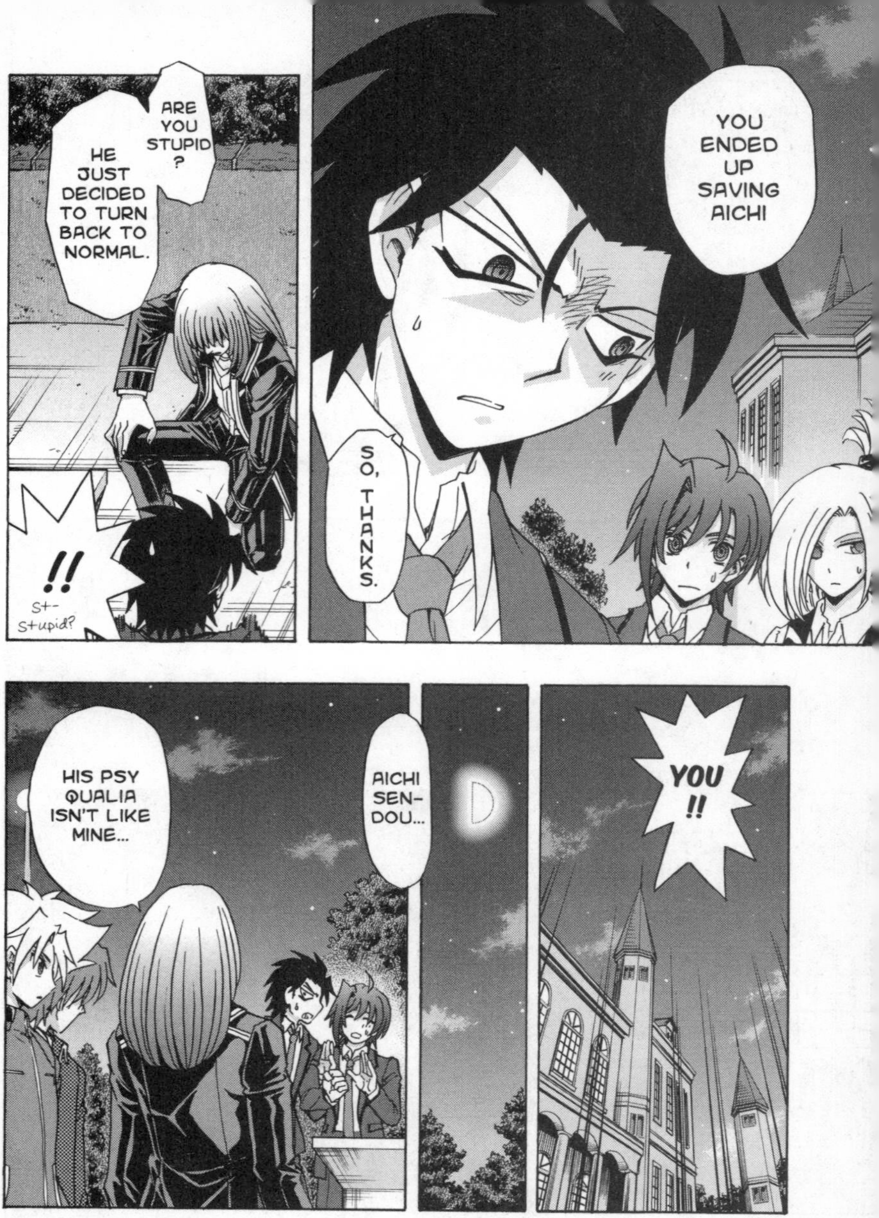
YOU ENDED UP SAVING AICHI
SO, THANKS.
ARE YOU STUPID?
HE JUST DECIDED TO TURN BACK TO NORMAL.
!!
St-stupid?
YOU !!
AICHI SEN-DOU...
HIS PSY QUALIA ISN'T LIKE MINE...

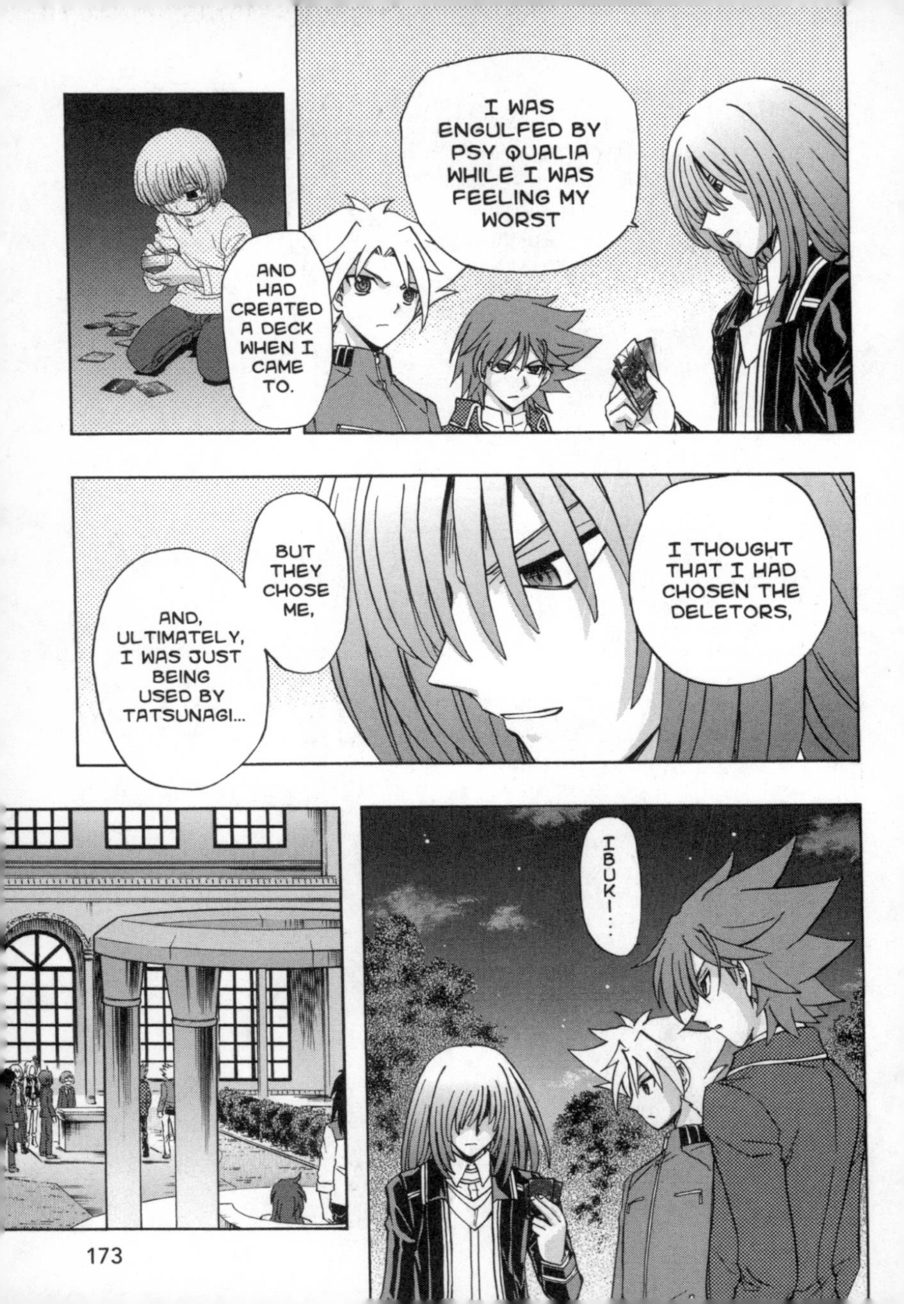
I WAS ENGULFED BY PSY QUALIA WHILE I WAS FEELING MY WORST
AND HAD CREATED A DECK WHEN I CAME TO.
I THOUGHT THAT I HAD CHOSEN THE DELETORS,
BUT THEY CHOSE ME,
AND, ULTIMATELY, I WAS JUST BEING USED BY TATSUNAGI...
IBUKI...

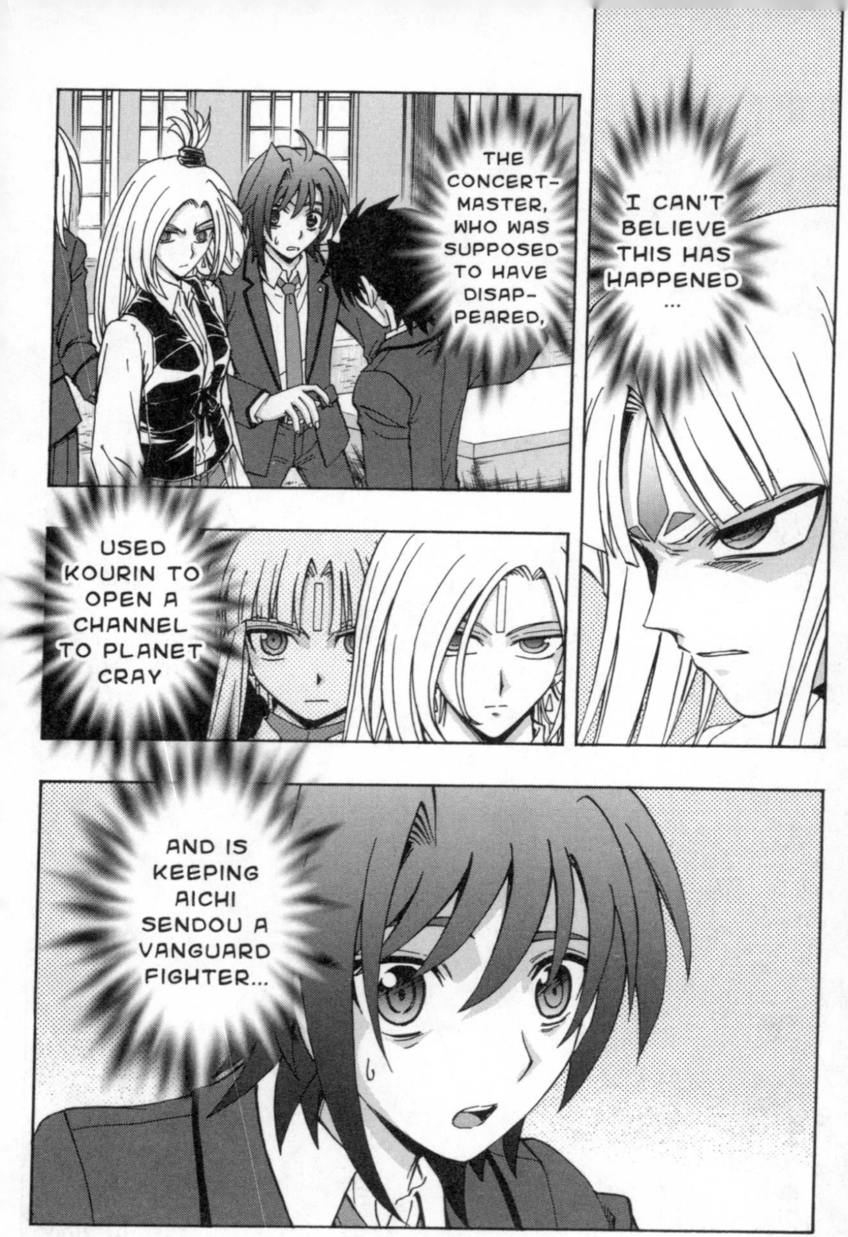
I CAN'T BELIEVE THIS HAS HAPPENED...
THE CONCERT-MASTER, WHO WAS SUPPOSED TO HAVE DISAP-PEARED,
USED KOURIN TO OPEN A CHANNEL TO PLANET CRAY
AND IS KEEPING AICHI SENDOU A VANGUARD FIGHTER...

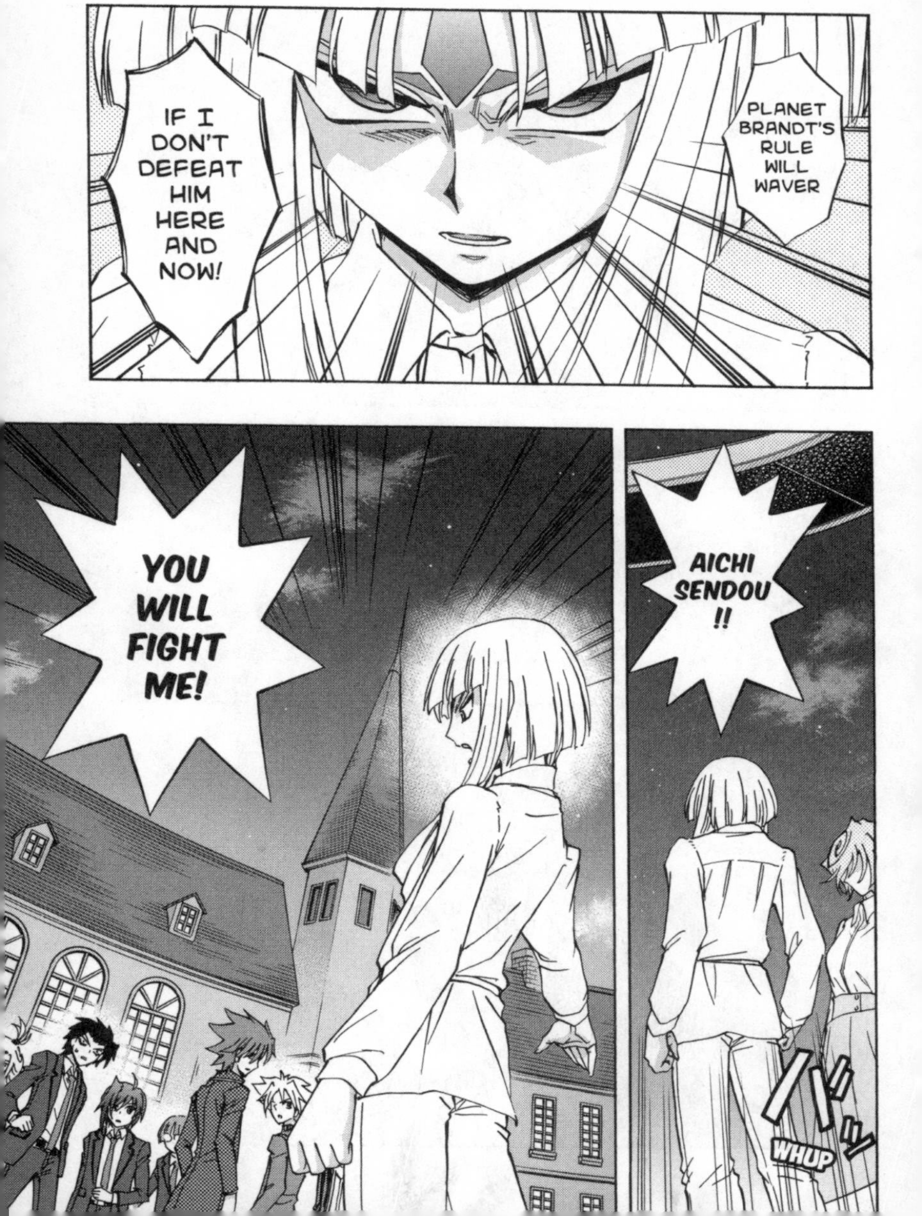
PLANET BRANDT'S RULE WILL WAVER
IF I DON'T DEFEAT HIM HERE AND NOW!
AICHI SENDOU !!
WHUP
YOU WILL FIGHT ME!

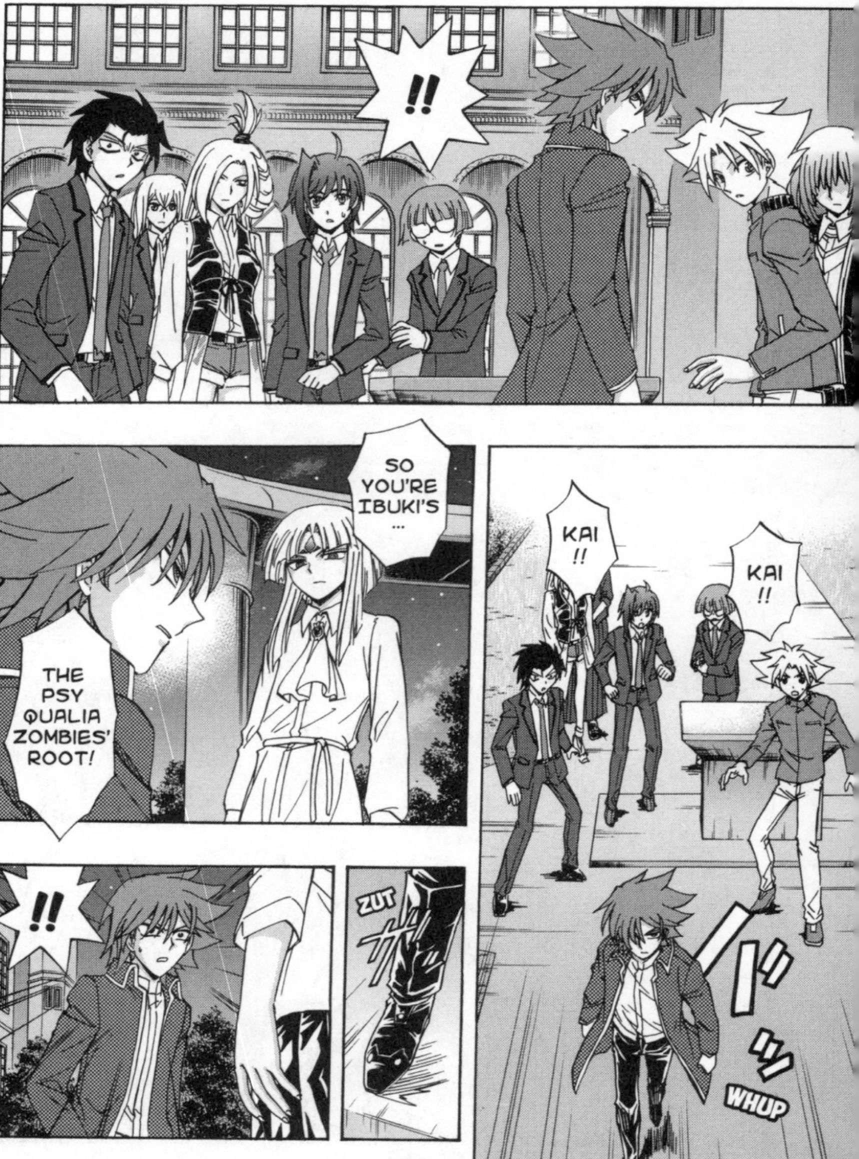
!!
KAI !!
KAI !!
WHUP
SO YOU'RE IBUKI'S ...
THE PSY QUALIA ZOMBIES' ROOT!
ZUT
!!

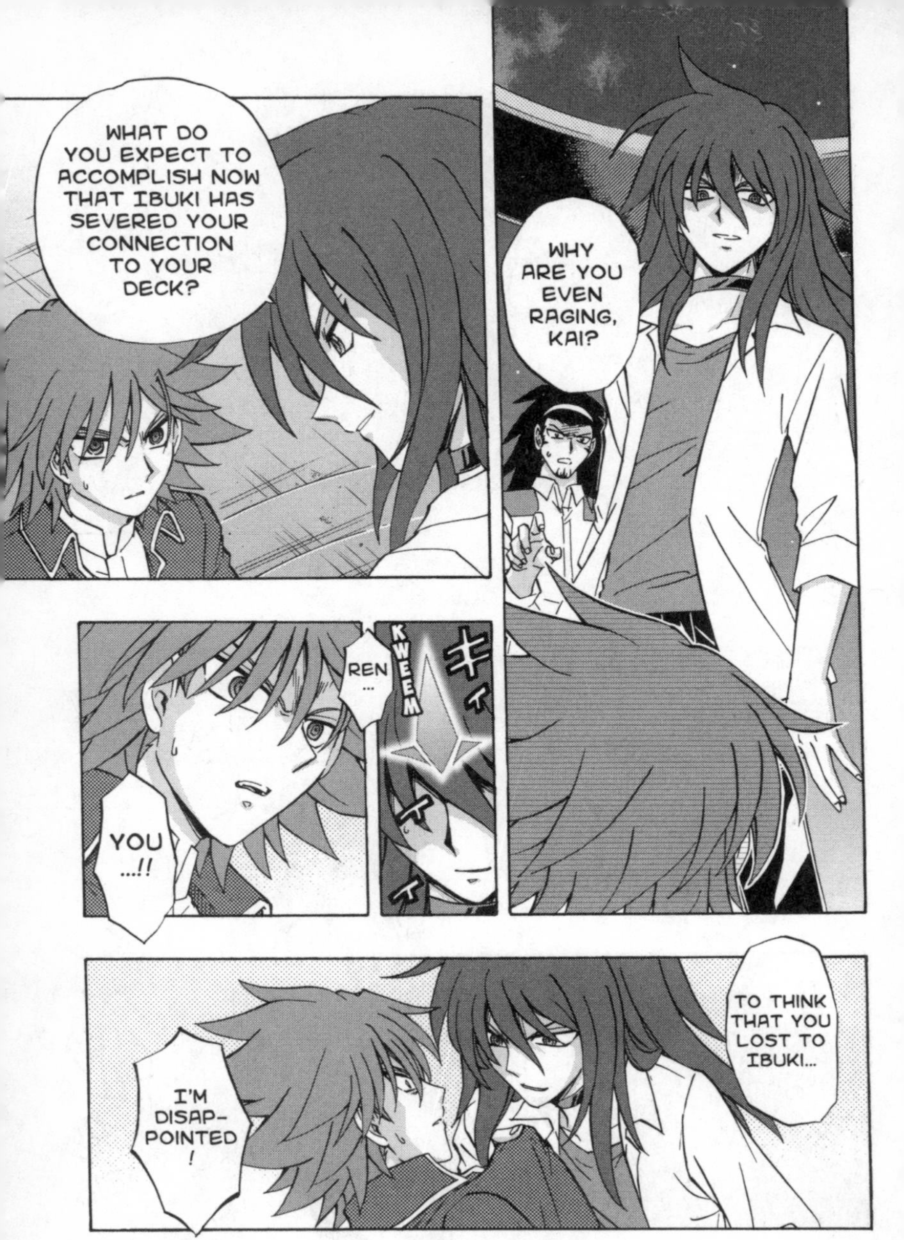
WHY ARE YOU EVEN RAGING, KAI?
WHAT DO YOU EXPECT TO ACCOMPLISH NOW THAT IBUKI HAS SEVERED YOUR CONNECTION TO YOUR DECK?
KWEEM
REN...
YOU...!!
TO THINK THAT YOU LOST TO IBUKI...
I'M DISAP-POINTED!

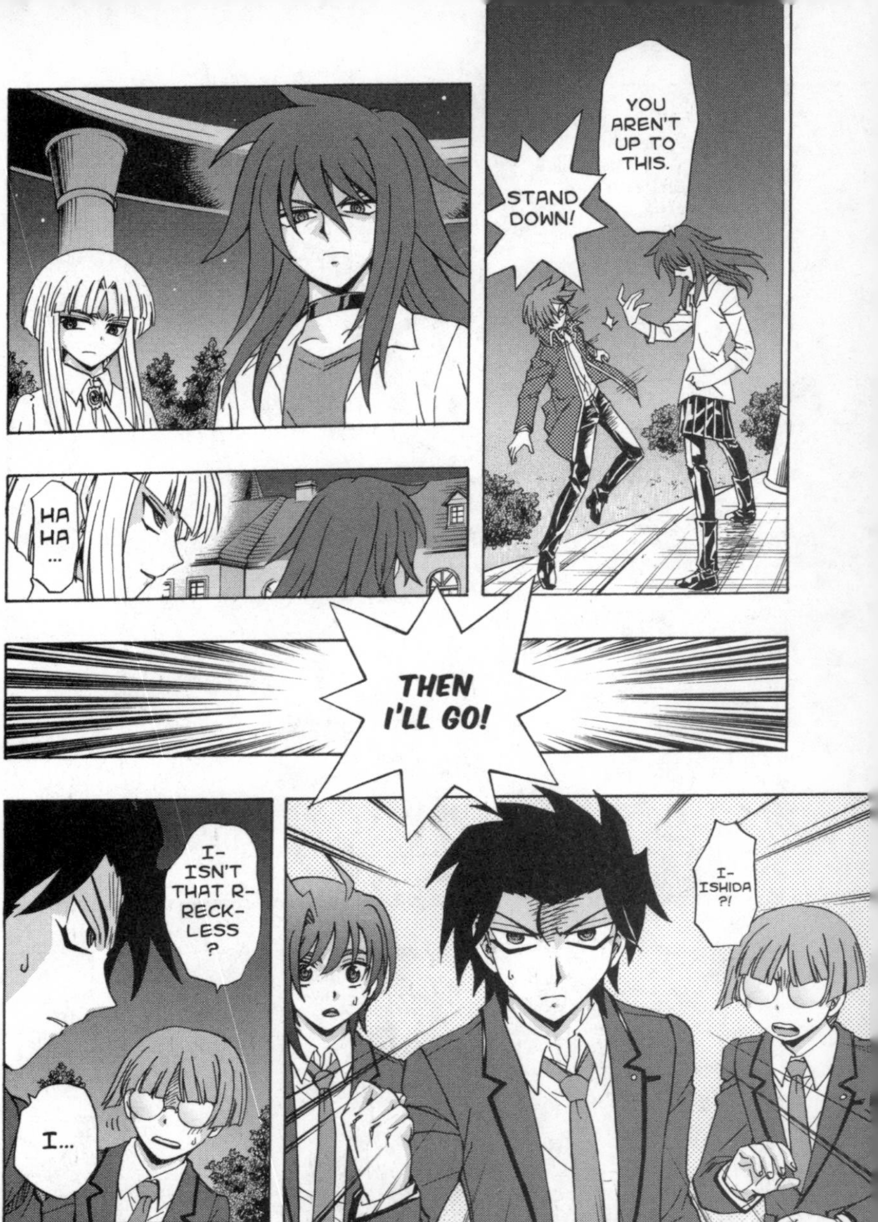
YOU AREN'T UP TO THIS.
STAND DOWN!
HA HA ...
THEN I'LL GO!
I- ISHIDA ?!
I- ISN'T THAT R- RECK- LESS ?
I...

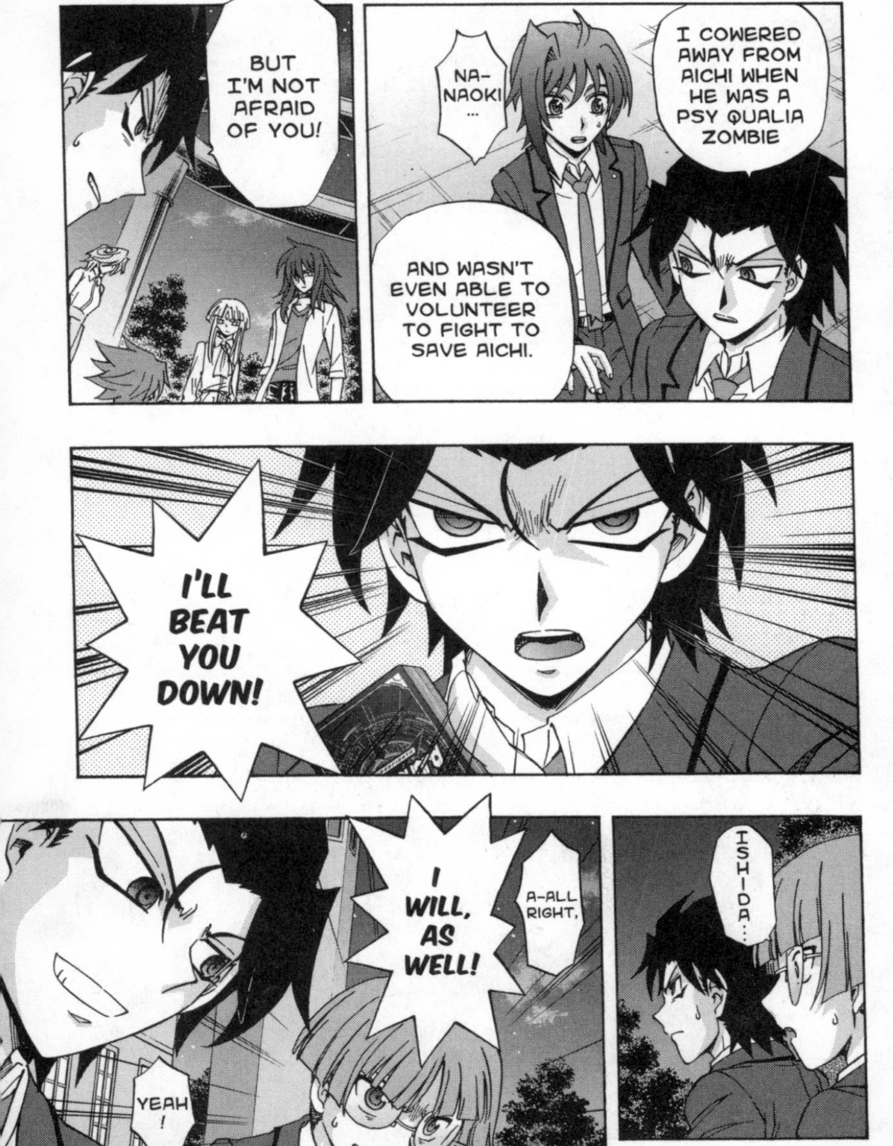
I COWERED AWAY FROM AICHI WHEN HE WAS A PSY QUALIA ZOMBIE
NA-NAOKI...
AND WASN'T EVEN ABLE TO VOLUNTEER TO FIGHT TO SAVE AICHI.
BUT I'M NOT AFRAID OF YOU!
I'LL BEAT YOU DOWN!
ISHIDA...
A-ALL RIGHT,
I WILL, AS WELL!
YEAH!

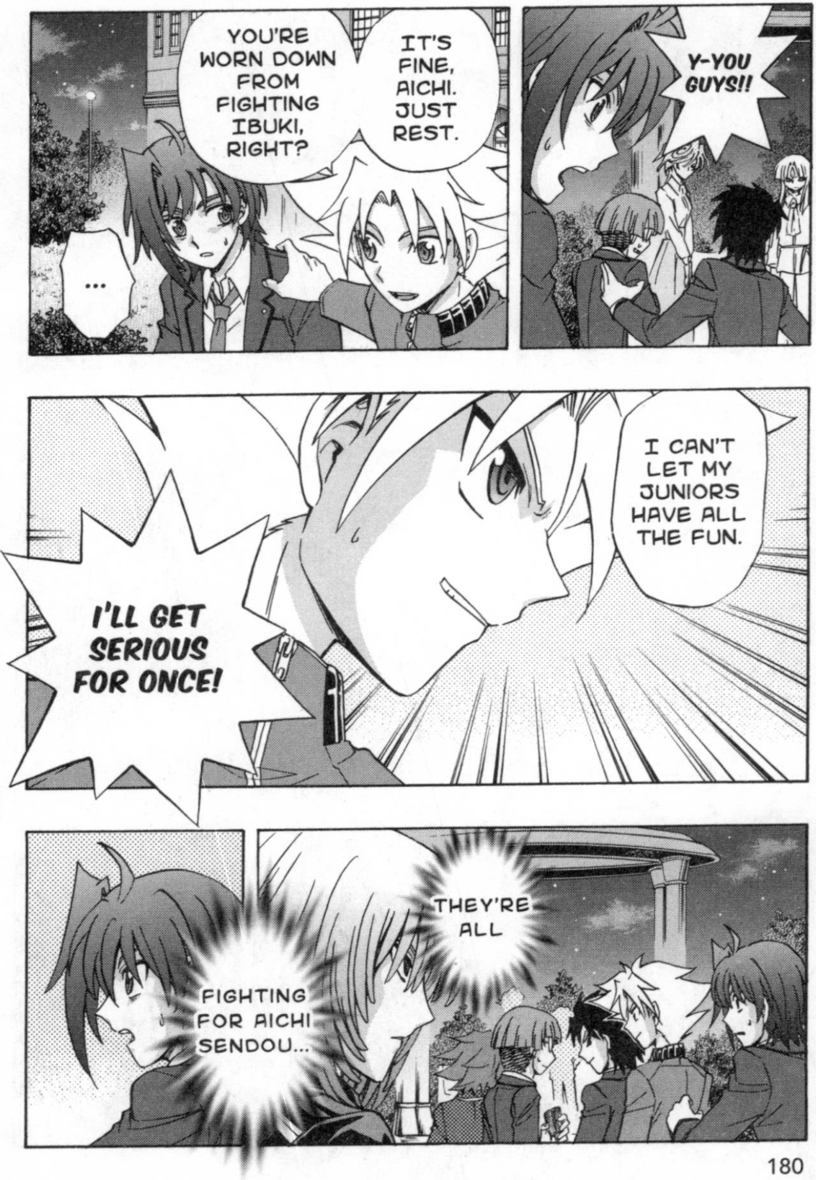
Y-YOU GUYS!!
IT'S FINE, AICHI. JUST REST.
YOU'RE WORN DOWN FROM FIGHTING IBUKI, RIGHT?
...
I CAN'T LET MY JUNIORS HAVE ALL THE FUN.
I'LL GET SERIOUS FOR ONCE!
THEY'RE ALL
FIGHTING FOR AICHI SENDOU...

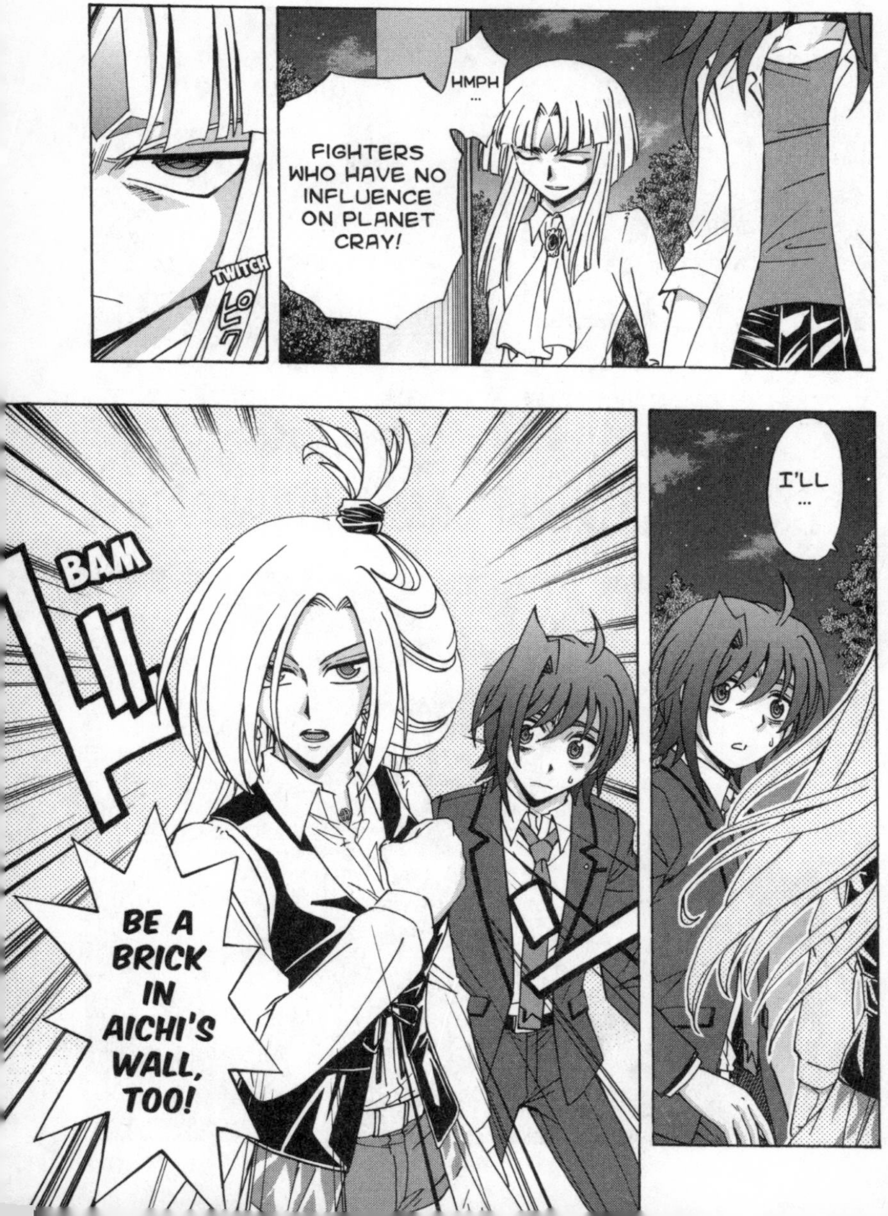
HMPH ...
FIGHTERS WHO HAVE NO INFLUENCE ON PLANET CRAY!
TWITCH
I'LL ...
BAM
BE A BRICK IN AICHI'S WALL, TOO!

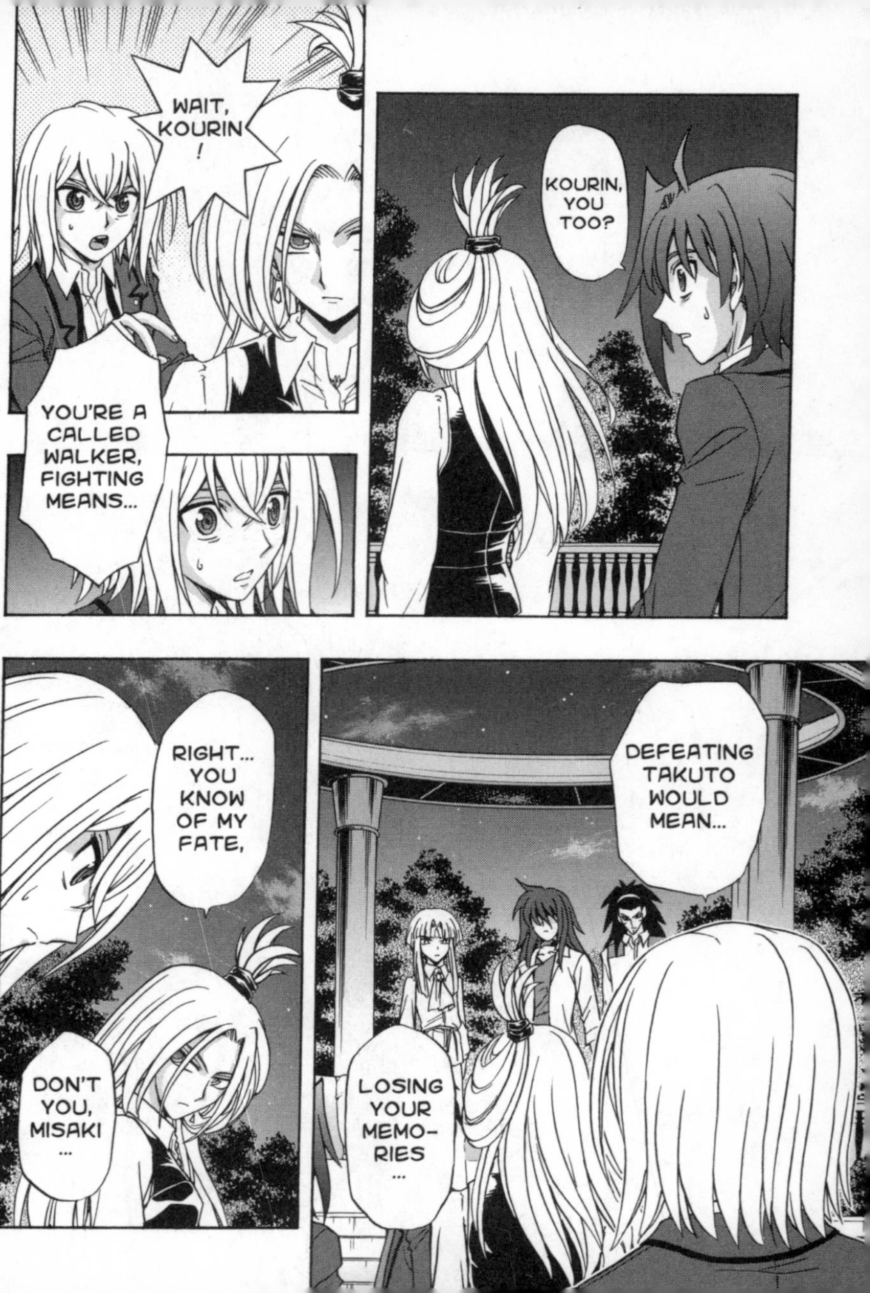
KOURIN, YOU TOO?
WAIT, KOURIN!
YOU'RE A CALLED WALKER, FIGHTING MEANS...
DEFEATING TAKUTO WOULD MEAN...
LOSING YOUR MEMORIES...
RIGHT... YOU KNOW OF MY FATE,
DON'T YOU, MISAKI...

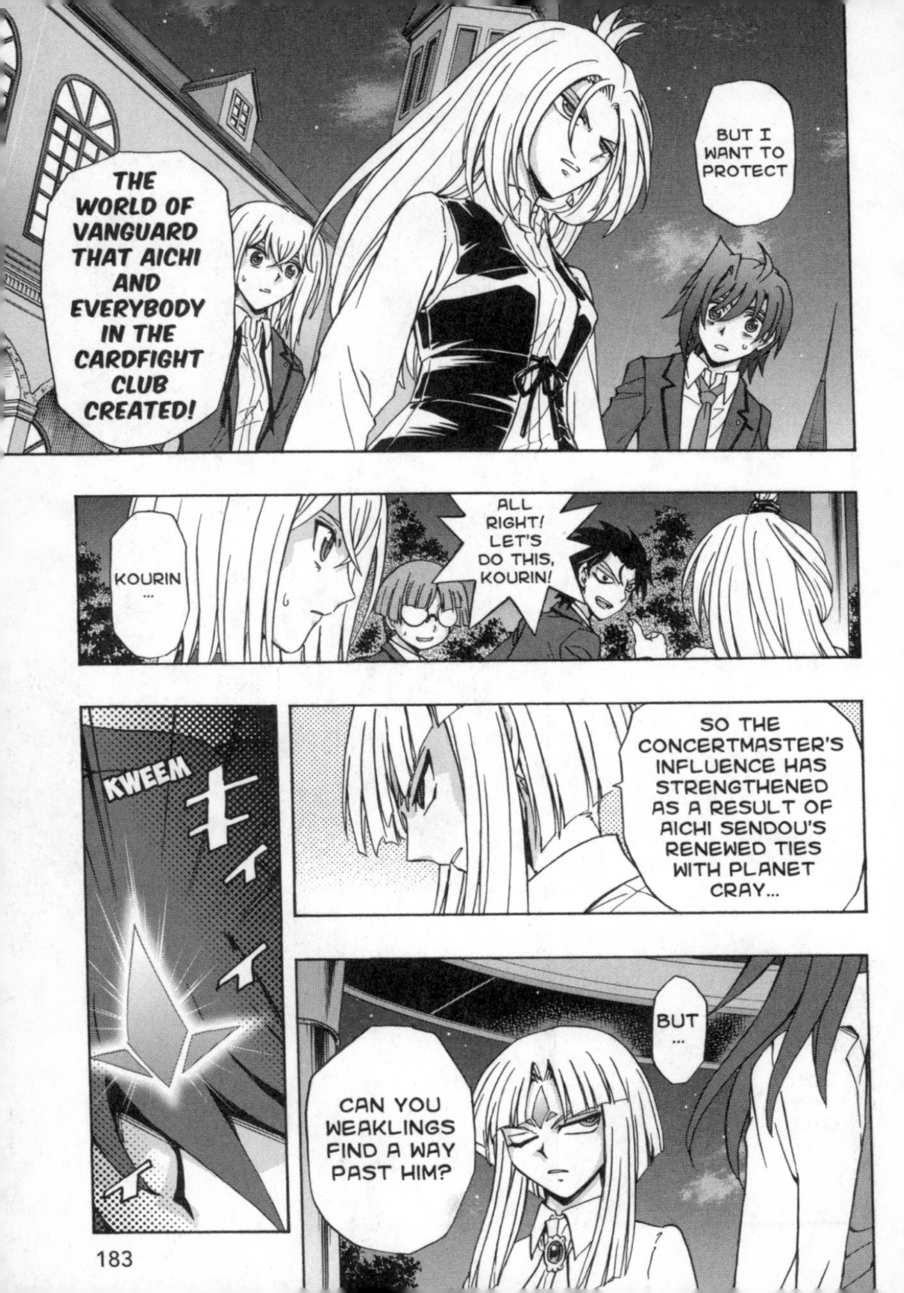
BUT I WANT TO PROTECT
THE WORLD OF VANGUARD THAT AICHI AND EVERYBODY IN THE CARDFIGHT CLUB CREATED!
ALL RIGHT! LET'S DO THIS, KOURIN!
KOURIN ...
SO THE CONCERTMASTER'S INFLUENCE HAS STRENGTHENED AS A RESULT OF AICHI SENDOU'S RENEWED TIES WITH PLANET CRAY...
BUT ...
CAN YOU WEAKLINGS FIND A WAY PAST HIM?
KWEEM

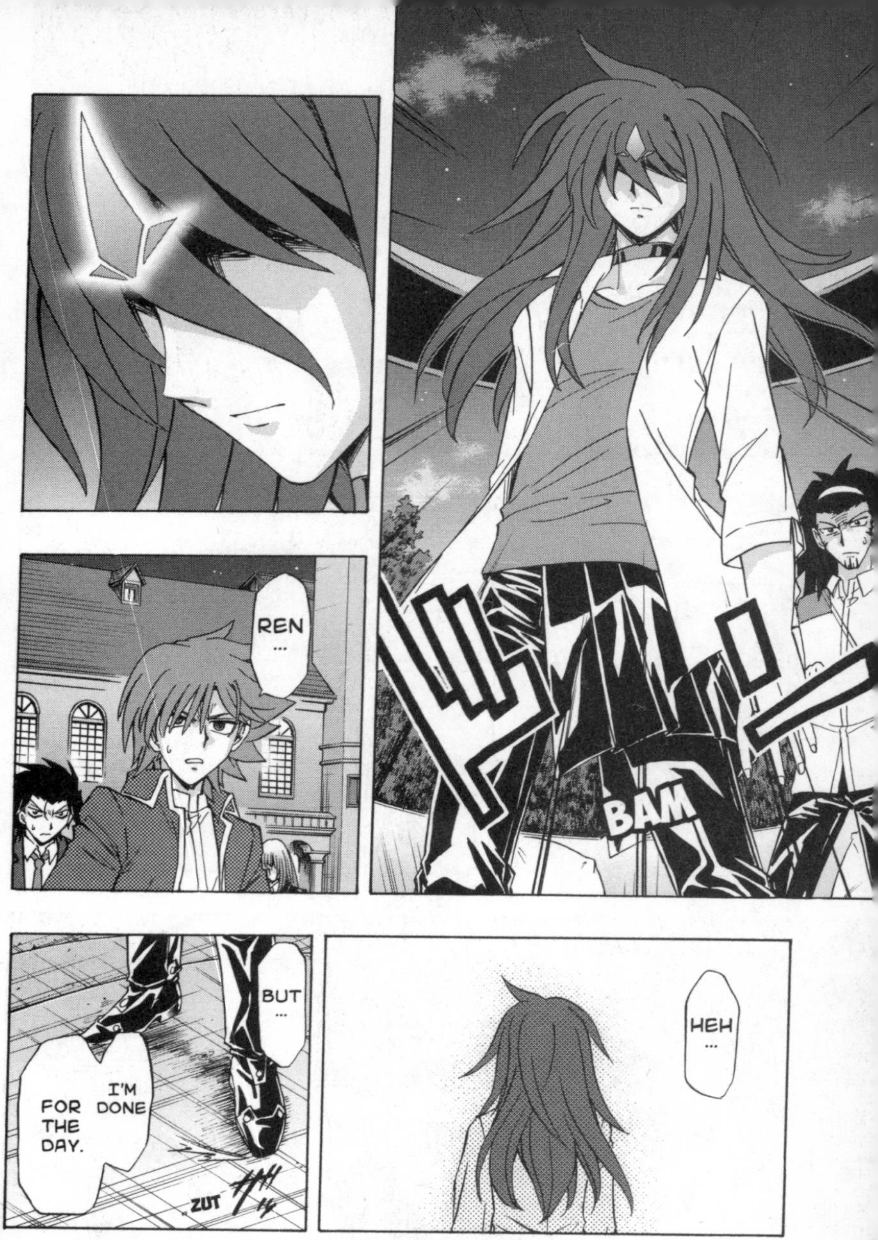
BAM
REN ...
HEH ...
BUT ...
I'M DONE FOR THE DAY.
ZUT

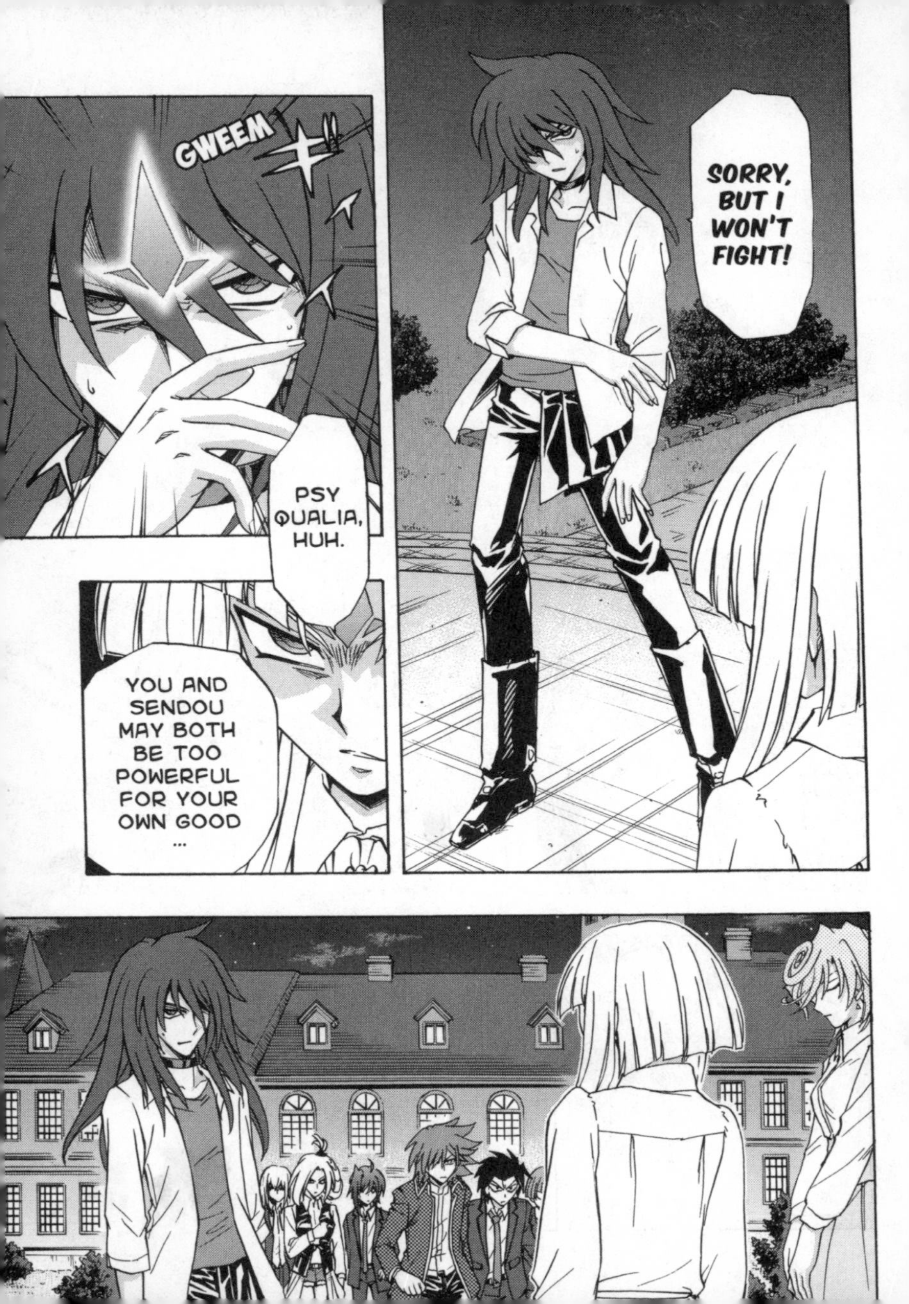
SORRY, BUT I WON'T FIGHT!
GWEEM
PSY QUALIA, HUH.
YOU AND SENDOU MAY BOTH BE TOO POWERFUL FOR YOUR OWN GOOD ...

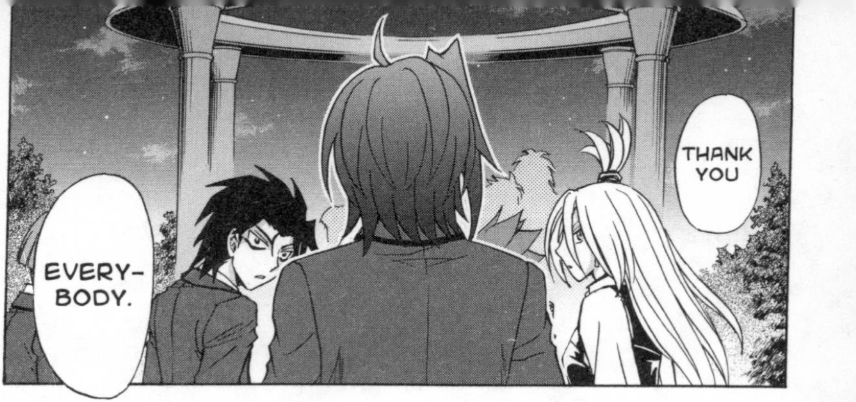
THANK YOU
EVERY-BODY.

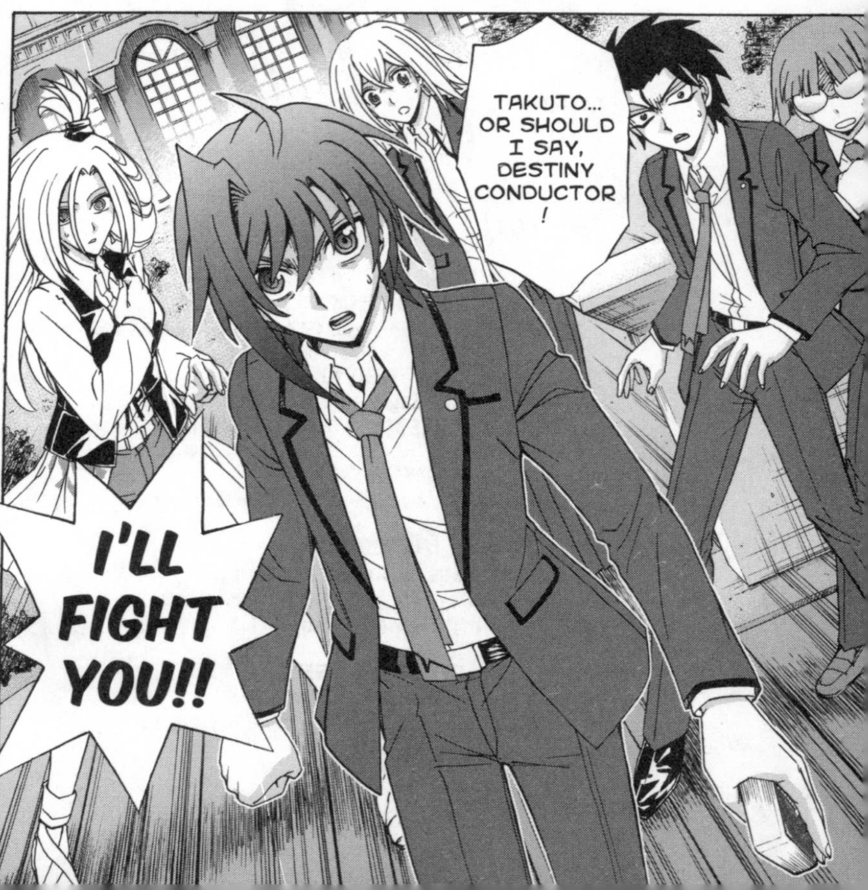
TAKUTO... OR SHOULD I SAY, DESTINY CONDUCTOR!
I'LL FIGHT YOU!!

CARDFIGHT!! VANGUARD VOL. 11
ORIGINAL DESIGNS OF THE FEATURED UNITS

CHAPTER 60
Death Feather Eagle / Daisuke Izuka
Grim Reaper / THORES柴本 (THORES Shibamoto)

CHAPTER 62
Flash Shield, Iseult / タイキ (TAIKI)

CHAPTER 64
Knight Squire, Allen / Ryo-ta.H
Override Deletor, Olg / 載克三好 (Norikatsu Miyoshi)
Yggdrasil Maiden, Elaine / TMS

CHAPTER 65
Yggdrasil Maiden, Elaine / TMS
Little Sage, Marron / 山崎奈苗 (Nanae Yamazaki)

All Other Units / 伊藤彰 (Akira Itou)

Ceya

CARDFIGHT! VANGUARD
VOLUME 11

Translation: Yota Okutani
Production: Grace Lu
Anthony Quintessenza

First published in Japan in 2016 by KADOKAWA CORPORATION, Tokyo.
English translation rights arranged with KADOKAWA CORPORATION, Tokyo through TUTTLE-MORI AGENCY, INC., Tokyo.
English language version produced by Vertical, Inc.

Translation provided by Vertical, Inc., 2018
Published by Vertical, Inc., New York

Originally published in Japanese as *Kaadofaito!! Vangaado 11* by KADOKAWA CORPORATION
Kaadofaito!! Vangaado first serialized in *Young Ace*, 2011-2017

ISBN: 978-1-945054-29-7

Manufactured in Canada

First Edition

Vertical, Inc.
451 Park Avenue South
7th Floor
New York, NY 10016
www.vertical-inc.com